HUMAN RIGHTS IN THE UNITED STATES

This book brings to light emerging evidence of a shift toward a fuller engagement with international human rights norms and their application to domestic policy dilemmas in the United States. The volume offers a rich history, spanning close to three centuries, of the marginalization of human rights discourse in the United States. Contributors analyze particular cases of U.S. human rights advocacy aimed at addressing persistent inequalities within the United States, including advocacy for the rights of persons with disabilities; indigenous peoples; lone-mother-headed families; incarcerated persons; lesbian, gay, bisexual, and transgendered people; and those displaced by natural disasters, most notably Hurricane Katrina. This book also explores key arenas in which legal scholars, policy practitioners, and grassroots activists are challenging multiple divides between "public" and "private" spheres (e.g., in connection with children's rights and domestic violence) and between "public" and "private" sectors (e.g., in relation to health care and business and human rights).

Shareen Hertel is Associate Professor of Political Science at the University of Connecticut, jointly appointed with the Human Rights Institute at the University. She is the author of *Unexpected Power: Conflict and Change Among Transnational Activists* (2006) and coeditor with Lanse P. Minkler of *Economic Rights: Conceptual, Measurement and Policy Issues* (2007). She has published in, among others, *Political Science Quarterly, Polity, International Studies Review, Global Governance, Human Rights Review,* and *Journal of Latin American Studies.* Hertel has served as a consultant to foundations, nongovernmental organizations (NGOs), and United Nations agencies in the United States, Latin America, and South Asia.

Kathryn Libal is Assistant Professor of Community Organization in the School of Social Work at the University of Connecticut. She has written on child welfare, children's rights, and state formation in Turkey. Libal is currently writing on international NGO advocacy for Iraqi forced migrants and the failures of the U.S. welfare state to fulfill the economic human rights of children. Her research has been published in *Human Rights Review, International Journal of Social Welfare, Violence against Women, Journal for Middle East Women's Studies,* and edited volumes on human rights, social welfare, international social work, and anthropology.

In memory of Peggy
And for Scott

Human Rights in the United States

BEYOND EXCEPTIONALISM

Edited by

Shareen Hertel

University of Connecticut

Kathryn Libal

University of Connecticut

CAMBRIDGE
UNIVERSITY PRESS

CAMBRIDGE UNIVERSITY PRESS
Cambridge, New York, Melbourne, Madrid, Cape Town,
Singapore, São Paulo, Delhi, Tokyo, Mexico City

Cambridge University Press
32 Avenue of the Americas, New York, NY 10013-2473, USA

www.cambridge.org
Information on this title: www.cambridge.org/9781107400870

First published 2011

Printed in the United States of America

A catalog record for this publication is available from the British Library.

Library of Congress Cataloging in Publication data

Human rights in the United States : beyond exceptionalism / [edited by] Shareen Hertel,
Kathryn Libal.
  p. cm.
Includes bibliographical references and index.
ISBN 978-1-107-00846-5 (hardback) – ISBN 978-1-107-40087-0 (paperback)
  1. Human rights – United States. I. Hertel, Shareen. II. Libal, Kathryn, 1968–
III. Title.
JC599.U5H754   2011
323.0973 – dc22   2010048058

ISBN 978-1-107-00846-5 Hardback
ISBN 978-1-107-40087-0 Paperback

Contents

Contributors

Mimi Abramovitz, DSW, is the Bertha Capen Reynolds Professor of Social Policy at Hunter College School of Social Work and The Graduate Center, City University of New York. An activist and scholar, she has authored many influential books on women, poverty, and social welfare policy. These include *Regulating the Lives of Women: Social Welfare Policy from Colonial Times to the Present* (1999); *Taxes Are a Women's Issue: Reframing the Debate* (The Feminist Press at CUNY 2006); *Under Attack, Fighting Back: Women and Welfare in the US* (2000; named an "Outstanding Book" by the Myers Center for Human Rights); and *The Dynamics of Social Welfare Policy* (Oxford University Press 2010). Abramovitz is currently writing a book titled *Gendered Obligations: The History of Activism Among Black and White Low-Income Women in the US since 1900.*

Cathy Albisa is a constitutional and human rights lawyer with a background in the right to health. Albisa also has significant experience working in partnership with community organizers on the use of human rights standards to strengthen advocacy in the United States. She cofounded, with Sharda Sekaran and Liz Sullivan, the National Economic and Social Rights Initiative (NESRI) to build legitimacy for human rights in general, and economic and social rights in particular, in the United States. Albisa (with Martha Davis and Cindy Soohoo) is an editor of the *Bringing Human Rights Home* series (Pennsylvania 2008) and has published on both economic and social rights, as well as reproductive rights issues, in the United States. Albisa has taught at Columbia Law School and Cornell Law School and currently teaches at the CUNY School of Law. She is Vice-Chair of the Board of Directors of the Center for Constitutional Rights and serves on the Board of Directors of the Center for Social

Inclusion. Albisa clerked for the Honorable Mitchell Cohen in the District of New Jersey. She received a BA from the University of Miami and is a graduate of Columbia Law School.

Joanne Bauer is Adjunct Professor in the School of International and Public Affairs at Columbia University, where she teaches business and human rights. She is also Senior Researcher and New York Representative of the Business and Human Rights Resource Centre, a London-headquartered organization working to increase the transparency of companies' human rights impact worldwide. Previously, she was Director of Studies at the Carnegie Council on Ethics and International Affairs, where she founded and directed two program areas: one on human rights; the other on environmental values. She is the founding editor of *Human Rights Dialogue* (a publication of the Carnegie Council); the editor of *Forging Environmentalism: Justice, Livelihood, and Contested Environments* (2006); and coeditor (with Daniel A. Bell) of *The East Asian Challenge for Human Rights* (Cambridge University Press 1999).

Bethany R. Berger, JD, is Professor at the University of Connecticut School of Law, where she teaches American Indian Law and Tribal Law. Her many articles have appeared in journals such as the *Duke Law Journal, California Law Review, Michigan Law Review*, and *UCLA Law Review*. She is the coauthor of *American Indian Law: Cases and Commentary* and a coauthor and member of the Board of Editors of *Cohen's Handbook of Federal Indian Law*, the preeminent treatise in the field. Berger is a graduate of Yale Law School.

Jean Connolly Carmalt is Assistant Professor of Law, Politics, and Society at Drake University. She holds a JD from Cornell University Law School (2003) and a PhD in Geography from the University of Washington (2010). She previously served as Legal Coordinator for the Center for Economic and Social Rights. Carmalt's research and teaching focus on the relationship between international human rights law and geographic literature, and she is the author of several articles and book chapters on that subject. Her dissertation is titled "Geographic Perspectives on International Law: Human Rights and Hurricane Katrina."

Davida Finger is Assistant Clinical Professor at Loyola University New Orleans College of Law, where she teaches the community justice section in the law clinic and the law and poverty course. In collaboration with community organizations, Finger has worked extensively on disaster-related litigation and policy, such as FEMA's rental assistance programs;

the State of Louisiana's Road Home Program for homeowners; wrongful public and private housing demolitions; public records matters; and various juvenile and housing issues. Finger is the 2011 Chair-Elect of the Association of American Law Schools' Poverty Law Section.

Shareen Hertel, PhD, is Associate Professor of Political Science at the University of Connecticut, jointly appointed with the Human Rights Institute at the University of Connecticut. She is the author of *Unexpected Power: Conflict and Change Among Transnational Activists* (Cornell 2006) and coeditor (with Lanse P. Minkler) of *Economic Rights: Conceptual, Measurement and Policy Issues* (Cambridge 2007). Hertel has published in, among others, *Political Science Quarterly, Polity, International Studies Review, Global Governance, Human Rights Review,* and *Journal of Latin American Studies.* She has served as a consultant to foundations, nongovernmental organizations (NGOs), and United Nations agencies in the United States, Latin America, and South Asia. She holds a doctorate in Political Science from Columbia University.

Rhoda E. Howard-Hassmann, PhD, FRSC, is Canada Research Chair in International Human Rights at Wilfrid Laurier University, where she holds a joint appointment in the Department of Global Studies and the Balsillie School of International Affairs. She is also a Fellow of the Royal Society of Canada. In 2006, the Human Rights section of the American Political Science Association named Dr. Howard-Hassmann its first Distinguished Scholar of Human Rights. In addition to her many published works on human rights since 1980, she is coeditor of *Economic Human Rights in Canada and the United States* (University of Pennsylvania 2006); coeditor of *The Age of Apology: Facing Up to the Past* (University of Pennsylvania 2008); and author of *Reparations to Africa* (University of Pennsylvania 2008) and *Can Globalization Promote Human Rights?* (Pennsylvania State University 2010). Howard-Hassmann has a long-standing interest in economic rights. Her current research project is on the right to food and the responsibility to protect, focusing more specifically on governments that starve their own citizens; it also encompasses the responsibilities of international organizations and transnational corporations.

Risa E. Kaufman, JD, is Executive Director of the Human Rights Institute (HRI) at Columbia Law School, where she is Lecturer-in-Law. Her work is particularly focused on implementing human rights treaty norms and obligations within the United States, including at the state and local levels, and developing strategies for promoting economic and social rights in the

United States. She also coordinates the Bringing Human Rights Home lawyers' network and teaches a seminar on economic justice and human rights in the United States. She has engaged in impact litigation, policy initiatives, public education, and scholarship focusing on welfare, housing rights, racial profiling, access to legal services, rights of incarcerated persons, and political participation. Kaufman holds a JD from the NYU School of Law, where she was a Root-Tilden-Snow Scholar. She clerked for Judge Ira DeMent in the U.S. District Court in Montgomery, Alabama.

Mie Lewis is a senior staff attorney with the Women's Rights Project of the American Civil Liberties Union (ACLU), where she works on behalf of women and girls in the criminal and juvenile justice systems. She has served as lead counsel in class-action lawsuits challenging the solitary confinement and unwarranted strip searching of incarcerated girls, as well as the sex discriminatory conditions of confinement of women prisoners in a men's prison. Previously, as the Aryeh Neier Fellow at Human Rights Watch and the ACLU, Lewis conducted a year-long investigation into human rights abuses against girls incarcerated in the state of New York. She earned her JD with distinction from Stanford Law School and served as law clerk to U.S. District Court Judge Susan Y. Illston.

Kathryn Libal, PhD, is Assistant Professor of Community Organization in the School of Social Work at the University of Connecticut. She holds a doctorate in cultural anthropology from the University of Washington. She has written on children and women's rights and child welfare in Turkey. Libal's current research focuses on two topics: international NGO advocacy for Iraqi forced migrants and failures of the U.S. welfare state to fulfill the economic human rights of children. Her work has been published in *Human Rights Review*, *Violence against Women*, *Journal of International Social Welfare*, the *Journal for Middle East Women's Studies*, and edited volumes on human rights, social welfare, international social work, and anthropology.

Janet E. Lord, LLM, LLB, is Senior Partner at BlueLaw International, LLP, a service-disabled, veteran-owned international law and development firm. A research associate at the Harvard Law School Project on Disability, she is an expert in international disability rights law. Lord participated in all of the negotiating sessions during the drafting of the UN Convention on the Rights of Persons with Disabilities, serving as legal advisor to Disabled Peoples' International and several lead governments, including Mexico, Ecuador, and Costa Rica. She has designed, managed, and implemented disability and development programs in more than twenty-five countries worldwide for a variety of agencies, including the World Bank, the Office of the High Commissioner for Human Rights, the UN Development Programme, the Pan American Health Organization, Handicap International, and CARE. She is adjunct Professor of Law at the University of Maryland School of Law and serves on the faculty of the American University School of International Service, where she teaches in the summer human rights program. She holds an LLM from George Washington University Law School and an LLM and LLB from the University of Edinburgh in Scotland.

Rachel E. Luft is Assistant Professor in the Department of Sociology at the University of New Orleans. Her primary areas of research specialization are race, gender, intersectionality, and social movements. Since Hurricane Katrina, she has been a participant observer in grassroots movement responses to the disaster. Her research and writing focus on the racial and gender politics of community organizing for just reconstruction, the politicization of displaced people, volunteer solidarity politics, and human rights. Her publications on Hurricane Katrina have appeared in several journals and collected volumes. Luft is also Senior Analyst in the Social Science Research Council's Research Network on Persons Displaced by Katrina.

Sally Engle Merry is Professor of Anthropology and former Director of the Law and Society Program at New York University. Her recent books include *Colonizing Hawai'i: The Cultural Power of Law* (Princeton University Press 2000); *Human Rights and Gender Violence: Translating International Law into Local Justice* (University of Chicago Press 2006); and *Gender Violence: A Cultural Perspective* (2009). She is past president of the Law and Society Association and President-Elect of the American Ethnological Society. The Law and Society Association awarded Professor Merry the Hurst Prize for *Colonizing Hawai'i* in 2002 and the Kalven Prize for overall scholarly contributions to sociolegal scholarship in 2007. The School of American Research awarded her the J.I. Staley Prize for *Human Rights and Gender Violence* in 2010.

Julie Mertus is Professor and the Co-Director of Ethics, Peace and Global Affairs program at American University. She has written widely on human rights and gender, conflict, the Balkans, U.S. foreign policy, and UN institutions. She is the author or editor of ten books, including *Bait and Switch: Human Rights and U.S. Foreign Policy* (Routledge 2008; named "human rights book of the year" by the American Political Science Association) and, most recently, *Human Rights Matters: Local Politics and National Human Rights Institutions* (Stanford University Press 2009) and *The United Nations and Human Rights* (2005). She has been the recipient of several fellowships and grants from the MacArthur Foundation, United States Institute of Peace, Ford Foundation, Soros Foundation, and the Open Society Institute.

Ken Neubeck, PhD, is Emeritus Professor of Sociology at the University of Connecticut, where he served as Director of the interdisciplinary undergraduate human rights minor. Now a resident of Eugene, Oregon, Neubeck volunteers as Executive Director of Amigos Multicultural Services Center (an immigrant rights organization) and is active with the Community Coalition for Advancement of Human Rights. He also serves on the City of Eugene Human Rights Commission, which is engaged in exploring ways in which international human rights principles and standards can be implemented across Eugene's city government operations (see www.humanrightscity.com). Neubeck is the author of *When Welfare Disappears: The Case for Economic Human Rights* (2006) and coauthor with Noel Cazenave of *Welfare Racism: Playing the Race Card Against America's Poor* (2001). His current scholarship focuses on grassroots efforts to implement the human rights framework in governmental and nongovernmental organizations at the local community level.

Jessica Shimmin is a doctoral candidate in the Department of Media, Culture, and Communication at New York University, where her research focuses on gendered spaces of personal safety, institutional approaches to social and personal welfare, and the boundary between public and private. Currently, her projects include research on the institutional production by professionals of safe shelter space for abused women and children in Massachusetts' domestic violence intervention services network.

Michael Ashley Stein, JD, PhD, is Cofounder and Executive Director of the Harvard Law School Project on Disability and Cabell Professor at William & Mary Law School. An internationally acclaimed disability rights advocate, Stein participated in the drafting of the United Nations Convention on the Rights of Persons with Disabilities and actively consults with international governments on their disability laws and policies. He acts as a legal advisor to Rehabilitation International, Disabled Peoples' International, and Special Olympics International, and advises a number of UN bodies. Stein has served as president of the National Disabled Bar Association and as pro bono counsel for Legal Aid Society's Juvenile Rights Division, and has most recently focused on filing disability rights briefs with the European Court of Human Rights. Stein earned his law degree from Harvard Law School and his doctorate from Cambridge University. He clerked for U.S. Supreme Court Justice Samuel A. Alito, Jr., and practiced law with Sullivan & Cromwell in New York.

Dorothy Q. Thomas is currently a research associate at the School of Oriental and African Studies at the University of London and was a 2008 Visiting Fellow at the London School of Economics' Centre for the Study of Human Rights. Thomas was the Founding Director of the Human Rights Watch Women's Division and served in that position from 1990 to 1998. She was a 1998 MacArthur Fellow; a 1995 Bunting Fellow of the Radcliffe Institute for Advanced Study at Harvard University; and, in 1998, received the Eleanor Roosevelt Human Rights Award from Bill and Hillary Clinton. Until January 2007, Thomas was the senior program advisor to the U.S. Human Rights Fund, a collaborative grant-making initiative supporting domestic human rights work in the United States. She is a member of the Board of the British Institute for Human Rights and the Ms. Foundation for Women and sits on the advisory boards of the ACLU Human Rights Project, the American Constitution Society Human Rights Working Group, and the Human Rights Watch U.S. Program. Thomas is a graduate of Georgetown University, which awarded her an honorary doctorate in 1995.

Jonathan Todres, JD, is Associate Professor of Law at Georgia State University College of Law, where he teaches courses on children's rights and health law. His research focuses primarily on children's rights issues, in particular, trafficking and commercial sexual exploitation of children and domestic interpretations of international children's rights law. Todres lectures frequently on children's rights issues and has testified before the UN Committee on the Rights of the Child and in Congressional briefings in the U.S. House of Representatives and U.S. Senate on trafficking and commercial sexual exploitation of children. He serves as a regular advisor to nongovernmental organizations involved in children's rights issues, including as Child Rights Advisor to ECPAT-USA. Todres is the author of numerous articles on children's rights and coeditor of the book *The UN Convention on the Rights of the Child: An Analysis of Treaty Provisions and Implications of US Ratification* (2006).

Alicia Ely Yamin, JD, MPH, is currently Joseph H. Flom Fellow on Global Health and Human Rights at Harvard Law School, Adjunct Lecturer on Health Policy and Management at the Harvard School of Public Health, and Senior Researcher (affiliated) at the Christian Michelsen Institute in Norway. She also serves as Special Advisor to Amnesty International's global campaign on poverty. Yamin is on the editorial boards of *Health and Human Rights, Human Rights Quarterly, Human Rights and the Global Economy,* and *Revista Iberoamericana de Derechos Humanos.* She was formerly Director of Research and Investigations at Physicians for Human Rights, where she oversaw all field investigations. Yamin is Chair of the Board of the Center for Economic and Social Rights. She also serves on, among others, the Reference Group of the International Budget Project's Partnership Initiative, the Advisory Boards of the International Initiative on Maternal Mortality and Human Rights, and the Center for Policy Analysis on Trade and Health.

Sarah Zaidi is the Executive Director of the International Treatment Preparedness Coalition, a global network advocating for longer, healthier, and more productive lives of people with HIV. A pioneer in human rights, in 1993, Zaidi cofounded, along with two colleagues, the Center for Economic and Social Rights (CESR), one of the first international organizations to focus exclusively on social justice issues through a human rights lens. Zaidi holds an undergraduate degree from Brown University and a doctorate from the Harvard School of Public Health. She has written extensively on issues of health and human rights and, most recently, co-authored *Human Rights at the UN: The Political History of Universal Justice* (Indiana University Press 2007), a critical analysis of the history of human rights at the United Nations.

Acknowledgments

We are indebted to many people for the development of this edited volume. Richard Ashby Wilson (Director, University of Connecticut Human Rights Institute) and Jeremy Paul (Dean, University of Connecticut Law School) marshaled the institutional support to host a conference on "Human Rights in the USA" in October 2009. The event was cosponsored by the Thomas J. Dodd Research Center, the University of Connecticut Humanities Institute, the Institute of Puerto Rican and Latino Studies, the Center for Latin American and Caribbean Studies, and the James L. and Shirley A. Draper Chair of Early American History.

The chapters in this volume were among the many rich and varied contributions initially presented at that event. Rachel Jackson has provided invaluable logistical support throughout the process. Aviva L. Ron has offered excellent copyediting and research support, and Kathy Birnie has graciously provided technical support at key junctures in the project. We are grateful to our contributors for their commitment to completing detailed and timely revisions. We are also grateful to our colleagues in the Economic and Social Rights Group at the University of Connecticut for their critical insights on the issues that undergird this volume. We appreciate the confidence and support of John Berger at Cambridge University Press and the comments of anonymous reviewers who read earlier versions of material included in the book.

Finally, we are encouraged by the efforts of thousands of grassroots activists, policy makers, and people in local communities throughout the United States who are already working tirelessly for the realization of human rights on multiple levels. We hope this book is useful in their efforts.

Foreword

Are Americans Human?
Reflections on the Future of Progressive Politics in the United States

Dorothy Q. Thomas

It is not easy being progressive in the United States today. Conservatives attack us as anathema to American values, and we portray them as a threat to progressive ones. President Barack Obama, the first avowedly progressive president since Franklin D. Roosevelt, is denounced by critics on the right as a "socialist" and decried by ones on the left as a "sell-out." Progressive Americans find ourselves caught between a political rock and a hard place: either we swallow our pride and use the opportunity of Obama's presidency to try to restore at least some semblance of progressivism to our country's policies, or we stick to our principles and risk losing the chance to govern it completely. What are we to do? Should U.S. progressives stand up for a country that continuously disappoints and even disavows us, or should we turn our back on one that still attracts our hope?

Obviously, no single answer to these questions exists, and the many underlying assumptions are open to debate. But rather than pitting one analysis of today's progressive American dilemmas against another, this volume takes a different approach: it suggests that we reconsider the state and fate of American progressivism altogether by placing it within the framework of human rights.

This is not an academic exercise. It has taken me all of my twenty-five years as a U.S. social justice activist, for example, to recast my own politics in terms of human rights, a shift that required me – as I hope this book will inspire you – to reexamine my sense of self, my connection to the various social justice movements of which I am a part, their relationship to one another and to the United States government, and the link between all of these things and what it means, in very practical terms, to be a progressive and an American in the world today.

As this volume attests, reframing progressive Americanism in human rights terms offers us fresh insights into some of the most intractable social and political problems confronting the United States – and the world. We are living in an unusually unstable and precarious period, not only for our politics but also for our planet. A great deal depends on what we choose to do. Yet, at such a decisive moment, how can we determine what it means to be progressive or what it will take to progress unless we are *very aware* of the larger historical context in which we operate, of the ways in which our past is encapsulated and our future enacted by what we choose to do? Adopting a human rights lens offers us this broader perspective. It gives us an overarching framework with which to review our past politics, envision our future objectives, and, ultimately, so the contributors to this volume hope, develop new ideas about what steps progressives can take today that will help us address the challenges we face now and will face in the future.

THE LESSONS OF HISTORY

One thing I have learned from applying a human rights lens to my own past experience as an activist is how divided I was from both America and other activists. At one level, this makes perfect sense. The United States was often the target of my activism (usually as a foreign policy matter), and my early work in the anti-apartheid, women's, and even human rights movements was often focused on specific groups. Upon reflection I find that something more worrisome was also at work. My antagonism toward the United States in the late 1970s and 1980s, like that of most of my fellow progressives, reflected a legitimate disappointment with its domestic and foreign policies. Unfortunately, it also coincided with the rise of the neoconservatives. Their determination to "take back America" was matched only by our inclination to move away from it. As a result, by the 1990s, it had become nearly unthinkable in almost any political circle to be both a progressive and a patriot. And by the time President Obama was elected in 2008, it was common for conservative pundits to question his loyalty, disparage his patrimony, and wonder aloud, as did one right-wing blogger, "if anyone had noticed that these minorities who hate this country are now running it?" (Applebome 2009).

As I reviewed this history, I discovered that progressive disaffection with the United States government, however justified, had morphed into a more profound alienation with another embittering side effect: when progressives began to turn off to America, we started to turn against one another. By some perverse political twist, we transmuted our loss of faith in the progressive ideals that America (at least arguably) represented into an inverse obsession with our own political legitimacy. To put it another way, the double whammy of our alienation from the United States and the conservatives' corresponding (and clever) denunciation of us as "un-American" led us, to varying degrees and for many different reasons, to locate our "true" identity in ever more narrow definitions of what it meant to be *authentically* progressive. Many American progressives who came of age during this period not only disavowed our country and denigrated some of our fellow activists, but also denied suspect dimensions of our own selves.

I take myself as a case in point. For almost as long as I have been a publicly recognized U.S. social justice activist, I have kept a patriotic skeleton in my progressive closet: I am also a descendant of Dorothy Quincy Hancock, one of America's founding mothers and the wife of John Hancock, the president of the Continental Congress and the boldface signer of the Declaration of Independence. What is significant to me now is not so much that I am indirectly descended from a signer of the American Declaration of Independence, but that, to retain my credibility as a leading progressive activist, I chose until this time in my life to hide it. In fact, I got into the not-unrelated habit of cloaking (or privileging) almost any aspect of my identity – be it my ancestry, my race, my class, my sexuality, my love of Terminator movies, or any other characteristic that might undermine (or advance) my credibility as a progressive activist.

From a human rights perspective, which assumes the dignity and equality of *all* people, these condemnatory and exclusionary undercurrents in progressive American politics now appear deeply reactive. I have consistently observed conservatives and progressives alike using exclusionary concepts of identity to defend rather than defeat more narrow interests – by, for example, selling out the so-called bad immigrants in order to secure legalization for the "good" ones, or by downplaying gay rights to advance equality for more "mainstream" groups, or by trading off race for gender or gender for race or both for something else, or by doubting the wisdom of youth to promote our own sage point of view. Human rights have helped me see that insofar as I participated in these dynamics – and I often did – I allowed a profound hypocrisy to infest my politics.

Every time progressives defend our legitimacy by denying the complexity of personal and/or political identity – whether our own, anyone else's, or even our country's – we compromise the principle and the power of progressivism itself, and we are complicit in the very structural inequities we seek to depose. If we are to have any meaningful chance to take advantage of Obama's presidency and what it represents in the interest of exerting a truly progressive influence on national policy, we will first have to stop squabbling over the scattered remnants of our deeply fractured identity and come together to create a much more affirmative, inclusive, and aspirational relationship not only to one another but also to the country as a whole.

ENVISIONING THE FUTURE

By looking through a human rights lens at my own past history, I've had to face my own complicity in a distorted form of progressive identity politics; these politics were intensified by years of conservative flag-baiting and often served to cut me off from my country, from many of my fellow activists, and even from myself. I do not say this to be condemnatory. Defensive progressivism, however internally contradictory, was necessary at a certain point in American history. But Obama had to overcome these divided politics to get elected, and now we activists, academics, policy makers, and philanthropists need to get our own act together. President Obama has put it this way:

> That is the story of America: of ordinary citizens organizing, agitating and advocating for change; of hope stronger than hate; of love more powerful than any insult or injury; of Americans fighting to build for themselves and their families a nation in which no one is a second-class citizen, in which no one is denied their basic rights; in which all of us are free to live and love as we see fit.... For while there will be setbacks and bumps along the road, the truth is that our common ideals are a force stronger than any division that some might sow. These ideals, when voiced by generations of citizens, are what made it possible for me to stand here today. These ideals are what make it possible for the people in this room to live freely and openly when for most of history that would have been inconceivable. That is the promise of America ... That is the promise that we are called to fulfill.
>
> (Obama 2009)

These remarks were made by a sitting president of the United States and they underscore the enormous opportunity we have, should we choose to take it, to broaden our perspective on what it means to be progressive *and* American, and to expand our influence on both national and global politics, even if it will not always turn out exactly as we envision it.

But are progressive Americans going to rise to the occasion? Can we envision a more unified and positive progressive American politics, even in the face of our own limitations, those of our national leadership, and the seeming intractability of our opponents? The broad perspective of human rights gives me a framework for such an alternative and affirmative brand of progressive American politics. Its emphasis on our common humanity mandates a profound degree of humility with respect to our own fallibility (never mind anyone else's), and as such it offers a powerful basis on which to assert and sustain a future of progressive unanimity, inclusiveness, and empathy that extends to those with whom we profoundly disagree.

Yet even if human rights offer progressive Americans a way to realign our politics with the values of connection, participation, and imagination on which social change inherently rests, I find myself wondering if we are really up for this level of inclusiveness. Can we ever find a way to connect to such a broad and expansive framework without fearing that it comes at the expense of the integrity of our own particular experience – a reasonable fear, given the lessons of American history?

Can human rights really help? Obviously, this is a question that each of us needs to answer for ourselves. Critics argue that the framework of human rights is too "foreign," too "abstract," and too "controversial" in the United States for it to be of much real use. The title of this Foreword, "Are Americans Human?" tries to address some of the assumptions behind these views. If we accept, for example, that human rights are foreign or abstract, it's almost as if we're saying the idea of human rights had nothing at all to do with the idea of the United States or that Americans are not actually part of the human race. The fact that Americans themselves as well as people in the rest of the world are asking this question (even if only by implication) suggests the precise loss of connection to ourselves, to one another, to our country, and to our fellow human beings that I feel bedevils all politics in the United States today and threatens our progress as a people and as a nation.

That human rights are controversial in the United States almost goes without saying, but we need to explore (in more detail than I have space for here) why and for whom this is the case. Suffice it to say that the controversy surrounding the realization of human rights in the United States is widespread and arises across the political spectrum with respect to a wide range of domestic and foreign policy issues including sovereignty, accountability, transparency, equality, unity, dignity, and liberty – all of which human rights aim to address. So perhaps the extent of the controversy makes sense.

What has been interesting for me to discover, however, is that there is an inverse relationship between the age of progressives and their willingness to risk such a systemic backlash to take up human rights in the United States. The younger the activists, the more willing they are to take such risks. This gives me great hope for the future of progressive American activism and of the United States, but I do not think it is fair to rely solely on the younger generation to make this shift. Progressive people of all ages and across the political spectrum need to adopt an alternative to the disaffection and disunity of our previous practice. We must do so, if for no other reason, than because it is obviously limiting our ability to progress, along with the ability of those who come after us. We need an alternative framework that challenges our country's and even our own inclination toward habits of superiority and exclusion but does not involve, as the progressive historian Sheila Rowbotham recently cautioned, "becoming trapped in a prescriptive construct" (Rowbotham as cited in Miller 2010).

I believe the human rights framework offers progressive Americans just such an alternative construct for our politics. As some of its potential practical innovations are discussed in detail in the following essays, I will reflect here on two of its more conceptual benefits.

Human rights respect national and other identities, but defy supremacy. If we choose to reconnect the principles of human rights to the ideals America at least arguably represents, it may help us recapture an affirmative relationship to the United States and therefore to its people without acceding to the exceptionalism, nationalism, and structural inequality alienating us in the first place. Nobody died and left the conservatives in charge of what it means to be an American. The primary progressive "value-added" of human rights is that as a framework for U.S. law, policy, and social mobilization, it provides a viable alternative to the ideology of supremacy *no matter who may practice human rights*. Nor does the form of human rights protection matter, whether focused around safeguarding people based on national identity, gender, race, class, sexuality, party, religion, or any other status. If we begin to promote a commitment to fundamental human rights as central to the progressive identity of the United States, we may be able to reclaim an affirmative relationship to our country as core to our own progressive identity. Patriotism would then be a way to uphold rather than usurp our shared commitment to fundamental equality.

Human rights recognize all peoples' equality and dignity but decry uniformity. If we choose to use human rights to frame our alternative vision of progressive American politics, it will provide us with a desperately needed corrective to the narrow and divisive character of much of our past practice, wherein many progressives cloaked our differences to fit into particular groups or downplayed our commonalities to protect our turf or got eaten up by some combination of both. Human rights offer American progressives an inclusive and affirmative antidote to the exclusionary side effects of our previous politics: one that recognizes we are different in virtually every respect and that those differences are usually compounded – and that we also have a lot in common. Human rights neither deny us our sense of individuality nor absolve us of our relationship to the broader community. Instead human rights offer American progressives a vastly more equitable and dynamic conception of personal and political identity, which simultaneously affirms that we are inherently different and that, in being born equal in dignity and rights, we all are also inalienably alike. This approach allows us to come together as progressive Americans based on both our identities and our values.

WHAT DOES IT MEAN TO BE A PROGRESSIVE AMERICAN IN THE UNITED STATES TODAY?

I recognize that as progressives our relationship to the United States as a country has been and probably always will be ambivalent. This ambivalence will be heightened or lessened by the nature of our own specific identities and experiences, by our race, our class, our culture, our past, our differences, our relative privilege. "Let America be America again," as Langston Hughes once put it. "(It never was America to me)" (Hughes [1936] 1994). But unless we intend to allow the "Birther Movement" or the "Tea Party Patriots" to bring down Obama's presidency and the entire agenda of progressive reform for the United States along with it, we are going to have to find a way to respect our relative ambivalence toward our country and perhaps even toward our fellow progressives without sacrificing our connection to it and to one another. As President Obama so eloquently put it, "that is the promise we are called to fulfill" (Obama 2009).

But, as I noted at the outset, it is difficult in such pressing and complex circumstances for progressive Americans to get perspective on the larger historical context we find ourselves in and then determine what we should do – both as individuals and as a movement. I had to move to England to figure out who I am as an American progressive, which the original Dorothy Quincy (who was present in Lexington, Massachusetts, when the shot "heard round the world" was fired) might find a bit ironic, to say the least. I now pay taxes both to Her Majesty Queen Elizabeth and to President Obama. This divided state of loyalty, however costly, perfectly encapsulates the unresolved question about my own identity and that of today's progressive Americans that lies at the heart of this book: Are we traitors or are we patriots? Are we Americans or are we humans? Or, might it not be possible, as it was at this country's founding, for us all to be both? As of this writing, I have decided to come home and find out.

REFERENCES

Applebome, Peter. 2009. "Giving Back Stature Stolen in Red Scare." *New York Times*, September 2. http://www.nytimes.com/2009/09/03/nyregion/03towns .html.
Hughes, Langston. [1936] 1994. "Let America Be America Again." In *The Collected Poems of Langston Hughes*, edited by Arnold Rampersad and David Roessel. New York: Alfred A. Knopf/Random House, Inc.
Miller, Jennifer. 2010. "The Outcast Redeemer." Review of *Edward Carpenter: A Life of Liberty and Love*, by Sheila Rowbotham. *Politics and Culture* 2 (May 24). http://www.politicsandculture.org/2010/05/24/the-outcast-redeemer-2/.
Obama, Barack. 2009. Keynote address, Human Rights Campaign Annual Dinner, October 10, Washington, D.C. http://blogs.suntimes.com/sweet/2009/ 10/obama_human_rights_campaign_sp.html.

Paradoxes and Possibilities: Domestic Human Rights Policy in Context

Kathryn Libal and Shareen Hertel

MOVING BEYOND EXCEPTIONALISM

The United States of America was founded on the principle of equality through law, even if this ideal has not always been realized. Indeed, the struggle to realize equality and full participation in society and governance is a perennial theme in U.S. history. At various junctures, realizing this ideal has been challenging, especially in the face of war, economic crises, or social unrest. Nowhere is this more evident than today, when growing opposition (both at the grassroots level and among political elites) to "big government" and "judicial activism" threatens to significantly limit the capacity of the state to address discrimination and social inequality. This opposition has sharpened in the wake of economic recession, heightened national security concerns, and rising nativism.

Human rights could provide a useful tool for addressing these challenges. Human rights are grounded in the notion of human dignity, and they obligate the state to assure the protection and provision of a full range of political, civil, economic, social, and cultural rights. Why, then, are human rights not central to discussions of public policy and legal reform in the United States? After all, the United States played an instrumental role both in founding the modern human rights regime in the immediate aftermath of World War II and in championing human rights as a foreign policy priority at various junctures over the ensuing six decades.

Yet many politicians, civil servants, members of the judiciary, academics, and pundits have long insisted that international human rights norms do not apply (or apply in only a limited manner) to the crafting, implementation, or evaluation of U.S. domestic laws and public policy. American citizens have tended instead to frame their grievances over personal abuse both in terms of constitutional rights and civil rights. Indeed, the Constitution (not human rights) is a focal point of national identity in the United States. The practical effect has been to extend "American exceptionalism" on human rights to the domestic realm. As Catherine Powell notes: "[H]uman rights has come to be seen as a purely international concern, even though it is fundamentally the responsibility of each nation to guarantee basic rights for its own people, as a matter of domestic policy" (Powell 2008, 1).

Americans thus resist scrutinizing domestic concerns – such as the effects of institutionalized racism and discrimination on other grounds (e.g., gender identity or disability) or the deepening of class-based inequality – in human rights terms. At both the institutional and popular level, human rights discourse in the United States has been anchored in the notion of freedom from abuse (negative rights) rather than entitlements to particular forms of social welfare or state-sponsored economic development to fulfill rights (positive rights). This dichotomy stems in part from the U.S. constitutional framework, which emphasizes civil and political rights and is less explicit on economic and social rights.[1]

The intellectual and political gulf between positive and negative dimensions of rights has thus become central to the United States' human rights identity over the past half-century. Although the interdependence and indivisibility of human rights was central to their initial conceptualization in international law, such lofty principles quickly became eclipsed by global politics during the Cold War. The reverberations were clear at the domestic level, in the United States' insistence that only civil and political rights are "real" rights. The U.S. Supreme Court, moreover, has never ruled that poor people constitute a protected group ("suspect class"), and thus there remains no fundamental right to subsistence in U.S. law (Kaufman 2005, 3; Davis 1995).

The institutional landscape mirrors this divide. Relevant federal, state, and local human rights agencies focus principally on questions of

---

[1] The U.S. Constitution sought to reverse the legacy of racial inequality in citizenship rights and political participation through the addition of the Fourteenth and Fifteenth Amendments. The Fourteenth Amendment, in particular, was grounded in the right to equal *protection from* harm rather than substantive guarantees of the *right to* state provision of entitlements – as evident in the landmark *Brown v. Board of Education* decision of the Supreme Court, which asserted the right to nondiscrimination rather than a substantive right to education (Patterson 2001; Steel 2001; Balkin 2001). Substantive guarantees of education and other economic and social rights have thus remained largely outside the purview of formal U.S. constitutional interpretation or reforms (Sunstein 2004).

procedural discrimination in the areas of civil and political rights. These institutions are largely separate in mandate and function from parallel agencies tasked with promoting domestic human welfare. Their work intersects only when individual discrimination is at stake, not when shortfalls in human well-being violate basic notions of rights fulfillment. As Stein and Lord observe in this book, "over-reliance on a minority-rights frame, involving rigid adherence to the formal equality mode" means that "equality measures that move beyond the elimination of simple prejudice are considered outside the province of law makers" (204).

As several chapters in this book underscore, the enduring legacy of racism has also contributed to the uneven realization of human rights in the United States. Since the 1970s, the bottom decile of wage-earners has seen wages increase less than 1 percent, whereas wages of those in the top decile have grown 27 percent (Opportunity Agenda 2010, 6). The patterns of these losses and gains follow racial lines. Asian Americans and whites earn the most; Latinos and Native Americans earn the least (American Human Development Report [AHDR] 2010, 2). Home ownership has modestly increased among higher income groups over the past three decades, whereas persistent discrimination in mortgage lending and home sales has resulted in declining rates of ownership among minorities (Glasberg, Beeman, and Casey forthcoming; Opportunity Agenda 2010, 6).

Health disparities are also pronounced. Whereas Asian Americans live the longest of any group in the United States, African-American life expectancy today is on par with that of the average American three decades ago (AHDR 2010, 1–2). African-American women are nearly four times more likely to die of pregnancy-related complications than white women, a level of disparity that has not improved in more than twenty years (Amnesty International 2010). In all but four states, Latinos either equal or surpass the national average in life span (AHDR 2010, 1–2), yet they lag significantly in educational attainment nationally, with only six in ten completing high school (Lewis and Burd-Sharps 2010, 8).

Moreover, the disproportionate incarceration of minorities in the United States has a multitude of human rights implications. As the Sentencing Project Reports (2010):

> More than 60% of the people in prison are now racial and ethnic minorities. For Black males in their twenties, 1 in every 8 is in prison or jail on any given day.... Increasingly, laws and policies are being enacted to restrict persons with a felony conviction (particularly convictions for drug

offenses) from employment, receipt of welfare benefits, access to public housing, and eligibility for student loans for higher education. Such collateral penalties place substantial barriers to an individual's social and economic advancement.

The UN Committee on the Elimination of Racial Discrimination underscored the interconnectedness of civil, political, economic, and social rights for ethnic and racial minorities in the United States in its most recent review (CERD 2008) of the International Convention on the Elimination of all forms of Racial Discrimination (ICERD). The United States ratified this landmark treaty on ending racial discrimination in 1994. In its 2008 Concluding Observations, the committee linked the disproportionate representation of "ethnic and national minorities in the prison population" to racial discrimination in the guarantee of equal treatment before the law, *and* to broader structural discrimination (2008, 5–6, ¶20).

Yet despite the collective dimension of these inequalities, American "rights talk," to use Mary Ann Glendon's phrase (1991), remains individualistic in nature with a strong emphasis on rights rather than responsibilities. Whereas human rights law posits rights as connected to corresponding duties (Whelan 2006; Baehr 2000), in practice duties have been eclipsed by rights in U.S. discourse. This "American rights dialect," Glendon argues, promotes a culture of rights in which "the winner takes all and the loser has to get out of town" (1991, 9, cited in Maltese 1993, 7). The American commitment to property rights above nearly all other rights, coupled with the virtual silence on collective duties, is a paradox of human rights discourse in America. So, too, is the consistent emphasis on individual over collective rights.

American notions of responsibility for fulfilling rights are also highly individual, with a tendency to blame the victim (especially in the case of the poor) for her or his situation rather than to consider the state's role in respecting, protecting, or fulfilling rights (Neubeck 2006) – including the state's duty to protect those within its borders from violations by nonstate actors, such as corporations (Bauer, Chapter 9 of this book). Indeed, the notion that poor people's rights are violated through systemic economic disadvantage or that the state has a responsibility to alter economic structures that perpetuate inequality has not been central to U.S. human rights for decades (Albisa, Chapter 4 of this book). In part, this stems from a myth of the individual's ability to secure one's own well-being and that of one's family solely through hard work and perseverance (Rank

2005). The failure to recognize structural disadvantage is also a result of the fealty that Americans hold toward property rights and market-based capitalism. Yet as constitutional scholar Noah Feldman (2010) observes:

> ... new and pressing constitutional issues and problems loom on the horizon – and they cannot be easily solved or resolved using the now-familiar frameworks of liberty and equality. These problems cluster around the current economic situation, which has revealed the extraordinary power of capital markets and business corporations in shaping the structure and actions of our government.... They require us to determine the limits of government power and the extent to which the state can impinge on collective and individual freedoms... Progressive constitutional thinkers... are out of practice in addressing such structural economic questions.

Supreme Court justices, moreover, have been reluctant to invoke foreign law – let alone international human rights law – in their jurisprudence (Ginsburg 2009), although lower courts are beginning to shift in this direction (Davis 2000). As Catherine Albisa shows in chapter four of this book, whereas questions of economic rights have often been adjudicated in the courts, they have not been recognized explicitly as human rights.

At the grassroots level, domestic social-justice advocates typically have not employed the language of international human rights in their critiques of U.S. public policy (Lewis 2008; Thomas 2008). Despite early twentieth-century efforts by American nongovernmental organizations (NGOs) to frame inequality in human rights terms (Anderson 2003), advocates in the United States have employed a nondiscrimination frame that resonates with U.S. case law and corresponding statutory protections of citizenship guarantees, as well as public discourse on human rights. Yet those working on behalf of noncitizens or other structurally marginalized groups within the United States have begun to engage more vigorously with international human rights institutions and processes. They have done so because of inadequate protections for these groups under existing U.S. law (Soohoo, Albisa, and Davis 2008) and because of strident anti-immigrant rhetoric at the popular level (Neubeck, Chapter 12 of this book).

Several trends are clear in the work of major U.S.-based human rights groups (including Human Rights Watch, Human Rights First, and Amnesty International-USA, among others). First, these groups are increasingly partnering with traditional civil rights organizations – such as the American Civil Liberties Union (ACLU) or the Center for Constitutional Rights – to address human rights violations in the United States and abroad. Second, conventional human rights groups have begun to move beyond a narrow civil rights frame to incorporate economic and social rights into their programming (Khan 2009). Third, all of these groups (human rights and civil rights groups alike) have begun to dedicate significant resources to monitoring and reporting on violations of noncitizens' rights.[2] They have focused on violations of civil rights in the context of detention and deportation as well as violations of health, housing, and labor rights involving structurally marginalized and immigrant populations (Human Rights Watch 2010a; Human Rights Watch 2010b; Amnesty International-USA 2009). Fourth, leaders in domestic human rights advocacy – particularly on economic and social rights – are drawn from a dynamic new universe of lawyers and grassroots activists, many of whom are linked through the U.S. Human Rights Network.

Indeed, the tide appears to be turning slowly but surely – with a widening set of actors exploring the application of international human rights law and discourse within the United States. Thus, the "domestication" of human rights is beginning to occur on multiple fronts. This is evident from the number of U.S.-based NGOs participating in the first universal periodic review of U.S. domestic human rights performance, conducted by the UN Human Rights Council (United Nations Human Rights Council 2010).

This book brings to light emerging evidence that U.S.-based scholars, activists, lawyers, and policy makers are shifting toward a fuller engagement with international human rights norms and their application to U.S. domestic policy dilemmas. This signals a growing recognition of economic and social rights and their implications for addressing historic patterns of discrimination and inequality within the United States. The book also underscores how civil rights concerns are increasingly framed as part of a broader human rights language and practice. Before proceeding to explore this contemporary shift, a brief discussion of historical milestones in U.S. human rights practice is in order.

---

[2] For example, in the wake of recent changes to state immigration law in Arizona (i.e., Law SB 1070), domestic human rights advocates have echoed international condemnation of a "disturbing pattern of legislative activity hostile to ethnic minorities and immigrants" (UN Office of the High Commissioner for Human Rights 2010). The Arizona law, they argue, increases the risk of racial profiling by law enforcement officials. This, in turn, violates the United States' commitments under ICERD. Labor rights advocates have also strategically engaged both regional and international human rights mechanisms to defend the rights of noncitizen workers (Asbed 2008; Compa 1999).

HISTORICAL ACCOUNT OF THE RISE OF HUMAN RIGHTS PRACTICES IN THE UNITED STATES

As historian Ken Cmiel has noted, "Few political agendas have seen such a rapid and dramatic growth as that of 'human rights'" (2004, 117). Whereas this has been most evident in the post-Cold War era in the United States, since at least the 1930s, human rights has been invoked as a framework or justification for action in a variety of campaigns challenging state-sanctioned oppression. The term "human rights" was rarely invoked prior to the 1940s in the United States, though antecedents to grassroots human rights activism could be seen in antislavery, labor rights, children's rights, and women's rights movements (Ishay 2004; Lauren 2003). Henry Gerber, for example, founded the short-lived Society for Human Rights in 1924 in Chicago to press for the rights of sexual minorities (Katz 1992).

The role of Eleanor Roosevelt as the first chair of the Human Rights Commission and key contributor in drafting the Universal Declaration of Human Rights is relatively well known (Glendon 2002). Less recognized has been the engagement of African-American organizations in human rights advocacy aimed at addressing the legacy of official segregation and discrimination against African Americans and other minority racial groups. In the decade after the creation of the United Nations, African-American leaders, galvanized by the National Association for the Advancement of Colored People (NAACP), mobilized to "make human rights *the* standard for equality" (Anderson 2003, 2). These early efforts bridged what would become ossified divides between civil and political rights and social and economic rights during the Cold War era. For example, in the 1940s–1950s, leading civil rights organizations such as ACLU and NAACP combined labor rights issues with challenges to segregation and discrimination in the workplace on the basis of ethnicity or race (Goluboff 2007).

Yet, as Carol Anderson (2003) has masterfully shown, U.S. treatment of human rights as a matter of foreign rather than domestic policy reflected a compromise with segregationist and anticommunist political leaders of the 1940s–1960s (see also Abramovitz, Chapter 3 in this book). As a number of scholars have argued, politics have profoundly shaped the U.S. government's participation – and nonparticipation – in international human rights processes (Anderson 2003; Hattery, Embrick, and Smith 2008).

Indeed, as the Cold War struggles between the United States and the Soviet Union deepened, the United States played a less fundamental role in drafting the major post-UDHR covenants: the International Covenant on Civil and Political Rights (ICCPR) and the International Covenant on Economic, Social, and Cultural Rights (ICESCR). The United States increasingly refused to recognize economic and social rights as "rights." The privileging of civil and political rights as core human rights was also reflected in the advocacy of the most prominent human rights organizations that emerged in Europe and the United States in the 1970s (Cmiel 2004; Moyn 2010). Until the 1990s, Amnesty International and Human Rights Watch, for example, rarely tackled economic and social rights in local and transnational campaigns (Lewis 2008). The majority of civil rights activists of the 1960s did not engage these rights either – with a few exceptions such as Martin Luther King, Jr., who turned to human rights discourses late in his life (Jackson 2006).

In 1966, Lyndon B. Johnson signed the International Convention on the Elimination of All Forms of Racial Discrimination (ICERD), although the treaty was not ratified until the tenure of the Clinton Administration. President Gerald Ford initiated the practice of selectively tying foreign aid to human rights performance, and in the 1970s he began to push for greater human rights participation internationally. President Jimmy Carter signed key treaties, including the ICCPR, ICESCR, and the Convention on the Elimination of All Forms of Discrimination against Women (CEDAW). But such efforts were framed as extensions of foreign policy intended to solidify U.S. involvement in the enforcement of human rights norms abroad (Cmiel 2004). Despite the Carter Administration's rather patchy and unsystematic support for U.S. participation in key human rights treaties, the United States ratified only a few of the key human rights treaties throughout the ensuing decades: the Convention Against Torture (in 1994); the ICCPR (in 1992); ICERD (in 1994); the Optional Protocol to the Convention on the Rights of the Child (CRC) on the Sale of Children, Child Prostitution, and Child Pornography (in 2002); and the Optional Protocol to the Convention on the Rights of the Child on the Involvement of Children in Armed Conflict (in 2002).[3]

As a number of contributors to this book argue, the election of Barack Obama as president and his subsequent appointment of key human rights leaders (such as Harold Hongju Koh and Michael Posner) to important positions within the administration signal an opportunity for fuller

---

[3] The United States also ratified the Protocol Relating to the Status of Refugees in 1968 and the Convention on the Prevention and Punishment of the Crime of Genocide in 1988.

participation and engagement in international human rights processes (Stein and Lord, Chapter 10 and Todres, Chapter 7 of this book). Koh, as legal advisor to the State Department, has underscored that obligations for human rights reporting must be addressed at both the state and federal levels. He has issued memoranda to state governors, for example, calling attention to the human rights treaties the United States has ratified (Koh 2010).[4] Access to these documents on a consolidated, officially hosted webpage (United States Department of State 2009) also responds to UN human rights criticisms about limited knowledge of human rights obligations and weak implementation at local, state, and federal levels throughout the United States (Committee on the Elimination of Racial Discrimination 2008, 3). Thus, the State Department's website includes links to the major human rights treaties to which the United States has acceded, including U.S. government reports and UN human rights committee recommendations concerning the ICCPR, CAT, ICERD, and the optional protocols of the CRC (http://www.state.gov/g/drl/hr/treaties/index.htm).

In addition, State Department lawyers are currently considering which other human rights treaties could be advanced to the Senate for ratification during President Obama's tenure. Advocates involved in ratification efforts cite internal debates over which treaty is likely to gain the Senate's support, signaling that the newest convention – the International Convention on the Rights of Persons With Disabilities – is a likely forerunner (Stein and Lord, Chapter 10 in this book). Other official documents underscore support for the Convention on the Elimination of All Forms of Discrimination Against Women (United States Department of State 2009). The Convention on the Rights of the Child is also under consideration, but advocates recognize that organized grassroots opposition to CEDAW and the CRC may present insurmountable barriers to ratification (Todres, Chapter 7 in this book). The International Covenant on Economic, Social, and Cultural Rights remains a distant prospect.

POWER AND LIMITS OF LEGALISM: INSTITUTIONAL ANALYSIS

Although the United States has a long and storied tradition of judicial activism on civil rights, there are both procedural obstacles and theoretical challenges that constrain a human rights approach to U.S. legal practice,

---

[4] See Koh's (2007) analysis of the relevance of applying international human rights principles in both domestic and foreign policy.

public policy design, and grassroots advocacy. Procedurally, international law is nonself-executing in the United States (Henkin 1995). It does not automatically enter into force upon the country's ratification of any given treaty, but instead requires an assessment of conformance with domestic law and policy first. This often means endless partisan wrangling within Congress over whether international norms are compatible with U.S. norms – even when the distinctions are exaggerated for political purposes.

There are numerous debates about the compatibility of U.S. and international human rights law. For example, the notion of a human right as a claim by someone, on someone, for something essential to human dignity establishes an individually based claim structure, which maps onto existing U.S. law well (Gewirth 1998). However, international human rights law also invokes the collective dimensions of rights in multiple ways – for example, through the formulation of "group rights," such as indigenous rights to land and cultural expression. These are afforded to the group as a whole, are nondivisible, and are one of the most contested and least well-established categories of rights in international law (Reidel 2010). As discussed by Bethany Berger (Chapter 11 in this book), the human rights of indigenous peoples in the United States repeatedly have fallen victim to a failure to implement group rights effectively.

Collective individual rights, in turn, are also controversial. These rights are individually enjoyed by specific people based on their membership in a group with a collective history of shared oppression. Remedies such as "temporary special measures" (e.g., legislative quotas for women) are required under CEDAW to redress historical patterns of economic, political, and social marginalization (Krook 2010).

Although the United States is not a party to CEDAW, temporary special measures are paralleled in U.S. law by the principle of "affirmative action." This remedy itself is increasingly under siege in the United States – challenged by citizens who regard it as a special privilege that affronts deeply held notions of a meritocracy (Dudas 2005; Amsterdam and Bruner 2002). Indeed, a corresponding series of lower court cases has been decided favorably on behalf of white plaintiffs who claim that race-based university selection criteria discriminate against them in violation of the Fourteenth Amendment's equal protection clause. Even when the Supreme Court has ruled that such criteria are justified in the interest of creating a diverse learning environment, such as in *Regents of the University of California v. Bakke* (1978) or *Grutter v. Bollinger* (2003), popular ballot initiatives have eliminated the remedy (e.g., California's Proposition 209; Michigan's Proposition 2; Washington's Initiative 200).

There is also the longstanding challenge – not unique to the United States, yet relevant – of transcending the public/private divide that has historically privileged state involvement in the "public" realm (i.e., formal sector employment or matters of formal political participation such as voting) over involvement in the "private" sphere of the home or the informal economy. Feminist legal scholars and their grassroots allies have shared the goal of breaking down the barriers between public and private spheres to increase state accountability for actions in defense of women's rights, regardless of the locus of abuse and in the interest of enhancing women's empowerment (Parekh, 2010; Romany 1993; Merry and Shimmin, Chapter 6 in this book). They have challenged the notion that privacy places the domestic realm off limits to the state, while at the same time adroitly invoking privacy in a skillful defense of reproductive rights.

On a practical level, many of these same feminist scholars and activists have waged lengthy battles to ensure enforcement of laws against domestic abuse and to safeguard access to a range of safe and legal contraceptive options for all women, regardless of income level – as Rhonda Copelon did, for example, in *Harris v. McRae* (1980). They have forged alliances with women working globally on similar issues within the UN human rights arena (Momaya 2010). And they have called on the state to take an active role not only in regulating the formal workplace to ensure equal pay for equal work, but also in recognizing the value of women's unpaid household work.

Human rights in the United States are also bedeviled by a persistent reluctance – both official and popular – to recognize economic rights as "real" rights. As discussed previously, economic rights are tied to notions of social citizenship that reach beyond the narrow bounds of the contemporary U.S. welfare state. This has not always been the case. As Abramovitz indicates in Chapter 3 of this book, a strong commitment to social rights as rights was foundational to the 1930s New Deal and Franklin Delano Roosevelt's "Four Freedoms" and was echoed in the subsequent UN Declaration of Human Rights. However, the privatization of health care and other forms of care work (such as elder care and childcare) over the past half century – coupled with the growing inaccessibility of affordable housing and higher education for many Americans – is helping fuel a growing wealth gap, which many in the United States still fail to view in human rights terms.

Indeed, there is increasingly strident public rhetoric that scapegoats the poor and undocumented while feeding a rising nativism (Goldsmith

and Romero 2008). For example, the online group Refugee Resettlement Watch characterizes organizations that work with immigrants and
refugees as being "run with tax dollars" and being used to "teach immigrants how to access 'resources' (welfare benefits), and then act as a
political voice for their respective ethnic group" (Refugee Resettlement
Watch 2010). The ambiguity and capriciousness of U.S. immigration
policy are not new (Zolberg 2006). However, contemporary growth in
the country's minority population is occurring precisely at a time when
the "mainstream" population increasingly feels at risk in the face of
"new security threats" in the post-9/11 era and constrained in the face
of eroding domestic prosperity. The broadening chasm in wealth generated by stagnating wages, reductions in health and retirement benefits,
erosion of housing values, decreasing job security amid the flexibiliza-
tion of the labor force, and outsourcing of industrial and service jobs
all have contributed to an intensifying racialization of contemporary
American immigration politics and to scape-goating of the poor. Yet
empirically, the pervasive experiences of poverty, inequality and insecurity are rooted less in the failures of individuals than in structural
inequality stemming from, among other factors, labor market dynamics
and weak social safety nets (Rank 2005; Howard-Hassmann and Welch,
Jr. 2006).

FROM ELITE ADVOCACY TO GRASSROOTS SUPPORT
FOR HUMAN RIGHTS

As several of our contributors note in this book (Finger and Luft, Chapter 15; Neubeck, Chapter 12; Albisa, Chapter 4), recognizing and realizing the legitimacy of human rights norms and processes "at home"
requires building a broader constituency for human rights than has been
achieved to date. Finger and Luft argue that this will require fostering a
"human rights culture," by which they mean "an engagement – philosophical, moral, and political, if not legal or systematic – with the notion
that human beings are entitled to a broader category of rights than those
promised by the U.S. Constitution. This orientation reveals itself in the
growing use of human rights framing devices by grassroots human rights
activists" (Finger and Luft in this volume, 302).

  Indeed, one of the legacies of American exceptionalism has been igno-
rance of – or sometimes outright hostility toward – the domestication of
human rights norms and practices. Basic familiarity with human rights
ideas through formal education has been limited (Apsel 2005), and even

among professionals who would be more likely to know about the United States' international human rights obligations, such knowledge remains scant (Finnegan, Saltzman, and White 2010). Moreover, the dominant idea associated with human rights focuses on violations, rather than the substantive, positive obligations states have to secure economic and social rights. Whereas educational efforts are unfolding in an effort to expand the "culture" of human rights in the United States, advocates and scholars recognize that this will be a long-term process of cultural transformation contested by sizeable constituencies, which remain skeptical or fearful of international processes such as human rights treaty monitoring.

As this book shows, a growing number of NGOs and grassroots organizations have begun to use human rights framing to address seemingly intractable social problems and harms. Such organizations mobilize by sharing resources, technical support, and media outreach efforts, as well as political access. One of the most visible instances of human rights coalition building among a variety of organizations and groups is the U.S. Human Rights Network. Formed following a Human Rights Leadership Summit held at Howard University Law School in 2002, and officially established in 2004, the network comprises some 300 member organizations. Founding member organizations included nationally recognized groups such as the ACLU, American Friends Service Committee, Amnesty International USA, Human Rights Watch, the Center for Constitutional Rights, and the NAACP Legal Defense Education Fund. Organizations such as Incite! Women of Color Against Violence, the Mississippi Center for Human Rights, Kensington Welfare Rights Union, and the Western Shoshone Defense Project also formed important local and regional links to movements addressing discrimination and structural inequality. Finally, Columbia University Law School and the Columbia University Mailman School of Public Health offered institutional support to the network.

Since 2004, the network's membership and visibility have expanded following its coordination of NGO participation in ICERD monitoring processes. In addition to playing an active role at the 2008 ICERD review in Geneva, the network has sponsored several human rights summits, participated in the U.S. Social Forum process, hosted webinars as well as on-site training in human rights advocacy, and participated in advocacy at the state and federal levels. In 2010, as the United States prepared to participate in the Human Rights Council's universal periodic review of its progress on human rights, the U.S. Human Rights Network helped coordinate documentation of rights violations and substantive legal and policy concerns (U.S. Human Rights Network n.d.). Through its website, the network has made available "shadow reports" of U.S. progress on key domestic concerns, such as civil rights, racial discrimination, corporate accountability, criminal justice, death penalty, economic and social rights, education, environmental justice, foreign policy, housing, the aftermath of Hurricane Katrina, labor (including migrant labor), and reproductive health, among other concerns.

This engagement of U.S.-based NGOs intent on applying human rights at home has been made possible in large part because of substantial philanthropic support by organizations such as the Ford Foundation, Public Welfare Foundation, Atlantic Philanthropies, Tides Foundation, and Open Society Institute as well as a number of smaller family foundations. Absent such financial support, it would have been difficult to launch campaigns in practical terms, and it would have been doubly difficult to gain political legitimacy for these efforts. In addition to foundations, universities foster connections between human rights practitioners and legal advocacy organizations. Institutions of higher learning are able to marshal financial and scholarly resources to support human rights research and advocacy.

These are largely elite-led efforts, but they have cultivated grassroots mobilization and promoted the development of human rights awareness among local groups and leaders who have the legitimacy to move a domestic human rights agenda forward at the popular level (see e.g., U.S. Human Rights Fund 2010; Ford Foundation 2004). Such grassroots rights promotion includes, for example, the National Economic and Social Rights Initiative's coordination and human rights training for the national "Schools with Dignity" campaign and its "Human Right to Healthcare Campaign," which include partnerships with local organizations in Vermont and Montana.[5]

Whereas efforts to promote human rights education and awareness at the grassroots level have increased in various places across the United States, opposition to the domestic application of human rights norms and practices presents a powerful challenge to local and national-level human rights organizers and advocates. Conservative think tanks (e.g., the American Enterprise Institute, the Heritage Foundation, and the American Eagle Forum) along with a host of Christian faith-based organizations use many of the same web-based and community-based tactics to publicize their opposition to U.S. participation in the international human

[5] Details of these campaigns can be found on NESRI's website (http://www.nesri.org).

rights system. They also oppose social policy reform that would introduce robust social supports in the form of entitlements, especially related to health, housing, and public assistance (Noble 2007; O'Connor 2002; Schreiber 2008). As Todres notes in Chapter 7 of this book, social conservatives continue to successfully block U.S. accession to the CRC, CEDAW, and the ICESCR even under the Obama Administration. Conservative political elites and their motivated constituencies frame participation in such treaties as a fundamental challenge to the "traditional family" and a covert means of infusing "socialistic values" that they regard as antithetical to U.S. values. The rhetoric claims exceptionalism as a badge of honor, such as the assertion by Steven Groves of the Heritage Foundation that UN human rights committees, such as CERD, have no jurisdiction or any "meaningful role to play" in ongoing debates about domestic social policy. "Those matters constitute legal, social, and cultural components of American life and must be left to the American people to consider and decide" (Groves 2008:3).

CONTRIBUTIONS TO THIS BOOK

We have engaged the insights of an interdisciplinary group of contributors to explore the evolution of human rights in domestic public policy, popular discourse, American legal theory, and corresponding institutional frameworks. The content of their chapters ranges from the founding of the country to the present. Whereas there is no single position among our contributors regarding the state of contemporary human rights in the United States, all recognize the significant shift toward a broader engagement with human rights by a wide range of actors across the country. Several of our contributors have been centrally involved in shaping scholarly discourse and policy outcomes in the areas they write on – from disability law to children's rights, from human rights approaches to addressing poverty to prison reform as a key civil rights issue. Indeed, the foreword is authored by Dorothy Q. Thomas, a protagonist in the U.S. human rights movement.

The chapters in Section I ground this book by providing an overview of key theoretical and institutional frameworks as well as historical milestones that have shaped the evolution and current state of human rights in the United States. Rhoda Howard-Hassmann situates the United States in comparative perspective with other industrialized democracies while also examining the theoretical underpinnings of human dignity as the structuring principle of human rights and its corresponding requirements.

Mimi Abramovitz then offers a comprehensive historical overview of the evolution of American social welfare policy in the twentieth century, highlighting ideological battles over the relationship between state and market and their impact on access to the basic requisites for fulfilling economic and social rights. Catherine Albisa explores the interplay between law and social movements, which she argues is foundational to creating "constitutive commitments" to economic and social rights. She critically analyzes a century's worth of U.S. Supreme Court rulings that have at times advanced and at other times hindered this process. Finally, Risa Kaufman assesses the significant role played by state and local institutions in translating international human rights norms and law into practice domestically.

The second section of the book explores several arenas in which U.S.-based legal scholars, policy practitioners, and grassroots activists are challenging multiple divides: first, between "public" and "private" spheres, specifically with reference to domestic violence and children's rights; second, between "public" and "private" sectors, specifically with reference to health care and corporate governance. Drawing on ethnographic research at the grassroots level, Sally Engle Merry and Jessica Shimmin analyze the intellectual, political, and institutional resistance in the United States to viewing domestic violence as a central human rights issue. Jonathan Todres unravels the paradoxical position of the United States on children's rights and assesses prospects for change in light of international policy shifts and domestic political reforms. Jean Connolly Carmalt, Sarah Zaidi, and Alicia Ely Yamin identify the roots of unequal access to health care in the United States and critique current health care reform policies from a human rights perspective. And Joanne Bauer presents a theoretical framework for analyzing the human rights responsibilities of private corporations along with a rich empirical assessment of the current state of practice by businesses operating in multiple sectors. The chapters in Section II thus provide well-grounded institutional analyses of how U.S. adoption of international law stands to affect contemporary public policy formation, judicial practices, and statutory law in each of these arenas. Bridging the "public/private" divides discussed in each of these chapters will also entail grappling with longstanding controversies over the nature of governance of human rights within the United States.

Contributors to Section III examine how advocates (both in the courts and at the grassroots level) have employed human rights strategies to address the inequalities experienced by particularly vulnerable individuals and groups. Michael Ashley Stein and Janet E. Lord discuss the evolution of human rights policies covering persons with disabilities in the United States, and Bethany Berger analyzes the evolution of indigenous peoples' rights from the country's founding to the present. Ken Neubeck explains the rights at risk of lone-mother-headed families, and Mie Lewis focuses on violations of the rights of incarcerated persons – especially children in detention. Julie Mertus chronicles the evolution of advocacy and policy change on the rights of lesbian, gay, bisexual, and transgendered people. And Davida Finger and Rachel E. Luft assess the rights at stake in the context of contemporary U.S. sheltering and disaster policies, drawing both on ethnographic research among survivors of recent hurricanes in Louisiana and on analysis of primary legal documents integral to the formulation of related state policy. This section grapples with multiple axes of discrimination and exclusion linked to racism, sexism, classism, anti-immigrant sentiment, and other forms of marginalization framed as human rights concerns.

As this book shows, we are at a critical juncture in the evolution of human rights as a concept and practice in the United States. In some quarters, the desire to link U.S. practice with international standards and institutions is enthusiastically embraced, whereas in others it is staunchly resisted. The conceptualization of human rights at stake in the United States has certainly broadened beyond traditional concern with civil and political rights. Moreover, movements to secure civil rights have been reinvigorated by an intersection with human rights discourse and grass-roots practice. The book highlights these intersections, even while recognizing the still unfinished character of the transition under way and the substantial opposition to bringing human rights home.

Whereas other books address the domestication of human rights in the United States, this edited collection significantly updates earlier work while highlighting new and emerging domains of interest (e.g., children's civil rights in prison; state accountability for internal displacement in the wake of natural disasters; business and human rights and the environment; disability rights; the rights of sexual minorities; and domestic violence as a human rights issue). It also engages a wide range of academic disciplines and policy voices in the discussion. This book thus moves the debate on the place of human rights in the United States forward on multiple fronts through a synthesis of this interdisciplinary work. We hope it also contributes to meaningful policy change that will help safeguard the rights of those most at risk in the United States, now and in the future.

REFERENCES

American Human Development Report Project. 2010. "AHDP Releases 'A Century Apart,' Revealing Alarming Disparities in Well-Being Among US Racial and Ethnic Groups." http://www.measureofamerica.org/wpcontent/uploads/2010/04/A_Century_Apart_Media_Release_04-28-2010.pdf.
Amnesty International-USA. 2009. *Jailed Without Justice: Immigration Detention in the USA*. New York: Amnesty International.
———. 2010. *Deadly Delivery: The Maternal Health Care Crisis in the USA* (London: Amnesty International). http://www.amnestyusa.org/dignity/pdf/DeadlyDelivery.pdf.
Amsterdam, Anthony G., and Jerome Bruner. 2002. *Minding the Law*. Cambridge, MA: Harvard University Press.
Anderson, Carol. 2003. *Eyes Off the Prize: The United Nations and the African-American Struggle for Human Rights, 1944–1955*. New York: Cambridge University Press.
Apsel, Joyce. 2005. *Teaching About Human Rights*. Washington, D.C.: American Sociological Association.
Asbed, Greg. 2008. "Coalition of Immokalee Workers: '¡Golpear a Uno Es Golpear a Todos!' To Beat One of Us Is to Beat Us All!" In *Bringing Human Rights Home: A History of Human Rights in the United States*, edited by Cynthia Soohoo, Catherine Albisa, and Martha F. Davis, Vol. 3, 1–23. Westport, CT: Praeger Publishers.
Baehr, Peter R. 2000. "Controversies in the Current International Human Rights Debate," Denver University Human Rights Working Papers #3. http://www.du/edu/humanrights/workingpapers/index.html.
Balkin, Jack M. 2001. *What Brown v. Board of Education Should Have Said: The Nation's Top Legal Experts Re-Write America's Landmark Civil Rights Decision*. New York: New York University Press.
Cmiel, Kenneth. 2004. "Review Essay: The Recent History of Human Rights." *American Historical Review* 109(1): 117–35.
Committee on the Elimination of Racial Discrimination. 2008. Concluding Observations of the Committee on the Elimination of Racial Discrimination: United States of America. Seventy-second Session. Geneva, February 18–March 7, 2008. CERD/C/USA/CO/6. Geneva: United Nations.
Compa, Lance. 1999. "NAFTA's Labour Side Agreement Five Years On: Progress and Prospects for the NAALC." *Canadian Labour & Employment Law Journal* 7(1): 1–30.
Davis, Martha F. 1995. *Brutal Need: Lawyers and the Welfare Rights Movement 1960–1973*. New Haven, CT: Yale University Press.
———.2000. "International Human Rights and United States Law: Predictions of a Court Watcher." *Albany Law Review* 64: 417–36.
Dudas, Jeffrey. 2005. "In the Name of Equal Rights: 'Special' Rights and the Politics of Resentment in Post-Civil Rights America." *Law and Society Review* 39: 723.
Feldman, Noah. 2010. "What a Liberal Court Should Be." *New York Times Magazine*, June 27: 38–43.

Finnegan, Amy C., Adam P. Saltzman, and Shelley K. White. 2010. "Negotiating Politics and Culture: The Utility of Human Rights for Activist Organizations in the United States." *Journal of Human Rights Practice* 2(3): 307–33.

Ford Foundation. 2004. *Close to Home: Case Studies of Human Rights Work in the United States.* New York: Ford Foundation.

Gewirth, Alan. 1998. *The Community of Rights.* Chicago: University of Chicago Press.

Ginsburg, Ruth Bader. 2009. Remarks for a symposium on "The Jurisprudence of Justice Ruth Bader Ginsburg: A Discussion of Fifteen Years on the U.S. Supreme Court." Moritz College of Law, Ohio State University, April 9. http://moritzlaw.osu.edu/lawjournal/symposium/2008–09/index.php.

Glasberg, Davita Silfen, Angie Beeman, and Colleen Casey. Forthcoming. "Preying on the American Dream: Predatory Lending, the Social Construction of Foreclosure and Resistance to Economic Injustice." In *In Our Own Back Yard: Human Rights in the United States,* edited by Bandana Purkayastha, William T. Armaline, and Davita Silfen Glasberg. Philadelphia, PA: University of Pennsylvania Press.

Glendon, Mary Ann. 1991. *Rights Talk: The Impoverishment of Political Discourse.* New York: The Free Press.

———. 2002. *A World Made New: Eleanor Roosevelt and the Universal Declaration of Human Rights.* New York: Random House.

Goldsmith, Pat Rubio, and Mary Romero. 2008. "'Aliens,' 'Illegals,' and Other Types of 'Mexicanness': Examination of Racial Profiling in Border Policing." In *Globalization and America: Race, Human Rights, and Inequality,* edited by Angela J. Hattery, David G. Embrick, and Earl Smith, 127–42. Lanham, MD: Rowman & Littlefield Publishers, Inc.

Goluboff, Risa L. 2007. *The Lost Promise of Civil Rights.* Cambridge, MA: Harvard University Press.

Groves, Steven. 2008. "Furthering the UN's Leftist Agenda: The UN CERD Committee Report," WebMemo Published by the Heritage Foundation, No. 1899, April 22.

Grutter v. Bollinger 539 U.S. 306 (2003).

Harris v. McRae 448 U.S. 297 (1980).

Hattery, Angela, David G. Embrick, and Earl Smith, eds. 2008. *Globalization and America: Race, Human Rights, and Inequality.* Lanham, MD: Rowman & Littlefield Publishers, Inc.

Henkin, Louis. 1995. "Editorial Comments – U.S. Ratification of Human Rights Conventions: The Ghost of Senator Bricker." *The American Journal of International Law* 89(2): 341–50.

Howard-Hassmann, Rhoda E., and Claude E. Welch, Jr. 2006. *Economic Rights in Canada and the United States.* Philadelphia, PA: University of Pennsylvania Press.

Human Rights Watch. 2010a. *My So-Called Emancipation: From Foster Care to Homelessness for California Youth.* New York: Human Rights Watch.

———. 2010b. *World Report 2010.* New York: Human Rights Watch.

Ishay, Micheline R. 2004. *The History of Human Rights: From Ancient Times to the Globalization Era.* Berkeley, CA: University of California Press.

Jackson, Thomas F. 2006. *From Civil Rights to Human Rights: Martin Luther King, Jr., And the Struggle for Economic Justice.* Philadelphia, PA: University of Pennsylvania Press.

Katz, Jonathan Ned. 1992. *Gay American History: Lesbians and Gay Men in the U.S.A.* New York: Meridian Books.

Kaufman, Risa. 2005. "Bridging the Federalism Gap: Procedural Due Process and Race Discrimination in a Devolved Welfare System." *Hastings Race & Poverty Law Journal* 1: 1–34.

Khan, Irene. 2009. *The Unheard Truth: Poverty and Human Rights.* New York: W.W. Norton & Company.

Koh, Harold Hongju. 2007. "Restoring America's Human Rights Reputation." *Cornell Journal of International Law* 40: 635–59.

———. 2010. "Memorandum for State Governors: U.S. Human Rights Treaty Reports." United States Department of State. http://www.state.gov/documents/organization/137292.pdf.

Krook, Mona Lena. 2010. *Quotas for Women in Politics: Gender and Candidate Selection Reform Worldwide.* Oxford, UK: Oxford University Press.

Lauren, Paul Gordon. 2003. *The Evolution of International Human Rights: Visions Seen.* Philadelphia, PA: University of Pennsylvania Press.

Lewis, Hope. 2008. "'New' Human Rights: US Ambivalence Toward The International Economic and Social Rights Framework." In *Bringing Human Rights Home: A History of Human Rights in the United States*, edited by Cynthia Soohoo, Catherine Albisa, and Martha F. Davis, Vol. 1, 103–44. Westport, CT: Praeger Publishers.

Lewis, Kristen and Sarah Burd-Sharps. 2010. *A Century Apart: New Measures of Well-Being for US Ethnic and Racial Groups.* New York: Social Science Research Council.

Maltese, John Anthony. 1993. Review of *Rights Talk: The Impoverishment of Political Discourse* by Mary Ann Glendon. *Law and Politics Book Review* 3(2): 7–8. http://www.bsos.umd.edu/gvpt/lpbr/subpages/reviews/glendon.htm.

Momaya, Masum. 2010. "Remembering Rhonda Copelon," Friday File, Association for Women's Human Rights in Development. http://awid.org/eng/Issues-and-Analysis/Library/Remembering-Rhonda-Copelon.

Moyn, Samuel. 2010. *The Last Utopia: Human Rights in History.* Cambridge, MA: Belknap Press of Harvard University.

Neubeck, Kenneth. 2006. *When Welfare Disappears: The Case for Economic Human Rights.* New York: Routledge.

Noble, Charles. 2007. "From Neoconservative to New Right: American Conservatives and the Welfare State." In *Confronting the New Conservativism: The Rise of the Right in America*, edited by Michael J. Thompson, 109–24. New York: New York University Press.

O'Connor, Alice. 2002. *Poverty Knowledge: Social Science, Social Policy, and the Poor in 20th Century U.S. History.* Princeton, NJ: Princeton University Press.

(The) Opportunity Agenda. 2010. *American Opportunity: A Toolkit.* New York: The Opportunity Agenda. http://opportunityagenda.org/files/field_file/American%20Opportunity%20-%20A%20Toolkit_2.pdf.

Parekh, Serena. 2010. "Getting to the Root of Gender Inequality: Structural Injustice and Political Responsibility." *Hypatia: A Journal of Feminist Philosophy.* Nov. 23, 2010: DOI 10.1111/j.1527-2001.2010.01159.x.

Patterson, James T. 2001. *Brown v. Board of Education: A Civil Rights Milestone and Its Troubled Legacy.* New York: Oxford University Press.

Powell, Catherine. 2008. *Human Rights at Home: A Domestic Policy Blueprint for a New Administration.* Washington, DC: American Constitution Society for Law and Policy. http://www.acslaw.org/files/C%20Powell%20Blueprint.pdf.

Rank, Mark Robert. 2005. *One Nation Underprivileged: Why American Poverty Affects Us All.* New York: Oxford University Press.

Refugee Resettlement Watch. 2010. "Lewiston, ME: Professor implies that refugees financially benefit Lewiston." http://refugeeresettlementwatch. wordpress.com/.

Regents of the University of California v. Bakke 438 U.S. 265 (1978).

Reidel, Laura. 2010. "What Are Cultural Rights? Protecting Groups with Individual Rights." *Journal of Human Rights* 9(1): 65–80.

Romany, Celina. 1993. "Women as Aliens," *Harvard Human Rights Journal* 6: 87–125.

(The) Sentencing Project. 2010. Online factsheets on "Racial Disparities" and "Collateral Consequences." http://www.sentencingproject.org/template/page .cfm?id=122.

Schreiber, Ronnee. 2008. *Righting Feminism: Conservative Women and American Politics.* New York: Oxford University Press.

Sohoo, Cynthia, Catherine Albisa, and Martha F. Davis, eds. 2008. *Bringing Human Rights Home,* Vols. 1, 2, 3. Westport, CT: Praeger Publishers.

Steel, Lewis M. 2001. "Separate and Unequal, by Design," a review of *Brown v. Board of Education: A Civil Rights Milestone and Its Troubled Legacy,* by James T. Patterson. *The Nation* 272, 5: 27–32.

Sunstein, Cass. 2004. *The Second Bill of Rights: FDR's Unfinished Revolution and Why We Need It More than Ever.* New York: Basic Books.

Thomas, Dorothy Q. 2008. "Against American Supremacy: Rebuilding Human Rights Culture in the United States." In *Bringing Human Rights Home: From Civil Rights to Human Rights,* edited by Cynthia Soohoo, Catherine Albisa, and Martha F. Davis, Vol. 2, 1–23. Westport, CT: Praeger Publishers.

United Nations Human Rights Council. 2010. "Summary Prepared by the Office of the High Commissioner for Human Rights in Accordance with Paragraph 15(c) of the Annex to Human Rights Council Resolution 5/1." A/HRC/WG.6/9/USA/3. Geneva: United Nations. http://www.ushrnetwork. org/sites/default/files/UPR%20Civil%20Society%20Report.pdf.

United Nations Office of the High Commissioner for Human Rights. 2010. "Arizona – UN Experts Warn Against a 'Disturbing legal pattern hostile to ethnic minorities and immigrants.'" May 10. http://www.ohchr.org/en/ NewsEvents/Pages/DisplayNews.aspx?NewsID=10035&LangID=E.

United States Department of State. 2009. "U.S. Human Rights Commitment and Pledges," Fact Sheet of the Bureau of Democracy, Human Rights, and Labor. April 16. Washington, D.C.: Department of State. http://www.state. gov/g/drl/rls/fs/2009/121764.htm.

United States Human Rights Fund. 2010. *Perfecting Our Union: Human Rights Success Stories from Across the United States.* New York: US Human Rights Fund/Public Interest Projects.

United States Human Rights Network. n.d. UPR Reports. Atlanta, GA: United States Human Rights Network. Accessed December 9, 2010. http://www .ushrnetwork.org/upr_reports

Whelan, Daniel. 2006. *Interdependent, Indivisible, and Interrelated Human Rights: A Political and Historical Investigation.* Unpublished Ph.D. Dissertation, University of Denver.

Zolberg, Aristide. 2006. *A Nation by Design: Immigration Policy in the Fashioning of America.* Cambridge, MA: Harvard University Press.

Structuring Debates, Institutionalizing Rights

2

The Yellow Sweatshirt: Human Dignity and Economic Human Rights in Advanced Industrial Democracies

Rhoda E. Howard-Hassmann

THE YELLOW SWEATSHIRT

Some years ago on a Saturday morning, I stopped downtown in my economically depressed city of Hamilton, Ontario, Canada, to give a couple of dollars to a youngish man with dirty-blond hair who was asking for money. I noticed that he was wearing a bright yellow sweatshirt and I complimented him on it. He replied that he had received it from his sister for his birthday; she had taken him to the local charity store to buy it. I was surprised – it had not occurred to me that a person who asked strangers for money might have a sister or celebrate his birthdays.

In advanced industrial democracies, the poor are largely invisible to the comfortable middle classes; they live in segregated economic zones, send their children to different schools, and patronize different social institutions. Middle-class people such as I can choose to acknowledge them or avoid them when we go to areas they frequent, in the meantime salving our consciences about this most intractable of social problems by giving money to charity or perhaps engaging in volunteer work. The poor's invisibility is one aspect of the indignity they suffer. Even though they enjoy formal legal equality with all other citizens, they are more acted upon than actors, intruders in the world of the autonomous and efficacious. A few among the poor are those who do not wish to work; many more are those who cannot find work. Others are those who cannot work for pay because of obligations of care for children, the disabled, or the elderly. Still others are so battered by life or so challenged by physical

I am grateful to Matthew Overall for research assistance for this chapter and to Shareen Hertel, Kathryn Libal, and Lanse Minkler for their comments on an earlier version. I also thank the Canada Research Chairs program for the funds and time to write the chapter and Wilfrid Laurier University for my position as chair.

or mental disabilities that they are incapable of work of any kind. All are grouped together in an undifferentiated category labeled "the poor," whose material needs and human dignity are constantly at risk.

In this chapter, I discuss violations of economic human rights as they relate most especially to the poor in advanced industrial democracies. My concern is that every person should live a "minimally decent life" (Hertel and Minkler 2007, 3). Decency requires that everyone live a life of human dignity; as stated in Article 22 of the Universal Declaration of Human Rights, "Everyone . . . has the right to . . . the economic, social and cultural rights indispensable for his dignity." I propose that human dignity is a socially constructed normative value that reflects the social conditions and possibilities of a society.

HUMAN DIGNITY AS A SOCIAL CONSTRUCT

A person cannot live a life of dignity without the fulfillment of her economic human rights: poverty is undignified and impedes participation in wider social and political life. "Economic and social arrangements cannot . . . be excluded from a consideration of the demands of dignity. . . . Degrading living conditions and deprivation of basic needs" are antithetical to respect for inherent dignity (Schachter 1983, 851–52). The Universal Declaration of Human Rights (UDHR) states in its preamble that "recognition of the inherent dignity and of the equal and inalienable rights of all members of the human family is the foundation of freedom, justice and peace in the world." Article 1 of the UDHR also states that "All human beings are born free and equal in dignity and rights."

Some scholars argue that the idea of human dignity is so vacuous as to be useless (Bagaric and Allan 2006). Indeed, the concept of dignity cannot be rooted in any empirical reference; like everything social, it is a social construct. Although some philosophers might argue that the basis for human dignity can be found in natural law, no such thing exists; whether or not God (or gods) exist, no law has been handed down from God to humans. Moreover, there is no state of nature from which to draw "natural" law. The state of nature varies among different human groups, however close to nature they might have been in the past. Nor is human dignity "prepolitical" or rooted in a social contract that precedes the organization of human groups (Nussbaum 2006, 53). Implicit social contracts are the results of active political negotiations over centuries between groups of citizens and their rulers.

Human dignity, then, is not inherent in humanity; it is an evolving, context-laden term (Shultziner 2003). As societies change and evolve, as more groups of citizens participate in social and political organization and decision making, the conception of human dignity evolves. Any "thick" conception of dignity reflects the normative system of the particular society in which the concept is rooted. Thus, although the UN and other legal references to human dignity are admirable normative principles, human rights and human dignity are not necessarily intertwined (Howard 1992). If they are intertwined in our modern-day thinking, it is because we have socially constructed them to be so.

In an earlier work, I defined human dignity as requiring three elements: personal autonomy, treatment by others as an equal, and societal concern and respect (Howard 1995). The first, autonomy, implies that the individual has her own sense of self, enjoys moral and ethical equality with others, and has the right to participate in moral and ethical decisions regarding not only her own private life but also the life of the community. Henkin contends that autonomy is at the heart of the American conception of human rights: the individual in a "hypothetical state of nature" is autonomous and retains that autonomy even as she combines with others to form a society (Henkin 1981, 1584). But it is difficult for any individual to exercise moral and ethical autonomy without a minimally decent standard of living that ensures, for example, that she is free from malnutrition and exposure to the elements (Hertel and Minkler 2007, 5). Treatment by others as an equal, the second aspect of autonomy, means citizens must enjoy equality of civil and political status and opportunity. The third aspect of autonomy, societal respect, means that others must respect an individual's choices and her sense of identity, social roles, and group memberships.

Luria states that "concepts of dignity, by which we perceive our life and [the life of] others around us, are like psychological glue through which social values that guide our life are attached to us and shape our conduct" (Shultziner 2003, 7, note 27). Because our social values are heavily influenced by our conception of individual rights and our underlying vision of humanity, it makes sense that we intertwine our vision of dignity with our belief in the necessity of human rights. In the Western world, human rights are becoming a social fact. Liberal democratic societies adhere to the principle that all human beings are entitled to equal human rights, merely by virtue of being human and regardless of status or achievement. Nevertheless, civil and political rights are supported much more strongly by this principle than are economic human rights, especially in the United States.

Because human dignity is a social construct, we can think about how it interacts with, and affects, enjoyment of economic human rights in advanced industrial democracies. Equality, autonomy, and respect are only the beginnings of a complex concept of human dignity suitable to life in advanced industrial democracies. A constructivist view of human dignity must consider what causes a human being to feel that he is dignified, that he is not humiliated, that he is socially valued. Dignity in advanced industrial democracies means that the individual's basic human needs are fulfilled – that he has enough to survive and live a minimally decent life according to the material standards of his own society. It also means not suffering the indignity of gross inequality. It means having a sense of purpose, usually found in paid work or in some socially valued analogue of it, such as volunteer work or the work of caring for others. It means that the individual and his family must feel secure against catastrophic threats such as natural disasters, and against the everyday problems of age, disability, and unemployment. It means the individual must be socially recognized, valued for himself regardless of status markers such as gender, race, or sexual orientation, and regardless of his comparative standard of living. Finally, dignity means the citizen must have the capacity, as well as the right, to participate in his community and government. None of this is possible, however, in a hyper-individualist world in which autonomy is viewed as the only necessary aspect of human dignity; human dignity in advanced industrial democracies requires that life be lived within a community, with a government that takes the standards of dignity seriously.

These requisites of dignity may seem a tall order, but in most advanced industrial democracies, a large proportion of the population enjoys such a sense of dignity. European social democracies strive to protect all their citizens against poverty and gross inequality; to ensure that they are employed and secure against the common threats of old age, illness, and disability; and to ensure that they are socially recognized members of the community and polity. Special social policies address the needs of immigrants; racial and ethnic minorities; and women, children, the elderly, and the poor. Addressing the needs of these social groups is considered a core function of government, not an unreasonable imposition on policy makers or taxpayers. The outlier among advanced industrial democracies, however, is the United States. Only in the United States does the ideology of individual self-reliance or autonomy have such a strong hold as to often outweigh the social obligations of citizens to each other and of the state to all citizens.

DIGNITY AND HUMAN BIOLOGICAL NEED

The minimum core obligations of economic, social, and cultural rights have been much discussed in recent years (Chapman 2007, 152–55). The starting point in defining this core "lies in identifying the grounds on which all humans deserve equal respect, or merit treating with equal dignity" (Beetham 1995, 46). In advanced industrial democracies, human dignity requires that all individuals enjoy access to adequate food, clothing, housing, medical care, and other needs identified as economic human rights; it is unjust, not merely unfortunate, if they do not (Young 2009, 185). One of the most important obligations of the government of an advanced industrial democracy, therefore, is to ensure that all citizens have access to economic human rights, especially the right to an adequate standard of living and to security in the event of standard life threats.

Some scholars suggest that human needs should be the basis of economic human rights (Bay 1982). It seems that it should be possible to distinguish a small core of biological needs common to all human beings, and that these should constitute rights priorities. Osiatynski suggests that national constitutions should protect "a minimum based on basic needs" whereas "all remaining social and economic needs can be left for social policy" (Osiatynski 2007, 74). He distinguishes between the wide variety of rights that might contribute to what he considers the "vague" concept of human dignity and those actual biological needs that must be fulfilled to survive as a human being.

This view makes sense when discussing economic rights priorities in developing countries. One might ask people, for example, "What is it you cannot do without?" assuming the answer would be rooted in material needs (Felice 1996, 21). However, this view of dignity contradicts the idea of need as rooted in social interpretation. It was not long ago in Western history, for example, that half of all children were expected to die before adulthood; yet Westerners are now shocked by infant mortality rates as low as five per thousand, and strive to reduce those rates to zero. What we "need" is what we think we can reasonably expect. Our life is not dignified if we are subjected to socially unnecessary suffering; that is, suffering that collective social effort should be able to ameliorate. Thus, although the U.S. government signed the 1966 International Covenant on Economic, Social and Cultural Rights (ICESCR) in 1977 but has not yet ratified it, that covenant's list of rights reflects the social expectations of large numbers of U.S. citizens.

However, economic human rights (like civil and political rights) are costly: the budgets of even the wealthiest states are finite, and there is always competition for resources. If human dignity is to be based on complete fulfillment of economic human rights as defined in international law, there may be very serious policy trade-offs. In Canada, for example, public provision of universal health care has required budgeting trade-offs in which other public goods such as education suffer. Nevertheless, if human dignity is to be preserved, social policy choices should not degrade some people by depriving them of collective resources, while others enjoy privileged access to those resources. Public policies meant to enhance human dignity should aim to erode, not reinforce, gross social inequalities.

DIGNITY AND MATERIAL EQUALITY

Human indignity is related to material inequality: the more unequal a society and the more the poor feel differentiated from the rich, the less likely the poor are to live lives of dignity. In this regard, the United States is particularly culpable: it is the most unequal of all advanced industrial countries. Moreover, it is far more unequal now than it was during the postwar boom. In part, this inequality is because of tax policies favoring the rich. For example, the top American income tax rate (taxing the highest income earners) in 2007 was only 35 percent, whereas in the mid-1950s it was 91 percent (Tomasky 2007, 13). In 2006, the top 10 percent of earners held 49.7 percent of U.S. income, compared to about 33 percent from the end of WWII until the 1970s. Even more seriously, the top 1 percent of earners held 22.9 percent of U.S. income in 2006, compared to only 9 percent of U.S. income in the 1960s and 1970s (Saez 2008, 2–3). In 2005, the CEO of Walmart earned more than 900 times the average Walmart worker's income, whereas in 1968 the CEO of General Motors took home about 66 times the average GM worker's income (Judt 2007, 22).

Table 2.1 uses data from the Organisation for Economic Co-operation and Development (OECD) to compare the United States with five other advanced industrial countries in various years since 2003. Of the five other countries, two – Sweden and the Netherlands – are among the most egalitarian in the OECD; Canada ranks in the middle of OECD countries in inequality; and the United Kingdom and Portugal, like the United States, are comparatively more unequal countries. With the exception

TABLE 2.1. *United States and other OECD countries' social protection*

	United States	Sweden	Netherlands	Canada	United Kingdom	Portugal
Life expectancy at birth 2004	77.8	80.6	79.2	80.2	78.9	77.8
Infant mortality (deaths per 1,000 live births) 2004	6.8	3.1	4.4	5.3	5.1	3.8
Poverty rate after taxes and transfers mid-2000s (40% current median income)	11.4	2.5	4.0	7.0	3.7	7.4
Public social expenditures as percentage GDP 2003	16.2	31.3	20.7	17.3	20.6	23.5
Income inequality after taxes and transfers mid-2000s (GINI coefficient)	.38	.23	.27	.32	.34	.38
Hours worked per year per person employed 2006	1,797	1,583	1,391	1,738	1,669	1,758
Prison population rate per 100,000 inhabitants 2004	725	81	123	107	138.7	129

Sources: Organisation for Economic Co-operation and Development 2008.

of Portugal, the United States had the lowest life expectancy in 2004 of the six countries. It had the highest infant mortality rate in 2004, the highest poverty rate by far, and the highest rate of income inequality (tying Portugal). It had the lowest public social expenditure rate as a percentage of its GDP; its citizens worked longer hours than in any of the other five countries; and its incarceration rate was astronomical.

In a comparison of OECD countries, Wilkinson and Pickett (2009) show that social problems are anywhere from three to ten times more common in more unequal than less unequal societies. The more unequal the society, the worse the educational attainment, the lower the adult literacy rate, and the higher the rate of teenaged births. Rates of mental illness and incarceration are five times higher in the most unequal than least unequal societies. Even social problems like obesity, often attributed to lack of individual self-control or poor eating habits, correlate with poverty. The United States is not only by far the most unequal of all the OECD countries, but it also has the worst record on a host of social problems (Wilkinson and Pickett 2009, 91, 107, 123, 172–74, 181).

More equal countries provide better social services than less equal countries. For example, Sweden provides parental leave for eighteen months at 80 percent of the parents' pay, permitting a further six months with less or no pay. By contrast, the United States permits twelve weeks of parental leave at no pay (Wilkinson and Pickett 2009, 112). Citizens of more unequal countries work longer hours than citizens of less unequal countries (Wilkinson and Pickett 2009, 223). As Table 2.1 shows, employed Americans in 2006 worked 1.14 times as many hours annually as employed Swedes, and 1.3 times as many hours as employed Dutch. These long working hours could be considered a violation of the much maligned right to paid rest and leisure time (Cranston 1989). This right is not merely a luxury or something that should be put on a "wish list" (Bagaric and Allan 2006, 258); it is a necessity in advanced industrial societies. Without pay for their weekly days of rest and vacations, many workers toil around the clock at several jobs all year round, their days off in one job merely allowing them to work at another.

The relationship between inequality and social problems holds within the United States itself; social problems are more severe in more unequal U.S. states and less severe in states that are more equal (Wilkinson and Pickett 2009). Nor can the differences between the United States and other OECD countries, or among U.S. states, be attributed solely to racial division. Nevertheless, the U.S. racial division is obvious. In 2007, the median household income for non-Hispanic whites in the United States was $54,920; for blacks, $33,916; and for Hispanics of any race, $38,679; this was an advantage of 60 percent for whites over blacks and 40 percent for whites over Hispanics. Among whites, 8.2 percent lived in poverty in 2007, compared with 24.5 percent of blacks and 21.5 percent of Hispanics. Similarly, 10.4 percent of whites, 19.5 percent of blacks, and 32.1 percent of Hispanics were without health insurance in 2007; among children, the uninsured rates were 7.3 percent for whites, 12.2 percent for blacks, and 20 percent for Hispanics (Denavas-Walt, Proctor, and Smith 2008: tables 1, 3, and 6 and figure 8). These disparities exist even though the United States ratified the 1966 International Convention on the Elimination of Racial Discrimination in 1994. Many individuals' health care is contingent on their being employed. In general, the health care system is multitiered depending on wealth, although at the time of this writing the Obama Administration was attempting to rectify this.

Social inequality is more than a material problem, however; it directly attacks human dignity. In effect, the poor are shamed, whereas the comfortable and rich are respected. In some American states, for example, welfare recipients are criminalized, forced to provide their fingerprints so that they can be identified in case of fraud (Ehrenreich 2009). This gross inequality also contributes to higher crime rates, as individuals threatened by negative social evaluation may turn to violence to ward off their shame and humiliation. Nonrecognition as an equal and valued member of society can cause an individual to feel even the tiniest of slights far more deeply than an individual sure of his own self-worth – hence the exaggerated reactions of some permanently unemployed young men to any perceived slight (Wilkinson and Pickett 2009, 37 and 133). Without work or acknowledgment as fellow citizens by society, some African Americans turn to crime as a means of personal validation (Wilson 2006, 109).

High social inequality also reflects social distance between the wealthy and the poor (Wilkinson and Pickett 2009, 27). This social distance undermines social trust; lack of social trust in turn undermines access to social capital such as job networks or personal contacts with professionals who can help individuals navigate around impersonal bureaucracies (Putnam 1995). To be poor, then, is to lack not only material well-being but social respect and membership in the wider community. When one is unemployed, loss of a sense of efficacy, self-respect, and social worth exacerbates material poverty.

DIGNITY AND THE RIGHT TO WORK

Human dignity requires that as much as possible individuals should consider themselves efficacious citizens who can work to support themselves and their families rather than feeling that they are a burden on society. This is confirmed by interviews I conducted in 1996–97 with seventy-eight civic leaders in Hamilton about poverty and the social obligations of those who live on welfare. Some of these civic leaders, whose average age was fifty, had been raised in severe poverty at a time when there were few if any "welfare" benefits for the poor or unemployed. At the time of the interviews, Ontario had a Conservative government, and there was a heated public discussion about "workfare" corresponding to simultaneous discussions in the United States. My respondents almost all believed that work was good for the individual because it provided a sense of efficacy. On the other hand, several mentioned that care had to be taken so that work provided for welfare recipients was not degrading. Some were concerned that individuals would take advantage of generous welfare payments to avoid work. In some cases, their concern stemmed not from a middle-class bias against the poor but from observations of their own neighbors or family members. Thus, respondents were simultaneously aware of the poor's need to enjoy self-respect and a sense of human dignity, and the moral hazard that some would prefer welfare to work (Howard-Hassmann 2003, 178–99).

Article 6, 1 of the ICESCR mandates "the right of everyone to the opportunity to gain his living by work which he freely chooses or accepts." This seems to imply that everyone who wants paid work must be guaranteed a job of his choosing. Yet completely full employment is not possible; there will always be some people who are unemployed as they change jobs. Full employment, moreover, may not give employers the flexibility they need to seek the workers most qualified for the jobs they offer and to dismiss incompetent or redundant workers. Harvey maintains that these are specious arguments and that full employment is possible in advanced industrial societies (Harvey 2007). Yet in several European countries, government restrictions on hiring and firing have exacerbated unemployment, because without the flexibility to dismiss their employees, employers are less willing to take risks and hire new, young, and/or unskilled workers. Similarly, high worker benefits often mean less employment and less flexibility; this has been a problem in Germany (Friedman 2005, 263, 287). Public policy decisions based upon the right to work can therefore have contradictory effects on different sectors of the community. By guaranteeing jobs and benefits to some, governments can also make it harder for others to enter and stay in the work force.

Goodhart suggests a basic income guarantee for those who are unwilling, not merely unable, to work. The only way to ensure that those who live on income transfers from the state do not suffer shame or indignity, he argues, is to institute a policy in which all citizens would receive a basic guaranteed income that would be clawed back via taxes from those who do not need it (Goodhart 2007). Goodhart's proposal is radical, indeed utopian. Moreover, it violates the common social norm that those who can, should support themselves. An individual's choice to rely on a guaranteed income transfer, rather than work, would anger those who work at jobs they do not enjoy, that do not give them any personal satisfaction, and that indeed might cause familial upset and stress. The provision of basic incomes for all risks the moral hazard that some who could work would choose not to, thus imposing both material and moral costs on those who do work (Massey 2006, 125).

Osiatynski, in disagreement with Goodhart, argues that one must try to contribute to the common good: "Entitlements to benefits without some form of contribution to others may violate the sense of fairness and justice" (Osiatynski 2007, 67). Moreover, dignity is often found through work, giving the individual a sense of purpose, a sense of being needed, and a sense that he is contributing to society as a whole. A policy that granted public funds to those who could work, but chose not to, would be disrespectful to those who do even the most demeaning jobs well with a sense of commitment and pride in achievement. Such a policy would also require large government disbursements up-front, to be recouped later when incomes are taxed. A more practical policy is a guaranteed annual income to be implemented via a negative income tax. This was unsuccessfully proposed by Canada's Liberal Government in 1973 (Myles and Pierson 1997, 455). Under this system, all citizens would be guaranteed a certain basic income, and those who did not earn or otherwise acquire it would receive it from the state. The income transfer would be automatic, based upon individuals' tax returns, and would not be characterized by the stigmatization and criminalization common in punitive welfare provisioning.

DIGNITY AND HUMAN SECURITY

An individual cannot feel a sense of dignity if she constantly feels insecure. In advanced industrial societies, financial insecurity is a threat when one cannot find work or can find only insecure, casual work. Changes in employment practices in some, but not all, OECD countries over the last three decades have radically increased the extent of insecurity, not only of the poor but also of those who had previously been securely middle class. Advanced industrial economies have experienced declining rates of unionization, rollbacks of benefits, and deliberate decisions by major corporations to employ as many part-time workers as possible to avoid paying benefits such as health insurance and pensions. Thus, many older workers have lost well-paid, secure full-time work and substituted two or even three lower-paid part-time jobs, while many younger workers seem relegated to permanent part-time, low-paid work, especially in the service industry.

Real wages have stagnated in the United States for more than twenty-five years. When Americans earn higher annual wages, it is partly because they work longer hours than their European counterparts (Stiglitz 2006, 10). The weekly paycheck of the average nonmanagement American worker declined by 22 percent between 1973 and 1993 (Friedman 2005, 198). Between 1999 and 2004 the median household income in the United States, adjusted for inflation, fell by about $1,500, or 3 percent (Stiglitz 2006, 45). Twenty-eight percent of U.S. private-sector workers earned less than $8.20 per hour in 1999 (Brocht 2000, 4). This "enforced casualization" of labor helps corporations keep "a fluid reserve of part-timers, temps and freelancers to help . . . keep overheads down and ride the twists and turns in the market" (Klein 2000, 231). The "McJobs" that these workers do are "low skill, low pay, high stress, exhausting and unstable" (Klein 2000, 237). Walmart, with an estimated 1.4 million employees in 2004, exemplifies these trends, keeping "the compensation of its [American] rank-and-file workers at or barely above the poverty line" (Head 2004, 81). This may be one reason why in 2005, 11 percent of Americans were considered "food-insecure" during all or part of the year (Nord, Andrews, and Carlson 2006). These low-paid workers are the new American "disposable people" (Bales 1999) in the sense that no one takes responsibility for their welfare.

The insecurity of contingent part-time work (Goldberg 2005, 420), with unpredictable hours and from which one can easily be dismissed, also contributes to social breakdown. Parents and caregivers who have little money and do not even know from one week or day to the next when they will be expected to work find it difficult to fulfill obligations of care to their children or disabled or elderly members of their families (Lewis 2005, 415). This is exacerbated by lack of a national childcare policy. Parents who cannot afford private childcare or find family members or friends to care for their children are subject to the constant insecurity of not knowing where their children are, whether they are properly fed, or whether they are in danger.

Aside from financial insecurity, human insecurity also derives from large-scale threats to well-being, such as terrorism, environmental damage, crime, new diseases, trafficking in drugs and people, and sudden economic downswings (Fukuda-Parr 2003). These large-scale threats do not affect everyone equally. The 2008–09 financial crisis was caused in part by the sale of subprime mortgage debt, particularly onerous for African Americans living in highly segregated areas (Squires, Hyra, and Renner 2009). African Americans also suffered more severely than others from the "natural" disaster of the hurricane that hit New Orleans in 2005. Governments of advanced industrial democracies cannot protect their citizens against all threats to their security. They can, however, provide adequate safety nets against the threat of financial insecurity, and they can institute plans to ensure that in the event of large-scale disasters, natural or otherwise, the poor are as well-protected as the rich. The stark evidence of racialized, class-biased treatment of those who endured the New Orleans hurricane are an indication that state and federal governments did not treat all their citizens with equal concern. African Americans did not seem to be part of the national community.

DIGNITY AND MEMBERSHIP IN THE COMMUNITY

In a previous section I argued that human dignity requires that the individual be able to act autonomously, both in her private life and as a member of the community. Some scholars, however, criticize the concept of autonomy for removing individuals from the community. Woods argues that Western culture perpetuates the myth of radical individual autonomy in which the individual is a free agent, motivated primarily by self-interest, who has no interest in collective identities and values (Woods 2005, 110–11). This seems to be a particularly American, rather than Western, view of autonomy. Autonomy does not necessarily mean that the individual is separated from or entitled to disregard family and community. Rather, autonomy means the ability to make life choices. Such choices are rendered easier by one's membership in society and one's ability to call on collective resources. All individuals live within a social context, although some are for various reasons disengaged from family and community. Individuals have obligations to others and others have obligations to them. Human dignity requires social membership and societal concern for the individual and the family (Howard 1995).

In the last two decades, the debate on human rights has come full circle from a stress on the individual to renewed stress on community and belonging. In part this is a result of protests against perceived excesses of individualism by commentators from the non-Western world, such as Lee Kwan Yew, the former president of Singapore (Zakaria 1994). The renewed stress on community is also a result of concern among Westerners about some of the anomic features of modern capitalist society and the sense of psychological homelessness that seems to characterize many people. Finally, some strands of feminist thought, especially the proposition that the feminist "ethic of care" is more community-oriented than the (allegedly male) ethic of individual rights, contribute to the renewed stress on community.

This new acknowledgment of community suggests limits on the degree of autonomy that is good for an individual. It suggests that individuals and communities have reciprocal obligations. The collectivity – the society at large – is obligated not only to the individual but also to families and groups of people who cannot support themselves on their own. The latter includes the permanently poor, such as some mentally ill people, some who are hostages to addictions of various kinds, and others who are entirely driven out of the job market because of lack of skills. Some social institutions are particularly good at overcoming the indignity and shame of poverty. Within the family, the better off often subsidize the worse off. Within religious organizations, success in the marketplace – or lack of it – is often subordinated to common beliefs and participation in common rituals. Likewise, ethnically based organizations sometimes overlook social status distinctions rooted in comparative wealth or poverty. These substate aspects of community, rooted in a civil society based not on the benevolence the rich sometimes show to the poor but rather on shared and equal membership, are as important as community grounded in common citizenship. Such aspects of community help those who suffer from indignity when participating in the wider society to recover their dignity in the private domain.

Community membership implies not only that one is an object of social concern but also that one participates in society. This includes political participation, especially fulfilling the obligations of citizenship, such as voting. Participation in government is generally seen as a political rather than an economic right, but it is germane to economic rights. If citizens do not vote, then they forgo an important means of participating in policy decisions pertaining to fulfillment of their economic human rights. Yet political participation often depends on one's prior level of enjoyment of economic human rights. Neuborne (2005) argues, for example, that there are three types of citizens in the United States: super, ordinary, and spectator. Super citizens are those who have a "hugely disproportionate role in deciding who runs for office, what the issues will be, and who will be elected," whereas ordinary citizens are those who merely vote, and spectator citizens are those who do not even do that. The latter group rose from 25 percent of the voting population in 1900 to more than half in 1996 (Neuborne 2005, 171). A campaign financing system biased toward the rich privileges "the autonomy of those with limitless wealth over the autonomy of those with limited funds" (Neuborne 2005, 173).

A conception of autonomy that undermines the individual's capacity to participate in the political process is the antithesis of the collective social responsibility necessary to ensure human dignity.

DIGNITY, ECONOMIC HUMAN RIGHTS, AND COLLECTIVE SOCIAL RESPONSIBILITY

Compared to other Western countries, the United States is a radically capitalist society that rejects the principle that a nation-state is also a community. This rejection is seen especially in its protection of civil and political rights and property rights, but not economic human rights. This system is manifested in two ideologies. The first is social minimalism (Howard 1995, 171–76), the idea of the individual as an "unencumbered self" (Sandel 1984). In this belief system, everything an individual does is a manifestation of her personal autonomy, but because she is allowed infinite choice, she is also expected to bear on her own the consequences of that choice. Society does not have any responsibility to assist the individual, even in a fundamental matter such as bearing and rearing children. In this view of the world a baby is a private consumer item no different from a car. Under the "Porsche preference" (Fineman 2006, 142) one can have a baby or a car, but in either case it is a private choice, and one is fully responsible for the cost and maintenance of that choice. On the other hand, the United States is also influenced by a conservative worldview, exemplified by the Christian right (Howard 1995, 176–81). In this view, one ought to be responsible to others, but this responsibility extends only to family. All must work to support themselves, except the elderly, the disabled, children, and their mothers, whom able-bodied adult male members of the family should support. There is no collective social responsibility for people outside one's family or perhaps one's own faith community.

Both in the minimalist and conservative worldview, societal responsibility to help others is "residual, only to help those who cannot help themselves, and only with respect to minimum necessities at poverty level" (Henkin 1981, 1590). There is no entitlement to social services, certainly no entitlement based in the concept of economic human rights. Rather, the U.S. tradition is to distinguish between the deserving and the "undeserving" poor (Katz 1989). The poor are considered morally weak (Ross 2005), a "deviant" class of people whom the morally strong, self-sufficient nonpoor could not help even if they wanted to. The American idea of state-supported social services as a privilege, not a right or entitlement, contrasts with welfare states in which "a fundamental philosophical concept... is that ... dependence... [is] not regarded as evidence of personal failure" (Ginsberg and Lesser 1981, 255).

This ethic of contempt for the poor is reflected in the welfare reform of the mid-1990s, which replaced the Aid to Families with Dependent Children (AFDC) program with Temporary Assistance to Needy Families (TANF), imposing work requirements on welfare recipients and imposing a lifetime limit of five years on assistance (Neubeck 2006, 95). TANF made "an individual's claim upon the collectivity once again contingent on good conduct; it reintroduce[d] a *conditionality* to social citizenship... Thus [it] reopens a distinction between active (or 'deserving') citizens and others" (Judt 2007, 24, emphasis in original). The name of the 1996 law changing AFDC to TANF, the Personal Responsibility and Work Opportunity Reconciliation Act (PRWORA), reveals the prejudices of those who passed it and of American society more broadly. Public opinion polls show that Americans are far less likely than citizens of western European nations such as Sweden, the United Kingdom, and Germany to believe that "the state should intervene to help the poor" (Neubeck 2006, 90). The PRWORA also reflects longstanding prejudices against African-American women as irresponsible, lazy, and sexually profligate.

Many families have needs that are not temporary, and they will not be able to survive if there is a lifetime limit of five years on state support. In many families, obliging the primary care-giver to seek paid work to demonstrate her worthiness to receive state support will deprive her dependents of the care they need. The ideology of autonomy stigmatizes dependency, yet dependency on others is a natural social condition. Indeed, society owes a social debt to those who perform the work of caring for the dependent, whether they be children, the disabled, or the elderly (Fineman 2006, 146). It appears in the United States that children born of parents who require state or community assistance in order to provide their children's basic material needs do not enjoy human rights. In a country that has ratified neither the ICESCR nor the 1989 Convention on the Rights of the Child, even the most minimal subsistence can be denied to children of parents who have run out of the time allotted for their temporary assistance, or who exhibit "unworthiness" by daring to have more children. In New Jersey in 2002, for example, a pregnant mother already on welfare could not expect any additional funds for her new baby (Fineman 2006, 150).

In contrast to the U.S. approach, European social democracies acknowledge collective social responsibility. Several differences between the United States and other advanced industrial democracies explain this contrast. The United States is one of the few Western countries that lacks leftist political parties, in large part because of its history of persecutions of communists, socialists, and trade unionists (Goldstein 1987). By contrast, pressure from the political left was important in establishing the British welfare state (Hage and Hanneman 1980, 67). When postwar European welfare states were established, there was also less concern about big government than in the United States and more faith in the ability and duty of governments to fulfill collective goals (Judt 2005, 69). The United States also has an implicit caste system, with African Americans occupying the undignified position of descendants of enslaved people. This may reduce the willingness of the majority white population to take responsibility for people it sees as "other," rather than as fictive national kin.

The United States constitutes a warning to other OECD countries that have seen an influx of non-Western immigrants in the past few decades, undermining a myth of social harmony based on a homogeneous "autochtonous" population as in the Netherlands. The presence of immigrants who are perceived as "others" – as well as of the indigenous Roma community – has given impetus to parties of the right in Europe. European social democracies are also not immune to tax revolts. In the last twenty years they have chosen to cut back on social supports to protect themselves against budget deficits. The idea of collective social responsibility nevertheless still seems more firmly entrenched in Europe than in the United States and shows the importance to human dignity of tempering personal autonomy with reciprocal obligations among the individual, the family, civil society, and the state.

SEVENTEEN UNDESERVED BLESSINGS

The Babylonian Talmud teaches that to give a coin to a poor person constitutes six blessings; to comfort him with words constitutes eleven; to do both constitutes seventeen, the numerical equivalent of the good.[1] I stopped to give money to the man in the yellow sweatshirt and chat with him for a while, so perhaps I did a tiny bit of good and earned my seventeen blessings. But I talked to him as a matter of choice, for the amount of time I found convenient. I could have just walked by, as I

---

[1] Babylonian Talmud, Tractate Bava Batra 9a. I am grateful to Rabbi Jordan Cohen of Temple Anshe Sholom, Hamilton, Ontario, Canada, for this reference.

frequently do to people who ask me for money. Beggars are only visible when the comfortable acknowledge them; otherwise, they are invisible. The man to whom I gave money that Saturday morning suffered, I imagine, from multiple indignities. He was reduced to begging to supplement what was probably an income insufficient to fulfill his basic needs. Perhaps if he received welfare he had enough for minimal subsistence, but he also wanted to exercise some personal autonomy in spending money on what the comfortable middle class might consider unnecessary and harmful frivolities, such as cigarettes. He lived in a state of severe insecurity; his housing was probably precarious, his food supply inadequate, and his access to Canada's universal health care system jeopardized if he did not have a permanent address to put on his health card. His capacity for participation in community life may have been limited by lack of resources such as a place to shower and wash his clothes or bus fare to get to the place where he hoped to volunteer. Without either employment or volunteer work, he might have felt devoid of a sense of purpose, of being a valued member of his community. All I know about him is that he had a sister who loved him enough to buy him a yellow sweatshirt for his birthday.

REFERENCES

Bagaric, Mirko, and James Allan. 2006. "The Vacuous Concept of Dignity." *Journal of Human Rights* 5(2): 257–70.
Bales, Kevin. 1999. *Disposable People: New Slavery in the Global Economy.* Berkeley: University of California Press.
Bay, Christian. 1982. "Self-Respect as a Human Right: Thoughts on the Dialectic of Wants and Needs in the Struggle for Human Community." *Human Rights Quarterly* 4(1): 53–75.
Beetham, David. 1995. "What Future for Economic and Social Rights?" *Political Studies* 53: 41–60.
Brocht, Chauna. 2000. *The Forgotten Workforce: More Than One in 10 Federal Contract Workers Earn Less Than a Living Wage.* Washington, D.C.: Economic Policy Institute.
Chapman, Audrey R. 2007. "The Status of Efforts to Monitor Economic, Social and Cultural Rights." In *Economic Rights: Conceptual, Measurement and Policy Issues*, edited by Shareen Hertel and Lanse Minkler, 143–64. New York: Cambridge University Press.
Cranston, Maurice. 1989. "Human Rights: Real and Supposed." In *The Philosophy of Human Rights*, edited by Morton E. Winston, 121–28. Belmont, CA: Wadsworth.
Denavas-Walt, Carmen, Bernadette D. Proctor, and Jessica C. Smith. 2008. *Income, Poverty and Health Insurance Coverage in the United States: 2007,*

edited by the U.S. Census Bureau. Washington, D.C.: Department of Commerce.

Ehrenreich, Barbara. 2009. "A Homespun Safety Net." *The New York Times*, July 12.

Felice, William F. 1996. *Taking Suffering Seriously: The Importance of Collective Human Rights*. Albany, NY: State University of New York Press.

Fineman, Martha Albertson. 2006. "Dependency and Social Debt." In *Poverty and Inequality*, edited by David B. Grusky and Ravi Kanbur, 133–50. Stanford, CA: Stanford University Press.

Friedman, Benjamin M. 2005. *The Moral Consequences of Economic Growth*. New York: Vintage Books.

Fukuda-Parr, Sakiko. 2003. "New Threats to Human Security in the Era of Globalization." *Journal of Human Development* 4(2): 167–79.

Ginsberg, Mitchell I., and Leonard Lesser. 1981. "Current Developments in Economic and Social Rights: A United States Perspective." *Human Rights Law Journal* 2(3–4): 237–56.

Goldberg, Gertrude Shaffner. 2005. "The Feminization of Poverty." In *Human Rights and the Global Marketplace: Economic, Social and Cultural Dimensions*, edited by Jeanne M. Woods and Hope Lewis, 418–20. Ardsley, NY: Transnational Publishers.

Goldstein, Robert Justin. 1987. "The United States." In *International Handbook of Human Rights*, edited by Jack Donnelly and Rhoda E. Howard, 429–56. New York: Greenwood Press.

Goodhart, Michael. 2007. "'None So Poor That He Is Compelled to Sell Himself': Democracy, Subsistence and Basic Income." In *Economic Rights: Conceptual, Measurement, and Policy Issues*, edited by Shareen Hertel and Lanse Minkler, 94–114. New York: Cambridge University Press.

Hage, Jerald, and Robert A. Hanneman. 1980. "The Growth of the Welfare State in Britain, France, Germany and Italy: A Comparison of Three Paradigms." In *Comparative Social Research Annual*, edited by Richard F. Tomasson, 45–70. Greenwich, CT: JAI Press.

Harvey, Philip. 2007. "Benchmarking the Right to Work." In *Economic Rights: Conceptual, Measurement and Policy Issues*, edited by Shareen Hertel and Lanse Minkler, 115–41. New York: Cambridge University Press.

Head, Simon. 2004. "Inside the Leviathan." *New York Review of Books* 51(20): 80–89.

Henkin, Louis. 1981. "Rights: Here and There." *Columbia Law Review* 81(8): 1582–610.

Hertel, Shareen, and Lanse Minkler. 2007. "Economic Rights: the Terrain." In *Economic Rights: Conceptual, Measurement and Policy Issues*, edited by Shareen Hertel and L. Minkler, 1–35. New York: Cambridge University Press.

Howard, Rhoda E. 1992. "Dignity, Community and Human Rights." In *Human Rights in Cross-Cultural Perspectives: A Quest for Consensus*, edited by Abdullahi A. An-Na'im, 81–102. Philadelphia, PA: University of Pennsylvania Press.

———. 1995. *Human Rights and the Search for Community*. Boulder, CO: Westview.

Howard-Hassmann, Rhoda E. 2003. *Compassionate Canadians: Civic Leaders Discuss Human Rights*. Toronto: University of Toronto Press.

Judt, Tony. 2005. *Postwar: A History of Europe since 1945*. New York: Penguin.

———. 2007. "The Wrecking Ball of Innovation." *New York Review of Books* 54(19): 22–27.

Katz, Michael B. 1989. *The Undeserving Poor: From the War on Poverty to the War on Welfare*. New York: Penguin Books.

Klein, Naomi. 2000. *No Logo: Taking Aim at the Brand Bullies*. Toronto: Vintage Canada.

Lewis, Hope. 2005. "Women (Under)Development: The Relevance of the 'Right to Development' to Poor Women of Color in the United States." In *Human Rights and the Global Marketplace: Economic, Social, and Cultural Dimensions*, edited by Jeanne M. Woods and Hope Lewis, 407–08. Ardsley, NY: Transnational Publishers.

Massey, Douglas S. 2006. "Race, Class, and Markets: Social Policy in the 21st Century." In *Poverty and Inequality*, edited by David B. Grusky and Ravi Kanbur, 117–32. Stanford, CA: Stanford University Press.

Myles, John, and Paul Pierson. 1997. "Friedman's Revenge: The Reform of 'Liberal' Welfare States in Canada and the United States." *Politics & Society* 25(4): 443–72.

Neubeck, Kenneth J. 2006. "Welfare Racism and Human Rights." In *Economic Rights in Canada and the United States*, edited by Rhoda E. Howard-Hassmann and Claude E. Welch, Jr., 87–102. Philadelphia, PA: University of Pennsylvania Press.

Neuborne, Burt. 2005. "Is Money Different?" In *Human Rights and the Global Marketplace: Economic, Social, and Cultural Dimensions*, edited by Jeanne M. Woods and Hope Lewis, 170–75. Ardsley, NY: Transnational Publishers.

Nord, Mark, Margaret Andrews, and Steven Carlson. 2006. *Household Food Security in the United States, 2005*. Washington, D.C.: United States Department of Agriculture.

Nussbaum, Martha C. 2006. "Poverty and Human Functioning: Capabilities as Fundamental Entitlements." In *Poverty and Inequality*, edited by David. B. Grusky and Ravi Kanbur, 47–75. Stanford, CA: Stanford University Press.

Organisation for Economic Cooperation and Development. 2008. *OECD Statistics: Social Protection*. Paris: Organization for Economic Cooperation and Development.

Osiatynski, Wiktor. 2007. "Needs-Based Approach to Social and Economic Rights." In *Economic Rights: Conceptual, Measurement and Policy Issues*, Edited by Shareen Hertel and Lanse Minkler, 56–75. New York: Cambridge.

Putnam, Robert D. 1995. "Bowling Alone: America's Declining Social Capital." *Journal of Democracy* 6(1): 65–78.

Ross, Thomas. 2005. "The Rhetoric of Poverty: Their Immorality, Our Helplessness." In *Human Rights and the Global Marketplace: Economic, Social, and Cultural Dimensions*, edited by Jeanne M. Woods and Hope Lewis, 853–60. Ardsley, NY: Transnational Publishers.

Saez, Emmanuel. 2008. "Striking It Richer: The Evolution of Top Incomes in the United States (Update Using 2006 Preliminary Estimates)." Berkeley: University of California, Department of Economics. http://elsa.berkeley.edu/~ saez/saez-UStopincomes-2006prel.pdf.

Sandel, Michael. 1984. "The Procedural Republic and the Unencumbered Self." *Political Theory* 12(1): 81–96.

Schachter, Oscar. 1983. "Human Dignity as a Normative Concept." *American Journal of International Law* 77(4): 848–54.

Shultziner, Doron. 2003. "Human Dignity–Function and Meanings." *Global Jurist Topics* 3(3): 1–21.

Squires, Gregory D., Derek S. Hyra, and Robert N. Renner. 2009. "Segregation and the Subprime Lending Crisis." In *EPI Briefing Papers*. Washington, D.C.: Economic Policy Institute.

Stiglitz, Joseph E. 2006. *Making Globalization Work*. New York: W.W. Norton.

Tomasky, Michael. 2007. "The Partisan." *New York Review of Books* 54(18):12–14.

Wilkinson, Richard, and Kate Pickett. 2009. *The Spirit Level: Why More Equal Societies Almost Always Do Better*. London: Allen Lane.

Wilson, William Julius. 2006. "Social Theory and the Concept 'Underclass.'" In *Poverty and Inequality*, edited by David B. Grusky and Ravi Kanbur, 103–16. Stanford, CA: Stanford University Press.

Woods, Jeanne M. 2005. "Justiciable Social Rights as a Critique of the Liberal Paradigm." In *Human Rights and the Global Marketplace: Economic, Social, and Cultural Dimensions*, edited by Jeanne M. Woods and Hope Lewis, 110–17. Ardsley, NY: Transnational Publishers.

Young, Katharine G. 2009. "Freedom, Want, and Economic and Social Rights: Frame and Law." *Maryland Journal of International Law* 24: 176–200.

Zakaria, Fareed. 1994. "Culture Is Destiny: A Conversation with Lee Kwan Yew." *Foreign Affairs* 73(2): 109–26.

3

The U.S. Welfare State: A Battleground for Human Rights

Mimi Abramovitz

The fulfillment of human rights is the bedrock of social justice. The 1948 Universal Declaration of Human Rights sparked an ongoing debate over the obligation of governments to ensure the welfare of individuals by protecting their social and economic as well as civil and political rights. Although political rights won early support, the achievement of social and economic rights has lagged. Many in the United States regard the fulfillment of social and economic rights (i.e., the right to work, health, income, housing, education, and employment) as conflicting with the workings of the market economy. Others think of social and economic rights as an impossible dream. Yet since the 1930s, if not before, the nation's top leaders have persistently promoted a human rights agenda, including social and economic rights. Despite such support in high places, the historical struggle to recognize the rights documented in this chapter was shaped by those who put profits before people and/or compromised with racism.

THE ORIGINS OF THE WELFARE STATE: AN ARENA OF STRUGGLE FOR HUMAN RIGHTS

The early struggle for human rights arose during the first major economic crisis of the twentieth century. The total collapse of the economy in 1929 signaled that the laissez-faire relationship between the market and the state could no longer assure profitable economic growth or social stability. Elites blamed their economic woes on the failure of the market and for the first time called on the federal government for help. Social movements seeking a better life for "the people" also called for government intervention. The resulting struggle over the role the government should play yielded New Deal programs that stimulated economic growth by redistributing income downward and enlarging the role of the state, especially the welfare state (Abramovitz 2004).

The welfare state thus became a site of political struggle due to its twin capacity for social control and social justice. Its programs exercised control by granting individuals access to benefits based on their compliance with dominant norms, by reproducing prevailing race, class, and gender hierarchies, and by offering benefits to dissenting groups to mute social unrest (Piven and Cloward 1971). The less well-known social justice potential of the welfare state stems from its capacity to meet basic human needs. Its programs have the potential to protect, if not liberate, people from the worst excesses of the market economy. Access to income outside the market and outside of marriage makes it possible for individuals to avoid the lowest paid, dirty, and dangerous jobs, and for women to escape unsafe and dangerous relationships. Like a strike fund, this economic safety net can reduce the fear of unemployment, which in turn can strengthen the bargaining power of individuals and social movements whose victories have expanded the welfare state (Abramovitz 2004).

The U.S. historical record reveals considerable support for human rights among the powers-that-be. This chapter details the repeated struggle to secure these rights during three key periods (i.e., the 1930s; the post-World War II era; and from the mid-1970s to the early 2000s), suggesting that greater progress in U.S. human rights fulfillment would have been achieved had the political process not favored economic interests and tolerated compromises with racism (Anderson 2003).

PROFITS BEFORE PEOPLE IN THE NEW DEAL ERA

More than a decade before the Universal Declaration of Human Rights, the architects of the New Deal legislated a wide range of programs that endorsed a belief in government's obligation to protect the right to health, income, employment, and housing (Gordon 1994). The earliest drafts of the 1935 Social Security Act (SSA) – the foundation of the U.S. welfare state – included comprehensive health, social insurance, and work programs. However, a highly truncated version emerged following the long and contentious battle between advocates of social and economic rights and powerful business groups whose interests were threatened by the prospect of fulfilling human rights (Brown 1999; Quadagno 1984).

Right to Health. The New Deal reformers revived the pre-World War I campaign for health insurance (HI), making the right to health a central feature of their program. However, vehement opposition from the health care industry, especially the American Medical Association (AMA), led the New Dealers to eliminate HI for fear that its inclusion would defeat the entire act (Rose 1994). But in 1938, they garnered AMA support in exchange for dropping the compulsory health insurance provision. Nonetheless, an alliance of Southern Democrats and Republicans blocked HI among many other reforms. Undaunted, in 1939, Democratic Senator Robert F. Wagner introduced a more limited bill. Nevertheless, opponents won the day. HI stayed off the agenda until the end of World War II (Starr 1982).

Right to Income. In his 1935 State of the Union address, President Franklin D. Roosevelt called for replacing the New Deal's emergency programs with a comprehensive, permanent social insurance program that would protect people from the loss of income due to old age, unemployment, sickness, disability, and loss of breadwinner support. However, the interests of the economic elite trumped the right to income. The original social security (SS) proposal contained a near universal right to income in old age. However, the final version offered much less. It 1) excluded farm and domestic workers; 2) favored work-based over need-based eligibility rules; 3) tied SS payments to labor market experience; 4) included a benefit formula that favored higher over lower paid workers; 5) created eligibility rules that served men better than women; and 6) funded the program with a contributory regressive payroll tax that lowered business costs. FDR included the payroll tax, believing that it would insulate SS from annual budget politics (Brown 1999; Leuchtenberg 1963).

The proposed SSA included a national public assistance (PA) program that approximated a right to income for the poor, except for its means test. Pressed by Southern Democrats, Congress turned PA into a state–federal partnership; removed the requirement that Aid to Dependent Children (ADC) provide "reasonable subsistence compatible with decency and health"; set benefits below the lowest prevailing wage; restricted ADC to children deprived of breadwinner support; and refused to aid poor two-parent households. These rules ensured local control of the programs, increased the supply of low-wage (black) workers, pressed wages down, and otherwise protected the profits of Southern planters (Gordon 1994).

New Dealer reformers regarded unemployment insurance (UI) as an important source of income for temporarily jobless (white male) workers. However, the idea sparked a number of major struggles over jurisdiction (national plan with uniform standards vs. variable state plans); financing (payroll tax vs. federal subsidy to the states); type of account (individual or pooled reserve); and use of a merit system to penalize employers who laid off workers (Baicker, Goldin, and Katz 1997). The initial plan approximated a national right to income for the jobless by offering decent benefits, uniform standards, federal funding, and pooled reserves. Pressed by business fearing that access to UI would strengthen the worker's bargaining power, Congress enacted a more limited plan (Brown 1999; Leuchtenberg 1963).

Right to Work. The New Deal also included work relief and job creation programs to help overwhelmed agencies, increase purchasing power, and address mounting protests by the jobless. On the assumption that the downturn was just an ordinary business slump, FDR's initial work relief programs were temporary. Once the depth of the crisis became apparent, the Federal Emergency Relief Administration (FERA) (1933) proposed a national program. To counter the stigma of its means test, the program provided for voluntary participation, "real" jobs, and cash (not in-kind) payments higher than direct relief or local wage rates. However, these more humanitarian rules benefited white middle-class men and some women more than other groups (Rose 1989; Leuchtenberg 1963).

In the end, profits trumped both the needs of people and the incipient right to work. The Chamber of Commerce, the National Association of Manufacturers, and the American Liberty League protested that work relief drove wages up, implied a critique of and drew workers away from low-wage employment, and promoted socialism. By November 1933, mounting business opposition put an end to the wage floor, to strike benefits, and to other protections. Not satisfied, in 1935 business lobbied Congress to replace FERA with a more standard work relief program. The resulting Works Progress Administration (WPA), the period's largest and most well-known program, weakened the right to work. It substituted mandatory for voluntary work, set benefits below market wages, capped participation at eighteen months, required WPA participants to accept low-paying private sector jobs, and paid men and whites more than women and persons of color. The WPA lasted until 1943, when the World War II demand for labor absorbed the unemployed (Rose 1995).

Various job creation programs more closely approximated the right to work. The Public Works Administration (PWA) provided jobs to thousands of adults in large-scale construction projects. The Civilian Conservation Corp (CCC) put young men to work in the national forests. The Civilian Works Administration (CWA) – a cross between relief and job creation – provided work to four million people paying close to private sector rates. The National Youth Administration (NYA) put thousands

of youth into education-related jobs. Once business challenged these programs as a threat to private enterprise, Congress scaled them back in
favor of more stigmatized, means-tested work relief (Rose 1989, 1994;
Brown 1999).

The original SSA contained an Employment Assurance program that
obliged the federal government to ensure permanent (not just emergency)
public employment to workers who exhausted or did not qualify for UI.
A strong expression of the right to work, it was actively supported by top
New Dealers including Harry Hopkins, the director of FERA (Hopkins
1999); by the White House, whose 1935 report stated "since most people
live by work, the first objective in a program of economic security must
be maximum work"; and by the President's Committee on Economic
Security, which concluded "while it will not always be necessary to have
public employment projects . . . it should be recognized as a permanent
policy of the government and not merely as an emergency measure" (Rose
1995, 53). The U.S. Conference of Mayors and the International City
Managers Association also supported the right to work (Brown 1999).
However, internal debates, intense business opposition, and problems
with existing job creation programs led Congress to exclude all permanent
work programs from the SSA and to relegate the jobless to means-tested
work relief programs.

Right to Housing. Despite FDR's faith in private housing, the New
Dealers supported the right to (public) housing. The PWA (1933) funded
the construction of public housing, schools, courthouses, city halls, and
highways to supply housing and create jobs. However, protests by the
Chamber of Commerce, the U.S. Savings and Loan League, and the
National Association of Real Estate Brokers undercut this early commitment. A circuit court ruling denying the government the right of emi-
nent domain also blocked PWA's construction of low-rent public housing
(Bratt 1986; Leuchtenberg 1963).

The housing industry favored government programs that benefited the
private housing market. For example, the 1934 National Housing Act
created jobs by insuring bank loans to (mostly white and middle-income)
families to repair, modernize, or purchase new homes, doing little to
help the more needy. The 1937 Housing Act funded the construction
of low-cost public housing despite industry complaints that it would
reduce the sale of private homes, push rents down, and compete with
private property. However, business won an "equivalent elimination"
provision that required the demolition of one substandard dwelling for
each new unit of public housing built, and another rule that stipulated

public housing must look different from – that is, less attractive than – private buildings (Bratt 1986; Williams 2004).

COMPROMISES WITH RACISM IN THE NEW DEAL ERA

The New Deal's human rights agenda lost out to compromises with racism as well as the profit motive. Its leadership opposed racial discrimination in principle but often failed to override opposition that took the racial status quo for granted or failed to enact programs that challenged it. Liberal Democrats frequently compromised with racism to win the legislative support of Southern Democrats and Republicans and to protect the Democratic Party from a disastrous north–south split (Piven and Cloward 1979). The New Dealers also ignored the power of institutionalized racism. Failing to account for the adverse impact of seemingly race-neutral regulations on persons of color, they naïvely believed that a higher standard of living for African Americans would right the wrong of racial inequality. Instead, programs that improved the conditions of poor and working-class whites often discriminated against blacks, placing the races on a different footing with regard to the right to income, work, and housing for years to come (Brown 1999; Neubeck and Casenave 2001).

Right to Income. This right was torpedoed by Southern interests, which feared that the fair treatment of the races would increase labor costs, forge an alliance between Southern black workers and Washington, D.C., and mobilize working-class coalitions to protest white racial hegemony (Lieberman 2006). Most blatantly, Congress immediately removed all SSA language that directly outlawed racial discrimination, thereby granting the states a license to discriminate (Neubeck and Casenave 2001). The ostensibly race-neutral SSA program also reproduced the racial hierarchies built into the labor market. For example, Roosevelt initially recommended that the SS and UI programs cover all workers. However, "administrative difficulties" led the act to exclude farm and domestic jobs – the two main occupations then open to blacks and Latinos. Likewise, benefit formulas based on years worked and wages earned adversely affected low-paid and part-time workers, especially workers of color and women who left work for family responsibilities (Abramovitz 1996). Such practices made it virtually impossible for blacks and Latinos to escape both their status as low-wage workers and their designation as social and political inferiors (Lieberman 2006).

The Southern Democrats' insistence on local/state control undercut the right to income, as did their opposition to a national public assistance program whose higher benefits they feared would disrupt local wage rates. The resulting federal–state partnership granting the states considerable discretionary administrative power left the door open to overt racial bias and patronage (Brown 1999; Gordon 1994). Congress refused to heed the warnings of the National Association for the Advancement of Colored People (NAACP) and the Federal Council of Churches that blacks would suffer if the law freed states to determine public assistance eligibility rules, benefit levels, and standards of need. Nor did the federal government use its powers to review and sanction these state practices (Neubeck and Casenave 2001).

Right to Work. This human right was also seriously compromised by racism. Despite antidiscrimination regulations, many of the New Deal work programs disproportionately rejected black and Latino workers, assigned them to manual labor regardless of their capabilities, and required that workers be hired by union contractors known to favor white over black workers. Work programs also placed a quota on black workers, routinely forced blacks to leave government when needed by private employers, and paid lower wages to blacks (assuming they needed less to live on than whites). Segregation was also common. The CCC imposed a 10 percent quota on black participants and housed them in segregated camps. FERA had difficulty finding sponsors for its racially segregated work projects. The 1935 Wagner Act, labor's Magna Carta, granted workers the right to organize, legalized collective bargaining, and created the National Labor Relations Board, but for years it allowed unions to exclude blacks and Latinos (Brown 1999; Rose 1994).

Seemingly race-neutral policies also deprived minorities of jobs. The Agriculture Adjustment Act (AAA) increased farm prices by paying white farmers to take acreage out of cultivation. This pushed black sharecroppers off the land. The National Recovery Administration (NRA) set the same wage rates for blacks and whites but did nothing when employers refused to hire blacks. Such racialized outcomes led blacks to rename the NRA "The Negro Removal Act." Many New Deal policies implicitly supported white workers who in turn opted for racial privilege rather than class solidarity (Brown 1999; Rose 1994).

Right to Housing. The New Deal's effort to establish the right to housing did not extend to black households. The model towns created by the Tennessee Valley Authority and other New Deal showcase communities excluded blacks (Leuchtenberg 1963). Rather than challenge the nation's racially segregated housing, the New Deal implicitly endorsed dual housing markets by granting programmatic control to localities whose leaders opposed both government initiatives and racial integration (Citizens Commission on Civil Rights 1986).

Federal policy also tolerated discrimination in the private housing market. The Federal Housing Administration (FHA), the Federal Home Loan Bank Board, and the Federal National Mortgage Association – created to promote homeownership – typically ignored racial discrimination in housing sales and/or openly discriminated. The profit-making FHA defined poor and black neighborhoods as bad credit risks unqualified for mortgage subsidies and home loans (Anderson 2003). The FHA, warning that selling to blacks endangered white property values, recommended both deed restrictions and zoning ordinances. These housing policies fueled the rigid separation of blacks and whites in public housing, limited mortgage assistance in neighborhoods of color, prevented blacks from buying private housing in white neighborhoods, and otherwise undercut the right to housing (Citizens Commission on Civil Rights 1986; Checkoway 1986).

SOCIAL MOVEMENTS IN THE NEW DEAL ERA: PRESSURE FROM BELOW

The New Deal put social and economic rights on the political agenda; however, massive protests played a key role. The unemployed councils comprising black and white jobless workers agitated for UI, work relief, and job creation, and against evictions and program cuts (Piven and Cloward 1979). The Townsendites, a popular movement of senior citizens during the Depression, supported a pension plan proposed by Frances E. Townsend (a California physician). The plan would have mandated that the Federal government pay $200 per month for Americans sixty years old or older. Black and white sharecroppers demanded federal relief (Quadagno 1984). Urban housewives marched for a better standard of living. Black communities organized the "don't buy where you can't work campaign" in major Northern cities. Huey Long's "share the wealth" program along with the Socialist and Communist parties agitated for a redistribution of wealth (Gordon 1994). The NAACP fought against discrimination and for local control of government programs. FDR's "Black Cabinet" agitated for antiracist federal policies (Judd 1999). The "rank and file movement" in social work drew on Depression-era public relief workers (later joined by radical social workers), who supported the unionization of public sector social workers and a strong human rights agenda (Fisher 1980). Although organized labor was hesitant about an expanded governmental role, trade union activism, combined with the new economic security provided by the welfare state, contributed to the progressive political climate that favored New Deal programs and opened the door to the civil rights movement (Brown 1999; Quadagno 1984). Despite their best efforts, these movements lacked the strength – and racial unity – to override powerful interests. Thus, the need to maintain business confidence and accommodate Southern interests eclipsed human rights claims.

Although leaders of the New Deal often put profits before people and compromised with racism, the historical record makes it clear that some people in power supported human rights in the 1930s. Despite the defeats, their efforts reversed historic assumptions about the government's obligation to society and created the foundation for the modern U.S. welfare state. The rise of conservatism in 1938 and U.S. entry to World War II stymied, but did not stop, these efforts.

POSTWAR YEARS: REVIVAL OF THE RIGHTS AGENDA AND THE BACKLASH

The struggle for human rights continued during and after World War II. It was fueled by large and militant social movements that pressed their claims on the state, by business leaders who accepted the welfare state as a partner in economic growth, and by the New Dealers' desire to advance their agenda. In 1941, President Roosevelt identified "Freedom from Want" as one of the Four Freedoms central to his State of the Union address (1941). In 1943, he called for a Second Bill of Rights (Harvey 2009). President Truman's 1945 postwar domestic program and the "Statement of Essential Human Rights" by the American Law Institute both recognized basic human rights (Backes and Arkin 2005). In 1948, the United Nations adopted the Universal Declaration of Human Rights, drafted under Eleanor Roosevelt's leadership. However, critics of Roosevelt's "cradle to grave" welfare immediately opposed the UDHR as a back door to larger government, federal control of the states, antilynching laws, and other measures that might "affect the colored question" (Anderson 2003). Yet, as in the New Deal era, postwar efforts to secure the right to health, income, work, and housing fell short.

In his 1949 State of the Union Address, Truman (1949) declared that: "Every segment of our population, and every individual, has a right to expect from his [sic] government a fair deal." Despite the conservative postwar reaction, he stood fast: "We should *expand* our Social Security benefits and coverage against the economic hazards due to unemployment, old age, sickness, and disability."

PEOPLE BEFORE PROFITS

Right to Health. Truman's Fair Deal relaunched Roosevelt's call for "a single unified system of national social insurance," including health insurance. In 1942, the report of the National Resources Planning Board (NRPB) – formed by FDR in 1933 – called for government-supported health care to provide freedom from sickness and accidents (Rose 1995). Starting in 1943, for nearly a decade Senators Wagner, Murray, and Dingell regularly tried to add universal, national health insurance to the SSA. But they could not overcome continued opposition of the health care industry or the conservative postwar climate. In 1943, the Insurance Economic Society of America defined government health insurance as "an issue of human rights versus state slavery" (Woolner 2009). In 1949, the AMA, Republicans, and Southern Democrats declared war on health reform, once again invoking the specter of "socialism" and "communism" to discredit Truman's proposal (Starr 1982; Foner 1999). Despite a few weak efforts in the 1950s, nothing succeeded until 1965 when Congress passed Medicaid for the poor and Medicare for the elderly, two groups that private insurers found too expensive to cover.

Right to Income. FDR's Second Bill of Rights declared that "social insurances must carry much of the load of providing adequate income for those without work and a general public assistance system for those left uncovered" (News from the Field 1943). To this end, the NRPB proposed a robust SSA expansion: federalize the social insurance and public assistance systems; expand social insurance to uncovered farm, domestic, and other workers; raise benefit levels; increase federal aid for general relief; make greater use of general revenues; and tighten federal oversight of public assistance programs (Rose 1995). Supported by this endorsement, Roosevelt (1944) stated, "Individuals are entitled to the right to earn enough to provide adequate food and clothing and recreation." Truman (1949) declared: "Government has the opportunity to help raise the standard of living of our citizens...."

In contrast to the deadlock over health insurance – and increasingly pressed by a strengthened postwar labor movement – Congress expanded the right to income. Although the changes fell far short of the comprehensive NRPB proposals, they raised benefits, liberalized eligibility rules, and protected more groups from the loss of income due to age, disability, unemployment, and retirement (Starr 1982). Some business leaders supported these social and economic rights because they increased consumer purchasing power, quieted unrest, and created the conditions for profit-making – especially for big business that could absorb the costs of reform. However, Southern Democrats who welcomed federal dollars to industrialize the South adamantly opposed higher benefits and greater federal controls. Combined with Republican insistence on tax cuts, these opponents limited the right to income (Brown 1999).

Right to Work. The 1943 NRPB Report also revived the right to work by proposing guaranteed employment for those who could not find work, permanent job creation programs (not work relief), national unemployment insurance financed with general revenues (not regressive payroll taxes), and a permanent Work Administration office to carry out "all kinds of socially useful work, not just construction." Roosevelt (1943) added that after the war the American people will "expect the opportunity to work, to run their farms, their stores, to earn decent wages."

Instead, unemployment mounted as soldiers returned and defense plants shut down. The initial effort to legislate a right to work – the 1945 Full Employment Act – guaranteed every American "able to work and seeking work" regular, full-time employment as a basic right. It won the support of labor, civil rights, and farm groups. Pressed by employers who feared that a full employment economy would drive up their labor costs, Congress gutted the bill. The Employment Act of 1946 removed the term "full" from the title and the body of the bill as well as related provisions; however, it did mandate Washington, D.C., to maximize employment, production, and purchasing power (Foner 1998; Rose 1995). Many in Congress preferred to address the specter of unemployed veterans by passing the Servicemen's Readjustment Act (The GI Bill) (Brown 1999).

Meanwhile, the postwar growth of unions threatened business, which successfully pressed Congress for the 1947 Taft-Hartley Act that severely restricted union activities won under the 1935 Wagner Act (Piven and Cloward 1979). President Truman (1949) unsuccessfully called for its repeal in 1949. Postwar prosperity eventually stalled the drive for full employment until the 1970s recession spurred the first job creation programs since the 1930s: the 1973 Comprehensive Employment Training Act and the 1976 Humphrey Hawkins Full Employment Act. But neither guaranteed the right to work.

Right to Housing. Truman's Fair Deal also advanced the right to housing amid the acute postwar housing shortage (Truman 1949). The

National Housing Act of 1949 – a sweeping expansion of the federal role – called for "the implementation . . . of a decent home and a suitable living environment for every American family." But the right to housing was eclipsed as the act turned the housing industry (i.e., real estate, construction, and homeowners) into one of the most powerful political groups in Washington, D.C. (Citizens Commission on Civil Rights 1986). The act guaranteed mortgage insurance to veterans and the middle class, created the mortgage interest tax deduction, and promoted private residential construction. However, urban renewal projects to revive downtown business districts destroyed low-income housing in adjacent "blighted" residential areas (Checkoway 1986).

Following Congressional approval of 800,000 low-income public housing units, the real estate lobby launched an all-out attack on the right to housing for low-income households. It warned that public housing was a "socialistic" threat to private enterprise. After Truman lambasted the attack as "propaganda," "misrepresentation," and "distortion," Congress approved the measure, but not without conceding that "private enterprise shall be encouraged to serve as large a part of the total need as it can." In the end, the program built only 25 percent of public housing units authorized in 1949, and the numbers dwindled until 1954 when Congress allowed localities to stop construction of unwanted public housing units (Bratt 1986; Checkoway 1986).

The law also restricted public housing to the "temporarily or deserving" poor. By the mid-1950s, this (mostly white) group had moved to the new suburbs. After this, "the projects" became stigmatized as housing for poor whites, Southern blacks, and people displaced by urban renewal and highway development. In the 1960s, public housing faced financial problems and a deteriorated housing stock. Washington, D.C. stepped in with rent and operating subsidies, later followed by demolition projects. However, in the 1970s, Nixon halted all federally subsidized public housing construction and began to move toward privatization, including vouchers for rentals in the private market. In the 1980s, Reagan slashed the operating and rental subsidies for all existing programs (Bratt 1986).

COMPROMISE WITH RACISM IN THE
POST–WORLD WAR II ERA

The 1938 elections put an anti-New Deal coalition of Southern Democrats and Republicans in control of Congress, leaving the Democratic Party dependent on their Southern flank for votes. Nonetheless, the 1942 report of the NRPB deplored discriminatory practices in public aid and made racial justice part of the postwar social welfare agenda. Black trade unionists and civil rights leaders who now equated the struggles for civil rights with the struggle for social and economic rights steadfastly defended a national universal welfare state. However, by the mid-1940s, the need to win Southern votes led Northern Democrats to regularly accept seemingly color-blind provisions that allowed Southern states to maintain control over their black and Latino labor force. Although statutorily color-blind, the racial stratification of the postwar welfare state undercut the right to income, work, and housing (Brown 1999).

Right to Income. Postwar prosperity did not lift all boats equally. More whites than persons of color benefited from economic and wage growth. The New Deal social insurance programs bolstered the rising wages of white workers by replacing a portion of their income lost through retirement or unemployment. However, the rules that tied eligibility to labor market participation effectively prevented black and Latino workers from accessing the more generous social insurance program and relegated them to means-tested public assistance (Brown 1999). Domestic workers (who opponents referred to as "girls" who worked for "women") continued to be denied access to social insurance benefits for "administrative" reasons. It took until 1950 for the SS program to include domestic workers and until 1954 to include hotel, laundry, agricultural, and state and local government workers (Kessler-Harris 2001).

The right to income was further curtailed by federal policy granting the states administrative control of public assistance programs and funding individual states based on need. The Republicans secured both of these policies by threatening to sink any social welfare legislation that included a nondiscrimination clause or federal control, often entering the provision into a bill themselves. State administration allowed officials and business elites to perpetuate the means test, meager benefits, and local control. This helped to maintain the subservience of black sharecroppers, while federal agricultural policy fueled the mechanization of farming, which undermined the sharecroppers' livelihood. In the late 1940s, using racially coded terms such as "unsuitable mothers," some sixteen states purged the welfare rolls. The cuts supplied white households with black domestic workers, although the stigmatization of black women undercut the increasingly militant civil rights movement (Brown 1999).

Right to Work. This right did not extend to persons of color who still struggled just to be hired. In 1941, the prominent civil rights activist A. Philip Randolph threatened to bring 100,000 black marchers to Washington, D.C., to protest Congressional resistance to fair employment in the military and in lucrative defense jobs. To forestall this, Roosevelt issued an executive order that barred discrimination in defense industries and federal bureaus and created the Fair Employment Practices Committee (FEPC) to address complaints. The FEPC became the first federal agency to deal exclusively with the employment problems of persons of color and to include African-American appointees. Strengthened in 1943, it endured constant attacks from Southern politicians, whereas employers and AFL unions ignored its directives. Nonetheless, in 1944 FDR supported a permanent FEPC while denouncing the poll tax and other racial barriers. Congress dissolved the short-lived FEPC in 1946. During the next four years, Southern filibusters defeated all eighty bills introduced to make it permanent. Only in 1964 did Congress establish the Equal Employment Opportunity Commission to fight employment discrimination (Rung 2005).

Ostensibly color-blind, the full employment initiatives of 1945 and 1946 implicitly benefited white men with no mention of rights for women or persons of color (Rose 1995). Blacks and Latinos lost out again when Congress effectively substituted the GI Bill of Rights for strong full employment and a national unemployment insurance program. The GI Bill itself was not discriminatory. However, to access its benefits, persons of color had to apply to discriminatory employment, financial, and education institutions.

In 1947, Truman tried to amend the Fair Labor Standards Act to make it unlawful to refuse to hire or fire a person based on their sex, race, religion, color, or national origin and to ensure that all federal personnel actions "be based solely upon merit and fitness" (Rayback 1966). In 1948, he issued an executive order establishing a Fair Employment Board (FEB) to regulate the federal workplace. Opponents who feared upsetting racial hierarchies or fueling an incipient alliance between working class and civil rights advocates, weakened both efforts (Rung 2005). In 1950, the National Manpower Council addressed structural unemployment. It recognized women's needs but not those of persons of color (Rose 1995). A right to work for persons of color did not materialize until the Civil Rights Act of 1964 that barred discrimination in public facilities and employment. Yet despite this *de jure* protection, African Americans' right to work continued to be violated *de facto*, as evident from their persistently high unemployment rate.

Right to Housing. Federal housing policy continued to compromise with racism. Despite the 1948 Supreme Court decision that outlawed racialized practices, the FHA provided mortgage insurance only to builders and buyers located beyond the inner city and supported racial covenants that prevented African Americans from moving into "white" neighborhoods (Checkoway 1986). In 1947, using federal funds, William Levitt built affordable white-only single-family tract homes for World War II veterans. This pattern of racial discrimination became the model for real estate developers across the country.

The 1949 Housing Act supported public housing but tied its expansion to an urban renewal program (i.e., "slum clearance") that destroyed more low-income housing than it built (Checkoway 1986; Wunder 2009). Blacks continued to face discrimination in public housing despite Truman's 1949 ban on federal aid to segregated projects and similar state bans. The Neighborhood Composition Rule required that public housing maintain the racial character of its neighborhood. The FHA technically offered apartments to blacks and whites on an "open occupancy" basis. But widespread segregation in the private market and local administrative control ensured that "separate but equal" housing prevailed (Bratt 1986). Local housing authorities housed blacks in segregated projects often on the edge of the city and drove public housing away from the (white) suburbs (Citizens Commission on Civil Rights 1986).

Once the 1954 *Brown* decision outlawed separate-but-equal facilities, the federal government rejected segregated projects. Yet Washington, D.C. left integration up to racially biased localities, saying that tenant selection was not a federal responsibility. In 1959, the U.S. Commission on Civil Rights recommended an executive order supporting equal opportunity in housing (Citizens Commission on Civil Rights 1986). In 1961, only thirty-two states practiced open occupancy. Although the 1964 Civil Rights Act finally prohibited discrimination in all federally assisted housing, many projects never became fully integrated (Bratt 1986). The urban renewal and highway development programs of the 1950s and 1960s resulted in significant displacement of blacks into overcrowded, substandard, and segregated neighborhoods – effectively reproducing the conditions they set out to improve (Citizens Commission on Civil Rights 1986).

RENEWED STRUGGLE: MORE PRESSURE FROM BELOW

Despite the postwar setbacks, the human rights dream did not disappear. Between 1945 and 1975, peace, steady economic growth, and victories of increasingly large and militant social movements such as trade unions and civil rights helped expand the welfare state. Increased access to an alternative source of income and newly won rights operated as an economic back-up that – like a strike fund – increased the bargaining power of these movements. The growing welfare state unexpectedly shifted the balance of power toward those with less who continued to battle for social and economic rights (Piven and Cloward 1979).

Although welfare state programs promoted profitable economic activity by increasing purchasing power and reducing social unrest, the new balance of power troubled business. In the more liberal political climate, the elite negotiated with social movements rather than opposing them outright, with trade-offs that benefited both parties. These informal "deals" or "accords" granted the social movements more equitable treatment in exchange for less turmoil in the labor market, the voting booth, and the streets (Abramovitz 1992; Bowles and Gintis 1982). By altering the dynamic of political struggle, the labor and civil rights accords moved the country closer to achieving social and economic rights even if such compromises could not be framed as human rights due to American exceptionalism.

THE LABOR ACCORD

Following World War II, organized labor's expanded membership and successful mass strikes gave unions the power to disrupt production (Boyer and Morais 1971; Rayback 1966). Business initially met labor's uprisings with harsh anti-union attacks. But the new balance of power caused business to shift to a negotiating strategy. Labor won automatic cost-of-living increases, paid vacations, improved pensions, greater control over the shop floor, fewer anti-union drives, and private health insurance to fill the gap left by Congress in the 1930s (Foner 1999; Rayback 1966). In exchange, labor agreed to longer contracts and to fewer and less militant strikes, and so on. Washington, D.C. backed the resulting accord with prolabor employment and social welfare policies, which also helped to stabilize previously unstable labor and management relations. This smoothed the way for the postwar productivity that increased both business profits and the overall standard of living (Bowles and Gintis 1982).

The 1955 merger of the AFL-CIO increased labor's electoral power and drew it into the political mainstream. In 1960, trade union dollars and votes helped Kennedy win a razor-thin victory over Nixon and then in 1964 handed the Johnson/Humphrey ticket a landslide victory over Goldwater. The Democratic Party returned the favor with the war on poverty,

Medicare, Medicaid, Food Stamps, and other important supports (Ray-back 1966). During the 1970s, a serious economic downturn led Congress to enact job creation programs including the Comprehensive Employment and Training Act (CETA), which provided public sector employment for the middle and working class. In 1975, the Equal Opportunity and Full Employment Act created a legal and enforceable right to employment similar to that called for in the 1940s. But Congress diluted the right in 1978 with the Humphrey-Hawkins Full Employment Bill, which offered only opportunities for paid work and minimal enforcement (Rose 1995). By this time, labor had begun to lose ground as the exportation of production abroad and the rise of conservatism at home fueled the second major economic crisis of the twentieth century.

THE CIVIL RIGHTS ACCORD

The postwar years witnessed a reorganization of race as well as labor relations as black voters became a political force and U.S. racism became an international embarrassment. Both events shifted the racial balance of power. The massive post-World War II migration of blacks to Northern cities made the black urban vote critical to Democratic presidential victories (McAdam 2000; Meier and Rudwick 1976). Meanwhile, the Democrats' entrenched stance on race led some black voters to actively consider bolting the party. The then-Soviet Union also mocked America's effort to export democracy by repeatedly pointing to ongoing segregation within U.S. borders (Anderson 2003).

Attempting to maintain black loyalty and to counter the Soviet critique, Truman advanced human rights. In 1947, he became the first president to address the NAACP and declare forthright support of civil rights. He established a civil rights committee whose report, *To Secure These Rights*, critiqued America's treatment of blacks. He also urged the government to end the poll tax; stamp out lynching, segregation, and discrimination in interstate travel and the armed forces; and support voting rights and a civil rights unit in the Justice Department (Gardner, Geroge, and Mfume 2003). After failing to attach an antidiscrimination amendment to the Fair Labor Standards Act, Truman issued two landmark executive orders: one established a fair employment board within the Civil Service Commission, and the other desegregated the armed forces (McAdam 2000).

In the late 1950s, the success of the Montgomery bus boycott and the *Brown v. Board of Education* Supreme Court decision (outlawing separate but equal facilities) emboldened the civil rights movement to adopt more militant tactics (Meier and Rudwick 1976; Sitkoff 1981). Tired of gradualism and tokenism, the leaders replaced the movement's "go slow" politics (i.e., self help, litigation, and lobbying) with direct action (e.g., sit-ins, pray-ins, boycotts, and Freedom Rides) that disrupted the racial status quo. The new militancy – especially the arrests, white mob violence, and police brutality they provoked – shifted the racial balance of power and public opinion toward the civil rights movement. It also intensified the Democrats' major dilemma: how to maintain the loyalty of both the black voters and the South.

Forced by the new racial balance of power to negotiate an accord with the civil rights movement, the Democratic Party agreed to more actively promote fair treatment in exchange for less disruptive direct action. In 1961, Kennedy issued an executive order against employment discrimination and appointed blacks to top positions in his administration, hiring more blacks than any previous president (Meier and Rudwick 1976). In exchange, he urged the movement to shift from disruptive direct action aimed at desegregating public facilities to a voter registration campaign. Kennedy wanted to capture the large untapped pool of Southern black voters but also viewed – wrongly – voter registration as less volatile. Working behind the scenes, the Kennedy Administration mobilized significant support from private foundations for voter registration projects that began in the South in spring 1962 and quickly gained traction (Piven and Cloward 1979). He won the support of key civil rights leaders ready to shift gears (McAdam 2000).

The escalation of violence in 1963 forced Kennedy to confront civil rights issues more directly. Televised coverage of the massive police attacks in Birmingham, Alabama, led Kennedy to publicly declare racial discrimination a moral issue. Following the 1963 March on Washington, Kennedy proposed a major civil rights bill that addressed discrimination in public accommodations, protected the political rights of Southern blacks, and supported fair employment practices. Kennedy later admitted to civil rights activists that the demonstrations "had brought results; they made the executive branch act faster and were now forcing Congress to entertain legislation which a fewer weeks before would have had no chance" (Piven and Cloward 1979).

During the 1964 Johnson/Goldwater presidential contest, the Democrats again persuaded the civil rights movement to curtail protests, fearing that the disruptions would cost the party white votes. After a landslide victory, Johnson honored his word. He supported the 1964 Voting

Rights law, antidiscrimination, affirmative action, and other measures that reduced racial barriers to voting, employment, education, and housing (Piven and Cloward 1971). He also launched the War on Poverty, the Great Society, Model Cities, educational reforms, and otherwise advanced social and economic rights, as well as civil and political ones.

These gains did not forestall the 1965 urban uprisings in black communities across the nation (McAdam 2000). The ensuing loss of white liberal support and the reduced effectiveness of direct action split the civil rights movement. The more militant wings moved toward separatism and black power, whereas the center moved toward electoral politics (Meier and Rudwick 1976). By the mid-1970s, middle-class African Americans were winning local and state office – gaining more power but being left more vulnerable to compromising their agenda.

NEOLIBERALISM: SOCIAL MOVEMENTS AND SOCIAL WELFARE UNDER ATTACK

The labor and civil rights accords designed to contain social movements paradoxically posed a new threat to the elite. That is, the welfare state reforms embedded in the accords undercut the exploitation of workers, weakened white hegemony, and otherwise raised the cost of doing business. Not surprisingly, the opponents of human rights looked for ways to push back. An opening appeared in the mid-1970s when the United States faced the second major economic crisis of the twentieth century. In contrast to the 1930s when many business leaders turned to the government for help, this time they blamed their falling profits on "big government," social welfare programs, "personal irresponsibility" – and the gains of the social movements. They concluded that the welfare state (put into place to address the crisis of the 1930s) was now part of the problem rather than part of the solution. They called for a reversal in public policy that would restructure postwar social, economic, and political institutions along old laissez-faire lines (Abramovitz 2004). This conservative paradigm, grounded in neoliberal economic principles and followed by every administration since the mid-1970s, sought to undo the hard-won New Deal and postwar gains by redistributing income upward and downsizing the state. Simultaneously, the Far Right sought to restore family values and a color-blind social order. Key neoliberal tactics included the well-known tax cuts, reduced social spending, privatization of public services, devolution of social welfare responsibility from the federal government to the states, and attacks on social movements that were best positioned to fight back. These opponents of human rights used antigovernment rhetoric, the well-worn race card, and fears of women's autonomy and gay rights to build public support for dismantling the welfare state.

Despite this history of slow and compromised victories, the battle for social and economic rights persists. In spring 2010, the American people finally secured an albeit limited right to health care and the reregulation of the financial services industry. Meanwhile, as contributions in this book show, more and more grassroots groups and service organizations around the country have adopted the human rights frame and are finding ways to bring human rights – especially social and economic rights – home.

REFERENCES

Abramovitz, Mimi. 1992. "The Reagan Legacy: Undoing the Class, Race and Gender Accords." *Journal of Sociology and Social Welfare* 19(1): 91–110.

Abramovitz, Mimi. 1996. *Regulating the Lives of Women: Social Welfare Policy from Colonial Times to the Present*. Boston: South End Press.

Abramovitz, Mimi. 2004. "Saving Capitalism from Itself: Whither the Welfare State?" *New England Journal of Public Policy* 20(1): 21–32.

Anderson, Carol. 2003. *Eyes Off the Prize: The United Nations and the African American Struggle for Human Rights, 1944–1955*. Cambridge, UK: Cambridge University Press.

Backes, Cynthia, and Cynthia Arkin. 2005. *The ALI Reporter*. Notes from the ALI Archives: The Statement of Essential Human Rights. http://www.ali.org/ali_old/R2703_11-Notes.htm.

Baicker, Katherine, Claudia Goldin, and Lawrence Katz. 1997. "A Distinctive System: Origins and the Impact of US Unemployment Compensation." National Bureau of Economic Research Working Paper 5889. http://www.econ.upenn.edu/~hfang/teaching/socialinsurance/readings/Baicker_etal98(4.1).pdf.

Bowles, Samuel, and Herbert Gintis. 1982. "The Crisis of Liberal Democratic Capitalism: The Case of the United States." *Politics & Society* 11(1): 51–93.

Boyer, Richard, and Herbert Morais. 1971. *Labor's Untold Story*. New York: United Electrical, Radio and Machine Workers of America.

Bratt, Rachel. 1986. "Public Housing: The Controversy and the Contribution." In *Critical Perspectives on Housing*, edited by Rachel Bratt, Chester Hartman, and Ann Meyerson, 335–61. Philadelphia, PA: Temple University Press.

Brown, Michael. 1999. *Race, Money and the American Welfare State*. Ithaca, NY: Cornell University Press.

Checkoway, Barry. 1986. "Large Builders, Federal Housing Programs, and Post War Surburbanization." In *Critical Perspectives on Housing*, edited by Rachel Bratt, Chester Hartman, and Ann Meyerson, 119–39. Philadelphia, PA: Temple University Press.

Citizens Commission on Civil Rights. 1986. "The Federal Government and Equal Housing Opportunity: A Continuing Failure." In *Critical Perspectives on*

Housing, edited by Chester Hartman and Ann Meyerson, 296–324. Philadelphia, PA: Temple University Press.

Fisher, Jacob. 1980. *The Response of Social Work to the Depression*. Cambridge, MA: Schenkman Publishing Co.

Foner, Eric. 1999. *The Story of American Freedom*. New York: Norton.

Gardner, Michael, Elsey Geroge, and Kweisi Mfume. 2003. *Harry Truman and Civil Rights: Moral Courage and Political Risks*: Carbondale, IL: Southern Illinois University Press.

Gordon, Linda. 1994. *Pitied But Not Entitled: Single Mothers and the History of Welfare 1890–1935*. New York: The Free Press.

Harvey, Philip. 2009. "Learning from the New Deal," paper presented at the Human Rights in the US Conference, University of Connecticut Storrs, CT, October 22–24.

Hopkins, June. 1999. *Harry Hopkins: A Sudden Hero, Brash Reformer*. New York: St. Martin's Press.

Judd, Dennis R. 1999. "Symbolic Politics and Urban Policies: Why African Americans Got So Little from the Democrats." In *Without Justice for All: The New Liberalism and Our Retreat from Racial Equality*, edited by Adolph Reed, 124–50. Boulder, CO: Westview Press.

Kessler-Harris, Alice. 2001. *In Pursuit of Equity*. New York: Oxford University Press.

Leuchtenberg, William E. 1963. *Franklin D. Roosevelt and the New Deal, 1932–1940*. New York: Harper Colophon Books.

Lieberman, Robert. 2006. "Race and the Limits of Solidarity: American Welfare State in Comparative Perspective." In *Race and the Politics of Welfare Reform*, edited by Sanford F. Schram, Joe Soss, and Richard C. Fording, 1–23. Ann Arbor, MI: University of Michigan Press.

McAdam, Doug. 2000. *Political Process and the Development of Black Insurgency*. Chicago: University of Chicago Press.

Meier, August, and Elliot Rudwick. 1976. *From Plantation to Ghetto*. New York: Hill and Wang.

Neubeck, Kenneth, and Noel Casenave. 2001. *Welfare Racism: Playing the Race Card Against America's Poor*. New York: Routledge.

News from the Field. 1943. "The National Resources Planning Board Reports." *American Journal of Public Health* 33(4): 461–63.

Piven, Francis Fox, and Richard M. Cloward. 1971. *Regulating the Poor: The Functions of Public Welfare* (updated edition). New York: Vintage Books.

Piven, Francis Fox, and Richard M. Cloward. 1979. *Poor People's Movements*. New York: Vintage Books.

Quadagno, Jill. 1984. "Welfare Capitalism and the Social Security Act of 1935." *American Sociological Review* 49(5): 632–47.

Rayback, Joseph. 1966. *A History of American Labor*. New York: Free Press.

Roosevelt, Franklin Delano. 1941. *The Four Freedoms*. http://www.americanrhetoric.com/speeches/fdrthefourfreedoms.htm.

———. 1943. State of the Union Address, 78th Congress. http://www.presidency.ucsb.edu/ws/index.php?pid=16386.

———— 1944. State of the Union Address, 79th Congress. http://www.fdrlibrary .marist.edu/archives/pdfs/state_union.pdf.

Rose, Nancy. 1989. "Work Relief in the 1930s and the Origins of the Social Security Act." *The Social Service Review* 63(1): 63–91.

———— 1994. *Put to Work: The WPA and Government Employment in the Great Depression*. New York: Monthly Review.

———— 1995. *Workfare or Fair Work: Women, Welfare and Government Work Programs*. New Brunswick, NJ: Rutgers University

Rung, Margaret. 2005. "Race, Labor & the State: Fair Employment Policy in Postwar North America." Midwest Political Science Association Annual Meeting April 10, Chicago. http://www.allacademic.com//meta/p_mla_apa_research_citation/o/8/6/4/5/pages86457/p86457-4.ph.

Sitkoff, Harvard. 1981. *The Struggle for Black Equality, 1954–1980*. New York: Hill and Wang.

Starr, Paul. 1982. *The Social Transformation of American Medicine*. New York: Basic Books.

Truman, Harry S. 1949. *Annual Message to Congress on the State of the Union, January 5, 1949*. http://www.presidency.ucsb.edu/ws/index.php?pid=13293.

Williams, Rhonda. 2004. *The Politics of Public Housing*. New York: Oxford University Press.

Woolner, David. 2009. "New Deal 2.0/Special Interests to FDR: 'National Health Care Is Un-American, A Threat to Capitalism, Nay, Slavery! (Sound familiar?).'" Eleanor Roosevelt Institute. http://www.newdeal20.org/2009/08/21/special-interests-to-fdr-national-health-care-is-un-american-a-threat-to-capitalism-nay-slavery-sound-familiar-4150/.

Wunder, William. 2009. "Harry Truman's Fair Deal: The Progressive Program of the Thirty-Third President." http://modern-us-history.suite101.com/article .cfm/harry_trumans_fair_deal #ixzzooF2TMQjr.

4

Drawing Lines in the Sand: Building Economic and Social Rights Norms in the United States

Cathy Albisa

Freedom is no half-and-half affair.[1]

INTRODUCTION

Despite identifying itself as a country that respects fundamental human rights, the United States is notorious for its opposition to universal economic and social rights. It lags behind every country with comparable levels of economic development in its recognition and protection of these rights. This is reflected in its high levels of income inequality and child poverty (Burd-Sharps, Lewis, and Martins 2008, 19, 132–49). Moreover, the positions it takes on the international stage – whether they involve questions of development, aid, or trade – are shaped and colored by the glaring absence of a cultural and political appreciation of what are often referred to as the "rights of the poor."

The paucity of analysis and scholarship from the legal community on this issue is startling. A significant exception to this silence is Cass Sunstein's *The Second Bill of Rights: FDR's Unfinished Revolution and Why We Need It More Than Ever* (2004), which details the relationship between law, jurisprudence, politics, and social movements with regard to economic and social rights in the United States. Sunstein argues that economic and social rights, although not constitutional in the United States, should be viewed the way President Franklin D. Roosevelt hoped they would be – as "constitutive commitments." He further explains that constitutive commitments represent basic principles that define our nation. Sunstein believes that some aspect of these rights, as well as other rights excluded from the Constitution, are already constitutive commitments,

[1] Franklin D. Roosevelt on the need to adopt a second bill of rights (Sunstein 2004, 42).

and there is potential to expand the universe of these commitments to include the full range of economic and social rights.

This chapter posits that as a general matter, such commitments – whether constitutional or not – emerge from the interplay between law and social movements. This chapter attempts to further define what a "constitutive commitment" might be, explores where we might look for evidence that a particular policy or approach is effectively a "constitutive commitment," and analyzes how we might learn from past successes in building these commitments in order to strengthen economic and social rights in the United States.

I. WHEN AN EIGHTEENTH-CENTURY CONSTITUTION ENTERS THE NEW MILLENNIUM

Among the most obvious places one might expect to find rights recognized and protected is in a nation's constitution and courtrooms. Although the U.S. Constitution plays some role at the margins, U.S. courts have clearly abdicated the field on most core economic and social rights issues. Is this due to the nature of our Constitution, including its age and narrow framework? Or have other factors influenced the lack of protection in the country's most important human rights document?

The U.S. Constitution, the oldest still in force in the world, has great strengths and glaring limitations. It has proven itself remarkably durable. Its legitimacy has survived a civil war, the threat to pack the court during the Great Depression – and more recently – the questionable outcome of a presidential election. In many circles it is revered, and, despite significant exceptions, it is considered a relatively enforceable document (Melusky 2006).

The U.S. Constitution also has proven unusually resistant to modernization. Whereas other countries have embraced international human rights law as well as deepened their practice of comparative jurisprudence, the United States lays claim to only a handful of cases in which human rights play a prominent role – and even in those instances the use of human rights is highly circumscribed. Similarly, where other countries have taken the lead on developing jurisprudential models for the enforcement of economic and social rights (Baderin and McCorquodale 2007), in the United States juridical silence is deafening on these issues.

It was not inevitable that the U.S. Constitution would stagnate on the question of economic and social rights (Sunstein 2004). The U.S. Supreme

Court in the 1930s initially resisted even allowing Congress authority to legislate in this arena, specifically on issues of labor protection. But after President Roosevelt threatened to "pack the court" and add six additional members if the Court did not uphold his legislative agenda, the Supreme Court decided *National Labor Relations Board v. Jones & Laughlin Steel Corporation* in 1937. Prior to this case, our federal constitutional law prohibited the national government from providing protection for a wide range of economic and social rights. In *Jones & Laughlin,* however, the Supreme Court reversed its longstanding position and upheld comprehensive labor reforms adopted during the Roosevelt Administration. The court's decision was based on the notion that labor regulation affected interstate commerce and therefore was constitutionally permissible. Although this did not obligate the government to protect rights, it did open the door for the Supreme Court to find that Congress was empowered to address a host of other human rights concerns through national legislation, including civil rights legislation to protect against race and sex discrimination.

Moreover, the dramatic change in the Supreme Court's reasoning indicated a deep shift in judicial perspective. For example, in 1923 the Supreme Court found in *Adkins v. Children's Hospital* that a minimum wage law was unconstitutional because it amounted to a "compulsory exaction from an employer for the support of a partially indigent person, for whose condition there rests upon him no peculiar responsibility, and therefore, in effect, arbitrarily shifts to his shoulders a burden which, if it belongs to anybody, belongs to society as a whole" (*Adkins v. Children's Hospital* 1923, 557–58). More than a decade later, in 1937 (the same year the Supreme Court decided the *Jones & Laughlin* case), the Supreme Court decided *West Coast Hotel v. Parrish*. Here it upheld a minimum wage law for women and described poor working women as "ready victims" due to their relatively weak bargaining power (*West Coast Hotel v. Parrish* 1937, 398). The Supreme Court also noted that in light of massive relief efforts at that time, prevailing subpoverty wages were unfair to society because "the community is not bound to provide what is in effect a subsidy for unconscionable employers" (*West Coast Hotel v. Parrish* 1937, 399).

As Sunstein observes: "What is most striking here is the reversal of what is considered a subsidy. In 1923, a minimum wage law was seen as forcing employers to subsidize the community; fifteen years later, the absence of a minimum wage law was forcing the community to subsidize employers" (Sunstein 2004, 30). This change in perspective was, no doubt, due in large part to the economic and social upheaval of the times and the rise of the labor movement.

Brown v. Board of Education in 1954 was the first major case directly addressing an economic and social right – the right to education. In this historic case that was driven by the civil rights movement, the Supreme Court held the longstanding practice of racially segregated public school systems unconstitutional. The case recognized the relationship between equality and the right to education, stressing:

> [I]t is doubtful that any child may reasonably be expected to succeed in life if he is denied the opportunity of an education. Such an opportunity, where the state has undertaken to provide it, is a right which must be made available to all on equal terms.
>
> (*Brown v. Board of Education* 1954, 493)

The Supreme Court also referred to education as a prerequisite to the meaningful exercise of other citizenship rights, implicitly acknowledging the interdependence of economic, social, civil, and political rights.

In the 1960s, the Supreme Court – perhaps influenced by the welfare rights movement – began to develop more jurisprudence specifically about the poor and appeared ready to acknowledge economic and social rights directly. In *Douglas v. California* in 1963, the Supreme Court held that poor people were constitutionally entitled to free legal representation on their first appeal of a criminal conviction. *Shapiro v. Thompson* in 1969 struck down a California law requiring new residents to wait six months before receiving welfare benefits. Although the Supreme Court's decision technically was based on the right to interstate travel, it noted that California's flawed policy denied poor people their means of subsistence. In *Goldberg v. Kelly* in 1970, the Supreme Court found that the scope of "property" interests covered under the U.S. Constitution's due process clause included welfare payments. The Supreme Court explained that because a government benefit provides an eligible recipient with "the very means by which to live," the government may not impair that recipient's interest arbitrarily and must provide a trial-like hearing prior to termination of benefits (*Goldberg v. Kelly* 1970, 264). Lower courts expanded the *Goldberg* holding to other contexts, such as housing (*Escalera v. New York City Housing Authority 1970; Caulder v. Durham Housing Authority 1970; Joy v. Daniels 1973; Williams v. Barry 1983*).

But beginning with *Shapiro v. Thompson* (1969), the Supreme Court noted that as a matter of national constitutional law, "[p]ublic assistance benefits are 'a privilege' and not a 'right,'" thus laying the groundwork for more recent circuit court rulings finding that limits on the time period that public assistance benefits are available do "not implicate a fundamental right" (*Turner v. Glickman* 2000, 424). Indeed, after 1970 the Supreme Court began to change course, becoming more hostile to economic and social rights. Judicial appointments by President Richard Nixon appeared to close the window on the development of these rights. In *Dandridge v. Williams* (1970), the Supreme Court confirmed that the Constitution contains no affirmative state obligations to care for the poor, upholding a state statute capping federal welfare grants below the level required to sustain a large family. The Supreme Court essentially stated that economic and social rights were not justiciable: "[T]he intractable economic, social, and even philosophical problems presented by public welfare assistance programs are not the business of this Court" (*Dandridge v. Williams* 1970, 487).

In *Lindsay v. Normet* in 1972, the Supreme Court rejected a challenge to a state's summary eviction procedure by tenants who refused to pay their rent on the grounds that the premises had been declared uninhabitable. In so doing, the court rejected even the negative components of economic and social rights, holding that there is no constitutional right to adequate housing and that "assurance of adequate housing and the definition of landlord-tenant relationships are legislative, not judicial, functions" (*Lindsay v. Normet* 1972, 74). In *Mathews v. Eldridge* in 1975, the Supreme Court deemed a posttermination proceeding sufficient to satisfy procedural due process, effectively undercutting its 1970 ruling in *Goldberg v. Kelly*. The Supreme Court even rejected the incipient right to education in *San Antonio Independent School District v. Rodriguez* (1973) by upholding a property tax-based school finance system that produced per-pupil spending disparities. The Supreme Court ruled such systems are problematic only when they deprive students of *any* educational opportunity (*San Antonio Independent School District v. Rodriguez* 1973, 54–56). Nearly a decade later, in *Plyler v. Doe* in 1982, the Supreme Court issued a schizophrenic decision striking down a Texas law that excluded undocumented immigrant children from public schools. On the one hand, the Supreme Court emphasized that education was not a right guaranteed under the federal Constitution. On the other, the Supreme Court stated education must be distinguished from social welfare legislation based on "the importance of education in maintaining our basic institutions, and the lasting impact of its deprivation on the life of a child" (*Plyler v. Doe* 1982, 221).

Moreover, although the Supreme Court did not try to justify its decision in *Plyler* based on existing discrimination jurisprudence, and although it explicitly rejected undocumented immigrants as a protected class, it nonetheless held that a state could not discriminatorily deny access to education to a class of children without fulfilling some substantial government goal. This holding was in stark contrast to the likely result under a "rational basis" standard of review, the standard normally applied in cases where no suspect class or fundamental right is at issue.

The Supreme Court found that none of the justifications proffered by the state of Texas in *Plyler* were sufficient to counterbalance the social costs of "denying [undocumented children the] ability to live within the structure of our civic institutions, and foreclos[ing] any realistic possibility that they will contribute in even the smallest way to the progress of our nation" (*Plyler v. Doe* 1982, 224). A subsequent decision, *Papsan v. Allain* in 1986, confirmed that the constitutional status of a right to "minimally adequate" education is still unsettled.

Plyler was an analytically muddled but ultimately ethical decision consistent with human rights norms. It is unclear, however, whether even that confused decision would stand today. The Supreme Court rejected the notion of positive state obligations in *Deshaney v. Winnebago County Department of Social Services* in 1989, stating that the federal Constitution's Due Process Clause "is phrased as a limitation on the State's power to act, not as a guarantee of certain minimal levels of safety and security," and thus "cannot fairly be extended to impose an affirmative obligation on the State. . . . Due Process Clauses generally confer no affirmative right to governmental aid, *even where such aid may be necessary to secure life*" (*Deshaney v. Winnebago County Department of Social Services* 1989, 195; emphasis added).

Despite the value afforded civil and political rights in U.S. jurisprudence, the Supreme Court rejected the principle of indivisibility and denied remedies where a failure to protect economic and social rights clearly undermined "fundamental" civil and political rights. In *Lyng v. International Union* in 1988, at the height of the Reagan counterrevolution, the Supreme Court upheld a 1981 statute that decreased or denied food stamp eligibility to households in which any member was participating in a legally protected labor strike, rejecting challenges based on the First and Fifth Amendments.

From the 1990s onward, the Supreme Court has continued to narrow legal avenues to protect the rights of the poor. For example, in *Department of Housing and Urban Development v. Rucker* in 2002, the

Supreme Court upheld the right of public housing authorities to evict residents when a household member or guest engaged in drug-related activity. In this decision, the Supreme Court stated it has no "constitutional doubts" that housing authorities could conduct no-fault evictions (*Department of Housing and Urban Development v. Rucker* 2002, 135). In other words, a public housing tenant may be evicted whether or not he or she knew (or even could have or should have known) about the illegal drug activity. This decision led to entire families being evicted from their homes because a household member or guest (often an adolescent) engaged in nonviolent drug-related activity.

As a result of this line of jurisprudence, the U.S. Constitution has been interpreted to contain no positive rights (with the notable exception of the right to be free from slavery); no explicit economic and social rights (with the exception of guarantees of non-interference with property rights and a limited right to education when the state enters the arena of public education – although in theory a state could choose to educate no one and that would still meet constitutional demands); and very little in the way of incorporating international human rights standards in general (with nothing in the way of incorporating them with regard to economic and social rights). That is our Constitution today – seemingly inflexible on these issues and increasingly outdated.

This state of affairs was not inevitable; the Constitution seeks to create the conditions for citizenship, which as Sunstein observes "might well require education and freedom from desperate insecurity" (Sunstein 2004, 115). Our Constitution is also inherently flexible enough to accommodate significant change in areas as diverse as racial segregation, sex discrimination, political dissent, wage and hour laws, commercial speech, and consensual sexual relations among homosexuals. In these critical areas, former constitutional prohibitions have yielded to permission and protections – often within a matter of only a few decades (Sunstein 2004, 123).

Most major Supreme Court departures from precedent follow a change in social consensus within the country. Even decisions perceived as pathbreaking, such as *Brown v. Board of Education*, sided with the nation's majority (Sunstein 2004). Indeed, in one form or another, fundamental shifts in constitutional interpretation have followed sustained social movements of various kinds. Racial segregation was ended by the civil rights movement; legal sex discrimination by the women's movement; legal suppression of political dissent by the labor and antiwar movements of the 1930s and 1960s, respectively; legal obstacles to the maximum hour and minimum wage laws by the labor movement; and antisodomy laws by the lesbian, gay, bisexual, transgendered and queer (LGBTQ) movement. Even the change of the status of commercial speech emerged from a movement – albeit one less characterized by human rights concerns – namely, the corporate rights movement, which has gained ground since the 1990s and in some ways threatens to overtake efforts to guarantee human rights.

Thus, we must explore other factors besides the less-than-persuasive argument that our Constitution was drafted at a time when economic and social rights were not firmly embedded and recognized by law. Tellingly, explicit protection of these rights is as scarce in legislation as it is in constitutional jurisprudence.

II. CONSTITUTIVE COMMITMENTS: DRAWING OUR LINES IN THE SAND

Although our Supreme Court has taken enormous constitutional leaps in the past, it is still difficult to reshape the contours of our country's Constitution. It is not necessary to do so in order to embed a set of rights and obligations within our nation's social fabric. There are some commitments we have made and enshrined in legislation that truly do appear as durable as constitutional rights, attaining what Louis Henkin has referred to as "near-constitutional sturdiness" (Henkin 1984, 43). As Sunstein notes, such commitments fall outside the Constitution, yet they "are widely accepted and cannot be eliminated without a fundamental change in social understanding.... they help create, or constitute, a society's basic values. They are also commitments in the sense that they are expected to have a degree of stability over time[,] . . . [and involve] a nation's understanding of what citizens [are] entitled to expect" (Sunstein 2004, 62, 64).

Although I am less optimistic than Henkin or Sunstein that this set of commitments is *ample*, there is distinct value in identifying criteria and indicators that would help us predict which commitments we have made, whether they will stand the test of time and political challenges, and which ones require more attention and effort to ensure their stability.

A. Are We There Yet?

Prior to the welfare reform efforts of the mid-1990s, Henkin observed that our "welfare system and other rights granted by legislation are so deeply embedded as to have near constitutional sturdiness" (Henkin 1984, 43). Has this assertion really withstood the test of time? Have we established a right to public assistance, or to education, or to be free of racial discrimination in employment or public accommodations, or to be protected when joining a labor union, or to Social Security?

That any child in the United States has a formal right to education is probably the most indisputable of the previous claims. "No public official at the federal, state or local level could reject that right as a matter of principle" (Sunstein 2004, 99). The notion of education as a constitutive commitment can be attributed in large part to the common schools movement of the early part of the twentieth century. Every state constitution includes a right to education of some sort, and even the Supreme Court has found support for the right to education in instances of discrimination and absolute exclusion. Although the right to education in our domestic law is not as robust as that found in the international domain and has significant limitations, it is true that no class of children can be excluded formally from any state school system (although informally children are often pushed out through abusive suspension and expulsion policies). On the contrary, children are – for the most part – legally required to attend school.

Almost equally indisputable are the rights protected in the Civil Rights Act of 1964. These include the right to be free from discrimination based on race or sex in employment and public accommodations. Racial discrimination in general has become a thoroughly discredited social approach. Although we accept disparate impacts in many areas of life, it is no longer politically acceptable to formally treat similarly situated people differently. Thus, *de jure* discrimination has gone the way of flogging for minor offenses – a historical horror we are happy to leave behind.

There have been many assaults upon the Civil Rights Act, and access to courts and remedies has been severely narrowed (in fact, plaintiffs rarely win cases at this point) (Chemerinsky 2002). Nonetheless, the act's core values – both legally and socially – remain immovable. The right to nondiscrimination in these discrete spheres is universal; even white people sue for racial discrimination. At least in theory, nondiscrimination is enforceable through court action. As a result, there is a great deal of voluntary compliance across society, with many businesses identifying and seeking to be "equal opportunity employers." There is a social consensus on the validity of nondiscrimination norms – a consensus that applies even to elected politicians.

Is the right to join a labor union also a constitutive commitment? The right to join a union is indeed constitutionally protected as part of the First Amendment. But in contemporary practice, this protection does not mean that the right to unionize obligates the government to protect individuals against retaliation for joining a union. First, the right is not universal. Farm workers and domestic workers are explicitly excluded from national laws that protect against retaliation for joining a union (1935 National Labor Relations Act § 152(3)). Second, there are still many public officials who are explicitly anti-union. It is publicly acceptable to take the position that unions are bad for the economy and for the nation as a whole. Although there are some constraints on what public officials can promote regarding anti-unionization, these are not parallel to the absolute lines drawn around racial discrimination in the public sphere. Not surprisingly, the labor movement has suffered major setbacks and defeats since the 1980s, with rates of unionization plummeting.

Finally, has Social Security for the elderly become a constitutive commitment? There are high levels of popular support for Social Security through government-managed retirement programs (American Association of Retired Persons 2010, 1–2), and there was considerable outcry when President George W. Bush proposed to privatize it (Beland and Shinkawa 2007). Yet I am still skeptical that access to Social Security has achieved the status of an enduring right in the United States. Social Security pensions are not universal. Unless you pay into the system, you are not entitled to any support. Current reversals in the fortunes of the stock market make government-run pension programs seem the wiser choice for stability and peace in old age – but this is a practical argument, not a moral imperative. Rights are the things we protect despite arguments about practicality. If the elderly had a right to Social Security, then it would not matter if they were undocumented or had simply recently arrived in the United States as refugees or legal immigrants. Indeed, it would not matter whether they had paid into the system for any reason. It would simply be their right to enjoy basic economic security in old age. I suspect that Social Security is perceived more as a contractual obligation than as a basic human right. Public officials who openly seek to privatize it are not demonized as morally repugnant. Although people might be outraged at the threat of privatization, officials who promote it are not deemed outrageous (as racists are) but rather simply wrong.

The remaining parts of our social safety net are on far more fragile ground than Social Security. Henkin (1984) commented that it was not so important that the United States did not recognize economic and social rights because our welfare system was so deeply entrenched that it had achieved "near-constitutional sturdiness." Just twelve years later, the entitlement to welfare was dismantled amid the reforms of 1996. Other aspects of the safety net are also attacked fairly regularly, including health coverage for the poor (Medicaid). But none of this should be terribly surprising, given that there has never been a social consensus that these programs confer or protect any sort of fundamental rights.

Unlike the Civil Rights Act, the legislative history of welfare is marked by phrases like "family assistance," "temporary assistance," "support," and later "personal responsibility," "transition," and "work." Although in substance welfare differs little from a right depending on the scope of the entitlement, it is radically distinct in terms of social perceptions. From its inception, welfare has been associated far more with charity than rights (Abramovitz 1996; Neubeck 2006). Additionally, welfare programs have not been universal. A person could be extremely poor and still not be eligible for cash assistance if she or he did not have children. Such benefits are not attached to the individual but rather to the family. If basic economic security were thought of as a right, it would make no sense to exclude any category of people.

After the reforms of 1996, it became impossible to argue that welfare was any sort of right (Mink 1999; Hancock 2004). There was no guarantee of receiving welfare if the state ran out of funds. Moreover, recipients became ineligible for welfare after a certain number of months – even if the need remained severe. In many states, additional children did not receive assistance if they were born into a family that already received welfare support. Instead, the family received a certain level of cash support, and if more children were born into the family the level remained the same. But if a child were born even a day before the family was on cash assistance, he or she would receive support from the state. The stated purpose of the 1996 reforms was to push people off the rolls. By this measure, the law was stunningly successful.

In sum, I believe we have achieved some constitutive commitments – specifically, education and the right to be free from *de jure* discrimination in private employment, housing, and public accommodations. I would include in the latter category sex discrimination. (Although I have not touched on it in this chapter, discrimination against the disabled is moving in the direction of a constitutive commitment.) I also believe that there are rights – such as joining a union and economic security in old age – where we have laid part of the foundation. These are considered significant human interests and have far more defenders than detractors. But there are also rights that remain disparaged – access to welfare and other social safety net programs – that matter most to the most vulnerable and excluded in our society.

B. Beyond the Robes

We have reached the first decade of the twenty-first century and are not much closer to achieving durable protection for economic and social rights than we were a century ago. This could be the result of our general lack of class consciousness or the absence of a socialist movement. It could also relate to the individualistic nature of American culture and issues of race (Sunstein 2004). We also have a winner-take-all system of government that does not allow for proportional representation. All of these factors likely play a role, and they interrelate in important ways.

There is little class mobility in the United States in both relative and absolute terms. There is less mobility in the United States than in the United Kingdom, which is thought to have an entrenched class structure and certainly has a history of strong class consciousness (Loury, Modood, and Teles 2005). Yet there has been, until recently, a widespread belief – not supported by empirical evidence – that a child in any American family had a better chance of climbing higher up the social ladder than his or her parents had. Though such attitudes have been changing as income inequality has grown and the country faces a frightening economic crisis, some commentators have posited this as an explanation for the relatively weak support for the rights of the poor (Royce 2009; Barusch 2009). If poverty is simply a transient condition that one might shed at any moment, then the reasons to invest in protecting the dignity of the poor may seem less compelling.

This explanation intersects with arguments that the individualistic nature of American culture leads to a puzzling gap in our rights framework. The individualist narrative also assumes poverty is a transitory condition because it is a result of individual – not collective – choices that can be changed based on simple acts of will (Royce 2009; Barusch 2009). This cultural interpretation also helps explain why socialist political parties and movements have not gathered greater force in the United States. Yet the significant constitutional changes already discussed in this chapter resulted from marked shifts in social consensus – so culture is far from static. Therefore, the more important question is why the United States has stubbornly clung to an impractical and unrealistic notion of individualism that does not reflect the reality of modern life (or life in almost any era, as the most typical state of human existence is interdependence).

Many commentators point to race as the primary source of inequality in the United States, arguing that individualism cloaks race, serving as an acceptable narrative in denying support to the most marginalized communities. There is some evidence to support this argument. Although President Roosevelt promised to bring the Second Bill of Rights to all people in the United States, in reality much of the legislation that succeeded was racist either on its face or in practice. For example, housing legislation intended to help returning veterans only provided housing support for what were deemed demographically appropriate neighborhoods, thus fueling segregation. As Maya Wiley, director of the Center for Social Inclusion, dryly notes: "You couldn't live near pigs or Black folks" (Wiley 2006). The civil rights movement did not gather enough force to prevent these outcomes. Thus, welfare recipients at the time were, in the public imagination, primarily white war widows and thus deserving of society's support and empathy. In fact, black women had a much more difficult time accessing these benefits.

If this theory is correct, then support for economic and social rights ironically diminished because of the success of the civil rights movement, which would have required the law to protect these rights for all people. This theory is buttressed by the story of the civil rights movement that Carol Anderson details in *Eyes Off the Prize* (2003). She traces how and why the movement abandoned its original quest for economic and social rights given the extreme backlash the pursuit engendered (Anderson 2003). Her historical analysis indicates that the country was not able to embrace what would have inevitably been racial integration at a far deeper level. It is also telling that when President Reagan chose to attack welfare, he invoked the image of the black "welfare queen" – an undeserving character who cheated society and left the welfare office in a Cadillac. Racism in the United States – and with it our inability to talk about race more fully and authentically – stifles progress on economic and social rights fulfillment far more than our hesitancy to discuss class.

Though all of these factors likely play a role in the continued marginalization of economic and social rights in America, the immutability of our electoral system is also problematic. Cultural changes, and even deeply entrenched racism, can be overcome (albeit slowly), but the lack of proportional representation in our system of government is a deep structural hurdle if it hinders the development of these rights. A system that requires a majority to win representation by definition creates little space for minority interests, which in a rich society might very well include the rights of the poor. Some commentators claim that proportional representation is more protective of these rights than winner-take-all elections (Amy 2002). Others argue that the more decisive issue is how campaigns are financed, particularly given unfettered corporate funding of campaigns following the Supreme Court's decision in *Citizens United v. Federal Election Commission* (Pasquale 2008).

Thus, any explanation of "U.S. exceptionalism" on economic and social rights must account for the complexity and range of factors at play. The health care reform debate, which began with promise, is a telling example. Initially, the public discourse focused on providing care, with then-candidate Barack Obama arguing in the 2008 presidential debates that health care was a right. But that echo became increasingly faint as the political conversation devolved into a debate over insurance reform, undergirded by the virtual guarantee of a vast pool of customers for the for-profit insurers and the likelihood that tax money would flow to these companies if necessary (Rudiger and Meier 2010). Indeed, the outcome of the health care reform effort focused on being "fair" to insurers – rendering a vigorous public option politically impossible and cementing in legislation the legitimacy of "tiers" of health care for different people based on wealth and class. The linking of a public health care option to much maligned "socialized medicine" played a large role in the debate as well. Notions of individualism, choice, and the failure to recognize class discrimination were all serious barriers to those seeking a more progressive health care system that would *provide* care to all based on their health care needs. Toward the end of the debate, there was little talk of human rights.

The arena of housing rights provides an even bleaker landscape. Support for housing as a human right is relatively low compared to that for health care and education. Still, more than half of the people in the United States believe housing should be considered a human right (Opportunity Agenda 2007, 4). National policy does not create an entitlement to housing. From an equity perspective, a great deal more government investment goes into upper-income housing (i.e., through the mortgage tax credit) than to housing for the poor and those of moderate income. Government officials also are mostly silent on the question of housing as a universal human right. Although many grassroots organizations – and some advocates – have been promoting a human right to housing, there are just as many housing groups that do not. The ongoing foreclosure crisis has also not provided a venue to build support for housing as a human right; instead, it has been framed as an ownership and financial crisis.

Additionally, in the midst of a severe housing crisis, localities have continued to demolish desperately needed public housing. Redevelopment of this type of housing stock has displaced significant numbers of residents. For the most part, public housing communities – as well as families dependent on housing vouchers – are composed of African Americans, Latinos, and other racial and ethnic groups facing disproportionate poverty. These communities are regularly subjected to demeaning stereotypes against people who are both poor and nonwhite. In New Orleans, which suffered particularly brutal demolitions after Hurricane Katrina in 2005, one survey showed that 100 percent of residents displaced from public housing were African American (NESRI forthcoming). Among the stated reasons for demolishing public housing was crime reduction – thus reaffirming the stereotypical assumption of criminality in these communities. After the demolitions, with little public housing left, murder rates soared in New Orleans.

It was in this context – relentless foreclosures, no coherent housing policy, a sinking economy, and demolition of the remaining public housing – that the UN Special Rapporteur on the Right to Housing Raquel Rolnick undertook her first assessment trip to the United States in fall 2009. Her visit received a reasonable amount of attention and helped lift morale in many of the most beleaguered communities across the country over the course of a six-city tour (including one Native American reservation). Lively town hall meetings were a centerpiece of the tour. Rolnick's message that housing was a human right, not a commodity, appeared to resonate with low-income residents and some housing officials.

Yet soon after Rolnick's visit the U.S. Department of Housing and Urban Development (HUD) proposed issuing private mortgages (not public funding) as a means of improving public housing in the United States. This first step toward privatization was particularly shocking in the face of the foreclosure crisis. It would have meant increasing the debt burden of low-income people in the short term and threatening the existence of affordable housing stock in the United States over the long term. Not surprisingly, grassroots housing rights groups have fiercely opposed this proposal, grounding their resistance in human rights arguments and principles (NESRI 2010, paragraph 22). Their efforts, however, are stymied not only by underlying racial dynamics in the country but also by misplaced notions of individualism; unless there are enough affordable housing units or well-paying jobs, no amount of individual effort can change the housing landscape.

Optimists, however, may still see 2009–10 as the years when seeds were planted for constitutive commitments to health care and housing as human rights. Courageous health care professionals who have been part of the single-payer movement faced arrest when they disrupted Congressional hearings and made rights-based arguments that full public financing for health care should be considered as a serious option. This could hardly be seen as an extreme position, considering that more than two-thirds of the American public agreed with them (CBS News/New York Times 2009). Additionally, a large human rights group, Amnesty International, for the first time took public positions on the human right to health care in the United States, and those positions involved support for a public financing system. Most significantly, the single-payer movement as a whole more strongly embraced health care as a human right in the wake of the defeat of a universal public health care option. Local and state campaigns grounded in a human rights framework are being waged across the country. In a similar manner, the visit of the UN Special Rapporteur on the Right to Housing galvanized grassroots communities to frame their struggles increasingly in human rights terms. Her ongoing engagement with U.S. activists is fueling a rights-based conversation that propelled HUD Secretary Shaun Donovan to announce publicly that housing was a human right – despite his formal policy positions to the contrary.

C. Making the Road by Walking

We have much further to go before the full range of economic and social rights become constitutive commitments in the United States. Constitutive commitments can be divided into three categories: those that are explicitly recognized in the Constitution, those that have been interpreted as part of the Constitution through case law, and those that have been adopted through legislation and deep social consensus (Sunstein 2004). Because the current Supreme Court is unlikely to render judgments grounded in human rights, and because constitutional change is daunting even under more favorable circumstances, the idea of forging a strategy to create constitutive commitments that fall outside the constitutional sphere is particularly appealing.

Doing so would require articulating the minimum elements of a constitutive commitment and then intentionally building layers of social consensus around and investment in such commitments. Important questions to ask include:

- Is it universal (or at least universal for some stage of life, such as for children or the elderly)?
- Is it equitable and equal, meaning does each person receive the same level of guarantee for the right – including those with particular needs? (A contrary example would be different tiers of health insurance for different people.)
- Is the language associated with it inclusive of the concept of rights and does it imply permanence?
- Is it socially unacceptable to deny its legitimacy as a right?
- Is it enforceable?
- Was it adopted after significant social changes and/or social movements?

Universality is key because it defines the basic essence of a human right. Moreover, it is what distinguishes a right from an interest – or in the even more pejorative term often used in the United States, a special interest. A right is held by everyone, regardless of his or her particular interest in it. Equity and *equality* on the one hand, and universality on the other, represent two sides of the same coin. Equity, in particular, raises the bar to the point where not only should each person be able to realize all their rights, but resources should be used in a way that prioritizes what each person or group needs to do so. Additionally, the language of rights, if it reflects a social consensus, increases the likelihood that it would be socially unacceptable for a public figure to argue against the right at stake, which makes the right practically immune from attack.

A constitutive commitment must also be reflected in some vehicle for enforcement against violations. Just because it may be socially unacceptable to attack a right in principle does not mean that it will not be consistently violated in practice. If a right is unenforceable, it loses credibility, and there is far less reason for anyone to be invested in protecting it. Thus, a genuine commitment must include an enforcement strategy.

Finally, "rights are born of wrongs" (Sunstein 2004), and here is where social movements play a critical role in transforming economic and social rights into constitutive commitments in the United States. Unless recognition of a right is the result of a sustained social movement activism, its foundation is far too unsteady. The Civil Rights Act provides a case exemplar. In President Lyndon Johnson's first State of the Union Address he said, "[l]et this session of Congress be known as the session that did more for civil rights than the last hundred sessions combined" (1964). But even with *full presidential support*, the legislative victory did not come easy:

> The 1964 civil rights Senate debate lasted over eighty days and took up some seven thousand pages in the Congressional Record. Well over ten million words were devoted to the subject by members of the upper house. In addition, the debate produced the longest filibuster in Senate history, as well as the first successful invocation of cloture in many years.
>
> (Schwartz 1970, 1089)

President Johnson then chose the Fourth of July to sign the bill in a dramatic televised ceremony.

Underlying this fierce debate and intense political theater were decades of community organizing, murders and political assassinations, and a whole country up in arms because of a powerful national movement that lay claim to the nation's founding ideals and challenged its ultimate hypocrisy. Even after the victory, much work remained. The Civil Rights Act was described as a desecration of American ideals by opponents in the Southern United States, who vowed to undermine and oppose it. But the very nature of their attack reflected that this had become a fight for the soul of the nation, a battle over ideology and ideals. The symbolism and the struggle were the things that made the Civil Rights Act as successful as any constitutional amendment would have been.

So how do we create the language, legitimacy, and social buy-in necessary to create constitutive commitments for economic and social rights? At minimum, advocacy and organizing strategies must break the isolation of the poor by creating platforms for leadership and the kind of storytelling that reclaims a person's dignity. This requires furiously rejecting the "victim advocacy model" – where an advocacy group "shows" a victim's side of the story, and then the "victim" falls silent while their representatives speak about solutions. Part of the story must include poor people themselves creating and conveying an image of the solution. Poor people must also become both the harbingers of the future definition of rights and stakeholders who engage in the conversation over how those ideals should be represented in the legal system.

This strategy for building constitutive commitments is grounded in the relationship and interactions between culture, law, and social movements. It requires working at multiple levels, lest short-term gains be swept away in the blink of an election cycle. In the daily work of activists, it means finding ways to scale the walls that exist between the poorest communities and the sites where decisions are made. Walls turned on their sides, after all, are bridges. Once we build and cross them, the conversation can never be the same again.

Creating alliances across social sectors and communities combined with consensus on what we want to achieve will dramatically increase the likelihood that constitutive commitments on economic and social rights take hold in the United States. The conceptual framework of human rights is essential to building that consensus: universality, interdependence of rights, public accountability, equity, equality, and participation. We can build those alliances by being willing to let the poor lead themselves and by committing to provide all the tools necessary for them to succeed. Constitutive commitments are not built in one or two election cycles. This is decades-long work. Perhaps the most important ingredient is sustained commitment to the vision and the approach. Changing a law might easily be characterized as an advocacy project. Changing a culture, however, must be a life's work.

REFERENCES

Abramovitz, Mimi. 1996. *Regulating the Lives of Women*. Cambridge, MA: South End Press.
Adkins v. Children's Hospital, 261 U.S. 525 (1923).
American Association of Retired Persons. 2010. *Social Security 75th Anniversary Survey Report: Public Opinion Trends*. Washington, D.C.: AARP.
Amy, Douglas J. 2002. *Real Choices/New Voices: How Proportional Representation Elections Could Revitalize American Democracy*. New York: Columbia University Press.
Anderson, Carol. 2003. *Eyes Off the Prize: The United Nations and the African-American Struggle for Human Rights, 1944–1955*. New York: Cambridge University Press.
Baderin, Mashood, and Robert McCorquodale, eds. 2007. *Economic, Social and Cultural Rights in Action*. New York: Oxford University Press.
Barusch, Amanda Smith. 2009. *Foundations of Social Policy: Social Justice in Human Perspective*. 3rd Edition. Belmont, CA: Brooks/Cole.
Beland, Daniel, and Toshimitsu Shinkawa. 2007. "Public and Private Policy Change: Pension Reform in Four Countries." *Policy Studies Journal* 35: 349–71.
Brown v. Board of Education, 347 U.S. 483 (1954).
Burd-Sharps, Sarah, Kristen Lewis, and Eduardo Borges Martins. 2008. *The Measure of America: American Human Development Report 2008–2009*. New York: Columbia University Press.
Caulder v. Durham Housing Authority, 433 F.2d 998, 1002–03 (Fourth Cir. 1970).

CBS News/New York Times. 2009. "Poll: Most Back Public Health Care Option." http://www.cbsnews.com/stories/2009/06/19/opinion/polls/main509 8517.shtml.

Chemerinsky, Erwin. 2002. "Closing the Courthouse Doors to Civil Rights Litigants." *University of Pennsylvania Journal of Constitutional Law* 5: 537–57.

Dandridge v. Williams, 397 U.S. 471 (1970).

Department of Housing and Urban Development v. Rucker, 535 U.S. 125 (2002).

Deshaney v. Winnebago County Department of Social Services, 489 U.S. 189 (1989).

Douglas v. California, 373 U.S. 353 (1963).

Escalera v. New York City Housing Authority, 425 F.2d 853, 861 (Second Cir. 1970).

Goldberg v. Kelly, 397 U.S. 254 (1970).

Hancock, Ange-Marie. 2004. *The Politics of Disgust: The Public Identity of the Welfare Queen.* New York University Press.

Henkin, Louis. 1984. "International Human Rights and Rights in the United States." In *Human Rights in International Law: Legal and Policy Issues*, edited by Theodore Meron, 25–67. Oxford, UK: Clarendon Press.

Johnson, Lyndon B. 1964. "State of the Union Address." http://teaching americanhistory.org/library/index.asp?document=99.

Joy v. Daniels, 479 F.2d 1236, 1242 (Fourth Cir. 1973).

Lindsay v. Normet, 405 U.S. 56 (1972).

Loury, Glenn, Tariq Modood, and Steven Michael Teles. 2005. *Ethnicity, Social Mobility, and Public Policy: Comparing the USA and UK.* New York and Cambridge, UK: Cambridge University Press.

Lyng v. International Union, 485 U.S. 360, 370–74 (1988).

Mathews v. Eldridge, 424 U.S. 319, 331 (1975).

Melusky, Joseph Anthony. 2006. *The Contemporary Constitution: Modern Interpretations.* Malabar, FL: Krieger Publishing Company.

Mink, Gwendolyn, ed. 1999. *Whose Welfare?* Ithaca, NY: Cornell University Press.

National Economic and Social Rights Initiative. Forthcoming. "Survey Findings." In *Constant Threat: How HUD and HANO Regulations Violate the Human Right to Housing by Displacing the Poor in New Orleans.* New York: NESRI.

National Economic and Social Rights Initiative, Coordinator. 2010. *Toward Economic and Social Rights in the United States: From Market Competition to Public Goods – Joint Submission to the UN Human Rights Council Universal Periodic Review of the United States of America.* New York: NESRI. http://www.nesri.org/UPRReportOnEconomic&SocialRights.pdf.

National Labor Relations Act. 2006. 29 U.S.C. § 152(3).

National Labor Relations Board v. Jones & Laughlin Steel Corporation, 301 U.S. 1 (1937).

Neubeck, Kenneth. 2006. *When Welfare Disappears.* New York: Routledge.

Opportunity Agenda. 2007. *Human Rights in the U.S.: Opinion Research with Advocates, Journalists, and the General Public.* Washington, D.C.: Opportunity Agenda.

Papsan v. Allain, 478 U.S. 265, 285 (1986).

Pasquale, Frank. 2008. "Reclaiming Egalitarianism in the Political Theory of Campaign Finance Reform." *University of Illinois Law Review* 2: 599–660.

Plyler v. Doe, 457 U.S. 202 (1982).

Royce, Edward. 2009. *Power and Poverty: The Problem of Structural Inequality.* Lanham, MD: Rowman and Littlefield.

Rudiger, Anja and Benjamin Mason Meier. 2010. "A Rights Based Approach to Health Care Reform." In *Rights-Based Approaches to Public Health*, edited by Elvira Beracochea, Corey Weinstein, and Dabney Evans, 69–86. New York: Springer Publishing Company.

San Antonio Independent School District v. Rodriguez, 411 U.S. 1 (1973).

Schwartz, Bernard. 1970. *Statutory History of the United States: Civil Rights.* *Part 2.* New York: Chelsea House Publishers.

Shapiro v. Thompson, 394 U.S. 618 (1969).

Sunstein, Cass. 2004. *The Second Bill of Rights: FDR's Unfinished Revolution and Why We Need It More Than Ever.* New York: Basic Books.

Turner v. Glickman, 207 F.3d 419 (Seventh Cir. 2000).

West Coast Hotel v. Parrish, 300 U.S. 379 (1937).

Wiley, Maya. 2006. Interview by the author, at the Center for Social Inclusion, September 6.

Williams v. Barry, 708 F.2d 789, 792 (D.C. Cir. 1983).

5

State and Local Commissions as Sites for Domestic Human Rights Implementation

Risa E. Kaufman

States and localities play a critical role in bringing the United States into compliance with its international human rights commitments. The human rights framework embraces the importance of local decision making and implementation, as well as a significant role for subnational incorporation of human rights obligations. Realization of human rights in affected communities requires strong cooperation and collaboration among local, state, and federal governments, and between government and civil society (Melish 2009). Moreover, state and local implementation of human rights may eventually help influence national policy and broader acceptance of international human rights norms (Burroughs 2006, 420–24; Davis 2008a, 436; Powell 2001, 249; Resnik 2006, 1581; Soohoo and Stoltz 2008, 475).

Indeed, human rights treaties are intended to be implemented at the local level with a great deal of democratic input. They provide mechanisms and opportunities for reporting on conditions within communities (both positive and negative), training government officials and agencies as well as the community to promote equality and nondiscrimination, conducting hearings to explore and examine the relevance of findings by international treaty bodies, and issuing recommendations for future

This chapter draws on research conducted for and recommendations made in a 2009 report by Columbia Law School's Human Rights Institute and the International Association of Human Rights Agencies under the auspices of the Human Rights at Home Campaign. A number of individuals provided critical research for this paper, including Joie Chowdhury, Sam Yospe, and Erin Foley Smith. I am also grateful to JoAnn Kamuf Ward, Peter Rosenblum, Robin Toma, Catherine Powell, Martha Davis, Eric Tars, Tara Melish, Marea Beaman, Debra Leibowski, Jamil Dakwar, Cynthia Soohoo, Lisa Crooms, Tanya Coke, Ejim Dike, and Daniel Belasco for their helpful comments and guidance on this project.

action. They also provide a set of standards that local governments should adhere to in administering their own laws and policies.

Subnational implementation of human rights, particularly in areas traditionally reserved for state and local regulation, is also consistent with the U.S. federalist system. In ratifying each of the human rights treaties it has signed, the U.S. Senate has noted that in light of federalism, human rights treaty obligations will be implemented by state and local governments to the extent that they exercise jurisdiction over such matters.[1] As Louis Henkin noted, international law allows the federal government to leave implementation of human rights treaty provisions to the states, although the United States remains internationally responsible for a state's failure to implement a treaty obligation (Henkin 1995, 346).

A growing body of literature describes ways in which states and localities are a critical site for human rights implementation. Martha Davis describes them as "laboratories of foreign affairs, testing policies before initiating full-blown national programs," with the hope that these programs may eventually "trickle up" to the national level (Davis 2008b, 128). Judith Resnik seeks to highlight collective state and local action, particularly through what she terms Translocal Organizations of Government Actors (TOGAs), as a force for enabling state and local officials to influence national and transnational policy, including through integrating international human rights norms (Resnik, Civin, and Frueh 2008, 732–65). Cynthia Soohoo, Suzanne Stolz, and Catherine Powell also note that local advocacy is important for human rights norm internalization and can support national implementation by countering criticism that human rights are somehow "antidemocratic" (Soohoo and Stolz 2008, 475; Powell 2001, 268).

This literature reflects increasing instances of subnational implementation of human rights within the United States. The most visible of these occur where state and local governments adopt standards from international human rights treaties into local law. Some ordinances and resolutions encourage local governments to take international treaty obligations into account when designing local policy and

---

[1] *Cong. Rec.* 138 (1992): 8071, recognizing that state and local governments shall implement obligations under the International Covenant on Civil and Political Rights (ICCPR) in areas within their jurisdiction; *Cong. Rec.* 140 (1994): 14326, same understanding regarding International Convention on the Elimination of All Forms of Race Discrimination (CERD); *Cong. Rec.* 136 (daily ed. Oct. 27, 1990): S17486, same understanding for Convention Against Torture and Other Cruel, Inhuman or Degrading Treatment or Punishment (CAT).

practice. Others require that the government assess how its policies and practices impact protected groups and take proactive steps to remedy disparities.

State and local human rights and human relations commissions can play an important role in subnational incorporation of human rights as well. There are more than 150 state and local commissions or agencies mandated by state, county, or city governments to enforce human and civil rights and/or to conduct research, training, and public education, and issue policy recommendations on human intergroup relations and civil and human rights (Saunders and Bang 2007). Although these commissions go by different names and have varying missions, they all generally operate to prevent and eliminate discrimination through a variety of means, including enforcing antidiscrimination laws and engaging in community education and training to prevent discrimination. Their core mission is encouraging and facilitating institutional change through policy and practice to eradicate discrimination and promote equal opportunity.

Many state and local commissions date back to the 1940s and 1950s, when human rights and race relations commissions were established to address racial tension and violence erupting around the country. Others were formed later – in the 1960s and 1970s – in reaction to the civil rights movement and in response to calls to eradicate racial discrimination (Saunders and Bang 2007). Resources for commissions come from governmental as well as private sources, yet resources are often scarce. Most agencies are organized into nonprofit associations that are international (e.g., International Association of Official Human Rights Agencies), national (e.g., National Association of Human Rights Workers), or statewide (e.g., California Association of Human Relations Organizations) in scope. As described more fully below, some state and local commissions are using an international human rights framework.

This chapter posits that, given their mission, history, and expertise, state and local human rights commissions can be effective sites for subnational implementation of international human rights treaty obligations and norms. Specifically, this chapter explores the role, both realized and potential, that state and local human rights agencies can play in helping implement the United States' international human rights obligations. This chapter also makes concrete recommendations for ways in which the federal government can play a more active role in supporting and coordinating state and local human rights agencies in monitoring compliance with and implementing human rights standards.

I. STATE AND LOCAL COMMISSIONS ENGAGING IN HUMAN RIGHTS IMPLEMENTATION

Several state and local human rights agencies are currently implementing international human rights standards locally, and much can be learned from these examples. In 2009, Columbia Law School's Human Rights Institute, in conjunction with the International Association of Official Human Rights Agencies, conducted interviews to learn about state and local agencies' efforts to engage an international human rights framework to advance their work. Researchers interviewed staff and commissioners from a number of state and local human rights and relations commissions, other state and local government entities, and human rights advocates. This section explores several instances of subnational human rights implementation revealed by the interviews.

Portland, Oregon

In March 2008, the City of Portland created a Human Rights Commission that incorporates a human rights framework. The commission, created in conjunction with an Office of Human Relations, is guided by international human rights principles (City of Portland 2008). Article II of its bylaws states:

> The Human Rights Commission shall work to eliminate discrimination and bigotry, to strengthen inter-group relationships and to foster greater understanding, inclusion and justice for those who live, work, study, worship, travel and play in the City of Portland. In doing so, the Human Rights Commission shall be guided by the principles embodied in the United Nations Universal Declaration of Human Rights.
>
> (City of Portland 2009)

Guided by the Universal Declaration of Human Rights (UDHR) principles, the commission has created a complaint mechanism that documents and reports a range of potential human rights violations, including abuse to the integrity of the person, denial of education, abuse of civil rights and liberties, incidents of bias, trafficking in persons, and abuse of workers' rights. The commission refers complainants to attorneys or supportive organizations whenever possible.

The Human Rights Commission also is engaged in education and outreach efforts. It declared 2009 a year of Human Rights Learning and committed itself to raising awareness about the existence of the UDHR, the rights it contains, and what the declaration means in practice to the residents of Portland (Johnson 2009).

Washington State

The Washington State Human Rights Commission, which is charged with enforcing the state's human rights statute, engages a human rights framework through public education and advocacy. In conjunction with the sixtieth anniversary of the UDHR, the commission drafted a proclamation for the governor's signature, declaring December 10, 2008, Human Rights Day.

The commission has also integrated human rights standards into its advocacy work (Brenman 2009). For example, in 2007, the commission embarked on a project to document, analyze, and address the severe lack of housing for farm workers in Washington. The commission explored the issue through the lens of discrimination against farm workers on the bases of race and national origin, drawing on its mandate to enforce prohibitions against such discrimination contained in the state's antidiscrimination statute and federal fair housing laws. In a report detailing its findings and recommendations for resolving the housing crisis, the commission discussed the relevant domestic legal standards and also drew on international human rights principles, specifically highlighting Article 25 of the UDHR:

> Everyone has the right to a standard of living adequate for the health and well-being of himself and of his family, including food, clothing, housing and medical care and necessary social services, and the right to security in the event of unemployment, sickness, disability, widowhood, old age or other lack of livelihood in circumstances beyond his control.
>
> (Washington State Human Rights Commission 2007)

San Francisco, California

The San Francisco Commission on the Status of Women was instrumental in enacting and implementing a local ordinance that directly incorporates international human rights principles into the city's functioning. Beginning in 1997, a number of citizens' groups worked with the San Francisco Commission on the Status of Women to hold hearings and engage in public education around human rights, particularly as they apply to women and girls in San Francisco. Following this educational process, the commission worked with citizens' groups to develop a local ordinance implementing the human rights principles of the Convention on the Elimination of All Forms of Discrimination Against Women (CEDAW) into local law (WILD for Human Rights 2006). In April 1998, the San Francisco Board of Supervisors passed the municipal ordinance, requiring government agencies and departments in San Francisco to implement the standards of CEDAW and "integrate gender equity and human rights principles into all of its operations" (City and County of San Francisco 1998).

Notably, the ordinance contains a more expansive definition of discrimination than previously recognized. Under the ordinance, the city must eradicate all policies that discriminate, including those that have a discriminatory impact, and proactively identify barriers to the exercise of human rights. The ordinance also calls for human rights education for city departments and employees. The Commission on the Status of Women is designated as the implementing agency and is required to conduct gender analyses of the budget, services, and employment practices of selected city departments to identify barriers and discrimination against women (Lehman 2009; Menon 2009).

As a result of such gender analyses, the commission identified myriad discriminatory practices, raising awareness around the need for policy changes to benefit both women and men. For example, the commission discovered that certain jobs were overwhelmingly held by men. To address this inequity, departments instituted policies that have resulted in more women accessing these jobs, including establishing emergency ride home programs, making information available about childcare for employees working nontraditional hours, allowing for telecommuting, and actively recruiting women for nontraditional jobs (WILD for Human Rights 2008; Lehman 2009; Menon 2009).

Beginning in 2001, the Commission on the Status of Women conducted a citywide gender analysis of work–life balance in thirty-nine city departments to identify any unintended consequences of its policies and practices on female employees. It catalyzed attention to the issue citywide and facilitated specific policy changes within individual city agencies. The information collected through the work–life balance study also helped support paid parental leave legislation passed in 2002 (Lehman 2009; Menon 2009).

Some departments found that their services had a discriminatory impact on city residents. For example, the Department of Public Works considered street lighting and noted in its gender analysis report that "a woman, in particular, may fear sexual assault, making her feel more vulnerable than a man." The department concluded that improving lighting on dark streets, parking lots, and public facilities "creates a more equitable outcome: both women and men feel safe walking down a street at night" (WILD for Human Rights 2008, 7).[2]

Eugene, Oregon

In 2006, Eugene's Human Rights Commission instituted a "Human Rights City" project dedicated to exploring ways in which the city government can implement international human rights standards and principles in its overall operations. Thus far, the commission has engaged in community education and outreach efforts, raising awareness about the potential for an international human rights framework to advance the equality and dignity of local residents.

After researching local implementation of human rights and actively networking with advocacy organizations, the project created an informational website that includes resources on local implementation efforts in the United States and the city of Eugene. The project has facilitated informal presentations to city employees and managers from various city departments and interdepartmental committees to acquaint them with international human rights principles and the Human Rights City concept and to convey that, in many instances, city staff already engage in human rights work. The project also has engaged in a series of symposia and summits to educate the community and local officials about international human rights principles (Neubeck 2009).

The commission is building support for a city council resolution committing the city's government to progressive implementation of the principles contained in the UDHR, embracing the full range of civil, political, economic, social, and cultural rights. Once the council passes such a resolution, the Human Rights Commission can play a role in advising and assisting the city manager and city staff in implementation (Neubeck 2009).

Los Angeles, California

The Los Angeles County Human Relations Commission documents and reports on human rights violations. Since 1980, the commission has compiled, analyzed, and produced an annual report on hate crime data in Los

---

[2] The CEDAW ordinance was amended in 2000 to include the requirement that agencies take account of the effect of various policies on racial and ethnic minorities.

Angeles County, based on data provided by law enforcement agencies, school districts, universities, and community organizations. The commission distributes the annual report to policy makers, law enforcement agencies, educators, and community groups throughout Los Angeles County and across the nation to raise awareness about the types, severity, location, and content of hate crimes in Los Angeles County; to improve efforts to prevent, detect, report, investigate, and prosecute these crimes; and to sponsor a number of ongoing programs related to combating hate crime. In 2002 and 2003, the commission contributed its data to a report by Human Rights Watch on racial discrimination (Toma 2009).

The commission also has promoted human rights at the international level. In 2001, the commission partnered with the U.S. State Department and local UN support groups to hold the only preparatory conference in the United States for the UN World Conference on Racism, Xenophobia, and Other Forms of Intolerance, which took place in South Africa in 2001. The executive director of the commission was invited to be part of the official U.S. delegation to the conference, prior to the U.S. government canceling its involvement in the conference. Despite the U.S. cancellation, the commission sent a delegation to the conference to share information on its work against racism, xenophobia, and other forms of discrimination, and to bring ideas and inspiration back to the community (Toma 2009).

The Human Relations Commission also draws upon international human rights standards in its advocacy efforts. For example, in its campaign to address rising violence against people who are homeless, the commission is drawing on international human rights standards to encourage law enforcement agencies to collect relevant data and to engage in public education highlighting the rights and standards regarding shelter and housing (Toma 2009).[3]

II. SUGGESTED BEST PRACTICES AND ADDITIONAL ACTIVITIES AND FUNCTIONS

As illustrated in the previous section, state and local agencies, including human rights and relations commissions, are well situated to engage in human rights compliance at the subnational level. Specifically, state and local human rights and human relations commissions can: (1) monitor and document human rights issues; (2) assess local policy and practice in

---

[3] Particularly applicable to the homeless is Article 25, paragraph 1 of the UDHR.

light of international standards; (3) engage in human rights education; (4) incorporate human rights principles into advocacy efforts; (5) investigate human rights complaints; and (6) coordinate and implement local policy to integrate human rights principles.

A. Monitor and Document Human Rights Abuses

First, state and local human rights agencies can facilitate the United States' international human rights compliance through the human rights treaty reporting process and other documentation efforts. As a party to several core human rights treaties, the United States is obligated to report periodically on its progress in advancing the rights set forth in the treaties to the relevant United Nations monitoring bodies. In addition, the United Nations Human Rights Council reviews the human rights records of all 192 United Nations member states once every four years through the Universal Periodic Review process. State and local human rights commissions can help the United States comply with its reporting obligations under these processes by providing information on human rights compliance at the state and local level.

For example, in February 2008 the United States had to report on its compliance with the Convention on the Elimination of All Forms of Racial Discrimination (CERD). The Pennsylvania Human Rights Commission became involved in this reporting process, providing information to the UN committee overseeing the convention, including disaggregated data on cases involving race, color, and national origin in employment, housing accommodation, and education (Glassman 2009).

The city of Berkeley recently committed itself to similar reporting. In September 2009, the Berkeley City Council approved a proposal from the Berkeley Peace and Justice Commission (the city's functional equivalent of a human rights or human relations commission) requiring the city to provide local statistical reports and information on local ordinances related to implementation of the major human rights treaties ratified by the United States to the county, state, and federal governments, and to the UN treaty bodies (Bohn 2009; Ginger 2009).[4] The reports would correspond with the U.S. government's periodic treaty reporting obligations.

---

[4] The text of the approved recommendation can be found at: http://www.ci.berkeley .ca.us/uploadedFiles/Clerk/Level_3_-_City_Council/2009/09Sep/2009-09-29_Item_19_ United_Nations_Treaty_Reports.pdf.

Significantly, recognizing the important role that state and local human rights and human relations commissions play in treaty reporting, Harold Hongju Koh, the legal advisor to the U.S. State Department, recently sent a letter to all state and local commissioners seeking information for the U.S. government's reports on compliance with its legal obligations contained in three of the human rights treaties the United States has ratified: CERD, the International Covenant on Civil and Political Rights (ICCPR), and the Convention Against Torture (CAT) (Koh 2010).

In addition to documenting and contributing information directly, state and local human rights and human relations agencies can help facilitate visits of international human rights experts and officials. In recent years, UN officials such as the Special Rapporteurs on Racism and on Housing have visited the United States with the goal of observing the status of human rights compliance in the United States and facilitating dialogues within communities about human rights. State and local human rights and human relations agencies can use such opportunities to engage their own communities in conversations on these issues and ensure that UN experts and officials accurately report on the status of human rights in their communities.

B. Assess Local Policy and Practice in Light of International Standards

Once an international treaty monitoring body, committee, or expert issues its findings on the United States' compliance with its human rights obligations, state and local agencies can hold hearings to assess state and local policy and practice in light of the findings and international human rights standards. State and local human rights and human relations commissions can then issue their own recommendations for legislation or administrative action at the state and local level based on their assessment.

For example, in the summary of concerns and recommendations it issued in 2008, the UN CERD Committee expressed concern with racial segregation in the United States (CERD 2008). The committee specifically referenced the need to eliminate obstacles that pose barriers to affordable housing and the need to effectively implement legislation adopted at the state and federal level to combat discrimination in housing. State and local commissions can use this opportunity to hold hearings and have a conversation about state and local policies around affordable housing and lending, and to promote policies that address the disparate racial impact of specific policies and practices at the local level. They can also identify best practices, which can serve as replicable models.

C. Engage in Education and Training

State and local human rights and human relations commissions may engage in education and training of the public and state and local officials about international human rights standards. They can work with local citizen groups to engage in public education and outreach around standards set forth in international human rights treaties the U.S. government has ratified as well as others that serve as the source of international human rights norms and obligations.

For example, in 2007, in conjunction with the sixtieth anniversary of the UDHR, the Anchorage, Alaska, Equal Rights Commission sent an email to municipal employees and others announcing that the day marked International Human Rights Day. The commission highlighted the basic principles contained in the UDHR, including the inherent dignity and equal and inalienable rights of all people. The email urged recipients to rededicate themselves to achieving equality and fairness for all (Jones 2009).

In addition, state and local human rights and human relations agencies can provide a clearinghouse of information for individuals who believe that their human rights have been violated. They can supply information on complaint mechanisms and local, national, and international avenues for redress, including information on the international human rights system as well as local human rights organizations that may be a resource. For example, the newly reestablished Milwaukee Equal Rights Commission is charged with making accessible a clearinghouse of information and publications related to human rights (Daitsman and Lindsley 2009). And the website of the Portland Office of Human Relations links to the website of the UN Office of the High Commissioner for Human Rights, which contains extensive information on human rights protection and promotion.

D. Incorporate Human Rights Principles into Advocacy Efforts

State and local human rights and human relations commissions can incorporate human rights standards to frame their missions and orient their advocacy initiatives. Through the framework of human rights, state and local agencies can better understand and articulate the interrelated nature of rights. For example, agencies can address issues of economic and social rights through the lens of discrimination. The ordinance reestablishing Milwaukee's Equal Rights Commission does this by charging the commission with promoting social and economic equity for all city residents as part of its objective of promoting equal rights, diversity, and nondiscrimination (Daitsman and Lindsley 2009).

An international human rights framework also enables commissions to identify and articulate issues in accordance with internationally recognized standards. Thus, the Washington State Human Rights Commission has articulated the human rights dimensions of the lack of housing for farm workers in the state (Brenman 2009). The Los Angeles County Human Relations Commission has placed the issue of hate crimes into a human rights context, highlighting international standards that prohibit such crimes (Toma 2009). And San Francisco has addressed ways in which certain employment policies and practices have a disparate, unintentionally adverse effect on women in violation of human rights standards prohibiting discrimination against women (WILD for Human Rights 2008).

E. Investigate Human Rights Complaints

Not all state and local human rights commissions have the authority to investigate complaints or enforce compliance with applicable laws. But for state and local human rights and human relations commissions authorized to investigate individual complaints, a human rights framework can provide a set of standards for assessing whether a violation has occurred. For example, guided by the principles contained in the UDHR, the Portland, Oregon, Human Rights Commission has designed its complaint form to address a broad range of potential rights violations that it might not otherwise consider (Johnson 2009; Office of Human Relations, City of Portland n.d.) Even if an agency is not authorized to enforce prohibitions on human rights violations, using a human rights framework as a basis of a complaint system enables state and local human rights and human relations commissions to engage in broader documenting and reporting efforts and raise awareness of human rights concerns within the community.

F. Encourage, Coordinate, and Implement Local Policy to Integrate Human Rights Principles

By raising awareness, building public support, engaging in monitoring, and providing other expertise and resources, state and local human rights and human relations agencies can encourage and assist other government agencies to incorporate human rights principles and standards into local law.

There are many examples of initiatives to incorporate human rights into local law. The San Francisco ordinance incorporating CEDAW is one model. In addition, the city of Chicago recently adopted a resolution encouraging incorporation of the principles of the Convention on the Rights of the Child (CRC), calling for the city to "advance policies and practices that are in harmony with the principles of the [CRC] in all city agencies and organizations that address issues directly affecting the City's children" (City of Chicago 2009).[5] The Seattle Human Rights Commission is currently working with elected officials to develop and promote a proposed ordinance whereby the city would adopt provisions and standards of the CRC, CEDAW, and the International Covenant on Economic, Social, and Cultural Rights (Solomon 2009; Nelson 2009). In New York City, the proposed New York City Human Rights in Government Operations Audit Law (Human Rights GOAL) seeks to integrate human rights principles of dignity and equality (based on CERD and CEDAW) into local policy and practice by requiring that the city train its personnel in human rights, undertake a human rights analysis of the operations of each city department, program, and entity, and create action plans for how the city will integrate human rights principles. The bill would create a task force consisting of community and government representatives to oversee local implementation and would provide avenues for community participation in the development of the human rights analysis and action plan (New York City Council 2010).

In addition to encouraging these efforts, state and local human rights and human relations agencies can play a robust role in their implementation. For example, a commission could monitor city agencies' compliance and potentially accept and investigate complaints of noncompliance with such resolutions and ordinances. It could also engage in education and training of local officials on applicable human rights standards and commitments. A commission could likewise raise public awareness of local human rights laws and their mandates, enabling individuals to secure the rights promoted by such laws (Babcock 2009).

[5] Chicago joined nine other cities and five states that have passed resolutions in support of the Convention on the Rights of the Child. Eighteen states, nineteen counties, and forty-seven cities have likewise passed resolutions in support of CEDAW, the Women's Convention. Three cities – San Francisco, Berkeley, and Los Angeles – have passed resolutions implementing the principles of CEDAW into local law.

III. APPROPRIATE FEDERAL ROLE

Although states and localities can be effective sites for human rights implementation, the federal government maintains a critical role in coordinating and supporting their efforts. Indeed, in its review of U.S. compliance with obligations under CERD, the UN CERD Committee voiced concern over the United States' "lack of appropriate and effective mechanisms to ensure a co-ordinated approach towards implementation of the Convention at the federal, state and local levels," and recommended establishing such mechanisms (CERD 2008).

Although principles of federalism and the Supreme Court's decision in *Medellin v. Texas* (2008)[6] may constrain or limit the scope of the federal government's power to *require* that state and local governments engage in these activities, the federal government can and should *encourage* these efforts. The federal government should also provide coordination and support where state and local human rights commissions endeavor to implement human rights treaty obligations at the local level.

Recognizing the role that state and local governments play in implementing the United States' international obligations, the federal government has nevertheless assumed its responsibility to oversee and facilitate state and local compliance with human rights treaty obligations. In ratifying human rights treaties, the United States recognizes this obligation to ensure that state and local governments implement their treaty obligations.[7] Indeed, under international law, the United States remains internationally responsible for any failure of its states to properly implement treaty obligations (Henkin 1995, 346).[8]

---

[6] In *Medellin*, the Supreme Court held unenforceable in domestic courts a decision by the International Court of Justice that the United States had violated its treaty obligations under Vienna Convention by failing to inform Mexican nationals of their rights under the convention.

[7] The federal government has assumed this responsibility, for example including in the "federalism understanding" it added to CERD the recognition that it assumes the obligation to, "as necessary, take appropriate measure to ensure the fulfillment of the Convention" by state and local authorities. (*Cong. Rec.* 1994, 140:S7634–02) (United States Reservations, Declarations, and Understandings, International Convention on the Elimination of All Forms of Racial Discrimination).

[8] Article 2(1) of CERD obligates the United States to "ensure that all public authorities and public institutions, national and local, shall act in conformity" with the convention and to "take effective measures to review governmental, national and local policies, and to amend, rescind or nullify any laws and regulations which have the effect of creating or perpetuating racial discrimination wherever it exists" (CERD, art. 2 [1][a] and [c] 1965).

The federal government already plays an important role in facilitating and supporting state and local human rights and human relations commissions in their efforts to enforce and monitor compliance with federal antidiscrimination laws. The Department of Housing and Urban Development provides grants to state commissions through its Fair Housing Initiatives Program to conduct fair housing education and outreach. The Equal Employment and Opportunity Commission (EEOC) contracts with state and local commissions to enforce federal antidiscrimination in employment laws at the local level. In these and other ways, the federal government should coordinate and support states and municipalities in their efforts to implement human rights treaty obligations as well.

A. Key Institutional Reform: A Federal Human Rights Monitoring Body

Heeding recent calls for institutional reform at the federal level, namely strengthening and transforming the current U.S. Civil Rights Commission to a U.S. Civil and *Human* Rights Commission, would help ensure effective human rights compliance in the United States, including subnational human rights incorporation (Powell 2008; Leadership Conference on Civil Rights 2009).

A new U.S. Civil and Human Rights Commission, as an independent and nonpartisan entity, would operate as a federal monitoring body with a mandate to examine the United States' compliance with international treaties and other international human rights obligations. Significantly, this enhanced commission should coordinate and support the efforts of states and localities to implement human rights close to home.

National human rights institutions around the world, including national human rights commissions, monitor and promote governments' compliance with human rights obligations by conducting research; issuing reports, opinions, and recommendations; issuing proposals to harmonize legislation and policies with human rights obligations; engaging in human rights education; contributing human rights reports to international and regional treaty bodies; and receiving complaints. Although the complaint function may not necessarily be tied into a judicial process, it may uncover issues that deserve attention and study and lead to recommendations for critically needed changes in relevant laws, policies, and practices. Suggested minimum standards for national human rights institutions are set forth in the principles relating to the Status of National Human Rights

Institutions (the "Paris Principles") endorsed by the UN General Assembly (UN General Assembly 1993).

Consistent with the role played by national human rights commissions elsewhere, a reformed U.S. Commission on Civil and Human Rights would be empowered to issue reports and recommendations to the executive branch and Congress; contribute to reports the United States submits to international bodies; develop programs for teaching and training on human rights issues; and conduct investigations and hearings into human rights complaints (Powell 2008; Leadership Conference on Civil Rights 2009).

Significantly, the Paris Principles explicitly call upon national human rights bodies to "setup local or regional sections" or "maintain consultation with the other bodies... responsible for the promotion and protection of human rights," highlighting the importance of engaging with state and local efforts (Paris Principles, Methods of Operation [e];[f]). By supporting and engaging with state and local efforts at human rights compliance and implementation, a U.S. Commission on Civil and Human Rights could both improve domestic compliance with human rights obligations and move one step closer to adhering to internationally recognized standards for national human rights bodies.

B. Strategies for Successful Engagement of State and Local Human Rights and Human Relations Commissions

A federal human rights monitoring body, such as a transformed U.S. Civil and Human Rights Commission, could provide critical support for subnational incorporation of human rights, specifically through dedicated staff, education and training, and funding.

1. Dedicated Staff. First, a federal human rights monitoring body should have staff dedicated to liaising and coordinating with states and municipalities, specifically through their human rights and human relations commissions and other relevant state and local officials. This dedicated staff should be based within the national and/or regional offices of the U.S. commission. For example, the U.S. Civil and Human Rights Commission should have dedicated staff charged with receiving reports, suggestions, and recommendations from state and local human rights and human relations commissions, as well as other relevant state and local officials, on matters falling within the jurisdiction of the U.S. commission. Dedicated staff should also be charged with soliciting input from and consulting with state and local human rights and relations commissions and other relevant state and local agencies on reports to international and regional human rights bodies. And they should initiate and forward advice and recommendations to state and local commissions and other relevant state and local officials on matters that the commission has studied or on observations or reports received from international and regional human rights bodies. The commission's mandate should also include dedicating staff to help state and local commissions and other relevant state and local officials collect, analyze, and report on human rights compliance at the state and local level to determine where compliance is strong and where it needs improvement. Staff could also organize and hold hearings on issues of state and local concern, including how state and local policy comports with the commission's findings as well as findings issued by international and regional human rights bodies; engage in educational efforts with the public and with state and local agencies to raise awareness of international human rights standards; assist state and local commissions and other relevant officials in identifying best practices for human rights compliance and implementation; and assist in drafting recommendations and guidance encouraging, allowing, or requiring governmental agencies to take international human rights standards into account in creating new policies and legislation.

2. *Education and Training.* Through a federal human rights monitoring body, the federal government should also mandate and offer guidance on civil and human rights training for key state and local human rights commissions and other relevant agency staff. Such a body would foster awareness of governments' obligations under civil rights statutes, human rights treaties ratified by the United States, and relevant international, regional, and national human rights mechanisms. This awareness in turn will clarify the obligations that state and municipal governments are expected to undertake for data collection and analysis and will facilitate dialogue with international and regional human rights bodies.

A U.S. Commission on Civil and Human Rights could also take a lead role, in conjunction with relevant federal agencies, in working with state and local commissions and other state and local officials to help U.S. delegations prepare for international human rights conferences and disseminate declarations or plans of action to appropriate government bodies. Likewise, the commission could work with state and local commissions to prepare for official mission site visits from international and regional human rights experts, including conducting previsit education with local commissions and other relevant state and local government agencies.

3. Funding. The federal government should also provide financial support for state and local governments to engage in civil and human rights implementation and compliance. Specifically, a federal human rights monitoring body, such as a U.S. Commission on Civil and Human Rights, could be authorized and funded to distribute and oversee a federal grants program supporting state and local agencies as well as community-based nongovernmental agencies in their efforts to undertake civil and human rights education, monitoring, reporting, and enforcement efforts.

There are several models for such a grants program. The EEOC contracts with state and local human rights and human relations commissions (Fair Employment Practice Agencies) to enforce several federal antidiscrimination laws (*U.S. Code.* Vol. 42, Sec. 2000e-8[b]). This arrangement allows state and local agencies to manage federal claims of discrimination through work-sharing agreements with the federal government. A U.S. Commission on Civil and Human Rights could enter into similar contracts with state and local human rights and human relations commissions to engage in periodic monitoring, reporting, and data analysis under the human rights treaties ratified by the United States.

Similarly, the Department of Housing and Urban Development Fair Housing Initiatives Program (FHIP) provides grants to state and local human rights commissions to conduct fair housing education and outreach (Housing and Community Development Act of 1987, 42 U.S.C 3616; PL 100–242, amended by Housing and Community Development Act of 1992, 24 CFR 125). A U.S. Commission on Civil and Human Rights could likewise issue grants to state and local agencies to develop and engage in general human rights education and training for the public, as well as education of state and local officials. Such education and training would include information on relevant civil and international human rights standards and mechanisms and would focus on helping staff within state and local commissions collect and analyze data and report on how well their jurisdictions are complying with civil rights laws and human rights treaties.

Another potential model is the Safe Schools/Healthy Students Initiative Grants, a collaboration of the U.S. Departments of Education, Health and Human Services, and Justice (Elementary and Secondary Education Act of 1965, as amended, Title IV, Part A, Subpart 2, Sec. 4121; 20 U.S.C 7131).

This discretionary grant program requires coordination with community-based organizations and allows local governmental agencies to apply jointly for federal funding to support a variety of activities and services. A U.S. Commission on Civil and Human Rights could similarly invite state and local human rights agencies and other state and local agencies to partner with community organizations and other members of civil society to create integrated approaches to civil and human rights education and compliance.

CONCLUSION

International human rights standards and strategies provide powerful tools for affirming and promoting the dignity and equality of all people and ensuring that everyone is able to fulfill his or her basic needs, as well as realize his or her full potential. These internationally recognized norms are central to the mission of state and local human rights and human relations agencies as they help ensure opportunity and equality within their communities. Thus, with the necessary support, state and local agencies can play an instrumental role in ensuring that the human rights ideals the United States was founded upon are reflected and realized at every level of government and accessible for all individuals.

REFERENCES

Babcock, Sandra (clinical director, Center for International Human Rights at Northwestern Law). 2009. Interview by Joie Chowdhury, February 27.
Bohn, Diana (member, Berkeley Peace and Justice Commission). 2009. Interview by Erin Smith, July 21.
Brenman, Marc (former executive director of Washington State Human Rights Commission). 2009. Interview by Sam Yospe, April 19.
Burroughs, Gaylynn. 2006. "More Than an Incidental Effect on Foreign Affairs: Implementation of Human Rights by State and Local Governments." *N.Y.U. Review of Law and Social Change* 30: 411, 420–24.
City and County of San Francisco. 1998. Local Implementation of the United Nations Convention on the Elimination of All Forms of Discrimination Against Women (CEDAW). Ordinance No. 128–98. Municipal Code, Administrative Code, Chapter 12K. April 13. http://sfgov.org/site/cosw_page.asp?id=10849.
City of Chicago. 2009. "Expression of Support for Convention on the Rights of the Child. Resolution R2009–143." *Journal of the Proceedings of the City Council of the City of Chicago, Illinois*, February 11: 55415–16. http://www .chicityclerk.com/journals/2009/feb11_2009/feb11_2009_part3optimize.pdf.
City of Portland. 2008. Ordinance No. 181670. Creation of the Office of Human Relations and the Human Rights Commission. City Council of the City of

Portland, Oregon. March 19. http://www.portlandonline.com/humanrelations/index.cfm?c=50680&a=227365.

———. 2009. January 7. "Bylaws: Human Rights Commission." http://www.portlandonline.com/humanrelations/index.cfm?c=49504&a=227082.

Committee on the Elimination of Racial Discrimination (CERD). 2008. "Concluding Observations on the United States of America." U.N. Doc. CERD/C/USA/CO/6, May 8.

Daitsman, Rose, and Linda Lindsley (co-coordinators of the Greater Milwaukee Human Rights Coalition). 2009. Interview by Joie Chowdhury, February 22.

Davis, Martha F. 2008a. "Upstairs, Downstairs: Subnational Incorporation of International Human Rights Law at the End of an Era." *Fordham Law Review* 77: 411–38.

———. 2008b. "Thinking Globally, Acting Locally: States, Municipalities, and International Human Rights." In *Bringing Human Rights Home*, edited by Cynthia Soohoo, Martha Davis, and Catherine Albisa, Vol. 2, 127–52. Westport, CT: Praeger Publishers.

Elementary and Secondary Education Act of 1965 (ESEA). U.S. Code. Title 20, sec. 7131.

Ginger, Ann (executive director, Meiklejohn Civil Liberties Institute). 2009. Interview by Erin Smith, July 6.

Glassman, Stephen (executive director, Pennsylvania Human Rights Commission). 2009. Interview by Joie Chowdhury, February 25.

Henkin, Louis. 1995. "U.S. Ratification of Human Rights Conventions: The Ghost of Senator Bricker." *American Journal of International Law* 89: 341–50.

Housing and Community Development Act of 1987. U.S. Code. Title 42, sec. 3616.

International Convention on the Elimination of All Forms of Racial Discrimination (ICERD), adopted 21 December 1965, 660 U.N.T.S. 195 (entered into force 4 January 1961), G.A. Res. 2106 (XX), 20 GAOR Supp. (No. 14) at 47, U.N. Doc. A/6014 (1965).

Johnson, María Lisa (director of the Office of Human Relations of Portland, Oregon). 2009. Interview by Joie Chowdhury, February 20.

Jones, Barbara (director, Anchorage Equal Rights Commission). 2009. Interview by Sam Yospe, April 6.

Koh, Harold Hongju (legal advisor, U.S. Department of State). 2010. Letter to State and Local Human Rights Commissioners, May 3.

Leadership Conference on Civil Rights. 2009. *Restoring the Conscience of a Nation.* http://www.civilrights.org/publications/reports/commission/lccref_commission_report_march2009.pdf.

Lehman, Ann (senior CEDAW policy analyst, San Francisco Department on the Status of Women). 2009. Interview by Erin Smith, July 7.

Medellín v. Texas, 128 S. Ct. 1346 (2008).

Melish, Tara J. 2009. "From Paradox to Subsidiarity: The United States and Human Rights Treaty Bodies." *Yale Journal of International Law* 34: 389–462.

Menon, Anu (CEDAW policy analyst, San Francisco Department on the Status of Women). 2009. Interview by Erin Smith, June 29.

Nelson, Julie (director, Seattle Office of Civil Rights). 2009. Interview by Joie Chowdhury, May 27.

Neubeck, Ken (community volunteer, Eugene Human Rights Commission). 2009. Interview by Joie Chowdhury, February 23.

New York City Council. 2010. *Human Rights Government in Operations Audit Law, Int 0283-2010.* http://legistar.council.nyc.gov/LegislationDetail .aspx?ID=679918&GUID=960F221E-C810-40E9-AF16-2EC4547ED586& Options=&Search=.

Office of Human Relations, City of Portland, Oregon. n.d. "Complaint Form: Report Human Rights Incidents." Accessed December 8, 2010. http://www .portlandonline.com/humanrelations/index.cfm?a=254809&c=50684.

Powell, Catherine. 2001. "Dialogic Federalism: Constitutional Possibilities for Incorporation of Human Rights Law in the United States." *University of Pennsylvania Law Review* 150: 245-96.

_____. 2008. *Human Rights at Home: A Domestic Policy Blueprint for the New Administration.* American Constitution Society for Law and Policy. http:// www.acslaw.org/files/C%20Powell%20Blueprint.pdf.

Resnik, Judith. 2006. "Law's Migration: American Exceptionalism and Federalism's Multiple Ports of Entry." *Yale Law Journal* 115: 1564-70.

Resnik, Judith, Joshua Civin, and Joseph Frueh. 2008. "Ratifying Kyoto at the Local Level: Sovereigntism, Federalism, and Translocal Organizations of Government Actors (TOGAs)." *Arizona Law Review* 50(3): 709-86.

Saunders, Kenneth L., and Hyo Eun (April) Bang. 2007. "A Historical Perspective on U.S. Human Rights Commissions." Executive Session Papers, Human Rights Commissions and Criminal Justice, No. 3. http://www.hrccj.org/hrccj/ pdfs/history_of_hrc.pdf.

Solomon, Rosalyn (commissioner, Seattle Human Rights Commission). 2009. Interviews by Joie Chowdhury, May 27.

Soohoo, Cynthia, and Suzanne Stolz. 2008. "Bringing Human Rights Change Home." *Fordham Law Review* 77: 459-500.

Toma, Robin (executive director, LA County Human Relations Commission). 2009. Interview by Joie Chowdhury, April 13.

UN General Assembly. 1993. "National Institutions for the Promotion and Protection of Human Rights" (Paris Principles). G.A. Res 48/134 (Dec. 20).

U.S. Congress. *Congressional Record Daily.* 1990. 101st Cong., 2d sess. Vol. 136, no. 150 (October 27): S17486.

U.S. Congress. *Congressional Record.* 1992. 102d Cong., 2d sess. Vol. 138, pt. 6: 8071.

U.S. Congress. *Congressional Record.* 1994. 103d Cong., 2d sess. Vol. 140, pt. 10: 14326.

U.S. Congress. *Congressional Record Daily.* 1994. 103d Cong., 2d sess. Vol. 140, no. 82 (June 24): S7634-02.

Washington State Human Rights Commission. 2007. *Farm Worker Housing and the Washington Law Against Discrimination.* Briefing Paper. http://content .knowledgeplex.org/kp2/cache/documents/17830/1783061.pdf.

WILD for Human Rights. 2006. *Making Rights Real: A Workbook for Local Implementation.* http://wildforhumanrights.org/publications/rightsreal/.

———. 2008. *Respect, Protect, Fulfill: Raising the Bar on Women's Rights in San Francisco.* http://www.wildforhumanrights.org/documents/resources/ respectprotect.pdf.

Challenging Public/Private Divides

6

The Curious Resistance to Seeing Domestic Violence as a Human Rights Violation in the United States

Sally Engle Merry and Jessica Shimmin

Over the last three decades, a global social movement has enshrined gender violence as a core violation of international human rights law (Merry 2006, 2009). However, the idea that domestic violence is a human rights violation has not had much impact on the U.S. movement against domestic violence. Human rights activists in the United States tend to focus on violations experienced by people in other countries rather than at home. Despite their influential role in devising international violence against women initiatives and their enthusiasm for seeing gender violence as a human rights violation in other countries, many leaders in the U.S. domestic violence movement fail to bring it home (Morgaine 2006, 2009).

Currently, the way domestic violence is framed within U.S. policy and activism makes it particularly resistant to human rights discourse. After briefly considering how gender violence has become defined as a global human rights violation, we consider the reasons for its limited impact on U.S. domestic violence activists. Using Massachusetts as a case study, we argue that the movement's intimate involvement with the state for financial support of domestic violence services reshapes the political perspectives of many domestic violence service providers and activists. As service providers, they have moved increasingly closer to the welfare system and its dominant characterization of state aid recipients. They share the view that battered women need to assert themselves as individuals and throw off their dependency on their partners and the state. Thus, these service providers have adopted, to some extent, a neoliberal understanding of welfare that insists that needy and dependant individuals take

The authors gratefully acknowledge the support of the National Science Foundation Law and Social Sciences Program #SES-0417730 and the Wenner Gren Foundation Dissertation Fieldwork Grant for support for some of this research.

responsibility for themselves. In this neoliberal regime, battered women become safe by achieving self-sufficiency and autonomy – qualities they perform by making choices and avoiding dependence on a partner or the state.

This perspective differs in significant ways from that of the human rights system. The human rights framework seeks to empower the most vulnerable; those who are discriminated against; and those who face social, economic, and cultural forms of exclusion and inequality (e.g., the 1979 Convention on the Elimination of All Forms of Discrimination Against Women, ratified by 186 states as of 2010). It examines the structures of exclusion and inequality, and seeks to protect the agency of those who are harmed in its delineation of violations (Ignatieff 2001). The human rights approach seeks solutions through structural change such as new government policies, reductions in poverty, and enhancements to individual coping strategies.

Whereas the human rights framework was compatible with the views of feminists who began the battered women's movement in the 1970s, it increasingly conflicts with the neoliberal orientation of the U.S. social welfare system. Today, the perspectives of people providing services to battered women in the United States have shifted. In the early years, activists argued that violence was caused by patriarchal structures, not a woman's failure to take responsibility for herself (Schechter 1982; Merry 2009). The early domestic violence movement in the United States was organized at a grassroots level with an agenda toward social change; therefore, a focus on structures of inequality made sense. However, with the professionalization of the battered women's movement during the 1980s and 1990s, domestic violence was formalized as a public health and safety problem. Professionalization allowed battered women's programs to both stabilize and provide services reliably. Yet it also diminished the role of battered women's leadership, moderated feminist political commitments, and produced a reliance on state and federal funding. In this context, domestic violence professionals adjusted their political commitments and developed new priorities and modes of advocacy. Now, domestic violence organizations are components of an extensive social service system that positions government as the medium of advocacy and opportunity. In this milieu, the universal language of human rights is not a compelling idiom for domestic violence advocacy.

As the domestic violence movement has become increasingly dependent on government support, its perspective has shifted to be more closely aligned with contemporary state policies (Markowitz and Tice 2002;

Merry 2001). In the process, structural analyses of violence have diminished whereas women have been "responsibilized" (i.e., held personally responsible for their problems). As domestic violence services are tied ever closer to welfare services, they are transformed by neoliberalism's emphasis on responsibility and privatization, both of which are opposed to collective analyses of the issue and social change responses (Morgen, Acker, and Weigt 2010; Ridzi 2009). Services have focused on making women responsible for themselves, making choices, and learning to conform to heteronormative family patterns through parenting classes and shelter life. In this way, domestic violence interventions in the United States increasingly parallel welfare reforms more generally, which also emphasize individual responsibility.

Another barrier to the use of a human rights framework for the domestic violence movement is the U.S. government's resistance to ratifying the convention that deals with women and gender violence – the Convention on the Elimination of All Forms of Discrimination Against Women (CEDAW). This refusal limits the legal scope of human rights as a way of dealing with gender violence. Despite its widespread global acceptance, the treaty remains stalled in the U.S. Congress. In addition to the historic resistance to ratifying international human rights treaties, some argue that there has also been a sense that the United States already has an adequate system of women's rights. However, these are less extensive than the protections offered by CEDAW. In the face of intransigent federal opposition, local activists have pushed for the passage of city ordinances to implement the terms of CEDAW. San Francisco is the most notable and successful example (Lozner 2004). There have been less successful efforts in New York City, Boston, and Los Angeles (Merry et al. 2010).

Although the original treaty did not mention gender violence, two general recommendations added to the text have elaborated this dimension of women's rights and the committee that monitors compliance with CEDAW routinely asks about it (Merry 2006). An initial recommendation against gender violence was developed in 1989, and in 1992, a broader recommendation that defined gender-based violence as a form of discrimination was added. The 1992 General Recommendation placed violence against women squarely within the rubric of human rights and fundamental freedoms. It made clear that states parties are obliged to eliminate violence perpetrated by public authorities and by private persons. This recommendation expanded the scope of monitoring open to the CEDAW committee, and it empowered the committee to investigate states' efforts to diminish violence against women.

ADVOCATING HUMAN RIGHTS FOR GENDER VIOLENCE

With some exceptions, local U.S. programs serving battered women still retain a civil rights focus, as does social science scholarship on domestic violence and sexual assault. Yet, there are domestic violence activists and advocates who have turned to human rights concepts in recent years (Schneider 2000, 2004). They build on a small but vibrant U.S. human rights movement, developed since the 1990s, that has focused on issues such as domestic violence, immigration rights, economic rights, welfare rights, sexual rights, reproductive health, the dilemmas of Hurricane Katrina victims, the rights of detainees, and the definition of torture. Organizations such as the U.S. Human Rights Network and the National Economic, Social, and Cultural Rights Initiative (NESRI) have imported human rights into discourse and policy advocacy on a variety of domestic issues. The new domestic human rights initiative is well documented in major contemporary scholarship (Soohoo, Albisa, and Davis 2008; Davis 2007). A human rights framework expands the focus beyond a relatively narrow civil rights approach, which requires only punishment of the offender, to a broader social justice one combining civil and political rights with social, economic, and cultural ones.

Some activists and scholars use the human rights framework to resist the neoliberal view of gender violence in favor of a more structural analysis. A human rights approach to domestic violence emphasizes the right to be free from violence as well as the right to health care, housing, education, and employment (Thomas 2000). Human rights approaches also build on ideas of intersectionality – combining gender with race, language, religion, and national origin as the basis for mobilization. Schneider (2004, 706–07) notes that communication has increased between domestic and international groups working on violence against women, including the increased use of international law in U.S. decisions and stronger links between organizations working inside and outside the United States. She attributes the shift to a growing frustration with the slow pace of litigating women's rights cases in the United States coupled with the internationalization of domestic organizations. She sees an increase in the use of human rights arguments in domestic women's rights litigation and heightened efforts to convince the U.S. government to ratify CEDAW (Schneider 2004, 707).

Some activists in the movement against gender violence have joined this wave. They are a relatively small but growing group, often working with communities that have particular sympathy for the human rights framework, such as immigrants and African Americans. Immigrant groups from countries where human rights are more widely recognized, such as South Asia, have created more human-rights focused domestic violence programs. For example, Das Gupta (2006) notes that South Asian immigrant rights groups in New York and New Jersey – such as Manavi (www.manavi.org) – use a human rights framework in their gender violence work, referencing human rights as well as civil and women's rights.

Women of color, especially African-American women, have been adroit at asserting human rights approaches. There is a long tradition of African Americans mobilizing human rights in an effort to shame the United States for its discriminatory practices. For example, Malcolm X used human rights as a counter to racial discrimination and inequality (Malcolm X and Haley 1964; Anderson 2003). In the late 1990s, African-American women took the lead in bringing a human rights framework to the issue of violence against women through a series of conferences and through the creation of INCITE!, an organization focused on the intersections of race, class, and gender in the analysis of violence (Smith, Richie, and Sudbury 2006).

The National Center for Human Rights Education (NCHRE), headquartered in Atlanta, Georgia, is a training and resource center for grassroots activists using human rights education to address social injustices in the United States. Loretta J. Ross, its founder and former executive director, believes that human rights provide a broader framework for thinking about violence against women than do simple rights approaches. She founded the center in 1996. However, Ross has a long history of feminist activism in the United States, including among women of color. In the 1970s, she was one of the first African-American women to direct a rape crisis center in the United States. She also was active in international women's human rights conferences in the 1980s. NCHRE was the fiscal sponsor for a national Color of Violence conference, where Ross was a featured plenary speaker in 2000. She explored the question of why the early domestic violence movement focused so much on criminalizing perpetrators while ignoring the fact that the criminal justice system often used violence against communities of color.

For battered women in minority communities with high rates of incarceration, this paradox presents excruciating choices. In her intervention, the Color of Violence Conference Coordinator Andrea Smith, a Native American activist and member of the Cherokee nation, argued that the criminalization approach is not appealing to poor women and women of color who face disproportionate incarceration of members of their communities and may feel excluded from domestic violence and rape crisis centers. She urged closer attention to the structural conditions that disproportionately affect women of color such as militarism, anti-immigration sentiment, and attacks on native treaty rights (Smith 2005). Both Ross and Smith thus embraced a human rights response to domestic violence as more focused on the structural conditions of violence than on criminalization.

Overall, however, the U.S. women's movement is a relative latecomer to the idea of using a human rights framework. Dorothy Thomas (2000) explains the surprising fissure between the United States and international women's rights activists. There is a long-standing fear in the United States that scrutiny under international standards might expose and challenge domestic abuse. By refusing to ratify many of the international human rights conventions, including CEDAW, the U.S. government prevents domestic groups from using these arguments in litigation. Activists in many parts of the world use human rights arguments because these arguments have moral authority, and because – in addition to their legal function – they provide effective tools for educating and mobilizing the public. In the past, U.S. activists rarely used human rights this way either. Some feel this approach detracts from the principle goals of holding perpetrators responsible and/or providing social services to abused women.

The nature of philanthropic funding also discourages U.S. women's activists from using a human rights framework. Most U.S. foundations that fund human rights work do so from their international offices; their domestic offices see human rights as outside their purview. Moreover, U.S. activists typically do not have human rights experience even though there are many American international human rights activists working on these issues outside the United States. In addition to these institutional barriers, Thomas blames the long-term isolationism of the United States and its tendency to think and problem solve in an insular manner. Activists think civil rights apply to "us" and human rights to "them" (Thomas 2000, 1123). Thus, the division between domestic advocacy based on a civil rights framework and international advocacy using a human rights perspective is a long-standing one. U.S. activists have clearly played a key role in promoting a human rights response to violence against women on the global stage; however, they have not done so at home.

Despite all these difficulties, some U.S. groups have enthusiastically adopted a human rights framework. Human rights offer these groups opportunities to expose violations and shame offenders, and to define social problems as collective in nature (i.e., grounded in racism and class differences rather than individual characteristics). Social and economic rights point to the importance of providing battered women housing and jobs while recognizing the way poverty contributes to violence. A human rights approach emphasizes the importance of providing violence survivors with housing, job training, and economic support (Schneider 2004). Moreover, human rights are attractive to feminist activists confronting an attenuated civil rights paradigm deemed weak and outdated. A human rights perspective also affords feminists a framework more open to the intersections of race, class, and gender, as well as to the economic and social dimensions of gender subordination. Yet mainstream domestic violence groups, with individualistic theories of injury and responsibility, find this interpretive framework less valuable. A more conventional approach provides easier access to social services, police, and welfare support, so that domestic violence groups find that they need to conform to those modes of thinking.

UNDERMINING HUMAN RIGHTS: THE STATE AND SERVICE PROVIDERS IN MASSACHUSETTS

Massachusetts provides a unique case through which to explore the changed political alignments of the battered women's movement. The feminist and anti-institutional foundations of Massachusetts' battered women's movement contrast with its rapid and thorough assimilation into contemporary state politics. To understand this context, this chapter presents Jessica Shimmin's analysis based on a year of fieldwork in the Massachusetts domestic violence shelter system. This includes forty interviews with domestic violence intervention professionals working in shelters, government, and leading nonprofit organizations, and those engaged in statewide political advocacy. This data provides evidence of the political advocacy approach adopted by battered women's advocates. At the same time, reliance on state funding means that politically entrenched government social service priorities define the limits of possibility for domestic violence nonprofits. Although human rights values and methods resonate in some aspects of an advocate's work, their integration within the state's political power structure and their individualized intervention strategies limit the utility and viability of human rights discourses.

After establishing a grassroots feminist presence in the 1970s, the battered women's movement ascended to political influence and social legitimacy in Massachusetts in the early 1990s. The social and political arrival of the movement corresponded with the beginning of sixteen years of Republican gubernatorial leadership, beginning in 1991. Phyllis Brashler's (2007) analysis of the Massachusetts domestic violence movement identifies the campaign and successful amendment of the Abuse Prevention Act of 1990 as marking the transition from activist protest tactics to institutional advocacy and lobbying. Aspiring to more ambitious influence, one of Brashler's informants explained: "The very things that we wanted would depend on resources that could only be provided by the government and by institutions" (Brashler 2007, 139). While advocates pursued political influence, the state government also became receptive to the battered women's movement. In response to escalating rates of domestic violence homicide, the first of Massachusetts' Republican governors, William Weld, established the Governor's Commission on Domestic Violence, an advisory body composed of administration leaders and battered women's advocates. In 1994, the state began constructing a comprehensive network of victim services through the Department of Social Services, now called the Department of Children and Families. The domestic violence movement integrated with state social services through a combination of its own ambition to effect social and political change, and the sympathetic leadership of Governor Weld.

Simultaneously, the state restructured social policy using free-market principles. Governor Weld defined the Massachusetts model as promoting self-sufficiency, personal responsibility, and work. Thus, he emulated federal reform efforts that culminated in the passage of the 1996 Personal Responsibility and Work Opportunity Reconciliation Act, also known as "welfare reform" (Katz 2008). To move people from dependency to work, welfare reforms in Massachusetts introduced time limits on cash benefits, child support enforcement, and work requirements for all welfare recipients. Although battered women's advocates recognize welfare as a crucial support for many victims, advocates did not argue that making cuts to the program would be detrimental to women's transition. Viewing welfare reform as inevitable, advocates supported the reforms and worked through the state to address aspects of the plan that compromised battered women's safety.

Whereas it is compelling to interpret the blending of domestic violence and welfare reform agendas as a cooptation of feminist politics, domestic violence professionals described parallels between welfare reformers' goals of self-sufficiency and their own commitment to women's empowerment. One of Brashler's informants recounted: "The battered women's community, historically, was on the same page as the other advocates at that table [who were against welfare reform], but economic

self-sufficiency was ultimately in the best interest of [their] clients . . .
which then put [them] on the side of the state agency people" (Brashler 2007, 141). Despite the ideological improbability of their convergence, this advocate found compatibility between welfare reform's self-
sufficiency discourse and the battered women's movement's commitment
to self-help. In the 1970s and 1980s, the domestic violence movement's
empowerment agenda aimed to rediscover women's personal capacities
and enhance access to legal entitlements, whereas 1990s-style welfare
reform advanced self-sufficiency in order to transform public benefits
into personal responsibilities. Growing antagonism toward dependency
in U.S. social welfare policy debates since the 1970s mediates the distance
between these rival agendas, making an unlikely collaboration appear
almost inevitable. Defining victimization as a state of dependency induced
by violence, the Massachusetts domestic violence movement pursues battered women's economic self-sufficiency from state welfare support. The
State reciprocates, even going so far as to define welfare dependency as
an extension of the battering dynamic. The ideological significance of
women's victimization and empowerment shifts over time. As domestic
violence advocates use these terms in changed social contexts, "victim of
domestic violence" and "women's empowerment" produce unexpected
conceptual alliances.

Another battered women's advocate described to Shimmin how she
came to support welfare reform:

> Our role was to help the women – the recipients – get waivers of all the
> [welfare reform] requirements. As we started to meet with the women,
> their question to us was, 'I don't want a waiver. I want a job. Can you help
> me with a job? Can you help me just get on with my life?' And I think that
> was a surprise for us from the advocacy world because we really came in
> here thinking we were going to battle the department and get these waivers
> all the time.

By pursuing waivers as a mode of resistance to welfare reform, this advocate already accepts the state social service bureaucracy as the terrain of
domestic violence advocacy. For this advocate, battered women's desire to
get out of the welfare system neutralizes welfare reform as a political issue.
This construction evidences a shift in battered women's politics toward
service provision and political pragmatism: because battered women do
not want waivers, there is no reason to resist the policy. Both informants
draw on the philosophy of the battered women's movement to arrive at

their support for welfare reform. However, the changed social and political context is again apparent. The informants no longer work in activist collectives but in a professionalized social service system where solutions resonate at an individual level rather than on a structural level. The shift in scale is most evident as advocates evaluate welfare reform based on its impact on individual clients apart from women's social status. This context changes the political meaning of women's empowerment such that welfare reform becomes the medium of battered women's initiative and self-help.

Because domestic violence programs rely on state funding to provide services, state systems exert a great deal of influence over nonprofits' activities. As a transitional housing professional explained, state money comes with strings: "You have to have beds full all the time and counting heads, how long you can keep them or not keep them. It's like having another supervisor and *they're not there.*" State money introduces bureaucratically defined priorities for domestic violence work, circumscribing domestic violence professionals' authority and autonomy. As state contracts define service priorities throughout the state, domestic violence professionals negotiate between their philosophy and the future of their programs. As the director of programs at Gateway, a domestic violence nonprofit explained, "We're sort of caught in the middle on the fact that we need this funding in order to keep ourselves open in the first place. So, 'We can't do this' is not an option, it's 'What can we do?'" The deputy director at the Ayuda[1] shelter program describes looking for ways to "comply with the [state] contract but also support families," suggesting that state-defined service goals translate into obstacles for battered women and children. Although state contracts support programs, they also constrain service delivery and philosophical stances. Thus, as the neoliberal state shrinks government responsibility by contracting domestic violence services to nonprofit organizations, it extends and compounds its influence by enmeshing domestic violence programs in a social service bureaucracy.

Nonetheless, the leaders of these nonprofits see benefits to working in and through the state. An executive director who began doing domestic violence work in the late 1990s described the shift from grassroots activism to nonprofit politics: "I felt [there was] a lot of the baggage of the 1980s, when the organization was formed and served it well in

---

[1] All person and organization names have been changed in the analysis of Massachusetts' domestic violence intervention services system.

the beginning. (You know, that antigovernment, push back at the police, don't trust government, don't trust anyone.) That kind of mentality served the organization well, but it was damaging it in 1999 when I started." As she described it, being "wise in the political world" enabled this director to transform a floundering grassroots domestic violence collective into a credible, hierarchical nonprofit. The shift from anti-institutionalism to political maneuvering is also apparent in this account from the executive director of the Voices Inc. program. Concerned to secure more funding for her programs, the executive director asked the Department of Children and Families (DCF) how it allocates state money:

> And he said, "[Barbara], grow up. Squeaky wheel gets the grease; it's all politics. They [other programs] all get it because their legislators went in and got it for them. If you don't like what you're getting, you need to get political." My thought was, jeez, I thought just doing good – and I mean this with all sincerity, I thought just doing – if we did the best, if we were really good, if we showed need we'd get money. Nuh-uh. Didn't work that way. So, and he said, "what you need to do is, you're good friends with folks in the community – start lining folks up."

In this account, DCF frames the director's belief in a meritocracy as childish. Instead, leveraging political influence through personal relationships is the only way local programs can ensure adequate support for their services. In both of these accounts, egalitarian, bottom-up operational strategies not only fail to sustain domestic violence organizations but also appear idealistic, immature, and dogmatic. Politics work for these leaders, and knowing how to play the political game confers a sense of rationality and competence on their organizations.

Hence, instead of challenging state authority, nonprofits increasingly approach the state as a political ally. Their sense of autonomy is notable given the influence the state exerts over nonprofits and nonprofits' dependence on the state for funding (Bumiller 2008, Morgaine 2009). Domestic violence professionals articulated a softer stance toward government when they talked about ways to enhance legislative "buy-in" for their goals. One coalition insider, "Mary," sought to persuade state officials by "connecting directly with the commissioners of Department of Public Health, the Department of Children and Families, you know, the Executive Office of Health and Public Safety and whatnot. So really working on that level and getting their buy-in as to this vision that we have." Similarly, the executive director of Women Together defined her approach to politics as "strategizing to achieve a goal and the compromises it takes to achieve them without compromising your principles. But, know-ing your audience and what will get them to buy in...that's a politi-cal skill." Focused on developing political relationships at the personal level of interests and needs, the "buy-in" is emblematic of the soften-ing political relationship between domestic violence professionals and government.

Yet for all of the emphasis on political maneuvering and diplomatic influence, data collection is still the primary way that the state listens to battered women's programs. In 2006, the Massachusetts Department of Children and Families conducted its most recent bid for domestic violence services, prioritizing "programs that are responsive to the individual needs of each person seeking help" (Department of Social Services 2006, 14). To this end, programs conduct an individualized risk assessment for every person or family served. Assessments build solutions to a family's prob-lems by identifying their existing strengths and resources. This "strength-based" process engages the victim in self-reflection and assessment. As the development coordinator at Women Together explained, "the way strengths-based counseling is supposed to work is you're supposed to get the woman to really, really assess the protective and the risk fac-tors." Individualized risk assessments transform safety into a clear choice. Strength-based models define battered women's transition to safety and empowerment as a process of learning to manage risks and make the right decisions.

In addition to making battered women responsible for choosing safety, detailed family risk assessments elicit useful information. Paperwork and data entry fields convert personal information into de-identified data pro-vided to the state as evidence of a program's efficacy. Once aggregated, these data produce a demographic profile of battered women, children, and risk. Although professionals lament the paperwork, they view data collection as contributing to their service provision. The deputy director of the nonprofit organization Ayuda explained: "The more we can show them [Department of Children and Families] that we're using their dollars wisely and efficiently, the more we're either going to get, or keep, or be level funded, or get more funding." In this account, demographic data collection shifts from being a state technique for ensuring organizational accountability to being a form of advocacy for battered women's services. This belief underpins the coalition's efforts to create a statewide database in response to what Mary, a coalition professional, describes as a "dearth of data in Massachusetts." The proposed database would aggregate the information that various programs provide to individual funding sources. The cumulative effect, Mary explained, will be to provide "a really clear and accurate full picture as to what the demand for services are [sic] as well as the delivery of services." Programs and the coalition will use the data to report to funders as well as to compete for more money. Again, this orientation transforms oversight techniques such as reporting into opportunities for knowledge production, program development, and resource acquisition.

Rather than fighting authority, battered women's advocates strive to influence government agendas. The statewide coalition in Massachusetts pursues this goal by lobbying on behalf of its member programs, which cannot lobby owing to their nonprofit status. The coalition occupies offices on Beacon Street at the center of state government activity in Boston. This address is emblematic of the coalition's effort to become influential in state politics. Gayle, a domestic violence professional in the coalition, described the organization as "focused on meeting the needs of our member programs, which are about 60 member programs. And, working to be part of shaping the ways domestic and sexual violence are addressed in the Commonwealth. And also participating in the national conversation about these issues." This bifurcated agenda configures local programs and service provision as separate from the politically powerful agenda-setting work of domestic violence advocacy.

In a domestic violence movement focused on service provision and political advocacy, very few domestic violence professionals frame their work in terms of human rights. Initiatives such as the White Ribbon Campaign, which encourages men to promote nonviolent masculinities, is influenced by human rights values without overtly identifying them as such. Work that explicitly frames itself in terms of human rights often takes a critical stance toward government. Most notably, the Battered Mothers' Testimony Project at the Wellesley Centers for Women used human rights methods to identify a pattern of discrimination against battered women in Massachusetts' family courts. Seeking to "uncover government practices that amount to human rights violations and to hold state actors accountable," the research politicizes victim's voices by recording and substantiating battered women's testimonies (Slote et al. 2005, 1374). The prioritization of battered women's voices and explicit use of human rights legal strategies makes the Battered Mothers' Testimony Project anomalous in a domestic violence service network oriented toward institutional systems.

USING HUMAN RIGHTS IN ADVOCACY FOR VIOLENCE
SURVIVORS IN NEW YORK CITY

In contrast to the reluctance of Massachusetts-based domestic violence service providers to use the human rights framework, a New York-based group engaged in advocacy with formerly battered women has found these ideas valuable. Our account of this advocacy organization builds on research by Diana Yoon in particular, as well as Peggy Levitt, Mihaela Serban Rosen, and Sally Merry (Merry et al. 2010).

The Voices of Women Organizing Project of the Battered Women's Resource Center (VOW) started in 2000 with the goal of enabling domestic violence survivors to become advocates on policy issues that affect battered women. VOW did not become a human rights organization in mission or discourse, but did adopt some of the human rights framework and techniques as an addition to its repertoire. They used human rights as a new way of framing their work (Snow 2004). Although the organization was primarily based on the ideas of the battered women's movement, it formed alliances with other New York City groups using human rights language to address diverse issues such as poverty, housing, and education. In its 2008 report on New York City family courts, VOW describes itself as:

> ...a grassroots advocacy organization of survivors of domestic violence who are working to improve the many systems battered women and their children rely on for safety and justice. VOW members represent the diversity of New York City and include African American, Caribbean, Latina, white, Asian, immigrant, lesbian, disabled and formerly incarcerated women. Since 2000, VOW members have documented system failures and developed recommendations for change, and they have educated policy makers, elected officials, the public and each other through trainings, meetings, testimony, and most recently, with this report.
>
> (VOW 2008, 15)

Voices of Women is heavily influenced by the discourse and strategies of the battered women's movement. Members talk about being survivors. Human rights ideals and principles are not a frequent topic of conversation, but do provide another system of values that can be used to critique court processes. For example, VOW's report on New York City family courts argued that government accountability is a universal human rights norm, and that institutions that provide public services should discharge their duties according to human rights principles such as accountability, transparency, and participation (VOW2008, 15).

The organization operates with a small staff of three and a modest budget. It relies heavily on its members – survivors of domestic violence who do advocacy work targeting courts, city agencies, and the legislature, as well as public education. They come from various backgrounds, but many are working class and poor women. It is one of the only organizations in New York with a mission to empower battered women in their transformation from victim to survivor to activist. The organization's focus on advocacy and activism distinguishes it from the service-delivery model of many other domestic violence organizations. The director has extensive experience in community organizing and leadership development and has worked with survivors of domestic violence for more than twenty-five years. The associate director came to VOW with expertise in direct services to battered women and advocacy on domestic violence policies. The organization's guiding principles and practices treat survivors' perspectives as an important source of authority and expertise on which to build advocacy strategies.

Staff and members have attended human rights training and sometimes talk about human rights conventions. They have also incorporated a human rights approach in pursuing VOW's advocacy agenda. In 2003, the organization initiated the Battered Mothers' Justice Campaign in collaboration with the Urban Justice Center's Human Rights Project. In an effort to document experiences of battered women in New York City family courts, VOW staff and the Human Rights Project designed a survey project and trained fourteen VOW members to conduct interviews with a lengthy questionnaire. In 2006, these trainees interviewed seventy-five domestic violence survivors about their experiences in New York City family courts. Women talked about losing custody of children to their batterers despite histories of being the primary caretaker, about inadequate measures for safety in the court building, and about the unprofessional conduct of judges and lawyers interacting with women who had raised claims of domestic violence. The data gathered provided the basis for a report, *Justice Denied: How Family Courts in New York City Endanger Battered Women and Children* (VOW 2008) that documented these problems, identified the articles of human rights conventions being violated, and offered recommendations for change. The report was presented to city and state government officials and made publicly available on the Web. Thus, the organization turned to human rights techniques as a strategy for social change, engaging in documentation and report writing to expose government's failures to live up to the standards of human rights treaties. VOW did not use legal complaints directly but drew more extensively on human rights values and techniques.

The VOW human rights documentation project was carried out largely by grassroots activists who were survivors of domestic abuse. The report harnessed human rights law to make moral claims about discriminatory treatment presented in the form of a human rights report. This activity depended on expert knowledge from human rights activists about how to create this documentation and how to present it; such expertise was shared by leaders of the Human Rights Project, one of whom was a key figure in the initiative to pass CEDAW and the International Convention on the Elimination of All Forms of Racial Discrimination (ICERD) as a city ordinance in New York. This set of ideas did not eclipse the organization's commitment to battered women's experiences as a critically important form of expert knowledge. Rather, the collaboration was facilitated by a resonance between human rights documentation techniques and the members' insight that documented evidence can make a crucial difference in dealing with government officials and in legal proceedings, as well as their frequently expressed belief that battered women's stories must be heard (Merry et al. 2010).

The Battered Mothers' Justice Campaign is just one instance of how human rights are meaningful for VOW. Individual members spoke about human rights as a powerful vision of justice – "Just the fact that you are born human give you rights." They noted that the universal scope of human rights advances ways to understand and advocate against violence in all its forms. In the words of VOW's associate director, human rights can "nurture a different possibility for the world."

The resonance of human rights values, however, runs alongside deep skepticism about its pragmatic utility in the American context. The director of VOW pointed out that human rights violations are typically understood as occurring in places outside the United States, and voiced skepticism about the power of human rights language to move domestic audiences: "It doesn't resonate here." One member commented that the Convention on the Rights of the Child has "no bearing whatsoever" when she talks to legislators about the need for better protection of children's rights. VOW is not unique in exhibiting skepticism about the pragmatic value of human rights. For donors and for activists working in fields such as domestic violence, welfare, and housing, the value added of the human rights framework is uncertain. Historically, it is *civil* rights that have delivered social movement claims (Anderson 2003), and those attracted to human rights tend to be groups that have found the current civil rights regime unsupportive, such as lesbian, gay, bisexual, and transgendered (LGBT) groups. Indeed, as Lauren points out, the emergence of the human rights movement in recent years follows a long period of retrenchment of civil rights (2008, 16–25).

CONCLUSION

Human rights offer technologies of justice making, alliances, and a broader framework for thinking about domestic violence. Although this approach resonates with the goals of the early battered women's movement of the 1970s, which viewed patriarchal and capitalist social structures as root causes of abuse, in the contemporary U.S. context human rights approaches lose traction amidst community and state pressures to move toward a neoliberal social welfare services approach. Ideas of personal responsibility and independence replace critiques of power and social structure as the domestic violence movement has become established and institutionalized in a neoliberal economic and political context. Yet, human rights ideas, with their structural analysis of the inequalities that contribute to gender violence, are still present in some pockets of gender violence work in the United States. Despite the pressures of funding and despite U.S. hostility to the domestic application of human rights ideas, there are signs that a human rights approach is being imported into the country in small but significant ways by activists who recognize its possibilities.

REFERENCES

Anderson, Carol. 2003. *Eyes off the Prize: The United Nations and the African-American Struggle for Human Rights, 1944–1955*. Cambridge, UK: Cambridge University Press.

Brashler, Phyllis C. 2007. "Flirting with Feminism: The State and the Battered Women's Movement in Massachusetts." PhD dissertation. Boston: Northeastern University.

Bumiller, Kristin. 2008. *In an Abusive State: How Neoliberalism Appropriated the Feminist Movement Against Sexual Violence*. Durham, NC: Duke University Press.

Cuthbert, Carrie, Kim Slote, Monica Ghosh Driggers, Cynthia J. Mesh, Lundy Bancroft, and Jay Silverman. 2002. *Battered Mothers Speak Out: A Human Rights Report and Video on Domestic Violence and Child Custody in the Massachusetts Family Courts*. Wellesley, MA: Wellesley Centers for Women. Retrieved from www.wcwonline.org/title380.html.

Das Gupta, Monisha. 2006. *Unruly Immigrants: Rights, Activism, and Transnational South Asian Politics in the United States*. Durham, NC: Duke University Press.

Davis, Martha F. 2007. "Human Rights in the Trenches: Using International Human Rights Law in 'Everyday' Legal Aid Cases." *Clearinghouse Review: Journal of Poverty Law and Policy*. November-December: 414–26.

Department of Social Services. 2006. *Domestic Violence Services Request for Responses (DSS DV07)*. Massachusetts Executive Office of Health and Human Services, March 2.

Ignatieff, Michael. 2001. *Human Rights as Politics and Idolatry*. Princeton, NJ: Princeton University Press.

Katz, Michael B. 2008. *The Price of Citizenship: Redefining America's Welfare State*. Updated Edition. Philadelphia, PA: University of Pennsylvania Press.

Lauren, Paul Gordon. 2008. "A Human Rights Lens on U.S. History: Human Rights at Home and Human Rights Abroad." In *Bringing Human Rights Home: A History of Human Rights in the United States*, edited by Cynthia Soohoo, Catherine Albisa, and Martha F. Davis, Vol. 3, 1–31. Westport, CT: Praeger Publishers.

Lozner, Stacy Laira. 2004. "Note: Diffusion of Local Regulatory Innovations: The San Francisco CEDAW Ordinance and the New York City Human Rights Initiative." *Columbia Law Review* 104: 768–800.

Markowitz, Lisa, and Karen W. Tice. 2002. "Paradoxes of Professionalization: Parallel Dilemmas in Women's Organizations in the Americas." *Gender and Society* 16 (6): 941–58.

Merry, Sally Engle. 2001. "Rights, Religion, and Community: Approaches to Violence Against Women in the Context of Globalization." *Law and Society Review* 35 (1): 39–88.

———. 2006. *Human Rights and Gender Violence: Translating International Law into Local Justice*. Chicago, IL: University of Chicago Press.

———. 2009. *Gender Violence: A Cultural Introduction*. London: Blackwell.

Merry, Sally Engle, Peggy Levitt, Mihaela Serban Rosen, and Diana H. Yoon. 2010. "Law from Below: Women's Human Rights and Social Movements in New York City." *Law and Society Review* 44 (1): 101–28.

Morgaine, Karen. 2006. "Domestic Violence and Human Rights: Local Challenges to a Universal Framework." *Journal of Sociology and Social Welfare* 33(4): 109–29.

———. 2009. "'You Can't Bite the Hand...' Domestic Violence and Human Rights." *Affilia* 24 (31): 31–43.

Morgen, Sandra, Joan Acker, and Jill Weigt. 2010. *Stretched Thin: Poor Families, Welfare Work, and Welfare Reform*. Ithaca, NY: ILR Press/Cornell.

Ridzi, Frank. 2009. *Selling Welfare Reform: Work-First and the New Common Sense of Employment*. New York: New York University Press.

Schechter, Susan. 1982. *Women and Male Violence: The Visions and Struggles of the Battered Women's Movement*. Boston: South End Press.

Schneider, Elizabeth M. 2000. *Battered Women and Feminist Lawmaking*. New Haven, CT: Yale University Press.

Schneider, Elizabeth M. 2004. "Transnational Law as a Domestic Resource: Thoughts on the Case of Women's Rights." *New England Law Review* 38 (3): 689–724.

Slote, Kim Y., Carrie Cuthbert, Cynthia J. Mesh, Monica G. Driggers, Lundy Bancroft, and Jay G. Silverman. 2005. "Battered Mothers Speak Out: Participatory Human Rights Documentation as a Model for Research and Activism in the United States." *Violence Against Women* Volume 11 (11): 1367–95.

Smith, Andrea. 2005. *Conquest*. Boston: South End Press.

Smith, Andrea, Beth E. Richie, and Julia Sudbury, eds. 2006. *The Color of Violence: INCITE! Anthology*. Boston: South End Press.

Snow, David A. 2004. "Framing Processes, Ideology, and Discursive Fields." In *The Blackwell Companion to Social Movements*, edited by David A. Snow, Sarah A. Soule, and Hanspeter Kriesi, 380–412. Malden, MA: Blackwell.

Soohoo, Cynthia, Catherine Albisa, and Martha F. Davis, eds. 2008. *Bringing Human Rights Home*. Vols 1, 2, 3. Westport, CT: Praeger.

Thomas, Dorothy Q. 2000. "We are Not the World: U.S. Activism and Human Rights in the Twenty-First Century." *Signs* 25: 1121–24.

Voices of Women Organizing Project (VOW). 2008. *Justice Denied: How Family Courts in New York City Endanger Battered Women*. New York. VOW. http://www.vowbwrc.org/pdf/justiceDeniedRep.pdf.

X, Malcolm, and Alex Haley. 1964. *The Autobiography of Malcolm X*. New York: Ballantine Books.

7

At the Crossroads: Children's Rights and the U.S. Government

Jonathan Todres

INTRODUCTION

As the world's sole superpower and one of only two countries that has not ratified the UN Convention on the Rights of the Child (CRC), the United States holds a unique position in the children's rights movement. It is arguably best positioned of any country to ensure the rights and well-being of children globally, yet it has not supported – and at times has hindered the effectiveness of – the most important tool for the child rights movement: the CRC. Today, policy makers and child advocates have arrived at a pivotal juncture in the children's rights movement, and a central consideration is the U.S. government's role in advancing children's rights at home and abroad.

On November 20, 2009, the international community celebrated the CRC's twentieth anniversary. In its first twenty years, the CRC achieved many milestones, becoming the most widely ratified human rights treaty (every country except the United States and Somalia is a party) and fostering positive changes in law, policy, and attitudes toward children in numerous countries. Although these achievements merit celebration, the convergence of several key developments makes this period not just one of celebration but also a critical juncture for children's rights and the U.S. government.

This chapter examines these recent developments and explicates their meaning for children's rights. The chapter argues, in particular, that these developments have created a pivotal moment for children and their rights, and that, without concerted action, this moment risks passing unnoticed to the detriment of millions of children. In particular, the chapter focuses on four significant developments having an impact on children and their rights: first, post-anniversary assessments of the CRC; second, the global economic crisis; third, the political shift in the United States with the election of President Barack Obama; and fourth, the evolving response to U.S. exceptionalism in the international arena. Following an examination of these issues, the chapter discusses steps for the U.S. government to take to reassume a leadership role in the children's rights arena and the importance of U.S. leadership in securing children's rights in the United States and around the world.

When assessing progress on human rights it is important not only to analyze substantive measures taken but also to examine the role of key actors and institutions. Institutions' influence is often ignored when assessing legal developments, but institutions play a critical role in how human rights law evolves. For example, the creation of customary international law depends on states' practices. Therefore, assessments of progress implementing children's rights must pay attention to the U.S. government's role in advancing children's rights at home and abroad.

Although human rights law mandates a domestic focus because it imposes obligations on states to ensure the rights of those subject to its jurisdiction, the global economy and constant movement of both goods and people suggest the need for a broader perspective. This is especially true when speaking of children, who are among the most vulnerable individuals in every country. Everyday occurrences serve as a reminder that when considering "human rights in the United States," it would be short-sighted to think only of children within U.S. borders. After all, unaccompanied minors enter the United States each day, so their treatment in their home countries affects whether they migrate and their circumstances or condition upon arrival. Children in developing countries are subjected to brutal labor conditions while making products to be sold and consumed in the United States, thus U.S. domestic actions affect the rights of children overseas. And American sex tourists travel to developing countries to sexually exploit minors. Accordingly, as this volume explores human rights in the United States, an important issue is the influential role of the U.S. government vis-à-vis initiatives to secure the rights of every child, both at home and abroad. On that point, and more generally for the children's rights movement, we stand at an important crossroads.

I. A CONFLUENCE OF EVENTS AFFECTING CHILDREN

A. Assessments of the CRC's Value

This critical juncture for children's rights has been sparked in part by the CRC's twentieth anniversary. Anniversaries are occasions for reflection, and the CRC's anniversary year has prompted important inquiries into progress achieved under the treaty in its first twenty years. Assessments of progress under the CRC are relevant not just for children in the 193 parties to the CRC, but also for U.S. children. As discussed later in this chapter, the U.S. government typically moves slowly toward ratification of human rights treaties. Therefore, appraisals of the CRC's first twenty years provide an opportunity for U.S. policy makers to evaluate the CRC's potential value to U.S. children and their families.

This section briefly examines achievements to date in terms of law and policy, impact on the ground, and work that still remains to ensure the rights and well-being of all children. As empirical work on the CRC's impact is in its early stages, this section draws upon select examples from various studies. Further, given that the United States has thus far refused to ratify the CRC, assessments necessarily must examine work done in other countries.

1. Law and Policy Developments. The CRC mandates that states parties take "legislative, administrative, and other measures" to protect the rights and well-being of children (CRC 1989, art. 4). Since the CRC's adoption, numerous countries have amended their laws to improve the lives of children. States parties to the CRC have strengthened laws related to children's health and education rights, their right to live free from abusive labor practices and other forms of exploitation, the administration of juvenile justice, adoption proceedings, and many other issues (UNICEF Innocenti Research Centre 2007). Dozens of countries have directly incorporated provisions of the CRC into their national law. In a number of cases, states have enshrined children's rights in new constitutions (UNICEF Innocenti Research Centre 2007, 2006). This wealth of new law represents an important source of protection for children. Implementation and enforcement of this law is essential to ensuring that all children realize the benefits of these legislative measures.

2. Impact on the Ground. Progress must be measured not just in the law but also in terms of actual impact on children's lives. Since the CRC's adoption, the world has become a better place for many children, suggesting that the children's rights movement, guided by the CRC, is having a positive impact (UNICEF 2009b). There has been progress on many issues vital to children's well-being, including infant and child survival, educational opportunities, and protection from exploitation. Although causation might be difficult to establish, the numerous child rights measures adopted since children's rights were elevated to the status of legally binding obligations in the CRC are evidence of a correlative effect.

For example, progress combating child mortality has been significant. The number of children who die before their fifth birthday has declined from 12.5 million in 1990 (the year the CRC entered into force) to less than 9 million in 2008 (WHO 2009, 10; Dugger 2009). This progress means that annually approximately 3.5 million children are able to realize their most precious right – their right to life – when previously their lives and contributions to their communities and countries would have been lost.

Meaningful advances also have been achieved in education. The latest UNESCO statistics show that globally the number of primary school age children out of school dropped from 103 million in 1999 to 75 million in 2006. Globally, 40 million more children were enrolled in primary school in 2006 than in 1999, reflecting both a decline in out-of-school numbers and an overall increase (Education for All Global Monitoring Report Team 2008).

Finally, efforts to combat economic exploitation of children have produced gains. Between 2000 and 2004, the number of child workers dropped 11 percent. Although the latest available data, from 2004, estimate the number of children involved in hazardous work at 126 million, that figure reflects a 26 percent reduction since 2000 (Capdevila 2006).

Progress in these and other areas represents dramatic improvements in the lives of millions of children and families around the globe. It indicates that the CRC's holistic rights framework offers children and their communities great benefits when successfully implemented.

3. Work Still to be Done. Although there has been significant progress in advancing the rights and well-being of children, the international community is still far from achieving the CRC's mandate. Efforts since its adoption have saved the lives of millions of children, as mentioned previously, but nearly 9 million children still die each year largely from preventable causes (Dugger 2009). Seventy-five million children of primary school age are not enrolled, the majority of whom are girls (Education for All Global Monitoring Report Team 2008). Moreover, the 191 million children ages five to fourteen who work for a living represent about one-sixth of the total population of children of that age (Hagemann, Diallo, Etienne, and Mehran 2006). Quite simply, although states have made important progress, they are well short of the CRC's ultimate goal – creating a world in which all children have the opportunity to develop to their fullest potential.

4. *Drawing Conclusions about the CRC.* The international community's record vis-à-vis children in the CRC era reflects a mixture of successes and shortcomings. Progress on securing children's rights in some countries has been groundbreaking, saving millions of lives and affording children the opportunity to develop to their fullest potential and contribute to their communities. In other countries, despite the CRC's mandate, governments have failed to meaningfully improve the lives of children and ensure their rights. The Committee on the Rights of the Child consistently urges governments to do better, but the international community rarely exerts significant pressure on governments that fail to fulfill their obligations under the CRC unless there is a broader pattern of gross human rights violations in that country. Moreover, because the world's sole superpower opts to not participate at all in the primary vehicle for advancing children's rights, even less pressure is felt by noncompliant countries. Thus, the CRC's anniversary, while cause for celebration, also provides the opportunity to identify shortcomings, one of which is the lack of strong support from the U.S. government. Therefore, any assessment of the CRC's impact must account for the fact that it has been hampered by a lack of support from the institution arguably best situated to ensure children's rights globally – the U.S. government.

By sitting on the sidelines, the U.S. government has not only hurt global child advocacy efforts, it also has done a disservice to children within its own borders. As discussed in more detail later in this chapter, millions of U.S. children go without regular access to health care; are out of, or underperforming in, school; and are subjected to various forms of abuse and exploitation – from forced labor and prostitution to domestic abuse and neglect.

In light of the above, what conclusions can be drawn about the CRC's first twenty years? Where countries have taken their obligations under the CRC seriously, the treaty has fostered improvements in the lives of millions of children and their families. Where countries have failed to implement the CRC or refused to ratify the treaty, children have suffered. In other words, the substantive law is strong, but much more is needed to ensure implementation and enforcement.

Acknowledging shortcomings in the implementation and enforcement of the CRC is essential. Equally important, deficiencies related to implementation or enforcement must not be misunderstood as suggesting the content of the CRC is without value. The CRC contains rights that each child holds by virtue of the fact that he or she is human. By comparison, when U.S. civil rights law is violated, we do not say the law is invalid. Nor do we dismiss the value of laws prohibiting murder simply because murders still occur and some perpetrators are never brought to justice. Like any law, the CRC is a tool that relies on government commitment to enforce it. Enforcement measures must be strengthened, but the CRC's first twenty years demonstrate that the treaty remains the most comprehensive tool available to ensure children's rights and well-being in the United States and elsewhere.

As the next section details, the CRC's twentieth anniversary coincided with a major challenge accelerating the need for action to ensure child survival and well-being.

B. Impact of the Global Economic Crisis

Globalization and economic growth have resulted in unprecedented wealth creation in the last fifty years. The hope has been that an integrated global economy would facilitate the spread of resources so all states would have greater capacity to provide for the well-being of children. That sharing of wealth was far from complete when the global economic crisis hit. The recent global economic crisis now presents a major challenge for children's rights because it is having a significant impact on programming and children everywhere.

Children are more vulnerable to human rights abuses than adults (Van Bueren 1995). They are more susceptible to feeling the effects of economic downturns and cutbacks in public expenditures on social programs. And the impact is significant. The World Bank has reported that in countries with high child mortality rates, the global economic crisis is spurring declines in household incomes, which might result in an average of 200,000 to 400,000 additional infant deaths annually between 2009 and 2015 (Sabarwal, Sinha, and Buvinic 2009). The global economic crisis is also causing an increase in hunger and malnutrition among children who do survive (UNICEF 2009a). As the global economic crisis exacerbates poverty, families may have to pull their children out of school so they can work (Mosel and Sarkar 2009). When youth leave school early, they enter the work force younger and with fewer skills, leaving them at heightened risk of various forms of exploitation, including commercial sex work, forced labor, and domestic servitude. Although the global economy might regain its health in the near term, exploitation and loss of educational opportunities will have a lifelong impact on children.

In short, the global economic crisis has implications across a broad range of children's rights. These implications also are relevant to children in poor and low-income families in the United States. Gains achieved over the past two decades might be eroded by the economic downturn. The additional challenge of the global economic crisis heightens the importance of this juncture for the children's rights movement. Now more than ever it is crucial that children's rights be secured; the survival, development, and lifetime prospects of millions of children are at stake in the United States and around the globe.

C. U.S. Exceptionalism Meets U.S. Human Rights Advocacy

1. A New Window of Opportunity. After eight years of former President George W. Bush's Administration, children's rights advocates, like other human rights advocates, see President Obama's Administration as an opportunity for the U.S. government to reestablish itself as a key partner in advancing human rights. Scholars have documented the human rights abuses of the Bush Administration (Mertus 2008; Koh 2003). The Bush Administration has been criticized for advancing a national security agenda at the expense of individual rights. As Harold Hongju Koh writes, the "[Bush] Administration's obsessive focus on the War on Terror . . . has taken an extraordinary toll upon US global human rights policy" (Koh 2007, 636).

President Obama's election offered new hope to human rights advocates. In his Inaugural Address, President Obama promised that the United States would not sacrifice human rights in the name of security, stating "[a]s for our common defense, we reject as false the choice between our safety and our ideals. Our Founding Fathers, faced with perils we can scarcely imagine, drafted a charter to assure the rule of law and the rights of man, a charter expanded by the blood of generations. Those ideals still light the world, and we will not give them up for expedience's sake" (*New York Times* 2009).

Recognizing this window of opportunity, human rights advocates are determined to hold the new administration to its promises. Numerous entities have proposed strategic plans for the new administration to "reaffirm and strengthen the longstanding commitment of the United States to human rights at home and abroad" (Powell 2008, 1).

Upon closer examination, the push for U.S. engagement in the international human rights movement is actually a call for two interrelated but distinct steps: first, it represents a desire to see the United States re-engage the international community, in stark contrast to the Bush Administration's largely unilateral approach to global issues. Second, it is a broader call for a new U.S. approach to human rights advocacy, both at home and abroad. Historically, the United States has been a strong supporter of the development of human rights instruments, engaging in the drafting of many treaties, but it has moved more slowly on ratification. It took the United States forty years to ratify the UN Convention on the Prevention and Punishment of the Crime of Genocide, even though it supported the ideals enshrined in the convention (Henkin 1995). Rather, as Mertus explains, "human rights are something the United States encourages for other countries, although the same international standards do not apply in the same manner in the United States" (Mertus 2008, 3). The United States has relied on the Bill of Rights as evidence that it recognizes rights and does not need to ratify human rights treaties, even though many human rights treaties cover individual rights not enshrined in the Bill of Rights. Therefore, calls today from the human rights community are not merely a reversal of Bush Administration policies, but something more. At their core, they represent a call for the U.S. government to incorporate human rights meaningfully not only into foreign policy but also into domestic policy with a view to recognizing and advancing the full panoply of individual rights for every person in the United States.

2. *Growing Domestic Demand.* Historically, on the domestic front, human rights language and principles have struggled to gain a foothold. When the issue is adults, it is seen as acceptable to speak of "civil rights" but not to extend more broadly to economic, social, and cultural rights. When the issue is children, the options are even more limited. To speak of child welfare is to engender empathy and support, but to speak of children's rights is to garner skepticism and mistrust. Yet despite this conventional wisdom, there is growing movement in support of a domestic human rights agenda that includes the full array of individual rights, from civil and political to economic, social, and cultural. And one component of that is a domestic children's rights agenda.

Following the UN Special Session on Children in 2002, at which the U.S. government delegation was perceived by many as obstructing progress on children's rights, a small group of U.S. child advocates decided the time was right to reinvigorate efforts to achieve U.S. ratification of the CRC. This decision resulted in the formation of the Campaign for U.S. Ratification of the Convention on the Rights of the Child in 2003, of which this author is a member. With the support of numerous entities ranging from child welfare groups and human rights organizations to professional associations (in the fields of law, pediatrics, education, social services, etc.) and faith-based organizations, the campaign now is a focal point for U.S. ratification efforts.

Support for the CRC and children's rights within the United States appears to be growing. Over the years, certain states and localities have decided to weigh in on the merits of U.S. ratification of the CRC. The state of Hawaii and the cities of Los Angeles (California), Chicago (Illinois), and Grand Rapids (Michigan) are the most recent additions to the list of states and localities endorsing U.S. ratification of the CRC. This list already includes New York, Rhode Island, South Carolina, Vermont, and the cities of Austin (Texas), Cambridge (Massachusetts), Cleveland (Ohio), Detroit (Michigan), Kansas City (Missouri), Minneapolis (Minnesota), New York City (New York), San Diego (California), and Savannah (Georgia). Although such measures are in some respects symbolic, given that foreign affairs is strictly the province of the federal government, they are meaningful because law and policy have an expressive function and, in this case, precisely because it is rare for a state or locality to view an international treaty as so important that warrants taking an official position.

In addition to calling upon the federal government to ratify the CRC, some state and city resolutions go further, pledging that their state or city will comply with the CRC's principles. For example, the city of Chicago pledged that it "will work to advance policies and practices that are in harmony with the principles of the Convention on the Rights of the Child in all city agencies and organizations that address issues directly affecting the City's children" (City of Chicago 2009). The state of South Carolina's resolution "calls on all agencies in South Carolina, especially those concerned with the housing, nutrition, education, protection, medical care, recreation, and economic opportunity for children, to ensure that even in increasingly difficult economic times their programs aim to achieve the goals of the Convention on the Rights of the Child" (State of South Carolina 1992). In a resolution that passed the day after the CRC was adopted, the New York City Council called on all city agencies "to ensure that their activities and funding processes comply with the Convention on the Rights of the Child" (City of New York 1989).

These resolutions demonstrate two important points: first, there is significant support for the principles enshrined in the CRC within the United States and from various regions of the country; and second, at the state and local levels, as well as at the grassroots level, there is a desire to comply with the CRC and a growing impatience with the federal government's failure to assume a leadership position vis-à-vis the CRC and more generally on children's rights. This impatience on the domestic front is mirrored by similar restlessness among the United States' global partners.

D. The Evolving International Response to the U.S. Government

As the world's sole superpower, and one of five nations with veto power on the UN Security Council, the United States holds a commanding position in the international arena. Without U.S. support and commitment, political measures advanced in the international arena face a tougher road. The same is true for children's rights initiatives. When asked to improve state practices vis-à-vis children's rights, many in other countries respond by asking how more can be asked of them when the United States will not even participate at all. Advocating for children's rights is more difficult without the full weight of the United States behind those efforts. The experience of the UN Special Session on Children showed how difficult it can be to advance children's rights when the United States is not on board.

At the UN Special Session on Children in 2002, a few issues created contentious debate that nearly derailed the adoption of a final outcome document establishing specific, time-bound targets to be achieved by governments to improve children's lives. The United States was at the center of the storm. Among the Bush Administration's concerns was language stating that the CRC was the most authoritative expression of child rights. As a result of U.S. government objections, the final outcome document avoided speaking about child rights in a number of contexts and described the CRC, together with its Optional Protocols, only as "contain[ing] a comprehensive set of international legal standards for the protection and well-being of children" (UN General Assembly 2002, ¶4). Although the Bush Administration succeeded at the UN Special Session in diluting support for the CRC and recognition of children's rights (preferring instead to speak only of child well-being), five years later the outcome was different, suggesting that the rest of the world may no longer be willing to wait indefinitely for the United States.

In November 2007, the UN General Assembly voted to create a new post, Special Rapporteur on Violence against Children. The measure was approved by a vote of 176 to 1; only the United States voted against it. The impetus for a UN Special Rapporteur on Violence against Children derived in part from the UN Study on Violence Against Children, published in 2006. That study (UN Secretary General 2006) was developed through regional consultations on issues of violence against children, including a North American consultation in which the United States participated. Yet when it came time to establish a special rapporteur post to ensure that prevention of violence against children is given sufficient priority, the United States voted no.

The creation of the special rapporteur post was actually one component of a larger resolution on children's rights that called on countries to eliminate child hunger, criminalize and penalize all forms of sexual exploitation and abuse of children, and work to prevent the abduction of children, especially in armed conflict situations. The United States contributes to remediation efforts on all of these issues, but it voted against the resolution because it believed the resolution gave too much prominence to the CRC (UN General Assembly 2007).

The resolution urged states that had not yet become parties to the CRC to do so, emphasizing that the CRC "must constitute the standard in the promotion and protection of the rights of the child" (UN General Assembly 2007). Because the Bush Administration did not support CRC ratification, the United States is now on record as voting against addressing many hardships experienced by children around the globe.

What is notable is not that the United States voted no, but rather that the rest of the world departed from the route it had followed during the UN Special Session on Children and decided to move forward without the United States. In doing so, the rest of the world sent a message to the United States: although it needs U.S. support, it will go forward without the United States if necessary to advance the interests of children.

In fact, in each of the years 2006, 2007, and 2008, the United States has stood alone as the only country to vote no on the UN General Assembly's annual Resolution on the Rights of the Child (Brief for Amnesty International 2009, 20). It has also found itself alone on other human rights votes. In 2008, the UN General Assembly voted 180 to 1 in favor of a resolution on the right to food, which stated that:

> [T]he Assembly would "consider it intolerable" that more than 6 million children still died every year from hunger-related illness before their fifth birthday, and that the number of undernourished people had grown to

about 923 million worldwide, at the same time that the planet could produce enough food to feed 12 billion people, or twice the world's present
population.

(UN General Assembly 2008)

The United States was the only no vote. With the 2008 Resolution on
the Rights of the Child, the United States was similarly on the short end
of a 180 to 1 vote. Its comments for the record noted that it could not
support the resolution because the resolution's preamble stated that the
CRC "must constitute" the standard in the protection and promotion of
children's rights, and that the operative paragraph stated that the General
Assembly "[u]rges states that have not yet done so become parties to"
the CRC and its Optional Protocols. A U.S.-proposed amendment sought
to water down that language to suggest that states "consider" becoming
a party, a much lesser step that even if the U.S. proposal had won the
day, the Bush Administration was unwilling to take (UN General Assembly 2008). Votes in which the United States stands alone in opposition
to advancing the rights and well-being of children have become more
common, and the rest of the world has signaled its willingness to pro-
ceed with initiatives to protect children, whether or not the United States
joins.

Given the United States' superpower status, the rest of the world is
not about to ignore it entirely. However, the international community
has indicated it will not allow the United States to hinder children's rights
measures that have overwhelming support globally. Therefore, the election of Barack Obama is potentially significant: it offers new possibilities
to people within the United States and globally, including the opportunity for the United States to reassume a leadership position on children's
rights.

II. ADVANCING BEYOND THE CROSSROADS

We are at a crossroads. The children's rights movement is maturing. The
CRC has begun its third decade, children's rights are included more consistently on international agendas, and law and policies protecting children are improving. Yet this progress is not sufficient, and more could
have been done to date. For the last twenty years, child rights advocacy and policy reform have proceeded without the full backing of the
United States. The question is whether the U.S. government will assume
a leadership role in the global child advocacy movement or whether it
will continue to remain on the sidelines. Assuming a leadership role will
entail three important steps.

A. Ratification of the CRC

First, the United States must ratify the CRC, which stands on the precipice of universal ratification. U.S. ratification would not only give legitimacy to the CRC, it also would bring about universal ratification of a human rights treaty for the first time and would open new doors for human rights generally. More important, although the CRC is imperfect (e.g., certain states parties have failed to make significant progress; its enforcement mechanisms are not strong), it remains the most comprehensive legally binding instrument on children's rights and well-being, one which the United States had a major role in drafting. Therefore, it is *the* primary tool for advancing children's rights. Moreover, the imperfect record on implementation reflects, in part, the reality of pressing for advances in the face of sometimes hostile opposition from the world's sole superpower.

President Obama has indicated that his administration will take a serious look at the CRC and explore whether the United States can ratify it (Heilprin 2009). Upon careful review, the concerns typically raised by opponents of the CRC – primarily, sovereignty issues and the question of parental rights – are not barriers to ratification. First, the United States has ratified human rights treaties in the past without ceding its sovereignty. More important, concerns expressed over U.S. sovereignty ignore two important points: the Senate will likely insist the CRC be deemed non-self-executing, and the Committee on the Rights of the Child does not have police powers, but rather the reporting process is a collaborative review of a state's practices with a view to identifying ways to further improve the lives and well-being of children.

Second, questions about parental rights also overlook the fact that the treaty will be non-self-executing. More important, such questions ignore the text of the CRC itself: nineteen provisions of the CRC acknowledge the importance of parents and families in the child's development and the exercise by the child of his or her rights. In fact, an in-depth comparison of U.S. law and the CRC reveals far more common ground than differences (Todres, Wojcik, and Revaz 2006). In areas where there are differences, opportunities exist to further strengthen U.S. law related to children, or if necessary consider making appropriate reservations to specific provisions of the treaty. In either instance, no difference rises to a level that would prevent the United States from participating entirely.

Although there may be no significant legal obstacles to ratification, there are political ones. The combination of the Obama Administration's commitment to review the U.S. government's position and growing domestic support for the CRC has provoked a sharp reaction by a small number of conservative political groups in the United States. These groups have sought to frighten Americans with doomsday scenarios and inflammatory rhetoric. They assert that the CRC represents "an assault on the [American] family," despite the strong support for parents and families enshrined in the CRC's text (ParentalRights.org 2010a). They claim the treaty "overrides even our Constitution" and would give the government the power to "override every decision made by every parent if a government worker disagreed with the parent's decision," even though neither statement reflects the realities of the CRC, U.S. law, or the manner in which the CRC would be implemented (ParentalRights.org 2010b).

Responding to human rights advocates' success in building support for the CRC within the United States, these groups have mobilized in select conservative states, pushing anti-CRC resolutions to counter growing support for children's rights (Tennessee House Joint Resolution 0369 2010; Oklahoma House Concurrent Resolution 1033 2009). More recently, they lobbied successfully to have a resolution introduced in the U.S. Senate in May 2010 that calls on President Obama not to send the CRC to the Senate for ratification (U.S. Senate Resolution 519 2010). Although the Senate resolution misrepresents the CRC, including the patently false assertion that pronouncements by the Committee on the Rights of the Child would be "binding and authoritative upon the United States" upon ratification, it is a vehicle through which a small number of conservative senators could delay U.S. ratification of the CRC for several years or more. Because human rights treaties require a two-thirds vote in the Senate for ratification, a small group of senators can effectively prevent the full Senate from considering the treaty's merits. Growing support for a domestic human rights agenda has mobilized CRC opponents in the United States. Notably, however, their anti-international, anti-children's rights rhetoric reflects the fact that their aims are much broader than the CRC.

The current debate over U.S. ratification of the CRC is ultimately not about the CRC. Rather, it reveals that the CRC is being used as a pawn in a broader culture war in a country that has become increasingly polarized socially. For the United States to assert leadership on children's rights, the CRC must be divorced from this broader culture war and recognized for what it is: the most comprehensive tool currently available to advance the rights and well-being of children. Given that, the U.S. government must reassert leadership by ratifying the CRC, a treaty whose content it shaped significantly more than twenty years ago.

B. Advancement of Children's Rights in Other Countries

The U.S. government stands positioned to be one of the most significant advocates for children globally – if it chooses. Although the United States has contributed significantly to child welfare initiatives through foreign assistance, as well as in emergency relief efforts, it has not pushed strongly for the realization of children's *rights*. Advancing children's rights would be qualitatively different, requiring not just humanitarian assistance but support for the development of programs and policies that foster the realization of children's rights. Moreover, the CRC contemplates international cooperation in facilitating states' fulfillment of their obligations under the CRC (CRC 1989, art. 4).

Assuming a leadership role in the children's rights movement around the world would require the United States to provide strong backing of the Committee on the Rights of the Child and country-level support to individuals and organizations seeking to advance a children's rights framework. Upon ratifying the CRC, the United States would be well positioned to strengthen the effectiveness of the Committee on the Rights of the Child. Although many countries take their international obligations seriously, others do not. U.S. participation could bolster the Committee's profile and the importance of the reporting process. The United States needs to direct some foreign assistance to the development of children's rights programming. It also needs to bring pressure on reluctant governments and insist that they take meaningful steps toward implementing the CRC and children's rights in general.

C. Development of a Domestic Child Rights Agenda

Children's rights matter at home as well. If the United States is to call upon other states to take their commitments more seriously, it must serve as a model – both in its participation in the international human rights system and with its practices within its own borders. Currently, the United States falls short of ensuring the rights and well-being of all children.

The United States performs below many other industrialized nations with respect to health indicators such as infant mortality, life expectancy, and premature and preventable deaths (Walker 2005, 17). It ranks tied for twenty-ninth among countries in under-five infant and child mortality, and "the gap between the U.S. infant mortality rate and the rates for the countries with the lowest infant mortality appears to be widening"

(MacDorman and Mathews 2008, 1–2). "Compared to other nations and especially western democracies, the U.S. record with respect to access to health care and public health services is not strong. Indeed, the [World Health Organization] ranked the performance of the U.S. health care system thirty-seventh among all nations due to disparities by race and income" (Kinney 2001, 1474).

Children in the United States today represent a disproportionate percentage of the poor and uninsured (Swan 1998, 74). In 2007, children represented 35.7 percent of Americans living in poverty (DeNavas-Walt, Proctor, and Smith 2008, 14). According to 2007 U.S. government data, 11 percent of children (or 8.1 million) in the United States had no health insurance coverage at all (DeNavas-Walt et al. 2008, 24).

Although research findings indicate that overall, 6 percent of children in the United States have no regular source of health care, uninsured children were fourteen times more likely than those with private insurance not to have a usual source of care (almost 30 percent versus approximately 2 percent based on 2006 figures) (Federal Interagency Forum on Child and Family Statistics 2008, 8). Research further shows that uninsured children are three times more likely than insured children to go without needed health care services and six times more likely to go without needed medical care (Newacheck et al. 1998, 516). In short, many children in the United States are not realizing their right to access needed health care, and that has implications for children's development and their capacity to pursue an education and other opportunities.

Education data similarly suggest significant shortcomings. In 2007, 27 percent of eighth graders scored below a basic reading level in the United States, and in the 2006 Program for International Assessment, fifteen-year-old students in the United States placed behind like students in thirty Organization for Economic Cooperation and Development countries in their average science and math proficiencies (Annie E. Casey Foundation 2007; U.S. Department of Education 2006). Moreover, although the national average dropout rate in 2007 was 8.7 percent, poor students drop out at ten times the rate of students from higher income families (U.S. Department of Education 2007). In certain areas, the high school dropout rate correlates with child labor data. About half of students who regularly perform farm work never graduate from high school (Child Labor Coalition 2007). In 1998, the U.S. General Accounting Office (GAO) estimated that 300,000 children worked in agriculture in the United States (GAO 1998, 2). As in other countries, many children in the United States face obstacles to realizing their right to education and end up entering the work force at an earlier age with fewer skills, and thus are at heightened risk of exploitation.

Research identified that 148,000 children per week were employed illegally in the United States (Kruse and Mahony 1998). These children are often exposed to increased safety risks. The National Institute for Occupational Safety and Health estimates that 230,000 workers under the age of eighteen are injured on the job each year and between sixty to seventy youth workers die due to workplace injury (Child Labor Coalition 2007). In addition, as many as 300,000 children are at risk of sexual exploitation in the United States (Estes and Weiner 2002).

The United States can – and must – do better. Notably, calls for the United States to ensure children's rights at home are coming primarily from its own people. As detailed in the previous section, there is support for the CRC and U.S. ratification in numerous cities and states. Moreover, there is broader support for human rights principles than the U.S. government has recognized. For example, 72 percent of Americans believe strongly that health care should be a right, and 82 percent believe strongly that equal access to quality public education is a right (Belden, Russonello, and Stewart 2007, 3–4). Eighty-one percent of Americans believe lack of quality education for children in poor communities is a violation of the right to education (Belden et al. 2007, 5). This is overwhelming support for core economic and social rights, which historically the U.S. government has been reluctant to recognize. Yet many of its citizens recognize access to health care and education as rights, on par with civil and political rights.

In short, there is significant support for children's rights and human rights in general in the United States. That does not mean the advancement of children's rights in the United States will be easy (the small, but vocal, opposition to the CRC is evidence that there are challenges ahead). However, the foundation exists, and the CRC offers a template for improving the lives and well-being of children in the United States. Ratifying the CRC would provide a mandate to improve the lives of U.S. children and enable the United States to leverage its significant clout to secure children's rights in other countries.

CONCLUSION

Whether the United States ratifies the CRC in the next few years depends on a number of variables, above and beyond questions about the CRC itself. Early indications are that the Obama Administration will seek to ratify the Convention on the Elimination of All Forms of Discrimination against Women (CEDAW) first. The debates over CEDAW are likely to influence the timing and prospects for CRC ratification. Moreover, midterm elections, debates over health care reform, and the economy might all shape whether President Obama has the political capital necessary to push for U.S. ratification of the CRC.

Although political results are uncertain, it is clear this is a crucial time for children's rights, heightened by the pressures from the global economic crisis. There has been significant progress. However, much work remains, as millions of children suffer human rights abuses daily. A groundswell has formed encompassing both those at the grassroots level in the United States and leaders and citizens of other countries. They are determined to improve the lives and well-being of all children and will not wait indefinitely for the U.S. government.

If the U.S. federal government seizes this moment and ratifies the CRC, then the country that established the world's first juvenile court and introduced the best interests of the child principle into its legal system more than a century ago can once again become a leader in the children's rights movement. If that occurs, the world will have much to be optimistic about in terms of protecting and nurturing its most valued resource: children. If the U.S. federal government fails to act, the global child advocacy movement will move forward, but it will have lost a most important potential ally, and children in the United States and elsewhere will suffer.

REFERENCES

Annie E. Casey Foundation. 2007. Kids Count Data Center. http://datacenter .kidscount.org/data/acrossstates/Rankings.aspx?ind=93.

Belden, Nancy, John Russonello, and Kate Stewart. 2007. *Human Rights in the United States: Findings from a National Survey*. Washington, D.C.: The Opportunity Agenda.

Brief for Amnesty International et al. 2009. As amicus curiae in support of Petitioners, *Graham v. Florida, Sullivan v. Florida*, Nos. 08–7412, 08–7621 (U.S. Supreme Court 2009).

Capdevila, Gustavo. 2006. "Child Labor – Slow Progress, Right Direction." *Global Policy Forum*. June 13. http://www.globalpolicy.org/component/ content/article/219-labor/46716-child-labour-slow-progress-right-direction .html.

Child Labor Coalition. 2007. *Children in the Fields: The Inequitable Treatment of Child Farmworkers*. http://www.stopchildlabor.org/Consumer campaigns/fields.htm.

City of Chicago. 2009. *Resolution of the City Council of Chicago – Expression of Support for Convention on the Rights of the Child. Res. No. R2009-143,* Feb. 11, 2009.

City of New York. 1989. *Resolution of the City Council of New York. Res. No. 1891,* Nov. 21, 1989.

DeNavas-Walt, Carmen, Bernadette D. Proctor, and Jessica C. Smith. 2008. *Income, Poverty, and Health Insurance Coverage in the United States: 2007.* Washington, D.C.: U.S. Government Printing Office.

Dugger, Celia. 2009. "Child Mortality Rate Declines Globally." *New York Times,* September 9.

Education for All Global Monitoring Report Team. 2008. *Overcoming Inequality: Why Governance Matters – Education for All Global Monitoring Report 2009.* Paris: UNESCO. http://unesdoc.unesco.org/images/0017/001776/1776 09e.pdf.

Estes, Richard J., and Neil A. Weiner. 2002. *Commercial Sexual Exploitation of Children in the U.S., Canada and Mexico.* Philadelphia, PA: University of Pennsylvania. http://www.sp2.upenn.edu/~restes/CSEC_Files/Complete_CSEC_020220.pdf.

Federal Interagency Forum on Child and Family Statistics. 2008. *America's Children in Brief: Key National Indicators of Well-Being, 2008.* Washington, D.C.: Government Printing Office.

Hagemann, Frank, Yacouba Diallo, Alex Etienne, and Farhad Mehran. 2006. *Global Child Labour Trends 2000 to 2004.* Geneva: International Labour Office.

Heilprin, John. 2009. "Obama Administration Seeks to Join UN Rights of the Child Convention." *Huffington Post,* June 22.

Henkin, Louis. 1995. "U.S. Ratification of Human Rights Conventions: The Ghost of Senator Bricker." *American Journal of International Law* 89: 341–50.

Koh, Harold Hongju. 2003. "On American Exceptionalism." *Stanford Law Review* 55(5): 1479–1527.

———. 2007. "Restoring America's Human Rights Reputation." *Cornell International Law Journal* 40(3): 635–59.

Kinney, Eleanor D. 2001. "The International Human Right to Health: What Does This Mean for Our Nation and the World?" *Indiana Law Review* 34(4): 1457–75.

Kruse, Douglas, and Douglas Mahony. 1998. *Illegal Child Labor in the United States: Prevalence and Characteristics.* NBER Working Papers 6479. National Bureau of Economic Research, Inc.

MacDorman, Marian, and T.J. Mathews. 2008. *Recent Trends in Infant Mortality in the United States.* NCHS Data Brief, No. 9. U.S. National Center for Health Statistics.

Mertus, Julie. 2008. *Bait and Switch: Human Rights and U.S. Foreign Policy.* 2nd Edition. New York: Routledge.

Mosel, Leah, and Urmila Sarkar. 2009. *Impacts of the Global Financial and Economic Crisis on Child Labour and Youth Employment.* ILO Regional

Office for Asia and the Pacific. http://www.ilo.org/public/english/support/lib/financialcrisis/download/childlabouryouthemp.pdf.

Newacheck, Paul W., Jefrey J. Stoddard, Paul C. Hughes, and Michelle Pearl. 1998. "Health Insurance and Access to Primary Care for Children." *New England Journal of Medicine* 338(8): 513–19.

New York Times. 2009. "Barack Obama's Inaugural Address," January 20.

Oklahoma House Concurrent Resolution 1033, May 13, 2009.

ParentalRights.org. 2010a. "The Threat from International Treaty Law." http://www.parentalrights.org/index.asp?type=B_BASIC&SEC={53D4DCA7–5899–4242-B244–54A253AFC137}.

———. 2010b. "20 Things You Need to Know About the UN Convention on the Rights of the Child." http://www.parentalrights.org/index.asp?Type=B_BASIC&SEC=%7BB56D7393-E583–4658–85E6-C1974B1A57F8%7D.

Powell, Catherine. 2008. *Human Rights at Home: A Domestic Policy Blueprint for the New Administration.* Washington, D.C.: American Constitution Society.

Sabarwal, Shwetlena, Nistha Sinha, and Mayra Buvinic. 2009. "The Global Financial Crisis: Assessing Vulnerability for Women and Children." World Bank Policy Paper. http://www.worldbank.org/financialcrisis/pdf/Women-Children-Vulnerability-March09.pdf.

State of South Carolina. 1992. *Concurrent Resolution S 790, A Concurrent Resolution to Support the United Nations Convention on the Rights of the Child and to Request Agencies Providing Services to Children to Aim to Achieve the Goals of the Convention.* Adopted April 30, 1992 (Senate) and May 5, 1992 (House).

Swan, Rita. 1998. "On Statutes Depriving a Class of Children of Rights to Medical Care: Can This Discrimination Be Litigated?" *Quinnipiac Health Law Journal* 2(1): 73–95.

Tennessee House Joint Resolution 0369, February 22, 2010.

Todres, Jonathan, Mark Wojcik, and Cris Revaz, eds. 2006. *The U.N. Convention on the Rights of the Child: An Analysis of Treaty Provisions and Implications of U.S. Ratification.* Boston: Brill Academic Publishers.

UNICEF. 2009a. *A Matter of Magnitude: The Impact of the Economic Crisis on Women and Children in South Asia.* Nepal: UNICEF Regional Office South Asia.

———. 2009b. *The State of the World's Children: Special Edition Celebrating 20 Years of the Convention on the Rights of the Child.* New York: UNICEF.

UNICEF Innocenti Research Centre. 2006. *The General Measures of the Convention on the Rights of the Child: The Process in Europe and Central Asia.* Florence: UNICEF.

———. 2007. *Law Reform and the Implementation of the Convention on the Rights of the Child.* Florence: UNICEF.

UN Convention on the Rights of the Child. 1989. G.A. res. 44/25, annex, 44 U.N. GAOR Supp. (No. 49) at 167, U.N. Doc. A/44/49 (1989), entered into force Sept. 2, 1990.

UN General Assembly. 2002. *A World Fit for Children*, 27th Special Sess. A/RES/S-27/2, October 11, 2002.

―――. 2007. *Third Committee Recommends Appointment of Special Representative on Violence Against Children.* November 27. http://www.un.org/News/Press/docs/2007/gashc3911.doc.htm.

―――. 2008. *Third Committee Draft Text Endorses Recommendations, Future Workplan of Human Rights Council's Working Group on Right to Development,* UN Doc. GA/SHC/3941. http://www.un.org/News/Press/docs/2008/gashc3941.doc.htm.

UN Secretary General. 2006. *Violence Against Children: United Nations Secretary-General's Study.* New York: UN. http://www.unviolencestudy.org/.

U.S. Department of Education. National Center for Education Statistics. 2006. *Program for International Student Assessment.* http://nces.ed.gov/surveys/pisa/pisa2006highlights.asp.

―――. 2007. *High School Dropout and Completion Rates in the United States.* http://nces.ed.gov/pubsearch/pubsinfo.asp?pubid=2009064.

U.S. General Accounting Office. 1998. *Child Labor in Agriculture: Characteristics and Legality of Work.* Washington, D.C.: GAO.

U.S. Senate Resolution 519, May 10, 2010. http://thomas.loc.gov/cgi-bin/query/z?c111:S.RES.519.

Van Bueren, Geraldine. 1995. *The International Law on the Rights of the Child.* Boston: Kluwer Academic Publishers.

Walker, David M., Comptroller of the United States. 2005. *21st Century Health Care Challenges: Unsustainable Trends Necessitate Reforms to Control Spending and Improve Value.* http://www.gao.gov/cghome/chcwg07222005/chcwg07222005.pdf.

World Health Organization. 2009. *World Health Statistics 2009.* http://www.who.int/whosis/whostat/EN_WHS09_Full.pdf.

8

Entrenched Inequity: Health Care in the United States

Jean Connolly Carmalt, Sarah Zaidi, and Alicia Ely Yamin

INTRODUCTION

In 1941, President Franklin D. Roosevelt proclaimed "freedom from want" to be one of the four essential liberties necessary to achieve human security. The polio-stricken president included in his definition of freedom "the right to adequate medical care and the opportunity to achieve and enjoy good health" (Roosevelt 1944, 41). This expansive vision of a right to health, which included both medical care and the preconditions to health, was subsequently incorporated into the Universal Declaration of Human Rights (UDHR) and has since been enshrined in many international and regional human rights treaties.

Roosevelt's vision was never fulfilled because the United States turned its back on economic and social rights. Despite spending far more per capita on health care than any other country, the United States continues to have some of the poorest health indicators in the industrialized world (Commonwealth Fund 2007). It is the only industrialized nation to deny its citizens universal access to medical services. Fully one-third of the population lacks health insurance for at least part of the year, and although this percentage is expected to decrease substantially as a result of the recently passed Patient Protection and Affordable Care Act (PPACA), those reforms still do not guarantee universal access. Add to this the lack of services for many Americans, discrimination in health care provision and inequitable outcomes between different racial groups, and pharmaceutical and insurance costs spiraling out of control, and it is clear U.S. health care is in a profound predicament.

This chapter is adapted with permission from a report by the Center for Economic and Social Rights (2004).

The severity of this predicament produced the political will to pass the PPACA of 2010, the largest reform to American health care in decades (PPACA 2010). At the time of this writing, it appears the PPACA's reforms will speak to certain issues raised here, particularly in terms of increasing availability of health care for underserved communities and providing access for some of the uninsured population. The PPACA is expected to decrease the number of uninsured individuals by 30 million, which would be a welcome and substantial improvement. Nonetheless, it does not provide universal coverage: between 18 and 24 million will likely remain uninsured, and it is unclear whether the PPACA will do much about underinsurance problems. Moreover, the reforms are structured as an expansion of a market-based model that leaves fundamental questions unanswered about justice and equity. This is not surprising – those same questions were conspicuously absent from the debates that produced the reform.

Because the PPACA was developed in a political environment that did not frame health as a human right, it expands an existing structure that is not designed to guarantee the highest attainable standard of health for everyone in the United States. Therefore, although the PPACA contains measures that improve upon specific problems discussed in this chapter (e.g., increasing minority representation among health professionals), it is only one development in a larger, continuing discussion about the overarching organization and goals of health care provision in the United States. It leaves unanswered questions about disparities and other issues discussed in the following sections.

Current discussions (including those that created the PPACA) regarding health care reform in the United States focus on how to contain cost and expenditures while improving quality of care. Many proposals for reform claim to be "consumer-driven," allowing health care consumers to extract greater value from the system, and much research has been devoted to applying cost-effectiveness analysis to a broad spectrum of health care services (e.g., Fisher, Staiger, Bynum, and Gottlieb 2007; Garber 2004; Howard, Kent, Vijan, and Hofer 2005; Kotlikoff and Hagist 2005). Much health law scholarship has been devoted to addressing how to reconcile the information, agency, and incentive problems in health care with a regime that still principally allocates health care through market mechanisms.

By contrast, a human rights approach to health care reform begins with different foundational premises. In a human rights framework, health claims – claims of entitlement to health care and enabling conditions – are reconceptualized as "assets of citizenship" (UN Millennium Project

Task Force 2005). The health care system, in this view, is more than just a delivery mechanism for services and products to consumers. Rather, it is a system through which to exercise citizenship and a core social system, more akin to the justice system than, for example, the post office, which provides a service and competes with a number of private providers. As such, the health system both reflects and contributes to the quality of democracy in a country. And like the justice system, the health system's relationship with the quality of democracy is not limited to citizens; rather, it extends to all the people currently in the country, regardless of their immigration status. In the United States, the fragmented, disparate, market-driven, commoditized pieces of health care reflect and contribute to entrenched inequities in American society.

This chapter gives substance to President Roosevelt's vision by using international human rights principles as a framework for health care reform in the United States. Acknowledging a right to health shifts policy debates from a narrow focus on "efficiency" (which itself can be a spurious notion when many costs – e.g., the loss of productivity due to employee health problems – are externalized) to questions of how to guarantee people an effective voice in policy and programming decisions that affect their well-being.

This chapter is divided into four parts. Part One examines the legal framework governing the right to health, with a focus on health care, in the United States. Part Two discusses the structure of the current U.S. health care system and its impact on health care delivery. Part Three examines how the U.S. system measures up to international human rights standards. Finally, Part Four presents the chapter's conclusions with respect to what needs to be done to align the U.S. health care system with international standards.

I. THE LEGAL FRAMEWORK FOR THE RIGHT TO HEALTH

The right to health is enshrined in international legal instruments, many of which were drafted with U.S. leadership. Among the most important are the Universal Declaration of Human Rights (UDHR) and the International Covenant on Economic, Social, and Cultural Rights (ICESCR) (UDHR 1948; ICESCR 1966). A focus on health *care* leaves aside many salient issues concerning the right to health and its implementation at the national level.[1] For example, the right to health requires not only that

---

[1] For a discussion of how and why the right to health should be framed in terms of power alignments and the ability to control one's own health, see Yamin (1996).

certain minimum standards of care be met or exceeded, but that basic preconditions to health also are met, including adequate shelter, food, and sanitation (CESCR 2000; Toebes 1998). In addition, as is the case with civil and political rights (e.g., the right to a fair trial), a government's responsibility to ensure the right to health is equally about process and outcome. Although the government must work to promote health, it cannot be held responsible for ensuring a particular individual's health unless that person's health problems stem directly from discrimination or other human rights violations. In other words, the right to health is not equivalent to a guarantee that one will actually be healthy.

A. The Right to Health in the UDHR and ICESCR

The Universal Declaration of Human Rights (UDHR) was one of the first great achievements of the United Nations (UN). Its preamble includes Roosevelt's "four freedoms," and its adoption marked the first time that international law protected the individual rights of citizens within their own countries (UDHR 1948, Preamble, ¶2). Eleanor Roosevelt led drafting discussions of the UDHR, and her influence is clear in both the UDHR and its two implementing covenants. The UDHR's provision on the right to health (Article 25) is complemented by the provision in the ICESCR (Article 2), which is meant to elaborate on the term's meaning (UDHR 1948; ICESCR 1966; see Appendix).

Under international law, the distinction between positive and negative rights has been increasingly challenged by a focus on three dimensions of state obligations that attach to all rights, whether civil and political or economic and social: the obligations to *respect, protect*, and *fulfill*. In relation to health, these obligations imply the following:

Respect. A government must refrain from directly infringing upon the right to health, as it would by cutting funding for doctors working in underserved areas or systematically discriminating against certain populations in its health care system.

Protect. A government is responsible for preventing third parties from violating the right to health. Eviscerating environmental regulations arguably breaches the obligation to protect right to health.

Fulfill. A government must take steps to ensure all citizens have access to basic health services as well as preconditions for health, such as sanitation and clean water.

The ICESCR sets out the core provision relating to the right to health under international law. However, although the treaty provisions recognize the right of everyone to enjoy "the highest attainable standard" of physical and mental health, they do not offer a recipe for implementation (ICESCR 1966).[2]

The UN Committee on Economic, Social, and Cultural Rights (CESCR), the primary body responsible for interpreting the ICESCR, has developed guidelines on how states should interpret the right to health (CESCR 2000). The first component of those guidelines is a *minimum floor* below which no country may fall. In the case of health, this means ensuring essential primary health care for the entire population. The committee listed four substantive interrelated elements essential to the right to health: *availability, accessibility, acceptability,* and *quality* (CESCR 2000, ¶¶ 9, 12).[3]

B. Substantive Elements Required to Fulfill the Right to Health

Availability. Governments must ensure that health care is available to all sectors of the population. This requires that "functioning public health and health care facilities, goods and services, as well as programmes, have to be available in sufficient quantity" (CESCR 2000). It also means that facilities have to be capable of actually providing care. Basic determinants of health must be present, such as potable water, adequate sanitation, trained medical personnel who receive domestically competitive salaries, and essential medicines. In the United States, although there are a substantial number of medical facilities and personnel, these are concentrated in urban and white areas, whereas rural and minority areas often have insufficient services (Grant Makers in Health 2002, 2). Although the PPACA reforms should help alleviate some of this lack of availability through, for example, increased funding of community health centers, it

---

[2] This phrasing is similar to the constitution of the World Health Organization. The right to health is also recognized in regional and international instruments including the American Declaration on the Rights and Duties of Man (1948), the European Social Charter (1961, 1996), and the African Charter on Human and Peoples' Rights (1982), the Convention on the Rights of the Child (1989), Convention on the Elimination of All Forms of Discrimination Against Women (1979), and International Convention on the Elimination of All Forms of Racial Discrimination (1965).

[3] There is overlap between these categories, but we have chosen a narrow definition of each. For example, we restrict "availability" to geographical availability and focus "accessibility" on economic accessibility.

is too soon to tell whether those measures will be sufficient to meet the current lack of care.

Accessibility. Health facilities, goods, and services must be accessible. Accessibility requires that basic health care services be affordable for every person in society, and "poorer households should not be disproportionately burdened with health expenses as compared to richer households" (CESCR 2000, ¶12). Access to information about health – including information about sexual health – is required. In the United States, the millions of people without health insurance, together with substantial bureaucratic, financial, and other barriers to obtaining care, reflect failures of accessibility.

Acceptability. Under international law, acceptable health care meets ethical standards and is culturally appropriate. This requires binding ethical guidelines for doctors and other medical practitioners. Acceptable health care also requires that ethical and cultural training be part of a medical education. In the United States, disadvantaged minorities typically receive poorer health care than white people, in part because there are disproportionately low numbers of minority caregivers and unequal treatment of patients based on their race (Smedley, Stith, and Nelson 2003).

Quality. The state must ensure that health facilities, goods, and services are scientifically and medically sound. Quality requires skilled medical personnel who prescribe medicines and medical procedures appropriately. Health facilities must be adequately supplied with, among other things, scientifically approved and unexpired medicines and hospital equipment, adequate sanitation, and skilled medical personnel (CESCR 2000, ¶12). Although some very high-quality health care is available in the United States for the wealthy, studies indicate inconsistent levels of quality throughout the overall health care system, including alarming numbers of avoidable errors (Institute of Medicine 2001, 13).

C. Procedural Protections Relating to the Right to Health

A number of procedural protections complement the four substantive requirements in the previous section. The primary procedural protections include *nonretrogression, nondiscrimination, participation, access to remedies,* and *information.*

Nonretrogression. Once a right to health is recognized, retrogression – or backsliding – is generally considered inconsistent with a country's obligations, and a government bears the burden of demonstrating that such retrogression was unavoidable and was as narrowly tailored in its effects and duration as possible.

Nondiscrimination. Any sort of discrimination – whether on an individual level or systemwide – is a human rights violation. International law explicitly prohibits discrimination on the basis of race, color, sex, language, religion, political or other opinion, national or social origin, property, birth, physical or mental disability, health status (including HIV/AIDS), sexual orientation and civil, political, social or other status (CESCR 2000, ¶18).

Remedy. When violations of the right to health occur, states must provide remedies. Remedies may redress individual abuses through civil or criminal penalties or they may seek to correct systemwide violations by introducing changes in policy or governing legislation.

Participation. States must ensure that patients are fully able to participate in decisions regarding their own health on both an individual and collective level. For example, patients should be able to fully participate in decisions about their own health and not be limited in that participation by, for example, insurance company policies about which medical services will be covered. Further, decisions regarding health policy and coverage should be made on the basis of a participatory, public, and transparent process.

Information. States are required to ensure that their population receives adequate information and education about medical practices and services (including those related to sexual and reproductive health) (CESCR 2000, ¶11). The procedural requirement for information overlaps with the substantive requirement of accessibility because information is a prerequisite to accessing care. It is also a prerequisite to effective participation.

The emphasis on process in a human rights framework shows that the right to health goes beyond the latest drugs, sterile needles, or any particular service. Rather, the government's obligation to respect, protect, and fulfill the right to health demands that policy makers approach health care reform with a view toward promoting improved health care as a dimension of social justice in the United States.

II. THE CURRENT U.S. SYSTEM

The United States is the only industrialized country that does not recognize a government's obligations to provide health care. At the federal level, the closest Americans have come to securing their right to health are programs like the State Children's Health Insurance Program (SCHIP), Medicare, and Medicaid, which are rooted in the idea that children, the elderly, and the poor should be guaranteed a minimum level of health services. Federal legislation also guarantees a limited right to emergency care in the United States. Important as these programs are, and important as it is to extend them, as happens under the PPACA, the exclusivity of their premise contradicts the notion of a universal right to health elaborated under international law.

In the U.S. federalist system, states are largely responsible for implementing the few health care entitlements that exist. There is considerable variation among states both in law and practice, which is another factor that breeds inequity from the standpoint of international human rights law.[4] In many cases, even essential services and limited benefits can be taken away when the legislature determines, which is inconsistent with a rights-based view of entitlements not subject to retrogression.

American law and policy generally approach health care as a commodity – either to be doled out to the needy as a matter of charity or to be regulated through the market. Nonetheless, there have been repeated attempts to establish national health insurance in the United States. In 1915, the American Association for Labor Legislation (unsuccessfully) campaigned for sickness insurance. President Harry Truman officially endorsed a national health insurance scheme proposed by the Wagner-Murray-Dingell Bill, but it never came to a vote in Congress (Social Security Administration n.d.). The result is that the U.S. system views health as a commodity and funds health primarily through employers or other private financing sources. However, from a rights-based perspective, the problem with U.S. health care is not the mixture of public and private funding per se, but rather the failure of the government to step in and level the playing field in the face of obvious inequities in the system.

A. The Legal Structure

Health care in the United States is financed and delivered according to terms set out in a complex array of regulations administered through an equally complex array of federal and state institutions and by public and private actors. Laws range from the specific, such as the requirement that managed care organizations approve hospital stays for mothers who have just given birth, to the general, such as the Employment Retirement

---

[4] Under international human rights law, even in a federalist system, the federal government is ultimately responsible for ensuring respect, protection, and fulfillment of certain minimum guarantees within its territory.

Income Security Act (ERISA) preemption provision, a federal statute that essentially prohibits individuals from suing their managed care organizations (USCS 42, Sec. 300gg-4 2006; USCS 29 §1144(a) 2006; *Aetna Health Inc. v. Davila* 2004).[5] The legal structure regulating health care is bifurcated into two main branches: laws that regulate government-run programs (e.g., Medicare) and laws that regulate private sector health care groups (e.g., HMOs).

The government's funding framework stems from a 1965 amendment to the Social Security Act signed into law by President Lyndon B. Johnson. The amendment created safety nets for two groups of vulnerable Americans: the elderly and the poor. The elderly (defined as those over 65) are eligible for Medicare, which is financed by federal funds. The poor are eligible for Medicaid, which is financed by a combination of federal and state funds. Federal funds also provide health insurance coverage for the military and federal employees.

In December 2003, the Medicare Prescription Drug, Improvement, and Modernization Act (MMA) introduced the most sweeping modifications to the Medicare and Medicaid programs since their creation. The MMA created a new group of prescription drug plans to fund those drugs and provided substantial incentives for private health care providers to enter the Medicare system. The MMA has been extremely profitable for pharmaceutical companies, although its complexity has resulted in tremendous overhead costs and the continuation of a system in which elderly and vulnerable Americans have the poorest health care coverage (Waxman 2006; Krugman 2007).

The MMA's privatization efforts mean that laws governing private sector health care funding are more important than ever. Under President Richard Nixon, the HMO Act (1973) kick-started the managed care industry by requiring all health care providers to accept patients from at least two managed care organizations. The act was fueled by concern that physicians had a financial incentive to provide more health services than necessary. HMOs were seen as a way to curb waste by penalizing doctors for providing unnecessary services. However, despite some success in eliminating waste, the organizations began to come under increasingly heavy criticism for depriving their members of needed treatments to save costs, ignoring unprofitable problems of quality, and creating burdensome administrative barriers to care.[6]

---

[5] ERISA is a federal statute that preempts state-based causes of action against applicable employee benefit plans. The purpose of ERISA is to allow broad removal to federal court to ensure a uniform regulatory regime over employee benefit plans.

[6] Many of these claims have gone to court. See *Pegram v. Herdrich* 2000.

Measures have been taken to curb the worst effects of managed care's cost-cutting in relation to patient care. However, one reason it is difficult to assess the scope of these concerns – or to address them systematically – is that health care is largely regulated through the courts, one case at a time. Litigation-based regulation does not effectively improve HMOs' responsiveness because the ERISA preemption provision exempts most managed care providers from state-based civil liability, including claims of wrongful death and other traditionally state-regulated torts.[7] Thus, most of the time, individuals cannot sue their HMOs.

B. The Financial Structure: Who Pays? Who Profits?

The United States spends more on health care per person than any other industrialized country (Anderson, Reinhardt, Hussey, and Petrosyan 2003). Total health costs continue to increase at approximately 7 percent per year, with costs projected to increase from $2.17 trillion to $2.88 trillion in 2010 (Plunkett Research 2006). Yet the United States has a lower-than-average physician-to-patient ratio, has one of the lowest rates of acute care beds per capita among industrialized countries, and is the only one that does not provide universal access to medical services (OECD 2009). The lack of available care is even more acute for minority patients, and in particular for patients who are black or Hispanic. Where all that money goes, if not toward increasing access and availability, is a central question for any rights-based reform.

There are many reasons health care in the United States is so expensive, ranging from high administrative costs to exorbitant drug costs. As health care becomes increasingly reliant on high-tech interventions, the Baby Boomer generation grows older, and as the American population grows in size, costs will continue to rise.[8] Health economists have been keen to explore how to contain the growth of these costs, but less scholarly attention has been devoted to the other manifestations of the failures of a market model: the profits made by health maintenance organizations

---

[7] Torts are civil – as opposed to criminal – wrongs that do not result from disputes over contracts. The Supreme Court has upheld the ERISA preemption, but dicta indicate a "rising judicial chorus urging that Congress and the Supreme Court revisit what is an unjust and increasingly tangled ERISA regime" (*DiFelice v. Aetna U.S. Health Care* 2003, Justice Becker, concurring, *Aetna Health Inc. v. Davila* 2004, Justice Ginsburg, concurring).

[8] For example, the increasing use of MRIs as a diagnostic tool is expensive. We are not suggesting MRIs should not be used, but only that their increased use is part of the reason health care costs continue to rise. Other uses of technology – such as using more email for communication – may help decrease costs, although it is unclear by how much.

and pharmaceutical companies, which dwarf those of other industries and suggest significant deadweight loss (U.S. Census Bureau 2003). For example, in 2001, as the overall profits of *Fortune 500* companies declined by 53 percent, the top ten U.S. drug makers increased their profits by 33 percent, from $28 billion to $37 billion. Managed-care organizations have also reported high profit growth, by as much as 73 percent in the second quarter of 2003 (a $1.8 billion increase over 2002) (Weiss Ratings, Inc. 2004). Lavish salaries accompany these profits. In 2002, William W. McGuire, the chairman and CEO of UnitedHealth Group, had a reported net worth of nearly $530 million. Another huge cost is lobbying. Pharmaceuticals spend the most on lobbying in the health care industry ($96 million in 2000), followed by physicians and health care organizations (Case Western Reserve University 2004). Of the 1,192 organizations involved in health care lobbying, the American Medical Association spent $17 million and the American Hospital Association $10 million. Meanwhile, HMO premiums for 2004 increased at an average rate of almost 18 percent, prompting more companies to require their employees to contribute to their health insurance plans (Hewitt Associates 2003).

Taken together, these figures represent hundreds of millions of dollars leaving the system without advancing research, delivering care, or paying medical providers. The newly passed PPACA introduces transparency measures and reins in some administrative spending, but it continues – and indeed, expands – reliance on a system structured around third parties whose incentives are to generate profit rather than to ensure people can achieve better health. The extent to which PPACA reforms affect insurance company profits also will depend on the way in which the measures are implemented (Hersch 2010).

III. INTERNATIONAL STANDARDS IN THE U.S. CONTEXT

Although the U.S. health care system provides some of the best care in the world for those who can afford it, overall the health care system falls far short of international human rights standards. Many of the existing problems will only continue to deepen because health care is considered a commodity rather than a basic right. This section will examine how the U.S. health care system fares with respect to the four essential elements to the right to health: *availability, accessibility, acceptability*, and *quality*.[9]

---

[9] The U.S. government has signed and ratified the International Convention on the Elimination of All Forms of Racial Discrimination, the International Covenant on Civil and Political Rights, and the Convention against Torture and Other Cruel and Inhuman or Degrading Treatment or Punishment. In addition, it has signed (but not ratified) the

A. Availability

For health care to be considered "available," facilities and personnel must exist in sufficient quantity and be located within reasonable proximity to all communities, regardless of their geographic location or racial, ethnic, or cultural makeup. In the United States, health care cannot be considered truly available, given the drastic shortages of care for people living in rural areas and for minorities. As of 2002, there were approximately 50 million people living in underserved areas in the United States (Grant Makers in Health 2002). Federal policy initiatives have successfully doubled the total number of doctors since 1970, but efforts have been based on the faulty assumption that market demand will even out geographical disparities. The PPACA makes an effort to address this issue by, for example, extending Medicare coverage in rural areas (PPACA 2010, §3121–3129) and providing federal funding for community health centers to overcome the larger structural problems associated with oversaturated urban markets and concomitant undersupply in rural and minority-dominated areas. Cities such as Washington, D.C., Boston, and San Francisco benefit from a ratio as high as one physician per 167 persons, whereas rural areas suffer severe medical service shortages (Grant Makers in Health 2002). Appalachia, for example, has less than one physician per 1,000 persons. Compounding the rural–urban divide is a significant racial gap in the availability of medical services. According to a study published in the *New England Journal of Medicine*, "communities with high proportions of black and Hispanic residents were four times as likely as others to have a shortage of physicians, regardless of community income" (Komaromy et al. 1996, 1305). In July 2000, the federal government designated 2,706 geographic areas, population groups, and facilities as "primary medical care health professional shortage" areas. The areas encompass 50 million people, a disproportionate number of whom are minorities (Grant Makers in Health 2002, 2).

The lack of health care facilities, goods, and services in rural and minority areas in the United States violates the requirement that health care be available. A human rights-based health care policy would entail maintaining training programs and incentives for those seeking to practice in underserved areas, but it would also prioritize ensuring availability for all populations in the United States. This does not mean putting a

ICESCR, the Convention on the Elimination of All Forms of Discrimination against Women, and the Convention on the Rights of the Child.

hospital on every corner, but it does require narrowing the gap in service availability between rural or minority areas and urban or white areas.

B. Accessibility

Even when health care is *available*, it may not be *accessible*. An accessibility requirement includes physical components, but it also includes economic accessibility. From 2002 to 2003, approximately one-third of the population lacked health insurance for at least part of the year, and in 2006, 15.8 percent of the population lacked health insurance for the full year (Families USA 2004).[10] Because meaningful access to health care without insurance is extremely limited, these numbers demonstrate a significant lack of health care accessibility in the United States. Moreover, even those with health insurance are frequently subject to large copayments or pharmaceutical bills that preclude true economic access to health care. The PPACA's goal is to decrease these numbers substantially, and it introduces welcome changes, such as banning the practice of denying insurance to those with pre-existing conditions. Although any decrease in the numbers of people who do not have access to health services is welcomed, there will still be millions of people who remain uninsured because the bill does not provide universal coverage.

The uninsured receive less preventive care, less appropriate care for chronic illnesses, and fewer hospital services when admitted (Institute of Medicine 2002). They are also more likely to die prematurely. Because they do not enjoy the benefit of negotiated discounts or set fee schedules, they tend to pay more for health services than those with insurance (Wielawski 2000). Ironically, people without insurance pick up a large portion of the nation's health care tab. In 2001, the uninsured spent $80.1 billion on health care (Hadley and Holahan 2003).

Overall, the lowest-income patients and those with chronic health conditions end up carrying the greatest health care burden as a percentage of their family income. The inequity of the U.S. system is reflected in the World Health Organization's statistical analysis comparing health systems around the world: the United States and Fiji tie, thus sharing the positions of fifty-fourth and fifty-fifth in terms of the fairness of financial contribution (World Health Organization 2000). This situation

---

[10] Those lacking health insurance for at least part of the year included only those under the age of 65, because that is the population ineligible for Medicare. The numbers vary by state; fourteen states had more than one out of three uninsured (Texas was highest, with 43.4 percent of the population uninsured).

contravenes human rights principles as set forth in the CESCR's guideline that "poorer households should not be disproportionately burdened with health expenses as compared to richer households" (CESCR 2000, ¶ 12(b)(iii); Hadley and Holahan 2003).

In addition to financial accessibility and inequity issues, the U.S. system includes barriers to access because of the way in which it is structured. With federal, state, and private funding sources, hundreds of individual insurance plans to choose from, and different referral procedures for different types of delivery systems, obtaining basic care can be a bureaucratic nightmare for patients. The PPACA introduces a change that will require standardization of certain forms, which will make a difference in barriers to access that arise from administrative complexities. But complex forms are just one symptom of an overly complicated system that makes it difficult for people to reach their highest attainable standard of health. When administrative burdens create barriers to accessibility, inhibit the ability to monitor health service delivery, and deprive people of a voice in their own treatment, those complexities become human rights concerns.

C. Acceptability

The United States has a strong history of requiring its physicians and other medical personnel to adhere to minimum ethical guidelines. Although some individual practitioners might violate these requirements, the vast majority of workers in the health profession uphold high ethical standards.

In addition to being ethically guided, however, acceptable health care must be culturally sensitive under international law. Unfortunately, in the U.S. health care system there is a significant gap in the quality of care received by minorities. In 1994, the UN Special Rapporteur on Racism found that in the United States "the consequences of racism and racial discrimination in the field of health are reflected in the disparity in access to health care, the infant mortality rates, and the life expectancy of Whites and Blacks or Latino Americans" (Glélé-Ahanhanzo 1995, ¶ 39). The situation has not improved since his visit. Minorities are more likely to die of cancer and heart disease, less likely to get preventive care and screening, and less likely to receive analgesia in emergency rooms for bone fractures (Smedley et al. 2003). This is not typically a result of deliberate discrimination on the part of individual medical workers but instead reflects systemwide inequalities.

In a country where minorities constitute more than one-quarter of the population (and are projected to constitute one-third by 2010), they represent less than 10 percent of the health care work force (Grant Makers in Health 2002). Although the minority health care problem affects each legal requirement for the right to health, it is particularly relevant to the requirement for culturally acceptable care. Research indicates minority patients have a higher level of comfort when treated by physicians of their own race, and they are more likely to follow through with necessary treatments and seek preventive care when they are satisfied with their physicians (Grant Makers in Health 2002; AAMC 2003). For African Americans, a physician's recommended treatment can be compromised by a "mistrust of health professionals that stems from racial discrimination and the history of segregated and inferior care for minorities" (Smedley et al. 2003, 131).

According to the Pew Health Professions Commission, "a substantial body of literature concludes that culturally sensitive care is good care" (Pew Health Professions Commission 1995, 31). The commission recommended that medical schools increase the number of minority students and integrate cultural sensitivity training into the basic medical curriculum. Increasing the number of minority students has also been shown to increase access to medical services in underserved communities.

Despite increasing concern about diversity issues, the problem remains entrenched in the U.S. health care system. Legal attacks on affirmative action policies have taken their toll; more than 60 percent of public medical schools have experienced declines in black, Latino, and other minority student enrollment since 1994, resulting in a collective decrease of 9.1 percent in the number of minority students enrolled (Smedley et al. 2003). State policies against affirmative action continue to result in declining minority representation in the medical field (AAMC 2003).

Human rights-based reform to the health care system would require all medical institutions to introduce cultural competency training for all medical personnel. It would also go further, requiring institutional changes to ensure that minorities have equal access to primary providers who come to know them and can speak their language or have constant access to interpreters; encouraging the training of minority health professionals; and ensuring institutional monitoring and enforcement of racial equality in treatment. The PPACA provides for some of these changes. For example, it provides scholarship and loan repayment incentives for minorities to enter the health profession, as well as grants for community health workers who can help bridge the gap for minority patients (Russell and

Davenport 2010). However, it remains to be seen whether those initiatives will actually result in increased diversity in the health care work force, and whether the structural problems that result in unequal treatment can be corrected through the PPACA's specific programs and reform measures.

D. Quality

The United States boasts some of the best physicians and most state-of-the-art medical technologies and techniques anywhere. However, despite these achievements, the quality of care delivered to patients varies widely, and high-quality care is unavailable to vast numbers of Americans (Institute of Medicine 2001, 13).

The Institute of Medicine (IOM) has called attention to the growing safety flaws and quality problems in the U.S. health care system.[11] The IOM has divided these quality problems into three categories: *overuse, underuse,* and *misuse* (Institute of Medicine 2001). **Overuse** occurs when health services are provided even though the potential risks outweigh any potential benefits. For example, one study found that 60 percent of patients reporting symptoms associated with the common cold filled prescriptions for antibiotics. **Underuse** stems from lack of insurance and lack of preventive care, including when those who are insured do not seek treatment for which potential benefits outweigh potential risks. One example of underuse is that approximately one-quarter of American children have not received appropriate immunizations. Finally, **misuse** includes errors by medical personnel, which can be difficult to document because instances often go unreported. According to the IOM, however, at least 44,000 Americans die each year due to medical errors, which is more than the number of people who die in car accidents or from HIV-AIDS (Institute of Medicine 2000, 26).

Poor quality health care is expensive. Unnecessary treatments cost money, as does correcting mistreatment and providing treatments that could have been avoided. However, waste and mistreatment are difficult to address under the current system in part because payment arrangements are developed by companies and organizations whose decisions are based on short-term cost containment, not on larger questions about quality of care (Institute of Medicine 2001, 36). Problems in quality

---

[11] The Institute of Medicine was chartered in 1970 as a component of the National Academy of Sciences. See www.iom.edu.

are largely because of the current system design, not because individual providers or products are deficient (Institute of Medicine 2003). Addressing these problems to meet international standards requires more than outcomes assessment performed by experts; it requires shifting public debates about health care reform in the United States.

IV. CONCLUSIONS

Neglect of basic medical services for much of its population and the commodification of health care belies the United States' reputation as a leader in the field of health. Regardless of how the PPACA plays out, the American health care system remains one in which health is viewed as a commodity instead of as a core social system. Reforms rooted in human rights principles can contribute to lasting improvement in the health care situation for the majority of Americans.

A. Health Care Must Be Universally Available and Accessible

Americans living in rural and predominantly minority-inhabited areas must have access to health services. Ensuring access means more than simply extending health insurance to the uninsured, however, and it includes more than the limited, albeit helpful, measures introduced by the PPACA. It also means ensuring that all people have access to health services, including those who are in the country without documentation. Moreover, the type of health coverage provided is as important as the number of people enrolled in a program.

Universal access to health services requires a fundamental change in the way the United States approaches health care. Millions of uninsured and underinsured Americans, minority Americans without access to appropriate services, and rural patients unable to access health care facilities all indicate that market forces simply will not fill gaps in health care coverage. Because the PPACA does not provide for universal coverage, and because it expands upon the market-based failures of the current system, many of these gaps will remain.

B. Increase Quality and Diversity Including Cultural Sensitivity

To meet international standards, the United States must ensure that health care is of good quality and culturally appropriate. This means enforcing existing regulations, expanding cultural competency training and protections for cultural differences, and undertaking institutional change that facilitates greater access to care for minorities. The U.S. government has historically scoffed at international treaty obligations, but as a state party to the International Covenant on the Elimination of All Forms of Racial Discrimination (ICERD), it is nonetheless legally bound to address systematic racial discrimination. In fact, the United States admitted that minorities receive "less adequate access to health insurance and health care," and the expert Committee for ICERD has recommended that the United States ensure the right of everyone to access public and private health care (United States 2000, 20; CERD 2001, ¶398).

The parallel and inferior health care system encountered by many minorities is inconsistent with a universal human right to health. Piecemeal laws created to provide greater access for minority patients are an important step in the process of recognizing the depth of these issues, but a more integral, human rights-based perspective requires placing race disparities in their larger social context and using internationally agreed-upon criteria to evaluate proposed policy solutions.

C. Health Care Policy Needs to Be about the Right to Health

Americans pay more per capita ($7,290 or two and one-half times the OECD average) for health care than the population of any other country in the world and receive far less for the money. The PPACA expands upon the current system in which a tremendous amount of money goes toward private-sector profits rather than toward increasing equity of access to quality care. Rights-based reform does not dictate financing mechanisms – any mixture of private and public funding may meet or fail human rights standards – but it does require that all Americans enjoy the minimum standards of availability, accessibility, acceptability, and quality when it comes to their health care.

All Americans should have access to basic health care as a matter of right, which means stepping back from narrow questions about cost-containment to examine the underlying purpose of the health care system. Framing debates about health care reform as a matter of fundamental rights underscores that people must have a voice in decisions affecting their well-being and demands a participatory reform process where those affected have the opportunity for genuine consultation.

Embracing Roosevelt's dictum that "freedom is no half-and-half affair" returns the human being to the center of health care legislation, policies, and practices. Reforms rooted in human rights begin with the idea that health services are a core social system and that no matter which components make up a particular health system, the overarching goal is to guarantee for everyone the highest attainable standard of physical and mental health. As Virginia Leary said of the United States in the early 1990s, "Tampering slightly with the US health system will not be sufficient" (Leary 1994, 87). The same is true today. Like the civil rights movement, the human rights movement can provide universal and populist language to the cause of health care reform. The time has come for the United States to fully recognize the universality of all human rights and to join others in implementing a health care system that fulfills Franklin D. Roosevelt's vision.

REFERENCES

Aetna Health Inc. v. Davila. 2004. 542 U.S. 200.
African Charter on Human and Peoples' Rights. 1982. OAU Doc. CAB/LEG/67/3 rev. 5; 1520 UNTS 217; 21 ILM 58 (1982).
American Association of Medical Colleges (AAMC). 2003. *Brief of the Association of American Medical Colleges et al. as amici curiae in support of the respondents at 12, Grutter v. Bollinger.* U.S. Supreme Court 2003: No. 02–241.
American Declaration of the Rights and Duties of Man. 1948. O.A.S. Res. XXX, adopted by the Ninth International Conference of American States.
Anderson, Gerard, Uwe Reinhardt, Peter Hussey, and Varduhi Petrosyan. 2003. "It's the Prices, Stupid: Why the United States Is So Different from Other Countries." *Health Affairs* 22(3): 89–105.
Case Western Reserve University. 2004. Press Release. *Case Study Shows Drug Companies Are Top Health Care Lobbyists.* http://www.case.edu/news/2004/3–04/lobbyists.htm.
Center for Economic and Social Rights. 2004. *The Right to Health in the United States of America: What Does It Mean?* New York: Center for Economic and Social Rights.
Committee on Economic, Social and Cultural Rights (CESCR). 2000. General Comment 14, The Right to the Highest Attainable Standard of Health. CESCR, 22nd Sess., para. 4, UN Doc. E/CN.12/2000/4 (2000).
Committee on the Elimination of Racial Discrimination (CERD). 2001. Concluding Observations of the Committee on the Elimination of Racial Discrimination: United States of America. UN Doc. A/56/18 (August 14, 2001).
Commonwealth Fund, The. 2007. *Mirror, Mirror on the Wall: An International Update on the Comparative Performance of American Health Care.* New York: The Commonwealth Fund.
Convention on the Elimination of All Forms of Discrimination against Women (CEDAW). Adopted December 18, 1979, GA res. 34/180, 34 UN GAOR Supp. (No. 46) at 193, UN Doc. A/34/46; 1249 UNTS 13; 19 ILM 33 (1980).
Convention on the Rights of the Child (CRC). Adopted November 20, 1989, GA res. 44/25, annex, 44 UN GAOR Supp. (No. 49) at 167, U.N. Doc. A/44/49 (1989); 1577 UNTS 3; 28 ILM 1456 (1989).

DiFelice v. Aetna U.S. Health Care. 2003. 346 F.3d 442, 453 (CA3 2003) (Becker, J., concurring).

European Social Charter. 1961. Council of Europe ETS 35. http://www.unhcr .org/refworld/docid/3ae6b3784.html .

European Social Charter (Revised). 1996. Council of Europe ETS 163. http://www.unhcr.org/refworld/docid/3ae6b3678.html.

Families USA. 2004. *One in Three: Non-Elderly Americans without Health Insurance, 2002–2003.* Washington, D.C.: Families USA.

Fisher, Elliott, Douglas O. Staiger, Julie P.W. Bynum, and Daniel J. Gottlieb. 2007. "Creating Accountable Care Organizations: The Extended Medical Staff." *Health Affairs* 26: w44–w57.

Garber, Alan. 2004. Cost-Effectiveness and Evidence Evaluation as Criteria for Coverage Policy. *Health Affairs Web Exclusive.* http://content.healthaffairs .org/cgi/content/full/hlthaff.w4.284v1/DC1.

Glélé-Ahanhanzo, Maurice. 1995. *Report by the Special Rapporteur on contemporary forms of racism, racial discrimination, xenophobia and related intolerance, on his mission to the United States of America, October 9–22.* UN Doc. E/CN.4/1995/78/Add.1 (Jan 16).

Grant Makers in Health. 2002. *Training the Health Workforce of Tomorrow, Issue Brief No. 12.* Washington, D.C.: Grant Makers in Health.

Hadley, Jack, and John Holahan. 2003. "How Much Medical Care Do the Uninsured Use and Who Pays for It?" *Health Affairs Web Exclusive* (1): W66–W81.

Hersch, Warern. 2010. "Fitch: PPACA May Hurt Margins." *National Underwriter.* March 25, 2010. http://www.lifeandhealthinsurancenews.com/News/ 2010/3/Pages/Fitch-PPACA-May-Hurt-Margins.aspx.

Hewitt Associates. 2003. http://was4.hewitt.com/hewitt/resource/newsroom/ pressrel/2003/06–23-03.htm.

Howard, Rodney, David M. Kent, Sandeep Vijan, and Timothy P. Hofer. 2005. "Reporting Clinical Trial Results to Inform Providers, Payers, and Consumers." *Health Affairs* 24(6): 1571–81.

Institute of Medicine. 2000. *To Err Is Human: Building a Safer Health System.* Washington, D.C.: National Academies Press.

———. 2001. *Crossing the Quality Chasm: A New Health System for the 21st Century* Washington, D.C.: National Academies Press.

———. 2002. *Care Without Coverage: Too Little, Too Late.* Washington, D.C.: National Academies Press.

———. 2003. *Priority Areas for National Action: Transforming Health Care Quality.* Washington, D.C.: Institute of Medicine.

International Convention on the Elimination of All Forms of Racial Discrimination (ICERD). Adopted December 21, 1965, 660 U.N.T.S. 195 (entered into force January 4, 1969), G.A. Res 2106 (XX), Annex, 20 U.N. GAOR Supp. (No. 14) at 47, U.N. Doc. A/6014 (1966).

International Covenant on Economic, Social, and Cultural Rights (ICESCR). Adopted December 16, 1966, 993 U.N.T.S. 3 (entered into force January 3, 1976), G.A. Res. 2200 (XXI), 21 U.N. GAOR Supp. (No. 16) at 49, UN Doc. A/6316 (1996).

Komaromy, Miriam, Kevin Grumbach, Michael Drake, Karen Vranizan, Nicole Lurie, Dennis Keane, and Andrew B. Bindman. 1996. "The Role of Black and Hispanic Physicians in Providing Health Care for Underserved Populations." *New England Journal of Medicine* 334(20): 1305–10.

Kotlikoff, Laurence, and Christian Hagist. 2005. "Who's Going Broke? Comparing Growth in Healthcare Costs in Ten OECD Countries." *NBER Working Paper No. W11833.* http://ssrn.com/abstract=875666.

Krugman, Paul. 2007. "The Plot Against Medicare." *The New York Times,* April 20.

Leary, Virginia. 1994. "Defining the Right to Health Care." In *Health Care Reform: A Human Rights Approach,* edited by A. Chapman, 87–105. Washington, D.C.: Georgetown University Press.

Organisation for Economic Co-operation and Development (OECD). 2009. *OECD Health Data 2009.* Paris: Organisation for Economic Co-operation and Development.

Patient Protection and Affordable Care Act of 2010 (PPACA). 2010. Pub. L. No. 111–148.

Pegram v. Herdrich. 2000. 530 U.S. 211; 120 S. Ct. 2143; 147 L. Ed. 2d 164.

Pew Health Professions Commission. 1995. *Critical Challenges: Revitalizing the Health Professions for the Twenty-First Century.* San Francisco, CA: University of California.

Plunkett Research, LTD. 2006. *Introduction to the Health Care Industry, Health Expenditures and Services in the US.* http://www.plunkettresearch.com/Industries/HealthCare/HealthCareTrends/tabid/294/Default.aspx.

Roosevelt, Franklin. 1944. *The Public Papers and Addresses of Franklin D. Roosevelt,* Volume 13 1944–45. New York: Harper.

Russell, Leslie, and Karen Davenport. 2010. *How Health Care Reform Will Benefit Hispanic Americans.* Washington, D.C.: Center for American Progress Action Fund.

Smedley, Brian, Adrienne Stith, and Alan Nelson, eds. 2003. *Unequal Treatment: Confronting Racial and Ethnic Disparities in Health Care.* Washington, D.C.: National Academies Press.

Social Security Administration. n.d. *Social Security History: Chapter 3: The Third Round 1943–1950.* Accessed July 7, 2010. http://www.ssa.gov/history/corningchap3.html.

Toebes, Brigit. 1998. *The Right to Health as a Human Right in International Law.* Antwerp: Intersentia-Hart.

United States. 2000. *Reports submitted by States Parties under Article 9 of the Convention, Third Periodic reports of States Parties due in 1999, Addendum, United States of America. Submitted October 10, 2000.* UN Doc. CERD/C/351/Add.1.

United States Code. 2006. Title 42: The Public Health and Welfare. Section 300gg-4.

United States Code. 2006. Title 29: Labor. Section 1144(a).

U.S. Census Bureau. 2003. *Quarterly Financial Report, Third Quarter 2003, Table D, p. xviii. Public Citizen Congress Watch, 2002 Drug Industry Profits:*

Hefty Pharmaceutical Company Margins Dwarf Other Industries. http://www
.citizen.org/documents/Pharma_Report.pdf.

UN Millennium Project Task Force on Child Health and Maternal Health. 2005.
Who's Got the Power? Transforming Health Systems for Women and Children.
http://www.unmillenniumproject.org/documents/maternalchild-complete.pdf.

Universal Declaration of Human Rights (UDHR). 1948. G.A. res. 217A (III), UN
Doc A/810 (1948).

Waxman, Henry. 2006. Analysis: Pharmaceutical Industry Profits Increase by over
$8 Billion After Medicare Drug Plan Goes into Effect. *U.S. House of Representatives.* http://oversight.house.gov/documents/20060919115623-70677.pdf.

Weiss Ratings Inc. 2004. http://www.weissratings.com/News/Ins_HMO/2004
0302hmo.htm.

Wielawski, Irene. 2000. "Gouging the Medically Uninsured: A Tale of Two Bills."
Health Affairs 19(5): 180–85.

World Health Organization. 2000. *The World Health Report 2000 – Health
Systems: Improving Performance.* Geneva: World Health Organization.

Yamin, Alicia Ely. 1996. "Defining Questions: Situating Issues of Power in the
Formulation of a Right to Health under International Law." *Human Rights
Quarterly* 18(2): 398–438.

9

Business and Human Rights: A New Approach to Advancing Environmental Justice in the United States

Joanne Bauer

For years, environmental justice advocates in the United States have relied mainly on domestic regulation and litigation to advance their claims. Recently they have also scored advances by bringing complaints against the U.S. government to international human rights tribunals and treaty bodies, including the Inter-American Commission for Human Rights, the UN Committee on the Elimination of All Forms of Racial Discrimination, and the UN Human Rights Council. These venues have carried new hope to U.S. activists after years of discouraging outcomes in domestic courts, where strict criteria for proof of contamination or of the intent of the offending corporations to discriminate have resulted in few satisfying judgments for victims of industrial pollution.

Alongside these efforts to hold the U.S. government accountable, a social movement has formed that uses the international human rights framework to address environmental degradation at its source – by insisting that polluting enterprises are responsible for complying with international human rights standards. The business and human rights (BHR) movement distinctively claims that international human rights law provides a hard legal benchmark against which companies can be judged and in accordance with which they must act, regardless of whether it is convenient, profitable, or will improve the company's reputation. BHR is conceptually distinct from another, older, and better known movement that seeks some of the same outcomes, namely corporate social responsibility (CSR). BHR insists that corporate compliance with human rights

The author is a senior researcher with the Business & Human Rights Resource Centre. This chapter was written in her personal capacity and not as a representative of the Resource Centre. The views, opinions, and analysis are the author's and not necessarily the same as those of the Resource Centre.

standards be legally obligatory rather than voluntary and an end in itself rather than a path to profit-making.

This chapter examines the promise that BHR holds for environmental justice advocacy in the United States. I will first analyze the distinction between CSR and BHR and demonstrate why CSR without human rights is not up to the task of protecting people from environmental harms. Next, I will address the legal force of corporate responsibility for human rights. Despite the fact that existing international treaty mechanisms refer exclusively to the state as duty bearer, there is an emerging body of soft law binding enterprises to international human rights, as well as a stream of litigation seeking to apply international human rights standards via domestic courts in the United States and elsewhere. I also point to examples of the incorporation of international human rights standards within corporate voluntary initiatives to demonstrate that the progression from soft law to legal norms is under way.

The second half of the chapter considers the application of BHR in the United States. I describe three cases of environmental injustice in the United States that show how BHR can be a useful tool for U.S. environmental groups in two ways. First, human rights provide a framework local community groups can use to unite people affected by the operations of multinational corporations across international borders. Second, BHR advocacy is beginning to generate support in civil society, creating an expectation that companies will integrate human rights considerations throughout their operations, and leading prominent multinationals to take steps to do so.

THE DISTINCTION BETWEEN "CORPORATE SOCIAL RESPONSIBILITY" AND "BUSINESS AND HUMAN RIGHTS"

To understand the BHR movement, it is helpful to compare it to the corporate social responsibility (CSR) movement, the better established and recognized movement that has attracted adherents across the business community. There is no consensus about what CSR is. However, a common element in most definitions is the call for industry to recognize the social consequences of its actions to align business practices with the input of an informed civil society to create a new business model. Rather than focusing on fixing the law, the CSR movement seeks to reform the corporation from within and raise the standards of corporate behavior beyond what is legally required.

Corporate social responsibility is an old idea with roots in the writings of the steel magnate Andrew Carnegie, who believed that the goal of businessmen should be "to do well *in order to* do good." He insisted that it was up to the more fortunate members of society to aid the less fortunate. The wealthy ought to be stewards of their property, holding their money "in trust" for the rest of society. As trustees they were entitled to do with it only what society deemed legitimate. Today, in contrast to Andrew Carnegie's vision, CSR advocates emphasize that virtuous companies will be rewarded in the marketplace, and thus can "do well *by* doing good."

There are several reasons for this trend. First, with the evolution of "globally integrated enterprises" (Palmisano 2006) – companies with large supply chains and global operations serving multiple markets – more companies are doing business in politically and economically fragile countries with weak and often corrupt leaders, who are unwilling or unable to enforce national environmental and labor laws where they exist. Beyond consumers and social justice advocates, who demand that companies operating in these situations meet and exceed legal standards, shareholders and business people concerned with the bottom line recognize the reputational and legal risks of being involved in human rights abuses – directly or indirectly.

Second, the Internet has helped bring corporate social and environmental impact into public view. How socially responsible a company appears not only impacts its brand reputation among consumers but also affects the company's ability to attract and retain employees. No one wants to work for a company that finds itself on a list of "The Meanest Companies of the Year."[1] Thus, the best way to appear good is to be good.

And third, over the last two decades institutions like the UN Global Compact, Business for Social Responsibility, and the International Business Leaders Forum have entered the scene, providing technical support and recognition to companies looking to develop corporate responsibility programs.

Yet for all its success at prodding companies to pay attention to their social and environmental roles, the CSR movement suffers from two fundamental problems. One relates to a lack of standards defining what

---

[1] This list was developed by Greenpeace Switzerland and the Berne Declaration and released at the World Economic Forum in Davos.

counts as corporate responsibility, leaving it up to businesses themselves to decide. The second relates to the overreliance on citizen oversight – sometimes referred to as "civil regulation" (Trebeck 2008, 11) – to make CSR work. These two problems are closely linked: because there are no clear standards for corporate responsibility, civil regulation cannot function well.

Much like Andrew Carnegie's vision, CSR is defined by business executives who make choices about what areas of social responsibility the company will focus on. For example, company executives may choose to contribute to community education, health care, or the arts. Or they may want to collaborate with a nongovernmental organization (NGO) to help educate communities in Africa about the risks of HIV/AIDS, or take steps to encourage staff diversity, or reduce carbon emissions. These are all commendable initiatives. But the problem with an approach that lets business define corporate responsibility is that it lacks common principles and common definitions of what it means to be a responsible business. Ultimately, CSR is whatever companies want it to be.

This ambiguity presents problems not only for stakeholders seeking to hold companies accountable for their actions, but also for businesses themselves. John Ruggie, the UN Special Representative of the Secretary-General for Business and Human Rights, has noted that those companies not adopting a rights-based corporate responsibility program "typically approach the recognition of rights as they would other social expectations, risks, and opportunities, determining which are most relevant to their business operations and devising their policies accordingly" (Ruggie 2007, 26). This discretionary approach leaves companies open to considerable risk, evident in the numerous corporate lawsuits, protests, and strong international criticism directed at companies that do not pay adequate attention to human rights.

The environmental area is where problems associated with a failure to take an integrated human rights approach, as BHR requires, frequently arise. Corporate environmental programs, such as those aimed at reducing greenhouse gas emissions or improving packaging, tend to be among the first CSR initiatives companies undertake for the simple reason that they see a way to profit from them. Companies can create efficiencies – and help the bottom line – while also improving brand image.

Yet these CSR programs also can be used to deflect attention from socially irresponsible practices the company may engage in. Conrad MacKerron of the shareholder advocacy group As You Sow identifies the problems of discretionary CSR in the practices of U.S. retail giant

Walmart. He argues that Walmart's environmental initiatives to reduce waste and improve energy efficiency among its vast network of Chinese suppliers not only ignore but also often come at a cost to workplace health and safety in those factories. These initiatives are expensive: to pressure suppliers to "go solar" or clean up wastewater discharge while making low-priced goods for U.S. consumers is not possible without cutting corners on worker pay and safety. MacKerron also reports on an overlooked consequence of Walmart's green agenda: solar panel makers in China are reportedly dumping silicon tetrachloride, a highly toxic byproduct of polysilicon manufacturing, directly onto fields in Henan Province rather than recycling it (MacKerron 2008).

CSR advocates agree that a "business-decides" approach to corporate responsibility is problematic. But, they counter, companies that practice CSR do operate under constraints: in their practices, they must do what the public expects of them. The concept of CSR rests on the idea that businesses operate with a social contract granted by society. Fulfilling that contract requires businesses to respond not only to their shareholders, but also more generally to civil society. Companies not behaving responsibly in relation to civil society demands risk losing their "social license to operate."

Civil regulation, however, often takes place haphazardly in ways that favor consumers with purchasing power at the expense of more vulnerable members of society. As Katherine Trebeck notes, even in a reasonably well-functioning participatory democracy with a strong civil rights tradition and the capacity to protest safely, citizen regulation is hard to achieve (2008, 8–23). Apathy or indifference can lead to vocal minorities dominating the decision-making process, whereas others may find they do not have the time or means to participate. Too often the inequities within society are replicated so that the "results of civil regulation will skew away from the interests of those affected" (Trebeck 2008, 13). Not unlike the case of Walmart in China, when it comes to CSR and the environment, too often companies are pushed to respond to a particular form of environmentalism reflecting middle-class interests. If CSR for many companies is about building brand value, then absent government regulation or other identifiable standards, consumers with purchasing power are the ones who often end up defining corporate responsibility.

Former U.S. Labor Secretary Robert Reich (2007) similarly expresses concern about the ability of citizens to regulate business behavior. Consumers derive benefits from inexpensive products made with cheap labor or cost-cutting initiatives that can result in harm to the environment and communities besides one's own, Reich argues. Hence, citizen–consumer interests are too conflicted to be counted upon to act as neutral arbiters of what constitutes responsible business. Instead, Reich calls for more government regulation as the only means to ensure that corporations behave responsibly.[2]

In sum, absent adequate domestic legal protections, CSR depends on oversight of business by society. Yet society alone cannot articulate the full range of protections its members need; therefore, business is free to decide whether or not to restrict its harmful impact and exercise its influence and capabilities to protect the rights of workers and communities. There is little incentive to do so if business finds it too difficult or if there is little payoff in the marketplace. For these reasons, human rights advocates have found CSR is not up to the task of preventing harm to people.

The BHR movement has emerged from this dissatisfaction. Its aim is to shift the focus from the *needs* to the *rights* of the affected community – and from acts of charity by businesses toward full accountability through international law.

Business and Human Rights – The Shift to "Rights" and "Accountability"

Whether it has a robust CSR program or not, nearly every company has mechanisms to ensure it complies with applicable local and national laws. However, as Phil Rudolph of the law firm Foley Hoag writes: "Literal compliance with the law is of course necessary. . . . But mere compliance is no longer likely to be sufficient to protect companies from potential moral and legal liability" (Rudolph 2004). What the human rights framework offers is a set of international legal principles to guide business conduct additionally with respect to its impact on human rights.

Applying human rights norms to businesses substantially raises the bar, compared both to CSR and to local and national laws. It requires paying attention to all of the human rights impacts of all business practices upon all stakeholders, who are broadly defined. In contrast to CSR, no act is good enough in and of itself or in isolation to fulfill a company's obligations. Whereas CSR adherents talk of the "business case" that can compel businesses to do the right thing, a human rights approach

---

[2] John Ruggie has responded to this critique of CSR, asserting that Reich has it "exactly backwards . . . If citizens and politicians were prepared to enact domestic legislation, there would be less need to rely on CSR in the first place" (Ruggie as cited in *The Economist*, 2007).

emphasizes that human rights are guaranteed by international law, hence, a company is obliged to "respect, protect, and fulfill" them regardless of whether it is profitable to do so. As Irene Khan, then secretary-general of Amnesty International, noted in a 2005 speech:

> Human rights are rooted in law. Respecting and protecting them was never meant to be an optional extra, a matter of choice. It is expected and required. It should be part of the mainstream of any company's strategy.
>
> (Khan 2005)

The conceptual grounding for assigning human rights responsibilities to business lies in the preamble of the Universal Declaration of Human Rights (UDHR), which calls upon "every individual and every organ of society" to promote and respect human rights – as evidence that international standards require companies to address human rights. The BHR movement builds on the argument that, in the words of Louis Henkin, "Every individual and every organ of society excludes no one, no company, no market, no cyberspace. The Universal Declaration applies to them all" (Henkin 1999, 25).

The assertion that businesses have human rights responsibilities under international law may seem to be a stretch: states, not corporations, are the explicit subject of international human rights law. John Ruggie underscored this point in his first interim report to the UN Human Rights Council. There, he assessed the Norms on the Responsibilities of Transnational Corporations and Other Business Enterprises with Regard to Human Rights, adopted by the United Nations Sub-Commission on the Promotion and Protection of Human Rights in 2003. He criticized the Norms "exercise" as being "engulfed by its own doctrinal excesses," specifically the drafters' claim that the Norms are both a restatement of international law and the first "non voluntary initiative." Because companies are not the explicit subject of international human rights law, Ruggie argued that both propositions cannot be right (2006).

Ruggie subsequently set out to define corporate responsibility for human rights by "identifying and fostering standards and processes within and among relevant entities – public and private national and international – that will make them more effective in dealing with human rights" (Ruggie 2010, 3–4). He has investigated paths that could be taken to improve corporate observance of international human rights – including mainstreaming human rights law into corporate law, investor-state contracts, and bilateral investment treaties. By the end of his first term in April 2008, Ruggie had developed a policy framework establishing as one of its three pillars the "corporate responsibility to respect" human rights (Ruggie 2008). This framework was adopted unanimously by the council, which extended Ruggie's appointment for a second three-year term with the mandate to operationalize the framework. Although Ruggie's language of "responsibility" and "respect" for companies versus "duties" and "protect" for states implies lighter obligations on companies than human rights activists had hoped for, the signal that human rights are integral to corporate practice is unmistakable.

Ruggie's appointment in 2005 built on a decades-long series of UN efforts to develop principles for the conduct of transnational businesses in response to their rise internationally.[3] Additionally, the Organisation for Economic Co-operation and Development (OECD) and the International Labour Organization (ILO) have developed guidelines recognizing the responsibility of companies to respect human rights; both instruments have been revised several times and remain in active use today.[4] In 1999, then-UN Secretary General Kofi Annan created the UN Global Compact, which recognizes that companies should respect international human rights standards and today has more than 5,200 corporate members. Beyond these key initiatives, there are many national, regional, and international soft law mechanisms establishing human rights legal obligations for companies, both direct and indirect.[5]

Over the past two decades a number of states – including the United Kingdom, Denmark, France, Sweden, and Australia – have enacted legislation making corporate disclosure mandatory rather than voluntary for a number of social and environmental impacts related in one way or another to human rights.[6] In July 2010, in a victory for the BHR

---

[3] Some of these early efforts, for example, the UN Centre for Transnational Corporations (UNCTC), began referencing the need for businesses to respect human rights in the mid-1970s (Jerbi 2009).

[4] In a significant advance toward accountability, in the 2000 revision of the OECD Guidelines for Multinational Enterprises, a dispute resolution mechanism via the establishment of National Contact Points (NCPs) was introduced; as of January 2010, of the ninety cases that have been filed with NCPs, 85 percent refer to human rights and supply chain violations and more than half refer to environmental impact (OECD Watch 2010, 12).

[5] These have been compiled by the Castan Centre for International Law's project on "Multinational Corporations and Human Rights." See http://www.law.monash.edu .au/castancentre/projects/mchr/.

[6] Two examples are the UK Companies Act of 2006, which requires company directors to consider environmental and social impacts and requires that the largest listed companies disclose those impacts; and Denmark's Social Responsibility for Large Businesses Law of 2009, requiring the 1,100 largest Danish companies to include information on their corporate responsibility policies and practices in their annual financial reports. This

movement, the U.S. Senate passed the financial services reform law containing two landmark provisions for company disclosure of U.S. companies: one regarding corporate payments to governments for access to oil, gas, and minerals; and a second regarding the importation of minerals from conflict-ridden Congo. Moreover, human rights criteria have been incorporated into loan review by the International Finance Corporation, an arm of the World Bank supporting private enterprise in the developing world.

Litigation in U.S. courts under the Alien Torts Claims Act (ATCA) also has given fuel to the BHR movement. Although not addressing human rights violations within the United States itself, this litigation has helped advance the idea that multinational corporations are legally bound by some elements of international human rights law. Part of the Judiciary Act of 1789, the ATCA allows non-U.S. citizens to file suit in U.S. district courts for violations of either a U.S. treaty or customary international law (including human rights law). After lying mostly dormant for nearly two centuries, ATCA was used in 1980 in *Filártiga v. Peña-Irala* when a U.S. court allowed a Paraguayan family to sue the former Paraguayan official who tortured their son.

Beginning in 1993, victims began to bring suits against U.S.-based multinational companies for "crimes against humanity," often involving environmental damage. Major cases against businesses include *Aguinda v. Texaco* (in which victims alleged that Texaco had spilled more than 3,000 gallons of oil per day during its operations in the Oriente region of Ecuador between 1964 and 1992), *Doe v. Unocal* (in which Burmese plaintiffs sued Unocal for working with the Burmese military to conscript forced labor, kill, abuse, and rape villagers while working on the Yadana gas pipeline project), and U.S. *Saro-Wiwa v. Shell* (in which Ogoni villagers in the Niger River Delta region of Nigeria accused the Shell Corporation of complicity in the government's torture and execution of environmental protesters of Shell's operations). To date there are just more than fifty corporate ATCA cases, most of which have been dismissed, with two victories for the corporate defendant and some fifteen cases still pending (Stephens 2008, 813).

Judith Chomsky, an attorney in the Shell case, declared: "The fortitude shown by our clients in the 13-year struggle to hold Shell accountable has helped establish a principle that goes beyond Shell and Nigeria – that

2009 law follows Danish laws passed in 1995 and 2001 requiring company reporting on environmental impact.

corporations, no matter how powerful, will be held to universal human rights standards" (Center for Constitutional Rights 2009). Despite the diverse outcomes of these cases,[7] ATCA cases have gone a long way to establish the principle that corporations can be held accountable in courts for violations of some components of international human rights law. According to John Ruggie, "the mere fact of providing the possibility of a remedy has made a difference" (Ruggie 2006, ¶62). Knowledgeable observers believe the operations and oversight of these companies have evolved considerably to the point where they would handle these situations much differently today, in part because of the influence of ATCA (Goldfarb 2008).

The best evidence of BHR's acceptance is the fact that companies themselves increasingly recognize their human rights responsibilities. One sign of this is the growing number of companies adopting corporate human rights policies across a range of sectors.[8] Yet the presence of a corporate human rights policy does not guarantee good corporate behavior. In fact, often a company will take this step following negative publicity, protests, or legal action. Nonetheless, by adopting a human rights policy the company demonstrates that it recognizes it has human rights responsibilities, defines them as such, and in so doing implies that it strives for consistent good conduct throughout its operations across the whole range of obligations defined by international human rights standards.

Why do companies pay attention to human rights? For some, it is a matter of principle, but for others it is a practical necessity. According to Avery, Short, and Regaignon, "Consumers, investors, local communities and other stakeholders are on the lookout for breaches of those international standards and are quick to bring them to global attention: this is what has been described as the 'goldfish bowl' world in which multinational corporations now operate" (2006). When a company is involved in human rights abuses, it risks not only legal action, but also protests against its facilities, loss of reputation and business, and a decline

---

[7] *Aguinda v. Texaco* was dismissed because the court deemed Ecuador to be a more appropriate venue. In *Doe v. Unocal*, Unocal settled for an undisclosed amount in 2005, following a ruling from the U.S. Court of Appeals that a corporation could be found complicit in a human rights violation if it provided "knowing practical assistance or encouragement which had a substantial effect on the perpetration of a crime." In June 2009, Shell agreed to settle the dispute with the Ogoni villagers. For more details on these and other corporate legal accountability cases, in both the U.S. and abroad, see: http://www.business-humanrights.org/LegalPortal/Home.

[8] The Business & Human Rights Resource Centre has identified more than 270 companies that have adopted human rights policies (BHRRC 2010).

in morale among employees. Even if a company is found not guilty of involvement in a rights violation in a court of law, it can be found guilty in the court of public opinion, which can be just as harmful to business.

Until an international treaty is developed explicitly assigning human rights duties to corporations, corporate respect for human rights is not strictly binding under international law. But corporate responsibility for human rights has already become what Ruggie calls "a well-established social norm" (Ruggie 2009). Louis Henkin and colleagues have argued that a norm is law when actors orient themselves to it with a sense of legal obligation (Henkin , Neuman, Orentlicher and Leebron 1999,295–305). No matter the reason for corporate recognition of human rights respon- sibilities, by joining voluntary initiatives (such as the Global Compact) or by adopting a corporate human rights policy, companies acknowledge international human rights standards as binding. In doing so, they push the soft law of BHR in the direction of hard law.

Bringing Business and Human Rights Home

How can the developments described in the previous section be put to use to advance the cause of environmental justice in the United States? In this section, I examine three cases of community struggles against polluting industries in the United States and the diverse ways in which the com- munities have made use of BHR, specifically: (1) residents of Mossville, Louisiana opposing fourteen petrochemical companies (all but one of which are U.S. companies) whose factories border their community; (2) the Western Shoshone of Nevada opposing the Canadian mining com- pany Barrick Gold and other mining companies; and (3) residents of Kanawha Valley, West Virginia opposing German-based Bayer Crop- Science Institute, whose local factory produces methyl isocyanate (MIC), the same chemical involved in the Bhopal, India industrial disaster of 1984.

The cases are drawn from the Business & Human Rights Resource Centre's website, a clearinghouse on the human rights impact of more than 5,000 companies worldwide.[9] They involve multinational

---

[9] Because "environmental rights" are not clearly enunciated in the International Bill of Rights, the criterion for the Resource Centre's "environment" category is corporate environmental harm that impacts the right to health (ICESCR article 12), food (ICESCR general comment 12), housing (ICESCR article 11), and access to water (ICESCR general comment 15). Depending on the case, other rights are often also affected, including the right to life (ICCPR article 6), liberty and security of person (ICCPR article 9), freedom

companies, both American and foreign, thus creating the potential to use international human rights law as a focus for advocacy to unite communities similarly impacted by a multinational corporate polluter. The ways in which each community aligns its struggle with human rights and mobilizes international support varies, as does the extent to which each community utilizes the BHR movement.

Mossville, Louisiana. Located in southern Louisiana in a region dubbed "Cancer Alley," Mossville is a historically African-American community surrounded by fourteen industrial facilities, including the largest concentration of vinyl production facilities in the country, an oil refinery, a coal-fired power plant, and several petrochemical manufacturers (Mossville Environmental Action Now 2007). The factories, which allegedly release millions of tons of toxins through air and groundwater contamination, are owned by: ConocoPhillips (oil refinery); Entergy (coal-fired power plant); Georgia Gulf (vinyl manufacturing facility); Lyondell (chemical manufacturing facility); PPG Industries (vinyl manufacturing facility); and Sasol (chemical manufacturing facility).

Studies conducted by the U.S. government and by independent researchers have found a high incidence of cancer and respiratory ailments within the community, which both medical researchers and community activists tie to dioxin poisoning by these industries. Community activists – organized as Mossville Environmental Action Now (MEAN) – fault the U.S. government for permitting the siting of these facilities so close to the residents. They blame the U.S. Environmental Protection Agency (EPA) and the U.S. Agency for Toxic Substances and Disease Registry (ATSDR) for carrying out health studies showing dioxin levels at three times the national average while leaving the source of the contamination unnamed.

Since the mid-1990s, MEAN has fought back against industrial polluters, notably in 1994 winning relocation for many families following a Condea Vista spill of 1 million pounds of ethylene dichloride that caused well-water contamination. After Condea Vista was acquired by the South African-based Sasol Corporation in 2002, the South African NGO environmental justice group Groundwork teamed up with MEAN as well as with the Boston-based South Africa Exchange Program on Environmental Justice. Together, they formed a united front against Sasol, which had

of thought, conscience, and religion (ICCPR article 18), freedom of expression (ICCPR article 19), adequate standard of living (ICESCR article 11), and the right to take part in cultural life (ICESCR article 15).

just gained a listing on the New York Stock Exchange. Their purpose was to inform investors of the company's "environmentally destructive" practices.[10] As Groundwork framed the injustice in human rights terms, this cross-border collaboration served as an early instance of a U.S. environmental justice group engaging in the then-fledgling BHR movement.

MEAN's engagement with BHR advanced when two lawyers who had helped the communities fight corporate polluters set up a public interest law firm, Advocates for Environmental Human Rights (AEHR), in New Orleans. MEAN began collaborating with AEHR, marking the beginning of an advocacy strategy clearly framed in terms of human rights.

In addition to documenting the impact on human health of the vinyl production facilities, MEAN and AEHR have engaged in shareholder advocacy to advance their human rights claims. In May 2008, residents attended a ConocoPhillips shareholder's meeting where they distributed a report on the environmental and health impact of the oil refinery and issued a statement in support of a shareholder resolution submitted by the Church Pension Fund for "corporate accountability to communities." The resolution called upon Conoco-Phillips to report how it will ensure that it is accountable for the environmental impact of its operations, noting that Conoco-Phillips ranked third in 2002 among the worst U.S. corporate air polluters "in terms of the amount and toxicity of pollution, and the numbers of people exposed to it" (Church Pension Fund 2008). In addition, AEHR has partnered with the New York-based Interfaith Center on Corporate Responsibility (ICCR), a coalition of 275 faith-based institutional investors that pushes companies to integrate human rights and other ethical practices into corporate and investor decisions. In June 2009, AEHR hosted an ICCR delegation to the region to assess the environmental and health impacts of the companies in the area, and the ICCR continues to support AEHR's efforts.

In that same year, AEHR took MEAN's case against the U.S. government to the Inter-American Commission for Human Rights. In March 2010, the commission agreed to accept the case, marking the first time it had taken jurisdiction over a case of environmental justice in the United States. The petitioners claim the U.S. government violated residents' rights to racial equality and privacy. As with the Western Shoshone case mentioned in the following discussion, a favorable ruling by the Inter-American Commission would undoubtedly bolster international recognition of the Mossville residents' human rights claims against the industrial polluters.

[10] See http://saepej.igc.org/.

The connection communities in Louisiana's Cancer Alley are making between their cause and those of groups in other parts of the world is revealed on the website of the Louisiana Bucket Brigade. This group assists Mossville and other Louisiana communities in conducting their own epidemiological studies to document the effects of industrial pollution. In 2009, the top story in the "Spotlight" column of its website read: "Victory Settlement in *Wiwa v. Shell* case!" and linked to a PDF of the settlement that compensated the Nigerian plaintiffs in the case.

The Business & Human Rights Resource Centre also helped increase the visibility of the Mossville case and framed it in human rights terms. The Resource Centre's database of individual companies' human rights impact is used globally by advocacy groups, journalists, investors, and UN officials, as well as by industry managers. In July 2007, when MEAN and AEHR published a detailed report (MEAN/AEHR 2007) about the poisoning based on U.S. government data, the Resource Centre contacted each of the companies named in the report, inviting them to respond to the allegations. Entergy, Georgia Gulf, PPG Industries, and Sasol responded: all claimed the mantle of environmental responsibility and either argued the toxic emissions were not as severe as the report claimed or placed the blame on facilities other than their own. ConocoPhillips and Lyondell did not respond, which the Resource Centre also reported alongside the original report.[11] The invitation to the companies to respond publicly to the allegations – and the framing of those allegations in human rights terms – put the companies on notice that they were being watched, and that the public expects them to comply with international human rights standards.

AEHR is a member of the U.S. Human Rights Network, which seeks to develop a human rights movement that can influence U.S. government policy to observe international human rights standards. AEHR's membership provides additional opportunities to develop its human rights strategy as well as connect with like-minded groups to advance its struggle against corporate polluters.

Western Shoshone. The Western Shoshone, whose U.S. territorial claims extend from Southern Idaho through eastern Nevada to the Mojave Desert of California, are engaged in an ongoing dispute over their land rights. The dispute centers on the contemporary validity of the 1863

---

[11] To view the responses see: http://www.business-humanrights.org/Documents/Mossvillereport-July2007.

Treaty of Ruby Valley, which recognized the Western Shoshone as land-holders. Because the land sits upon rich mineral deposits and is the source of 64 percent of the gold mined in the United States and the second-largest gold mining region in the world, it is highly sought after. The federal government claims 90 percent of the territory to be "federal lands" based on the theory of "gradual encroachment" (i.e., that occupation by non-natives nullifies Western Shoshone claims to the lands).

Numerous mining companies have won concessions from the U.S. government and are now operating on these lands. Through the Western Shoshone Defense Project (WSDP), the Western Shoshone have mounted a legal battle over their ancestral lands, both in U.S. courts and in international human rights bodies. In 1993, Mary and Carrie Dann, two Western Shoshone leaders, took their case to the Inter-American Commission of Human Rights. They argued that the American Declaration of the Rights and Duties of Man (a precursor to the UDHR) binds all member states of the Organization of American States (OAS), including the United States. They contended that the decision of the U.S. government to grant concessions to Barrick Gold (a Canadian multinational) and other companies violated five rights under the declaration: the right to property, the right to equality under the law, the right to cultural integrity, the right to self-determination, and the rights to judicial protection and due process of law. The commission rendered a ruling favorable to the Shoshone in January 2003, recommending that the U.S. government find judicial and legislative remedies for infringement of Western Shoshone property rights consistent with the declaration.

In 2000 and 2005, WSDP petitioned the Geneva-based Committee on the Elimination of All Forms of Racial Discrimination (CERD) for urgent action with respect to the allegedly unlawful operations of transnational corporations on Shoshone lands. In March 2006, CERD ruled that the Canadian government (the home country of Barrick Gold) should take "appropriate . . . measures to prevent the acts of transnational corporations on indigenous territories," and the U.S. government should stop all commercial activities on tribal land (Rizvi 2007). WSDP's Julie Cavenaugh-Bill has noted the importance of the human rights framework to their struggle: "International human rights laws and bodies are essential to receiving justice. We need international mechanisms to serve as an independent review of the inadequacies of the US judicial system and federal Indian law" (Ford Foundation 2004, 34).

So far, these victories at the Inter-American Commission and CERD appear to have had little influence in U.S. courts, where judges have been unsympathetic to cultural rights claims. In November 2008, WSDP sought an injunction against the Cortez Hills Expansion Project of Barrick Gold. The project involves explosions and open-pit mining on the sacred site of Mt. Tenabo, with substantial environmental and cultural rights implications.[12] WSDP filed a lawsuit in a Nevada federal court against the U.S. Bureau of Land Management over its approval of the Cortez Hills project, and subsequently Barrick Gold voluntarily joined the suit as a defendant-intervenor. In February 2009, the judge rejected WSDP's application for preliminary injunction, arguing that the costs of the injunction outweigh the religious and cultural concerns. Later that year on appeal, WSDP won a preliminary injunction. But in June 2010, the Ninth Circuit Court of Appeals issued a decision affirming the lower court's decision and remanding the environmental claims to a lower court for further proceedings under the National Environmental Policy Act.[13]

BHR's potential in this case rests mainly with its power to bring international pressure to bear on multinationals like Barrick Gold to comply with international human rights standards. Despite the resistance of U.S. courts to human rights arguments, the rulings of international human rights bodies are significant in legitimizing the Western Shoshone's claims, which in turn strengthens their efforts to mobilize international support. An international coalition of NGOs has been pushing the company to cease its harmful operations worldwide, including the Cortez Hills project. The coalition created an online portal featuring news stories, testimonies, and background information related to Barrick Gold's activities internationally (protestbarrick.net), and in 2007 the coalition began organizing a "Global Day of Action against Barrick Gold" (May 2) as a way of "uniting once isolated communities . . . in their actions to halt big mining projects." This international advocacy network presents an opportunity for the Western Shoshone to develop a corporate responsibility front in its human rights campaign to compliment its legal battles against the U.S. government.

Notably, the Western Shoshone are active in the Economic, Cultural and Social Rights Network (ESCR-net), a coalition of NGOs around the

---

[12] In addition to denying Shoshone access to its spiritual site, there are concerns about the disruption of gravesites and the pollution of land, air, and water. Reportedly, the company plans "to construct a large cyanide heap leach processing facility, dump over 1.5 billion tons of mine waste on Mt. Tenabo, and pump over 16.5 billion gallons of groundwater from Mt. Tenabo to keep the pit dry for mining" (Wolf 2009).

[13] A full account of this case is available at: http://www.business-humanrights.org/ Categories/Lawlawsuits/Lawsuitsregulatoryaction/LawsuitsSelectedcases/BarrickGold lawsuitreWesternShoshonetribesUSA.

world that has provided input into the Ruggie process. Also, an award-winning documentary on the Western Shoshone case was featured at a two-day conference on Ruggie's UN Policy Framework, organized in 2009 by the UN Office of the High Commissioner for Human Rights (OHCHR).

In response to all these pressures, Barrick Gold has dedicated significant space on its website to corporate responsibility, making explicit reference to its commitment to international human rights and, in particular, defending its involvement with the Western Shoshone.

Kanawha Valley, West Virginia. When a 1984 industrial explosion involving the chemical methyl isocyanate (MIC) occurred at a Union Carbide facility in Bhopal, India, killing and injuring thousands of people, citizens of the Kanawha Valley in West Virginia took special notice. Dubbed by locals as the "chemical capital of the world," Kanawha Valley is the home to Bayer CropSciences Institute, the German pesticide manufacturer that houses the largest stockpile of MIC in North America. In the aftermath of Bhopal and following an incident of chemical leakage at the West Virginia facility (then owned by Union Carbide), local residents formed People Concerned about MIC to raise awareness of the dangers of the substance and the potential for a Bhopal-like disaster to happen in their backyard. This mobilization is documented in the 1991 film, *Chemical Valley*. The film makes specific rights claims that the company practiced racism in siting the facility and denied the community access to information while threatening local health and safety. The film also accused the company of sowing division between local company employees who wanted to preserve their jobs and livelihoods, and other community members.

In August 2008, an explosion *did* take place in the pesticide unit, which uses MIC as feedstock. The explosion killed two workers. A Congressional subcommittee investigation found that a 5,000-pound vessel was thrown fifty feet north during the explosion, just missing a storage tank holding seven tons of MIC. The Chemical Safety Board investigation revealed numerous safety lapses at the plant that day. The investigations also turned up an effort by CEO William Buckner to use chemical plant security regulations developed as part of American's antiterrorism measures to hide information about the incident. In August 2009, Bayer CropSciences announced it would decrease its stockpile of MIC by 80 percent and shut down production of the two MIC-based pesticide ingredients.

Throughout the twenty-five year history of People Concerned about MIC, the West Virginian group has maintained its connection to victims in Bhopal, recently hosting a May 2009 forum featuring three residents from Bhopal who participated as part of a twenty-five city tour across the United States sponsored by the International Campaign for Justice in Bhopal. Although this sustained international connection might have spurred the community to adopt the human rights framework as a strategy for corporate accountability, it has not yet done so. The early successes the movement had in creating the foundation for key statutory provisions, including the Community Right to Know and Emergency Planning laws and the Toxic Release Inventory, might have obviated the need to look beyond U.S. legislative remedies (Larson 2010).

Today, Kanawha Valley waits restlessly for the company to make good on its promise to reduce its stockpile of MIC as advocates attempt to draw attention to the persistent dangers of the remaining stockpile. Given increasing international expectations that companies comply with human rights standards, the community could benefit from adopting a BHR strategy. In 2008, the German-based Coalition against Bayer Dangers (CBD) interviewed Maya Nye, executive director of People Concerned about MIC. Nye's responses point to the potential for even greater transnational advocacy underpinned by the concept of human rights. When asked by the German interviewer what groups from "outside" could do to support the people of Kanawha Valley, Nye replied: "Groups from outside can support us by keeping the pressure on . . . [k]eeping us informed on how other organizations and countries are dealing with similar issues . . . providing us with studies or ideas of economic alternatives to dirty jobs that would be viable in our community. One of the biggest forms of assistance from outside groups would be forming a coalition for environmental justice" (Nye 2008).

CONCLUSION

Twenty years ago, Robert Bullard articulated an environmental justice framework in his seminal book *Dumping in Dixie*. Forcefully arguing that industrial pollution disproportionately impacts poor African Americans, he called for new legislation – a "Fair Environmental Protection Act" – that would build upon the Civil Rights Act of 1964. Today, the vulnerability of poor, disenfranchised communities to industrial pollution persists. Civil rights has taken us only so far – more is needed.

The promise of the international human rights framework to prevent industrial harm to all communities is now greater than ever. Embracing international human rights does not require civil rights activists to abandon the principles of the civil rights movement. In fact, the characteristics of Bullard's framework align well with those of the BHR movement, reflecting the principle of nondiscrimination, the duties of companies to prevent harm, and the rights of victims to access justice (Bullard 2000, 121–25). But Bullard's framework requires recognition that civil rights activists might have been unwitting accomplices to the long-held belief in American exceptionalism – and, in turn, that American-based human rights activists have for too long turned their backs on human rights victims at home.

The cases analyzed in this chapter reveal four ways in which communities in the United States are already using elements of the BHR approach to hold companies accountable for environmental harms: (1) by building international solidarity among communities similarly impacted by a single multinational corporation to seek accountability and pressure the company into integrating human rights considerations into its operations; (2) by bringing their cases to international human rights bodies and winning a judgment, thereby lending further legitimacy to their case, both domestically and internationally; (3) by working with investors concerned about corporate human rights abuses to develop shareholder advocacy campaigns; and (4) by getting involved in the international standard-setting process around BHR to push for a human rights-based accountability mechanism.

The cases show that communities in the United States are beginning to grasp what their counterparts in developing countries have long understood: the critical importance of developing an international legal and advocacy strategy to combat injustice. Clarice Friloux is a community leader in Grand Bois, Louisiana, another "Cancer Alley" town. In reflecting upon her experience fighting ExxonMobil and other corporate offenders in litigation that tore her community apart, Friloux recounts the moment when she realized that their human rights had been violated:

A year into the litigation I began to think in terms of our human rights being abused. I used to think it was just because most of us are Native Americans. Then when I started meeting other communities, I began to realize that we were not the only ones. Most of the communities who have environmental problems like ours are low-income and minority. When I started seeing these communities being destroyed just like mine, I realized that for all of us, our rights are being abused. The facility and the oil companies have taken away our clean air and clean water – every basic thing that human beings need.

(Friloux 2000)

As with many other victims, the connection with human rights is made at the moment of identification with similarly harmed communities. In turn, community-to-community linkages enable victims to trace a pattern of abuse by a corporate offender based in one country for abuses committed in other countries and thereby strengthen the case for human rights protections beyond borders. As international norms assigning human rights responsibilities to corporations strengthen, U.S. environmental justice advocates will have even greater leverage to insist that companies adhere to international human rights standards and to hold them accountable.

For multinationals, international human rights advocacy networks present a strong incentive to act proactively. Unlike governments accused of human rights abuses, multinationals have a broader set of stakeholders extending far beyond national lines: consumers, suppliers, employees, business-to-business clients, shareholders, government regulators, international organizations, world media, and others. As global economic players, companies understand they must safeguard their international reputations; increasingly they are realizing that responding to human rights concerns is integral to doing so. It is in the company's interest to have in place the internal mechanisms (e.g., a human rights policy, routine human rights impact assessments, procedures to uphold the principle of free prior and informed consent) that demonstrate a genuine commitment to respecting human rights and keep it out of trouble. This should be welcome news for shareholders and communities everywhere.

REFERENCES

Avery, Chris, Annabel Short, and Gregory Tzeutschler Regaignon. 2006. "Why All Companies Should Address Human Rights." September. http://www.business-humanrights.org/Links/Repository/228498.

Bullard, Robert D. 2000. *Dumping in Dixie: Race, Class and Environmental Quality*. 3rd Edition. Boulder, CO: Westview Press.

Business & Human Rights Resource Centre (BHRRC). 2010. Human Rights Policies section. http://www.business-humanrights.org/Documents/Policies.

Center for Constitutional Rights. 2009. Press Release. http://ccrjustice.org/newsroom/press-releases/settlement-reached-human-rights-cases-against-royal-dutch/shell.

Church Pension Fund. 2008. "Community Accountability 2008 – Conoco Phillips." http://www.ehumanrights.org/docs/Community-Accountability-Shareholder-Phillips.pdf.

(The) Economist. 2007. "In Search of the Good Company." September 6.

Ford Foundation. 2004. *Close to Home: Case Studies of Human Rights Work in the United States*. New York: The Ford Foundation.

Friloux, Clarice. 2000. "Big Oil in Louisiana and a Community's Bottom Line." *Human Rights Dialogue* 2(2). http://www.cceia.org/resources/publications/dialogue/2_02/articles/617.html.

Goldfarb, Michael. 2008. "Open Wounds." *The American Lawyer*. http://www.law.com/jsp/law/PubArticlePrinterFriendly.jsp?id=1202424880572.

Henkin, Louis. 1999. "The Universal Declaration at 50 and the Challenge of Global Markets." *Brooklyn Journal of International Law* 25(1): 17–25.

Henkin, Louis, Gerald L. Neuman, Diane F. Orentlicher, and David Leebron. 1999. *Human Rights*. New York: Foundation Press.

Jerbi, Scott. 2009. "Business and Human Rights at the UN: What Might Happen Next." *Human Rights Quarterly* 31(2): 299–320.

Khan, Irene. 2005. "Should Human Rights Be Your Business?" Speech delivered to Japan Association of Corporate Executives, Keizai Doyukai, Tokyo, June 2, 2005. http://asiapacific.amnesty.org/apro/APROweb.nsf/pages/IreneKhan_KeizaiDoyukai.

Larson, Denny. 2010. "West Virginia: Where the Chemicals Run Deep." Air Hugger blog, July 30. http://airhugger.wordpress.com/2010/07/30/west-virginia-where-the-chemicals-run-deep/.

MacKerron, Conrad. 2008. "Prius Envy and the Greening of Wal-Mart: A Blind Spot for the Human Cost." Green Biz.com, June 29. http://www.greenbiz.com/blog/2008/06/29/prius-envy-and-greening-wal-mart-blind-spot-human-cost.

Mossville Environmental Action Now (MEAN) and Americans for Environmental Human Rights. 2007. "Industrial Sources of Dioxin Poisoning in Mossville, Louisiana: A Report Based on the Government's Own Data." July. http://www.corporatecrimereporter.com/documents/mossville.pdf.

Nye, Maya (Executive Director, People Concerned about MIC). 2008. Interviewed by the Coalition against Bayer Dangers. November 25. http://www.cbgnetwork.org/2744.html.

OECD Watch. 2010. Quarterly Case Update. February 1–12. http://oecdwatch.org/publications-en/Publication_3338/at_download/fullfile.

Palmisano, Samuel J. 2006. "The Globally Integrated Enterprise." *Foreign Affairs* 85(3): 127–36.

Power, Stephen. 2009. "Political Alliances Shift in Fight Over Climate Bill." *The Wall Street Journal*. October 6.

Reich, Robert. 2007. *Supercapitalism: The Transformation of Business, Democracy and Everyday Life*. New York: Vintage Books/Random House.

Rizvi, Haydar. 2007. "U.S. and Canada Found Guilty of Racism." *Inter Press Service*. August 7. http://ipsnews.net/news.asp?idnews=43487.

Rudolph, Phil. 2004. "Foley Hoag foreword." In *The Changing Landscape of Liability*, *SustainAbility*, December. http://www.sustainability.com/insight/liability-article.asp?id=180.

Ruggie, John. 2006. "Interim Report of the Special Representative of the Secretary-General on the Issue of Human Rights and Transnational Corporations and Other Business Enterprises." U.N. Doc. E/CN.4/2006/97. February 21. http://www2.ohchr.org/english/issues/globalization/business/reports.htm.

———. 2007. "Implementation of General Assembly Resolution 60/251 of 15 March 2006 entitled, 'Human Rights Council'; Report of the Special Representative of the Secretary-General on the issue of human rights and transnational corporations and other business enterprises, Addendum: Human Rights Policies and Management Practices: Results from questionnaire surveys of Governments and Fortune Global 500 firms." A/HRC/4/35/Add.3. February 28. http://www2.ohchr.org/english/issues/globalization/business/reports.htm.

———. 2008. "Protect, Respect, and Remedy: A Framework for Business and Human Rights." *Report of the Special Representative of the Secretary-General on the Issue of Human Rights and Transnational Corporations and Other Business Enterprises.* April 7. New York: UN.

———. 2009. Statement to an NGO Consultation. March 5. New York: UN.

———. 2010. "Business and Human Rights: Further Steps Toward the Operationalization of the 'Protect, Respect and Remedy' Framework." *Report of the Special Representative of the Secretary-General on the Issue of Human Rights and Transnational Corporations and Other Business Enterprises, John Ruggie.* A/HRC/14/27. April 9. New York: UN.

Stephens, Beth. 2008. "Judicial Preference and the Unreasonable Views of the Bush Administration." *Brooklyn Journal of International Law* 3(3): 773–83.

Trebeck, Kathryn. 2008. "Corporate Social Responsibility and Democratization: Opportunities and Obstacles." In *Earth Matters*, edited by Ciaran O'Faircheallaigh and Saleem Ali, 8–23. Sheffield, UK: Greenleaf Publishing, Ltd.

Wolf, Lisa. 2009. "Native Americans Ask Court to Stop Gold Mine on Sacred Mountain." *Environmental News Service*, June 6. http://www.ens-newswire.com/ens/jun2009/2009–06-06–093.asp.

From the Margins to the Center: Making Harms Visible through Human Rights Framing

10

The Law and Politics of U.S. Participation in the UN Convention on the Rights of Persons with Disabilities

Michael Ashley Stein and Janet E. Lord

INTRODUCTION

On July 30, 2009, the United States signed the United Nations Convention on the Rights of Persons with Disabilities (CRPD), reversing the Bush Administration's general disengagement with the convention. America historically has considered itself the global leader in disability civil rights law and policy, and largely deserves this reputation. Signature by the United States signals an intention to ratify the treaty, and President Barack Obama's Administration is submitting its convention ratification package to the U.S. Senate in short order. Notably, the CRPD (2007) is the first human rights treaty to be signed by the United States since the Convention on the Rights of the Child (1989) in 1995.

The worldwide momentum in favor of CRPD ratification poses both a challenge and an opportunity for the United States as a recognized disability rights leader. Ratification would signal an American return to active participation in the UN human rights system, supporting other efforts made by the Obama Administration in that direction, such as joining the UN Human Rights Council. It also would help reinstate the global leadership of the United States in disability law and policy after its relative disengagement from the globally supported CRPD treaty negotiations by the Bush Administration. Yet the prospects for such reinstatement must be set against the political landscape of American nonparticipation in human rights treaties and the challenges of a ratification effort for an American disability community rooted in a tradition of domestic civil rights advocacy and largely disconnected from the global human rights movement.

The convention's possible ratification by the United States begs several related questions on the law and politics of ratification: How consonant is the framing of disability human rights in the CRPD with existing American disability civil rights laws and policies? What are the implications of American human rights treaty policy and ratification practice, and, more generally, for the CRPD ratification process in particular? What consequences might flow from convention ratification for the United States and for American disability rights advocates? This chapter addresses each of those matters in turn.

I. CONCEPTS AND LIMITS OF AMERICAN DISABILITY CIVIL RIGHTS

A. *International Disability Rights Framings*

The United Nations estimates that one person in ten has a disability, and that some 80 percent of people with disabilities live in a developing country (United Nations Population Fund 2005, 3). Disabled persons tend to be among the most severely impoverished. According to World Bank estimates, one of every five of the globe's poorest people has a disability (Elwan 1999, 15). In developing countries, it is estimated that 2 percent of people with disabilities have access to rehabilitation and appropriate basic services, and less than 2 percent of children with disabilities receive any education (Despouy 1993). Women and girls with disabilities experience double discrimination on the grounds of gender and disability. Their literacy rates are dramatically lower, and their poverty and unemployment rates significantly higher than male counterparts (Lewis and Sygall 1997). Moreover, poverty and social exclusion lead to multiple disadvantage and discrimination on many fronts (UN Secretary General 1992, ¶5). The numerous barriers limiting access by people with disabilities to education, employment, housing, health care and rehabilitation, transportation, and recreation also limit their participation in political decision making at all levels where their input is needed to formulate laws, policies, and practices that could improve their lives (Betts and Flower 2001, 7).

Early international instruments approached persons with disabilities within a medical or charity construct that, in some instances, circumscribed human rights protections seemingly accorded to all human beings in the Universal Declaration of Human Rights (UDHR, 1948) and under the International Covenant on Civil and Political Rights (ICCPR, 1966) and the International Covenant on Economic, Social, and Cultural Rights (ICESCR, 1966). As an example, the Declaration on the Rights of

Mentally Retarded Persons arguably qualifies the scope of rights for people with intellectual disabilities in providing that "the mentally retarded person has, to the maximum degree of feasibility, the same rights as other human beings." Its goal for societies is limited to promoting "their integration as far as possible in normal life" (DRMRP 1971, 93).

In contrast, the United Nations High Commissioner for Human Rights heralded the CRPD as a rejection of the understanding of persons with disabilities "as objects of charity, medical treatment, and social protection" and as an embrace of disabled people as "subjects of rights" (Arbour 2006, 5). The text of the convention itself, and indeed the process by which it was negotiated, signal a definitive break from international – and many prevailing domestic – approaches focusing on understandings of disability within a medical/charity model framework, and as a deviant departure from the norm (Stein and Lord 2008b).

B. American Disability Rights Framings

The earliest expressions of American disability rights advocacy sought to reframe the situation of persons with disabilities by referring to the socially constructed barriers inhibiting their full participation in society. This approach, originating from Michael Oliver (1983) and called the "social model of disability," contrasts with the historically dominant medical model that considered "handicapped" individuals naturally excluded from mainstream societies. A medically based, individualized pathology has caused disabled persons historically to be excluded from social opportunities – as in the case of receiving social welfare benefits in lieu of employment – or to be accorded limited participation in those opportunities – for example, receiving their education at separate schools (Fries 1997, 6–7). Consequently, the absence of persons with disabilities from their respective societies has been viewed as an inevitable if unfortunate circumstance not suited for remediation. The primary thrust of interventions associated with a medical approach is directed at cures or correction and remediation through rehabilitation narrowly defined. Such measures play a role in facilitating human rights principles of independence and autonomy, but on their own and in isolation from measures directed at breaking down external barriers that reinforce disadvantage – whether physical, legal, policy, or attitudinal in character – they limit and constrain disability equality.

The social model is in striking opposition to the medical model and attributes a central role to the constructed environment and the attitudes it reflects toward creating what society labels a "disability." Thus, factors external to any given person's impairments determine how disabled she or he will be in terms of functioning within society (Silvers 1998, 75). Interventions stemming from a social–contextual understanding of disability focus on the removal of constructed barriers experienced by people with disabilities in their daily lives, to their exclusion and disadvantage. This acknowledgment of the impact of multiple barriers to participation in all areas of life for disabled persons – and the centrality of the social construction of disability – results in a far-reaching and holistic understanding of what foments disability exclusion (Stein 2007, 90). In human rights terms, such an approach is grounded in the fullness of the UDHR and the combined framework of the ICCPR and ICESC. However, the disability rights movement in the United States framed its claims to equality not in human rights but in the familiar and more bounded American civil rights model.

C. American Legal Expressions of Disability Civil Rights

American disability rights discourse has been dominated by precepts drawn from the social model of disability that largely tracks American civil rights. As a conceptual matter, disability advocates in the United States view discriminatory attitudes as the central obstacle to integration. To quote path-breaking advocate and political scientist Jacobus tenBroek, American policy makers historically considered people with disabilities as "mentally inferior and narrowly circumscribed in the range of their ability – and therefore inevitably doomed to vocational monotony, economic dependence, and social isolation" (tenBroek as cited in Matson 2005, 242). And so, following the course of predecessor civil rights movements, disability rights proponents have applied the social model through a civil rights prism in line with strategies pursued by racial minorities and women. Accordingly, American disability advocates pressed their claims using antidiscrimination approaches embedded in civil rights statutes, especially Title VII of the Civil Rights Act of 1964 (Burgdorf 1991). The most significant result of these advocacy efforts was the 1990 promulgation of the Americans with Disabilities Act (ADA), signaling the social model's legislative, and one could argue theoretical, victory in the United States.

The U.S. Congress heard testimony on the exclusion of people with disabilities from American society. As a result of that testimony, Congress was persuaded that the overall status of Americans with disabilities was dismal, and it concluded the group was historically "relegated to a position of political powerlessness in our society" and "continually encounter[s] various forms of discrimination." Moreover, Congress stipulated in the ADA's Finding section (ADA 2000) that this exclusion had arisen from "unfair and unnecessary discrimination and prejudice." Hence, the ADA was premised on the social model's premise that the repercussions of having a disability are mutable. To remedy artificial exclusion, Congress enacted the ADA as a civil rights statute, mandating that persons with disabilities be treated as equal to the general population. Notably, the ADA was heralded as an "emancipation proclamation" for people with disabilities by both Senator Tom Harkin (Congressional Record S9689 1990) and Senator Ted Kennedy (Congressional Record S10789 1989).

Notwithstanding significant achievements of the disability rights movement in adopting the ADA along with other supporting pieces of legislation, constraints inherent in the American civil rights model also have been manifested in the disability civil rights context (Rosenberg 2008). Specifically, inequalities caused by the systemic and multidimensional disadvantages of disabled persons have proven impervious to diffuse statutory remediation. In the same manner that Carol Anderson finds civil rights alone inadequate to resolve deeply entrenched racial inequalities (Anderson 2003), the ADA is not designed to remedy the historical socioeconomic exclusion of persons with disabilities, at least not as interpreted and applied in practice (Stein 2000). Moreover, although the strength of the social model lies in diverting attention away from medical pathology and toward socially constructed barriers that exclude, American disability advocates grafted the social model onto a minority rights framework (Hahn 1987, 553). Therefore, the ADA's recognition of people with disabilities as a "discrete and insular minority" creates a protected class and suggests the possibility – all too patent in ADA jurisprudence – that judicial application may turn more on who is (and is not) included in the defined class rather than on the potentially discriminatory conduct in question.

D. *Limiting Implications of American Disability Civil Rights*

The American disability rights agenda has exerted a powerful influence on other nations' disability laws and policies. Nonetheless, and perhaps ironically, U.S. disability rights law, policy, and advocacy are not as robust as they could be. This is due, in large measure, to advocates adhering too rigidly to the formal equality model espoused by the civil rights movement through which similarly situated people are treated similarly, and equality measures moving beyond the elimination of simple prejudice are considered outside the province of lawmakers. Hence, these advocates have yet to seek equality measures allocating preferential treatment to persons with disabilities to create social equity (e.g., affirmative action), or acknowledging difference in the form of economic and social rights (e.g., subsidizing higher costs associated with disability) (Stein and Stein 2007).

As a result, the ADA cannot bring about disabled citizens' full social inclusion, and so its promise to achieve equality through traditional civil rights protection goes unfulfilled (Burkhauser 1997). That people with disabilities remain socially marginalized can be seen by their unemployment and poverty rates, which may reach up to 63.1 percent and 24.7 percent, respectively (Erickson and Lee 2008, 3). Remarkably, even the sacrosanct right of voting remains unrealized in practice. Disabled Americans continue to be excluded from voting due to inaccessible venues and the failure to provide reasonable accommodations in respect of this fundamental right (General Accounting Office 2009).

Despite the strength of U.S. antidiscrimination laws, full inclusion of socially marginalized groups requires comprehensive protection entailing negative proscriptions on exclusion and the facilitation of inclusion. This is because standard antidiscrimination prohibitions can prospectively prevent prejudicial harm, whereas equality measures are needed to remedy inequities that exist due to past practices. Moreover, failing to counteract the unequal position of people with disabilities perpetuates their social stigma and the attitudes and structures maintaining subordination.

To illustrate the incomplete nature of U.S. disability policy, consider the effect of the absence of equality measures from the ADA. Title I was intended as the most expedient method of bringing about social and economic equality for people with disabilities. Nevertheless, it took nearly a decade to pass initiatives allowing disabled persons receiving public assistance to maintain their health care coverage while transitioning to employment under the Ticket to Work, Work Incentives Improvement Act, and the Workforce Investment Act. During this period, and despite Senator Bob Dole's efforts (Dole 1994), no job training programs were promulgated on behalf of the disabled, although they were developed for other historically disadvantaged groups as part of dramatic welfare reforms (Zatz 2006). Indeed, to date, no systemic federal job program exists on behalf of workers with disabilities. Hence, the ADA forbids employment discrimination; however, the means by which disabled Americans can obtain and keep employment have not been provided (Stein and Stein 2007).

II. THE LAW AND POLITICS OF U.S. CRPD RATIFICATION

A. The CRPD as a Disability Human Rights Treaty

As a modern human rights treaty, the CRPD combines civil and political rights with economic, social, and cultural rights to manifest the Vienna Declaration's notion that human rights are truly "indivisible and inter-related and interconnected" (World Conference on Human Rights 1993, ¶5). The CRPD cements into place the precepts of the social model of disability while advancing a holistic human rights framework that goes beyond the social model's boundaries. Notwithstanding the success of disability rights advocates in invoking the social model, the transformation of persons with disabilities from a socially and economically marginalized group to one enjoying full inclusion in society requires invoking both negative and positive rights. Antidiscrimination prohibitions can guard against future exclusion; however, equality measures are necessary to close existing equity gaps. Furthermore, neglecting to use positive measures to eradicate inequities between persons with disabilities and mainstream society would result in the continued subordination of people with disabilities (Stein and Stein 2007).

The CRPD gives the principle of equality a prominent role in its framework. Article 1 specifies its purpose "to promote, protect and ensure the full and equal enjoyment of all human rights and fundamental freedoms by all persons with disabilities, and to promote respect for their inherent dignity." Article 3 sets forth specific principles upon which the convention is based and through which the convention must be interpreted and applied – the first such articulation in an international human rights convention (Stein and Lord 2008b, 495). Among the Article 3 principles are respect for dignity, autonomy, and difference; nondiscrimination and equality of opportunity; full social inclusion; equality between women and men; and respect for children's evolving capabilities. The commitment to equality is further underscored in the Preamble by numerous framings of social disadvantages and societal barriers experienced by persons with disabilities. Obligations required to achieve the objectives of the convention are laid out in Article 4. Notable among these provisions with horizontal application are duties to adopt and amend legislation; institute disability as a cross-cutting issue across all programming; eliminate discrimination; promote universal design; provide accessible information; and include people with disabilities and their representative organizations in planning activities affecting their lives.

Article 5 authorizes the provision of special measures and prohibits "all discrimination on the basis of disability." Article 2 defines discrimination specifically as:

> Any distinction, exclusion, or restriction on the basis of disability which has the purpose or effect of impairing or nullifying the recognition, enjoyment or exercise, on an equal basis with others, of all human rights and fundamental freedoms in the political, economic, social, cultural or any other field. It includes all forms of discrimination including denial of reasonable accommodation.

This formulation is notable because it presents a robust disability equality model that explicitly recognizes the transformative impact of reasonable accommodation. Lawson has suggested such a model could give rise not only to individualized accommodations but also to "anticipatory reasonable accommodation duties." Similar disability legislation in the United Kingdom requires the prospective removal of barriers and steps to maximize access to products, information, and the built environment (Lawson 2008, 31).

In addition to the previously mentioned articles of general application to be applied horizontally across the CRPD, the convention includes several other potentially far-reaching provisions with similar effect. Among the other articles of general application are provisions underscoring the rights of women with disabilities (Article 6) and children with disabilities (Article 7). Other individuals with disabilities subject to multiple forms of discrimination are acknowledged in the Preamble. Rounding out the articles of general application, Article 8 addresses some of the underlying determinants of disability discrimination by requiring states parties to raise public awareness. In support of this, the treaty provides a nonexhaustive list of illustrative measures (Article 8). Article 9 seeks to dismantle barriers hindering the effective enjoyment of rights by persons with disabilities. It addresses a broad spectrum of accessibility concerns within both the public and private spheres by obligating public and private products or services be "open or provided to the public" (Article 9).

As a comprehensive human rights treaty, the CRPD's substantive articles cover the spectrum of life activities of persons with disabilities. In doing so, the convention clarifies, within the context of disability, the human rights that all persons are entitled to under existing international human rights law instruments as well as under customary international law. These elemental human rights include fundamental freedoms such as the right to life (Article 10), freedom from torture (Article 15), the right to education (Article 24), employment (Article 27), political participation (Article 29), legal capacity (Article 12), access to justice (Article 13), freedom of expression and opinion (Article 21), privacy (Article 22), participation in cultural life, sports, and recreation (Article 30), respect for home and family (Article 23), personal integrity (Article 17), liberty of movement and nationality (Article 18), liberty and security of the person (Article 14), and adequate standard of living (Article 38).

By providing a comprehensive rights catalog, the convention endeavors to ensure the substantive equality of persons with disabilities, putting into sharp focus the realization of all human rights. Consequently, the CRPD advances a markedly different conception of the relationship between persons with disabilities and the state than those offered by traditional models of disability or traditional civil rights formulations of disability rights. Under the convention, human rights are directed and responsive to individual needs and cast toward the development of the "capacity of all individuals on the basis of their inherent worth and potential" as opposed to charitable impulse (Stein 2004, 119). The conceptual implications of conferring individual rights claims on persons with disabilities are profound; this framework serves to displace the notion of the state as beneficent welfare provider, provides fertile ground for theorizing and putting into practice civil, political, as well as economic, social, and cultural rights, and places in clear relief the inextricably holistic nature of human rights obligations (O'Cinneide 2009, 167).

B. American Disability Rights as Human Rights

In terms of substance, the CRPD's aims are consistent with those of American disability law and policy. Overall, U.S. law can be viewed as either being in alignment with the convention's mandates or capable of reaching those levels through more rigorous enforcement and – potentially in some instances – through additional legislative action (Stein and Waterstone 2008). Indeed, the core principles articulated in the CRPD are firmly embedded in American disability law – respect for human dignity, nondiscrimination and autonomy, reasonable accommodation, and participation (Stein and Lord 2008a).

Where gaps arise between the two sets of legal mandates, they do so because U.S. domestic disability rights laws, as described previously, operate from a different perspective than that of international law. Yet, because discernable gaps can be narrowed or eradicated through improved implementation and/or Congressional action, ratifying the CRPD ought not to be an issue given the ample tools at the disposal of the Senate to address concerns regarding particular provisions. Employing reservations, declarations, and understandings is certainly the bane of human rights advocates who view their use as undercutting the spirit of human rights treaty participation. Nonetheless, when used prudently and subjected to scrutiny by reference to the purported and actual effect, they can be a necessary expedient to achieve ratification. Even so, general cultural resistance to the ratification of human rights treaties and a corresponding ambivalence on the part of the American disability community poses substantial – yet not insurmountable – political barriers to ratification.

C. Resisting the CRPD

Following authorization by the UN General Assembly to consider development of a specialized disability human rights treaty in December 2001, government delegations from around the world debated the necessity of such an instrument. During the first two ad hoc sessions of the CRPD negotiations, held in July 2002 and June 2003, the United States argued that disability was a domestic rather than international concern. Further, the argument was put forth that the ADA's preeminence militated against signing or ratifying an international agreement relating to disability rights (Boyd 2003). As a lone voice of dissent, the U.S. delegation looked on as the rest of the world enthusiastically pressed forward in support of drafting a new disability-specific human rights convention. Somewhat paradoxically – as well as disingenuously – the United States argued that its position toward participation in any resulting treaty was "neutrality." It did not oppose the treaty, which it observed might be a good thing for other countries; however, it held that such a treaty would not offer the United States any tangible benefits given the domestic disability framework already in place (Boyd 2003).

Consistent with a "neutrality" position, the Bush Administration sent a skeletal delegation to initial negotiating sessions and did not permit those members in attendance to formally intervene on substance until the seventh ad hoc session (Seventh Session of the Ad Hoc Committee on a Comprehensive and Integral International Convention on Protection and Promotion on the Rights and Dignity of Persons with Disabilities 2003). Notably, the text forming the foundation for the resulting treaty was developed in 2004 between the third and fourth sessions at a special working group of the ad hoc committee. The ensuing American disengagement was glaring in view of the United States' extensive experience in the disability rights field, much of which was intrepid at home and highly influential abroad (Stein and Stein 2007, 1203–04). The Bush Administration's aversion to cooperation also was particularly striking because of references within the CRPD to concepts and principles originating in American disability law (e.g., the concept of reasonable accommodation) and its inherent values (i.e., the emphasis on independence and autonomy) (Articles 2 and 3).

The professed nonaligned status of the United States yielded at the behest of the American right-to-life movement, and interventions thereafter concentrated on limiting sexual and reproductive rights. Further reinforcing American inhospitality to global delegates from around the world was its failure during the five-year negotiation period to host a single reception or informal facilitation at its New York UN Mission – practices undertaken by a number of developing countries with poorly resourced missions. Ultimately, reluctance by the United States to negotiate with a view to joining the treaty deprived state delegations of American expertise in a number of areas ranging from architectural barriers (addressed in the Architectural Barriers Act of 1968) to inclusive education (addressed in the Individuals with Disabilities Education Act of 2006).

Poignantly, due to the Bush Administration's general disengagement, the American delegation was effectively marginalized during the ad hoc committee sessions as delegations focused their lobbying efforts on winning the support of involved states, including the European Union sitting as a regional body. Moreover, delegations paid little attention to American objections voiced on the floor, knowing that accommodation would not win eventual support. As a strategy for effective American participation in an international negotiation, the Bush policy was an abysmal failure.

Regrettably, U.S. disengagement also resulted in scant interaction with American (and other) nongovernmental organizations. Such groups made the strategic decision to avoid interfacing with a delegation whose instructions sidelined them from the process. Although this was perhaps an expedient position to assume given competing lobbying priorities, it did little to forge potentially important relationships in what is now a politically more favorable climate for human rights treaty ratification. For example, witness the principal governmental actors in the current ratification process, several of whom were on the U.S. delegation to the ad hoc committee for all or substantial parts of the negotiation process.[1]

D. Resisting Human Rights Treaties

Despite the Bush Administration's aversion to human rights treaties (Mertus 2008), resistance to these instruments – and international law in general – originated more than half a century earlier (Foot 2008, 720). Although the United States contributed significantly to the development of the international human rights movement, which included the participation of Eleanor Roosevelt and other Americans (Glendon 2001), Senator John W. Bricker of Ohio brought an abrupt end to this pioneering role in the early 1950s (Tananbaum 1988). Senator Bricker proposed an amendment to the U.S. Constitution making all treaties nonself-executing (Henkin 1995, 348). Indeed, Bricker's stated purpose was to "bury the so-called" International Covenant on Civil and Political Rights "so deep so that no-one holding high public office will ever dare to attempt its resurrection" (Tananbaum 1988, 25). Significantly, such a measure would have precluded individuals from invoking human rights treaty provisions in domestic courts absent implementing legislation. President Dwight D. Eisenhower defeated the Bricker Amendment; however, success came at a cost, with that administration promising not to accede to any international human rights treaties (Henkin 1995, 348–49).

The legacy of Senator Bricker, who saw international human rights as a major threat to preserving domestic discrimination – and especially the *de jure* racial discrimination he supported – lives on in enduring U.S. resistance to participating in human rights treaties (Henkin 1995; Bruch 2006, 627, n. 13). Trenchantly, the United States has the poorest ratification record of human rights treaties among all industrialized

---

[1] Gilda Brancato was head of the U.S. delegation during the early ad hoc committee process and now leads the Department of State's preparation of the ratification package the Obama Administration is reviewing for Senate submission. Likewise John Wodatch, having served more than forty years in the Department of Justice asserting American civil rights law, was part of the CRPD negotiation and is now participating in the ratification effort.

nations, having ratified only three of the nine core human rights treaties (Pereira 2004, 488–89). Curiously unquestioned, U.S. nonparticipation in human rights treaties has been justified on a number of grounds: (1) the American federal system is exceedingly complex; (2) U.S. domestic law is vastly superior to international treaty systems, and/or ratification might undermine federal protections; (3) human rights are exclusively a domestic concern and the U.S. Constitution does not permit the use of treaty power to regulate such matters; and/or (4) treaties present potential conflicts between their obligations and those of the Constitution. Conservative legal academics defend this practice by arguing it is necessitated by the presumed sovereignty of domestic legal norms (McGinnis and Somin 2007, 1239–40). Yet as inaccurate as these now reflexive responses are in the opinion of highly respected international law scholars and practitioners (Buergenthal 1995, 284–98), and as counter-factual as they are given the many international treaties entered into by the United States (Hathaway 2008) and other highly developed federal states such as Brazil, Germany, and Nigeria, they remain serious obstacles to securing American participation in numerous multilateral treaty efforts – human rights treaties in particular.

Finally, the standard for U.S. ratification of human rights treaties is substantially higher than that of the international community of states, with the U.S. State Department's review process following a methodology that puts the threshold of assessment at near perfect compliance with the treaty obligations under question (UN Human Rights Committee 2005). In other words, the method tests existing American law against a highly unrealistic bar no comparably responsible ratifying state (e.g., Australia, Canada, New Zealand) follows. This pre-ratification position is in some senses laudable and preferable to instances where states ratify and then rush through poorly crafted domestic level legislation, or worse, ratify to achieve a higher international reputation without intending to comply (Hathaway 2002, 1989). Yet such a position taken at the level of domestic legislation would render few instruments passable. And, unlike other potential human rights treaty ratifications that might garner U.S. consideration – the Convention on the Rights of the Child and the Convention on the Elimination of All Forms of Discrimination Against Women (1979) – disability law is an area in which the United States claims a precedence (Congressional Record S8121 2009, 8123) it can reaffirm. Indeed, ratification would provide the American disability community a constructive tool to press for more complete implementation of the American domestic disability law framework. For example, outrage at the human rights abuses suffered by people with disabilities left behind during Hurricane Katrina (Lord, Stein, and Waterstone 2008) could be channeled through CRPD Article 11, which covers situations of risk, including natural disasters and humanitarian assistance.

E. Toward U.S. Ratification?

Notwithstanding general American resistance to participating in human rights treaties (Nash 2009), many in the U.S. human rights movement find hope in promises undertaken by President Obama during his campaign to sign and support their ratification, including the CRPD. Indeed, by signing the CRPD on July 30, 2009, voicing support for its ratification, and providing technical assistance (UN Enable 2009), the Obama Administration has demonstrated the commitment of the United States to rejoining the global community (Ogilvy and Ya'alon 2009, 193–94) and to continuing American leadership in the area of disability law and policy. Support for disability rights is further reflected in appointments across the government, including positions of Special Assistant to the President, Senior Advisor on Disability Issues within the Federal Emergency Management Agency, and the announcement in July 2009 of a Senior Disability Human Rights Advisor at the Department of State.

These significant developments aside, challenges facing U.S. ratification of the CRPD and other human rights treaties cannot be underestimated. Although American leadership in disability rights provides compelling legal grounds for pressing ahead with CRPD ratification, political obstacles remain. These relate not only to the general atmosphere of parochialism that conditions human rights treaty participation within the U.S. Senate (and across the American conservative civil society sector), but also to the lack of consistent and ongoing engagement in human rights advocacy within the disability civil rights-oriented American disability community. Indeed, the disability rights movement in the United States, focused understandably on retaining existing rights protections now under further threat in light of the recession, is not experienced or well-versed in international human rights law or ratification of human rights conventions. Moreover, fractures existing within the community with regard to disability civil rights (Bagenstos 2009) also are present in connection with a consensus around disability human rights and CRPD ratification. In addition, like the international disability community, the American disability community holds the mainstream human rights movement at arm's length, thereby undermining efforts to broaden a coalition to campaign in favor of CRPD ratification.

CONCLUSION

The CRPD lays out a progressive framework for disability human rights that is unfulfilled. Although its substantive obligations in many respects closely mirror the American disability rights legal framework, its holistic vision presses for a more robust, fully implemented, substantive equality human rights framework. This agenda is one that traditional civil rights law, and indeed disability rights advocacy, is not poised to achieve. Ratifying the CRPD gives the United States an opportunity to meet the challenge of this unfulfilled promise for persons with disabilities, as well as for other disadvantaged groups vying for a fuller human rights vision. It also opens the door for a homeward-bound human rights movement to take hold, at long last, in the United States.

REFERENCES

Americans with Disabilities Act. 2000. 42 U.S.C. §12101.

Anderson, Carol. 2003. *Eyes Off the Prize: The United Nations and the African American Struggle for Human Rights, 1944–1955.* New York: Cambridge University Press.

Arbour, Louise. 2006. "Statement on the Ad Hoc Committee's adoption of the International Convention on the Rights of Persons with Disabilities." December 5. http://www.ohchr.org/English/issues/disability/docs/statementhcdec06.doc.

Architectural Barriers Act. 1968. 42 U.S.C. §§ 4151–4156.

Bagenstos, Samuel R. 2009. *The Law and Contradictions of the Disability Movement.* New Haven, CT: Yale University Press.

Betts, Jen, and Jonathan Flower. 2001. "Towards a Level Playing Field: A Call to Make Development Programs More Inclusive." In Discussion Paper 11, *All Things Being Equal: Perspectives on Disability and Development,* 7–12. Milton Keynes, UK: World Vision. http://www.worldvision.org.uk/upload/pdf/Disability_paper.pdf.

Boyd, Ralph F. 2003. Statement. Second Session of the Ad Hoc Committee on a Comprehensive and Integral International Convention on Protection and Promotion of the Rights of Persons with Disabilities, June 16–27. New York: United Nations. http://www.un.org/esa/socdev/enable/rights/contrib-us.htm.

Bruch, Elizabeth M. 2006. "Whose Law Is It Anyway? The Cultural Legitimacy of International Human Rights in the United States." *Tennessee Law Review* 73(4): 669–710.

Buergenthal, Thomas. 1995. *International Human Rights in a Nutshell.* 2nd Edition. Eagan, MN: West Group Publishing.

Burgdorf, Jr., Robert L. 1991. "The Americans with Disabilities Act: Analysis and Implications of a Second-Generation Civil Rights Statute." *Harvard Civil Rights and Civil Liberties Law Review* 26(2): 413–522.

Burkhauser, Richard V. 1997. "Post ADA: Are People with Disabilities Expected to Work?" *Annals of the American Academy of Political and Social Science* 549: 71–83.

Congressional Record S10789. Vol. 135. 1989.

Congressional Record S9689. Vol. 136. 1990.

Congressional Record S8121. Vol. 155. 2009.

Convention on the Elimination of All Forms of Discrimination against Women. Adopted December 18, 1979 (entered into force Sept. 3, 1981). G.A. Res. 34/180. UN Doc. A/34/46 (1981).

Convention on the Rights of the Child. Adopted November 20, 1989 (entered into force September 20, 1990). G.A. Res. 44/25, UN Doc. A/44/49 (1989).

Convention on the Rights of Persons with Disabilities (CRPD). Adopted January 24, 2007 (entered into force May 3, 2008). G.A. Res. 61/106. UN Doc A/RES/61/106 (2007).

Declaration on the Rights of Mentally Retarded Persons. Adopted December 20, 1971 (entered into force September 24, 1973). G.A. res. 2856 (XXVI), 26 UN GAOR Supp. (No. 29) at 93, UN Doc. A/8429 (1971).

Despouy, Leandro. 1993. *Human Rights and Disabled Persons*: Study Series 6. Geneva and New York: Centre for Human Rights.

Dole, Bob. 1994. "Are We Keeping America's Promises to People with Disabilities?" *Iowa Law Review* 79(4): 925–34.

Elwan, Ann. 1999. "Poverty and Disability: A Survey of the Literature." Social Discussion Paper Series. Washington, D.C.: World Bank.

Erickson, W., and C. Lee. 2008. *2007 Disability Status Report*. Cornell University Rehabilitation Research and Training Center on Disability Demographics and Statistics. http://www.ilr.cornell.edu/edi/disabilitystatistics/.

Foot, Rosemary. 2008. "Exceptionalism Again: The Bush Administration, the 'Global War on Terror,' and Human Rights." *Law and History Review* 26(3): 707–26.

Fries, Kenny. 1997. "Introduction." In *Staring Back: The Disability Experience from the Inside Out*, edited by Kenny Fries, 6–7. New York: Plume.

General Accounting Office. 2009. *Voters with Disabilities: More Polling Places Had No Potential Impediments than in 2000, but Challenges Remain*. Washington, D.C.: GAO. http://www.gao.gov/new.items/d09685.pdf.

Glendon, Mary Ann. 2001. *A World Made New: Eleanor Roosevelt and the Universal Declaration of Human Rights*. New York: Random House Publishing, Inc.

Hahn, Harlan. 1987. "Advertising the Acceptably Employable Image: Disability and Capitalism." *Policy Study Journal* 15(3): 551–70.

Hathaway, Oona A. 2002. "Do Human Rights Treaties Make a Difference?" *Yale Law Journal* 111(8): 1935–2042.

———. 2008. "Treaties End: The Past, Present, and Future of International Lawmaking in the United States." *Yale Law Journal* 117(7): 1236–1362.

Henkin, Louis. 1995. "U.S. Ratification of Human Rights Conventions: The Ghost of Senator Bricker." *American Journal of International Law* 89(2): 341–50.

Individuals with Disabilities Education Act. 2006. 20 U.S.C. § 1400, 1415.

International Covenant on Civil and Political Rights (ICCPR). Adopted December 16, 1966 (entered into force March 23, 1976). G.A. Res. 2200A (XXI), U. N. GAOR, Supp. No. 16 at 52, UN Doc. A/6316 (1966).

International Covenant on Economic, Social, and Cultural Rights (ICESCR). Adopted December 16, 1966 (entered into force January 3, 1976). G.A. Res. 2200A (XXI), UN GAOR, Supp. No. 16, UN Doc. A/6316 (1966).

Lawson, Anna. 2008. *Disability and Equality Law in Britain: The Role of Reasonable Adjustment*. Oxford, UK: Hart Publishing Ltd.

Lewis, C., and S. Sygall, eds. 1997. *Loud, Proud, and Passionate: Including Women with Disabilities in International Development Programmes*. Rome: UNESCO.

Lord, Janet E., Michael A. Stein, and Michael Waterstone. 2008. "Disability Inclusive Development and Natural Disasters." In *Law and Recovery from Disaster: Hurricane Katrina*, edited by Robin Paul Malloy, 71–82. Burlington, VT: Ashgate.

Matson, Floyd W. 2005. *Blind Justice: Jacobus tenBroek and the Vision of Equality: 242*. Washington, D.C.: Government Printing Office.

McGinnis, John O., and Ilya Somin. 2007. "Should International Law Be Our Law?" *Stanford Law Review* 59(5): 1175–1247.

Mertus, Julie A. 2008. *Bait and Switch: Human Rights and US Foreign Policy*. 2nd Edition. London: Taylor and Francis.

Nash, Kate. 2009. *The Cultural Politics of Human Rights: Comparing the US and UK*. Cambridge, UK/New York: Cambridge University Press.

O'Cinneide, Colm. 2009. "Extracting Protection for the Rights of Persons with Disabilities from Human Rights Framework – Established Limits and New Possibilities." In *The UN Convention on the Rights of Person with Disabilities: European and Scandinavian Perspectives*, edited by Oddny Mjoll Arnardottir and Gerard Quinn, 163–98. Leiden, Netherlands: Martinus Nijhoff Publishers.

Ogilvy, Graham, and Belhas v. Ya'alon. 2009. "The Case for a Jus Cogens Exception to the Foreign Sovereign Immunities Act." *Journal of International Business and Law* 8(1): 169–95.

Oliver, Michael. 1983. *Social Work with Disabled People*. New York: The Macmillan Press.

Pereira, Anita. 2004. "Live and Let Live: Healthcare Is a Fundamental Human Right." *Connecticut Public Interest Law Journal* 3(2): 481–503.

Rosenberg, Gerald. 2008. *The Hollow Hope: Can Courts Bring About Change?* 2nd Edition. Chicago, IL: University of Chicago Press.

Seventh Session of the Ad Hoc Committee on a Comprehensive and Integral International Convention on Protection and Promotion on the Rights and Dignity of Persons with Disabilities. 2003. List of Participants. UN Doc A/AC.265/2006/INF/1: 12 (January 12).

Silvers, Anita. 1998. "Formal Justice." In *Disability, Difference, Discrimination: Perspectives on Justice in Bioethics and Public Policy*, edited by Anita Silvers,

David Wassermand, and Mary Mahowald, 13-146. Lanham, MD: Rowman and Littlefield.

Stein, Michael Ashley. 2000. "Empirical Implications of Title I." *Iowa Law Review* 85(5): 1671–90.

———. 2004. "Same Struggle, Different Difference: ADA Accommodations as Antidiscrimination." *Pennsylvania Law Review* 153(2): 579–673.

———. 2007. "Disability Human Rights." *California Law Review* 95(1): 75–121.

Stein, Michael Ashley, and Janet E. Lord. 2008a. "Jacobus tenBroek, Participatory Justice, and the UN Convention on the Rights of Persons with Disabilities." *Texas Journal on Civil Liberties and Civil Rights* 13(2): 167–85.

———. 2008b. "United Nations Convention on the Rights of Persons with Disabilities: Process, Substance, and Prospects." In *The International Human Rights Law in a Global Context*, edited by Felipe Gomez Isa, 495–514. Bilbao, Spain: University of Duesto Press.

Stein, Michael Ashley, and Penelope J.S. Stein. 2007. "Beyond Disability Civil Rights." *Hastings Law Journal* 58(6): 1203–40.

Stein, Michael Ashley, and Michael E. Waterstone. 2008. *Finding the Gaps: A Comparative Analysis of Disability Laws in the United States to the United Nations Convention on the Rights of Persons with Disabilities.* National Council on Disability (May 12). http://www.ncd.gov/newsroom/publications/2008/pdf/ncd_crpd_analysis.pdf.

Tananbaum, Duane. 1988. *The Bricker Amendment Controversy: A Test of Eisenhower's Political Leadership.* Ithaca, NY: Cornell University Press.

UN Enable. 2009. "Second Session of the Conference of States Parties List of Side-Events." http://www.un.org/disabilities/documents/COP/CSP2-SideEvents1Aug09-Website.doc.

UN Human Rights Committee. 2005. "Consideration of Reports Submitted by States Parties under Article 40 of the Covenant: United States of America." U.N. Doc. CCPR/C/USA/3 (November 28). http://www.unhchr.ch/tbs/doc.nsf/898586b1dc7b4043c1256a450044f331/01e6a2b492ba27e5c12570fc003f558b$/FILE/G0545268.pdf.

United Nations Population Fund. 2005. *The Promise of Equality: Gender Equity, Reproductive Health and the Millennium Development Goals.* UN Sales No. E.05.III.H.1: 3. http://www.unfpa.org/upload/lib_pub_file/493_filename_en_swpo5.pdf.

UN Secretary General. 1992. "Social Development: Questions Relating to the World Social Situation and to Youth, Aging, Disabled Persons and the Family, Implementation of the World Programme of Action Concerning Disabled Persons and the United Nations Decade of Disabled Persons." U.N. Doc. A/CONF.47/415 (September 11, 1992).

Universal Declaration of Human Rights. 1948. G.A. Res. 217A (III): art. 5. UN GAOR, 3d Sess. U.N. Doc. A/810 (December 12, 1948).

World Conference on Human Rights. 1993. "Vienna Declaration and Programme of Action." UN Doc. A/CONF. 157/23: para. 5 (July 12).

Zatz, Noah D. 2006. "From Welfare to What?" *Hastings Law Journal* 57(6): 1131–88.

11

The Anomaly of Citizenship
for Indigenous Rights

Bethany R. Berger

All ye men of Congress, we wish you to help us. You do things all over
the world. I want you to help us keep this thing citizenship away from us.
That is all I have to say; but what I know I tell the truth.
Pa-Hang-Ga-Ma-Ne, the man that walks in front, Omaha,
1888 Petition to Congress

Citizenship has an anomalous status in the struggles of native peoples for human rights. Citizenship is often understood as a regrettable but necessary prerequisite to securing human rights, and the gradual extension of citizenship to broader segments of the population is seen as the triumph of human rights in the United States. Although this is largely true, it overlooks an important ambiguity with respect to American Indians that highlights the deficiencies of a human rights model that takes the state and the individual as its fundamental categories. The struggle for indigenous rights throughout history has not been only – or even primarily – to gain rights for native people as individuals separate from tribal communities, but to secure their right to self-determination as political entities distinct from states. International human rights law has only just begun to formally recognize this right, but it was at the heart of the earliest debates on international law. Although some native people sincerely did seek citizenship, in U.S. history calls to provide citizenship to American Indians were repeatedly linked to efforts to deny them self-determination. This chapter first unpacks this history and then discusses developments in both domestic and international human rights law that begin to move beyond the citizen–state dichotomy to more effectively recognize the rights of indigenous peoples.

THE EMERGENCE, IMPACT, AND DECLINE OF THE
CITIZEN–STATE DICHOTOMY ON AMERICAN INDIANS

The status of the indigenous peoples of the Americas forms a key part of the early development of international human rights. In the early 1500s, Bartolomé de las Casas protested that the natural rights of man prohibited Spanish enslavement of the indigenous South Americans and expropriation of their land. De las Casas' calls catalyzed Franciscus de Victoria's 1532 lectures on the rights of the Indians and the law of war. In these lectures, Victoria began to develop notions of the basic equality of political communities and the obligations of each government to respect certain universal laws (Victoria [1557] 1917). Under the law of nations, he argued, the political and property rights of indigenous peoples demanded respect and recognition, and were not vitiated by their lack of Christianity, European claims of "discovery," or different governmental structures or customs (130–48). Victoria's work influenced Hugo Grotius and Emerich de Vattel in laying the foundations of international law as we know it today.

Victoria formulated his ideas before the Treaty of Westphalia or the complete emergence of the nation-state concept. Therefore, his work does not restrict who can claim the benefits of the law of nations and blends claims of what we might consider individual rights with those of state rights. Victoria can be interpreted to support a claim that all people have individual rights and rights to self-government as political communities. The distinction between the two is not fundamental, and both are necessary to achieve human thriving. However, as international law developed over the eighteenth and nineteenth centuries, it narrowed the definition of states entitled to claim the protections of international law to those fitting within a European or Anglo-American mold (Anaya 2004, 20–22).

This development in legal theory was accompanied by changes in legal practice. Although North American practice initially recognized the national status of Indian communities through treaty-making and boundary-drawing agreements, European-Americans increasingly saw such agreements as expedients to placate savage groups. Congress ultimately ended treaty-making with Indian tribes in 1871.[1] Even when the national status of Indian tribes was more fully recognized, their political rights were frequently ignored. Thus, colonial and national governments frequently claimed lands based on agreements made with

---

[1] 16 Stat. 566 (March 3, 1871), codified at 25 U.S.C. § 71.

individuals they knew lacked authority from their tribes (e.g., Kades 2000, 1081), a practice that Victoria had condemned in the sixteenth century (Victoria [1557] 1917, 148). Similarly, even as the founders urged strict adherence to humanitarian law toward British soldiers and civilians during the American Revolution, they celebrated the burning of Cherokee villages and scalping of Indian civilians (Calloway 1995, 49). Indians – both as individuals and as political communities – were being placed outside the protections of international law.

Native people, for their part, primarily focused on protecting their national rights to self-government, territory, and the fulfillment of treaty agreements. Inclusion within the U.S. polity as citizens was initially only a minor part of this struggle and was even seen as hostile to the protection of tribal rights. "Indian" and "citizen" were often opposing terms in Indian treaties, and U.S. lawmakers were usually willing – even eager – to offer citizenship to Indians as a reward for and inducement to assimilation (Cohen 1942, 153; Porter 1999, 111–12). Treaties offered citizenship to those who accepted federal conditions to abandon their tribes[2] or who swore an oath of allegiance to the United States and could prove that they had "adopted the habits of civilized life."[3] A number of such treaty provisions explicitly provided that accepting citizenship would "dissolve their tribal relations."[4] A few treaties even extended citizenship to all tribal members not opting out within a fixed period and stipulated that after such period, the group's recognition as an Indian tribe would be "dissolved and terminated."[5] In the 1860s and 1870s, as Congress moved toward governing Indian affairs by legislation rather than treaty, various statutes allowed individual tribal members to become citizens by proving civilization and swearing allegiance to the United States.[6]

Some Indian individuals and even tribes did agree to citizenship. Many did so as the only alternative to leaving their homes for the Indian Territory west of the Mississippi. Others thought that citizenship would give

---

[2] See, e.g., Treaty with the Choctaw, 7 Stat. 333, art. 13 (1830) (allowing those who wished to remain east of the Mississippi to receive an allotment of land and become citizens of the state).

[3] See Treaty with the Delawares, 14 Stat. 793, Art. 9 (1866); Treaty with the Kickapoo, 12 Stat. 1249, Art. 3 (1862); Treaty with the Pottawatomie, 12 Stat. 1191, Art. 3 (1861).

[4] See Treaty with the Sioux, 12 Stat. 1037, Art. 8 (1858); Treaty with the Delawares, 14 Stat. 793, Art. 9 (1866).

[5] Treaty with the Wyandott, 10 Stat. 1159, Art. 1 (1855); Treaty with the Ottawa of Blanchard's Fork and Roche de Bouef, Art. 1 (1862).

[6] See 17 Stat. 631, 632 (March 3, 1873) (Miami Indians); 16 Stat. 335, 361–62 (July 15, 1870) (Winnebago Indians); 13 Stat. 541, 562 (March 3, 1865) (Stockbridge Indians).

them stronger legal protection for their lands, while others were coerced or misled into accepting citizenship. Still others wanted the full incorporation within the United States that citizenship implied. Ely Parker, for example, the Seneca man who had served as brigadier general in the Civil War and later became the first Indian Commissioner of Indian Affairs, petitioned Congress for citizenship in 1862.[7] But the recipients of citizenship often protested against it. After receiving citizenship under an 1843 act, a large portion of the Stockbridge Indians refused to accept its validity and persuaded Congress to revoke the legislation and enter into a treaty restoring their status as a tribe.[8] Similarly, the Wyandotte, who had entered into an 1855 treaty accepting citizenship and dissolving the tribe, found its impact so damaging they successfully petitioned for an 1867 treaty in which they "began anew a tribal existence."[9] One of the three bands of Kickapoo Indians was so resistant to a treaty demanding they accept the habits of civilization that they refused to accept citizenship until 1985, long after all Indians had been made citizens by congressional act in 1924 (*New York Times* 1985).

In the 1870s, tribal protests defeated a federal proposal allowing all Indians to assume citizenship. Congress had proposed extending citizenship to all Indians willing to swear an oath of allegiance and prove their civilization; those becoming citizens would not thereby lose their right to any tribal lands or annuities.[10] The Choctaw, Chickasaw, Seminole, and Creek tribes sent delegations to Congress opposing any such measure as destructive to their sovereignty and in violation of their treaties with the United States.[11] They had no objection to individuals voluntarily leaving tribal lands and becoming citizens, but this right was already provided them by treaty. However, allowing those who had sworn allegiance to the United States to remain in their midst would destroy the fabric of the tribe. The petitioners also argued that citizenship would be harmful

---

[7] H.R. No. 37–84 (April 18, 1862).

[8] Treaty with the Stockbridge Tribe, 9 Stat. 955 (1848).

[9] See Treaty with the Seneca, Mixed Seneca, Shawnee, Quapaw, Etc., 15 Stat. 513, Preamble & Art. 13 (1867); *see also Karahoo v. Adams*, 14 Fed. Case 134 (C.C. Kan. 1870) (holding that plaintiff had not accepted citizenship and could not be ejected from her land).

[10] See Citizenship of Indians, H.R. Ex. Doc. 43–228 (April 24, 1874).

[11] Memorial of the Delegates and Agents of the Choctaw and Chickasaw Nations of Indians Remonstrating against the passage of Senate Bill 107, to enable Indians to become citizens, S. Misc. Doc. 45–8 (December 10, 1877); Remonstrance of the Seminole and Creek Delegates against the passage of Senate Bill No. 107, to enable Indians to become citizens (January 14, 1878).

to their people, citing the example of 2,000 Kansas Indians who had been made citizens by similar legislation.[12] The Kansas Indians had since lost their property and sought to return to the Indian Territory and "become reconstructed as Indian tribes."[13] The petitioners claimed that out of a dozen bands affected by such citizenship legislation, for all but a few the results were disastrous.

Debates in the Reconstruction Congress reveal a similar ambiguity. Opponents of the Fourteenth Amendment argued that it would confer citizenship on the Indians and sought an amendment to explicitly exclude tribal Indians from the citizenship clause.[14] In contrast, proponents of Reconstruction opposed the amendment, but not because they wanted to include tribal members within the grant of citizenship. Rather, they argued that Indians maintaining relations with their tribes were already excluded from the citizenship clause by the requirement that one had to be both "born in the United States" and "subject to the jurisdiction thereof."[15] These arguments were based on the independence of Indian peoples, not their inferiority. For example, Senator Lyman Trumbull argued that "it would be a breach of good faith on our part to extend the laws of the United States over the Indian tribes with whom we have these treaty stipulations."[16] Senator Jacob Howard insisted that asserting tribal Indians were subject to the full and complete jurisdiction of the United States would be inconsistent with "the national character in which they have been recognized ever since the discovery of the continent and its occupation by civilized men."[17] Ultimately a proposal to explicitly exclude "Indians not taxed" from the Fourteenth Amendment failed, with Democrats comprising all but three of those voting for it, and Republicans comprising all of those voting against.[18]

---

[12] S. Misc. Doc. 45–8 (December 10, 1877) at 3.

[13] S. Misc. Doc. 45–8 (December 10, 1877) at 3.

[14] See Cong. Globe 2939, 39th Cong., 1st Sess., June 4, 1866 (Sen. Thomas Hendricks) (arguing that conferring citizenship on "the negroes, the coolies, and the Indians" would undermine the just pride that this rank belonged "to the inhabitants of the United States who were descended from the great races of people who inhabit the countries of Europe"); Cong. Globe 1067, 40th Cong. 2d Sess., February 8, 1868 (Sen. Reverdy Johnson) (arguing that citizenship should not be extended to the "negroes, Chinese, and Indians" as "the rights and liberties of the white men of this country are greater than can ever legally be accorded to the inferior races").

[15] U.S. Constitution. Amndt. 14, § 1, cl. 1.

[16] Cong. Globe 2894, 39th Cong. 1st Sess., May 30, 1866.

[17] *Id.* at 2895.

[18] *Id.* at 2897.

Soon after, however, the United States abandoned treaty-making with the Indian tribes and began a period of coercive regulation that increasingly denied tribes any measure of independence (Anderson et al. 2010, 90, 105). Extension of citizenship was part of this process. The 1887 Dawes Allotment Act, the defining legislation of the period, provided for allotment of tribal territories to individual Indians and the sale of any remaining land to homesteaders and railroads.[19] Individual property ownership was intended to be "a mighty pulverizing engine for breaking up the tribal mass" and separating the individual from the tribe (Gates [1900] 1973, 342). One of the act's provisions was that every Indian to whom an allotment was made or who had been born within the United States and who had voluntarily taken up "a residence separate and apart from any tribe" and "adopted the habits of civilized life" would become a citizen of the United States.[20] The following year, reacting to concerns that white men were marrying Indian women simply to obtain allotments, Congress passed a law forbidding any allotment rights by marriage and adding that all Indian women who married white men would thereby become citizens of the United States.[21] The measure was designed to encourage the couple to "come back to the confines of civilization" and impress upon the woman that she "must no longer remain in that country or a member of a tribe."[22]

The citizenship ceremony of the time explicitly linked citizenship, the end of tribal identity, and gendered concepts of assimilation. If the Indian accepting citizenship was male, he would first, in a symbolic gesture, "shoot his last arrow, and accept the plow"; the federal official would then declare, "This act means that you have chosen to live the life of the white man – and the white man lives by work. From the earth we must all get our living. . . . Only by work do we gain a right to the land. . . ." For a woman the ceremony was different: she would first renounce her allegiance to the tribe, and then accept a "work bag and purse." The federal official would then say, "This means you have chosen the life of the white woman – and the white woman loves her home. The family and home are the foundation of our civilization" (Valencia-Weber 2004, 349).

Such measures were intended to both encourage assimilation and hasten the termination of federal responsibilities for Indian people.

---

[19] 24 Stat. 388 (February 8, 1887).
[20] 24 Stat. 390, Sec. 6 (February 8, 1887).
[21] See Act of August 9, 1888, ch. 818, 25 Stat. 392 (1888).
[22] Cong. Rec. 6886 (July 26, 1888).

Citizenship was initially understood to end immunity of Indians from state law or taxation as well as federal obligations of support and protection. Although policy makers had hoped the magic of individual land ownership would result in speedy incorporation of Indians into the general public, such measures instead made the Indian population even poorer and more dependent on federal support. The plaintive 1888 petition by the Omaha tribe underscores the impact of this policy. This is the testimony of one of the petitioners:

> A woman came here among the Indians and gave me a name (that of citizen), but the Government gave me a name before that, and I want to take the name that the Government gave me. She ... kind of forced me to take that name, but I want to go by the name I had. That is the reason I asked God to help me.
>
> ...God made wild animals; made me live on them. They are now all gone, and that is the reason I have to hold the plow for a living.... Our Government told us to go to work and break the prairie; so we did, but our tools and machinery and harness are rotten and worn out; that is why we want you to buy tools and harness to work with.[23]

The federal government also intervened more directly in Indian lives, providing boarding schools, health care, tribal police, and courts, all rapidly expanding the cost of the Indian program. Ignoring that in many cases these programs were in fulfillment of treaty obligations, Congress sought to use citizenship as a reason to terminate such obligations, enacting laws, for example, that denied entrance to Indian schools to those whose parents were citizens and who themselves had less than one-quarter Indian blood.[24]

Of course, some measures extending citizenship were motivated by egalitarian desires. For example, it was largely abolitionist sentiments that led Massachusetts to enact the 1869 Massachusetts Indian Enfranchisement Act, making all Massachusetts Indians full citizens of the Commonwealth (Plane and Button 1993, 592–93). A number of African Americans who had married into Massachusetts Indian communities used the language of racial equality and Reconstruction to argue for the law (601–02).

---

[23] Petition of members of the Omaha Indian tribe in regard to citizenship and taxation, and praying for the payment of their annuities, S. Misc. Do. 50–26 (January 9, 1888).

[24] 63d Cong., 2d Sess., c.222, 38 Stat. 582, August 1, 1914; see also Citizenship of Indians, H.R. Rep. 52–1130 (recommending passage of bill that all Indians who had received ten years of schooling would become citizens at the age of twenty-one and "thereafter receive no more aid or support from the Government...the object being to fix a time and mode of bringing to a close the much-vexed 'Indian question'").

But most people in those communities opposed the act out of fear that by making formerly communally held property subject to state taxation and individual sale, the law would destroy the communities and the culture sustaining them (603–04). Despite this, Massachusetts passed the Enfranchisement Act, oblivious to the ambiguity of citizenship for these Indians and convinced intermarriage had rendered them no longer "real Indians" at all (593).

A similar ambiguity played out in Indian reactions to federal citizenship. In part due to the allotment's effect of breaking up tribal territories as well as the integrating effect of federal boarding schools and, later, service in World War I, an increasingly vocal minority of Indian people desired the benefits of citizenship. Both the Supreme Court and lower courts rejected a number of petitions by Indian people that they should be considered citizens for voting and other purposes.[25] On varying grounds, both lower and state courts generally reached similar conclusions. But although these Indians were actively pursuing citizenship, many others were fighting against its implications, challenging claims that as a result of citizenship they were subject to state marriage laws,[26] state taxation of their lands,[27] and state criminal prosecution.[28]

Whatever the desires and interests of the Indians involved, by virtue of various federal measures two-thirds of all Indians were U.S. citizens by 1924.[29] By this time, the Supreme Court had established the United

[25] *Elk v. Wilkins*, 112 U.S. 94 (1884) (holding that a man who had separated from his tribe and gone to live in a non-Indian community was not a citizen absent naturalization, and so was not entitled to vote in Nebraska); In Unclear re: Liquor Election in Beltrami County, 163 N.W. 988, 989 (Minn. 1917) (holding that because children of Indian mothers and citizen fathers were likely illegitimate, they took the status of their mothers and therefore could not vote in state elections); *McKay v. Campbell*, 16 F. Case 161 (D. Or. 1871) (holding that son of a British father and Indian mother born in Oregon Territory while it was a joint British-United States territory was not a citizen born subject to the jurisdiction of the United States). One California court, in contrast, held that a California Indian whose community had never been federally recognized as a tribe was indeed a citizen entitled to vote. *Anderson v. Matthews*, 163 P. 902 (California 1917).

[26] *Moore v. Wah-me-go*, 83 P. 400 (Kansas 1904) (holding effect of Indian divorce invalid because spouse was a citizen subject to state marriage and divorce laws); *Palmer v. Cully*, 153 P. 154 (Oklahoma 1915) (holding that petitioner was not lawfully married to the deceased, so that she had no right to his estate when she alleged she was defrauded into signing over the estate to another).

[27] *New Mexico v. Delinquent Tax List of Bernalillo County* for 1899, 76 P. 307 (New Mexico 1904); *see also U.S. v. Hester*, 137 F.2d 145 (10th Cir. 1943) (holding that as citizens Indians were subject to forced sale of their land for failure to pay state taxes).

[28] *Kitto v. State*, 152 N.W. 380 (Nebraska 1915).

[29] Joseph E. Otis, The Indian Problem: Resolution of the Committee of One Hundred Appointed by the Secretary of the Interior, H.R. Doc. 68–149 at 6 (January 7, 1924).

States did not lose power over those Indians who had become citizens, something that had been debated previously.[30] Advocacy organizations also were placing pressure on the United States to extend citizenship to all Indians. Still, a committee appointed to assess federal Indian policy found that "Indians, as a whole, are not much concerned with citizenship."[31] Nevertheless, on June 2, 1924, Congress declared that all Indians born within the territorial limits of the United States were citizens.[32]

Although citizenship provided benefits to Indian people, it also fueled arguments for destruction of their distinctive tribal rights. The 1924 act did lead some states that had previously denied noncitizen Indians the right to vote to extend it to all Indians; although New Mexico, Utah, and Arizona continued to deny Indians voting rights based on wardship, taxation, or reservation residence until after World War II (Berger 2009, 654–56). However, in the same period, federal and state policy makers used Indian citizenship as a rallying cry to end the special status of Indian people, leading to claims that reservations, immunity from state taxation, and everything else that made tribal members legally distinct was inconsistent with their status as citizens.[33] These arguments led to what is now called the Termination Policy, which guided federal Indian policy between the late 1940s and the 1960s, and resulted in termination of the federal relationship with some Indian tribes and the extension of state jurisdiction over many more (Anderson et al. 2010, 142–51). Policy makers justified these measures on grounds that otherwise Indians would still be "set apart from other citizens of the state."[34]

Again, some Indian people initially agreed that true equal citizenship meant ending the distinctive legal status of tribes and their territory. Others thought ending this status was the only way to escape the pervasive control of the Bureau of Indian Affairs. But by the mid-1950s, native people unified against any concept of "equality" that denied the group rights of tribal communities. Throughout the next decade, tribal communities and supra-tribal organizations would organize to demand

---

[30] *United States v. Waller*, 243 U.S. 252, 459–60 (1917); *United States v. Nice*, 241 U.S. 591, 601 (1916); *Tiger v. W. Inv. Co.*, 221 U.S. 286, 311–16 (1911).

[31] Otis, The Indian Problem 40 (1924).

[32] 43 Stat. 253 (June 2, 1924).

[33] See, e.g., An Investigation to Determine Whether the Changed Status of the Indian Requires a Revision of the Law and Regulations Affecting the American Indian, H.R. Rep. 78–2091 (December 3, 1944).

[34] Hearings before the Subcommittee on Indian Affairs of the Interior and Insular Affairs Committee, House of Representatives, to Amend Title 18, United States Code, Entitled "Crimes and Criminal Procedure," H.R. 1063 at 9 (June 29, 1953).

self-determination not as individual citizens but as tribal groups (Wilkinson 2005, 178–82).

In 1970, President Richard Nixon officially embraced self-determination as the guiding principle of federal Indian policy,[35] and this principle has guided Congressional enactments in Indian affairs ever since. The concept of self-determination recognizes the equality of individual Indians and seeks to ensure that they have the tools and encouragement to participate in social, political, and economic life on an equal basis with other citizens. But even more important, it recognizes the importance of the tribal community and seeks to strengthen the ability of tribal leadership to govern the conditions of life in tribal territories and for tribal people. Although the concept of self-determination has been challenged as creating unfair special rights, federal policy has made strides toward recognizing that individual equality and respect for tribal governments are not at odds, but rather are both necessary to ensure the well-being of native people.

THE CITIZEN–STATE DICHOTOMY IN INTERNATIONAL LAW REGARDING INDIGENOUS PEOPLES

These U.S. developments parallel those on the international stage. In the nineteenth and early twentieth centuries, international law recognized no governmental rights for indigenous peoples, seeing them at best as populations under trusteeship to be guided into assimilation (Anaya 2004, 27–33). Over the course of the twentieth century, however, the establishment of international law principles of self-determination and equality created space for discussion and eventual agreement on distinctive rights for indigenous peoples. As in U.S. law and policy, however, the citizen–state dichotomies initially used in implementing these concepts had to be modified to acknowledge indigenous peoples' claims.

Today, rights of equality and self-determination are established principles of international law. The 1945 UN Charter declares one of its fundamental purposes to be "to develop friendly relations among nations based on the principles of equality and self-determination of peoples."[36] The charter extended rights of self-determination beyond member states, placing obligations of "sacred trust" on states with responsibility for

---

[35] See Richard M. Nixon, Special Message on Indian Affairs (July 8, 1970) (announcing policy of "Self-Determination without Termination").

[36] UN Charter, Art. I, para 2.

"territories whose peoples have not yet attained a full measure of self-government... to take due account of the political aspirations of the peoples, and to assist them in the progressive development of their free institutions, according to the particular circumstances of the each territory."[37] Article 1 of both the International Covenant on Civil and Political Rights (ICCPR) and the International Covenant on Economic, Social, and Cultural Rights (ICESCR) further defines the self-determination principle, declaring that "All peoples have the right of self-determination. By virtue of that right they freely determine their political status and freely pursue their economic, social and cultural development."[38] The UN Charter also underscores the principle of equality for groups subject to discrimination, pledging its members to promote and encourage "human rights and fundamental freedoms for all without distinction as to race, sex, language, or religion."[39] Equality and protections from discrimination are further emphasized in both the ICCPR and the ICESCR.[40] Both self-determination and equality have been recognized and elaborated on in numerous other global and regional international agreements.

The equality and self-determination principles have contributed to successful movements for decolonization and protection of minority rights; both, in turn, lent ideological credence to demands for indigenous rights (Anaya 2004, 53–56). Still, neither decolonization nor minority rights movements provided an adequate conceptualization of the claims of indigenous peoples. Although the decolonization movement contained many principles applicable to the struggles of indigenous peoples, the decolonization process was limited to geographically separate territories.[41] Indigenous peoples, however, were geographically incorporated within states and rarely sought full political independence. On the flip side, the protection of international law for minorities, while providing crucial support for the indigenous rights movement, did not capture

---

[37] UN Charter, Art. 73.

[38] International Covenant on Civil and Political Rights, December 16, 1966, G.A. Res. 2200A (XXI), art. 1 (entered into force March 23, 1976); International Covenant on Economic, Social and Cultural Rights, December 16, 1966, G.A. Res. 2200A (XXI), art. 1 (entered into force January 3, 1976).

[39] UN Charter, Art. I, para. 3.

[40] International Covenant on Civil and Political Rights, Preamble & art. 2, 20, 25–27; International Covenant on Economic, Social and Cultural Rights, Preamble & art. 2.

[41] See GA Res. 1541(XV), December 15, 1960 (principles guiding the determination of whether an entity was a non-self-governing territory entitled under the UN Charter, Art. XI, Sec. 73.).

aspects of indigenous demands. Minority rights protections focused on full incorporation within the majority. However, a necessary element of indigenous rights is respect for their distinct status and institutions. A model of minority rights that emphasizes integration, therefore, is not helpful to – and may even undermine – this goal.

Both the support of self-determination and minority rights movements and their limitations are reflected in the origins of the UN Declaration on the Rights of Indigenous Peoples. The working group that drafted the declaration was formed in 1982 in response to a study commissioned by the Sub-Commission on Prevention of Discrimination and Protection of Minorities.[42] Indigenous peoples from around the world quickly became involved in its work, traveling each summer to articulate their claims to the working group. The initial title of both the study and the working group referred to "Indigenous Populations," a term that did not reflect indigenous peoples' claims to collective rights distinct from those of other minority populations (Daes 2001, 260). When the group changed its name to the "Working Group on Indigenous Peoples," however, the change to "peoples" fed state concerns that the term implied demands for self-determination (Anaya 2004, 59–60, 98).

Since 1993, when the initial draft was completed, the declaration has emphasized self-determination as a matter of both equality and human rights. The declaration affirms that "indigenous peoples are equal in dignity and rights to all other peoples, while recognizing the right of all peoples to be different, to consider themselves different, and to be respected as such."[43] It proclaims these basic principles in its first three articles:

Article 1. Indigenous peoples have the right to the full and effective enjoyment of all human rights and fundamental freedoms recognized in the Charter of the United Nations, the Universal Declaration of Human Rights and international human rights law.

Article 2. Indigenous individuals and peoples are free and equal to all other individuals and peoples in dignity and rights, and have the right to be free from any kind of adverse discrimination, in particular that based on their indigenous origin or identity.

---

[42] See ECOSOC Res. 1982/34 (May 7, 1982).
[43] Declaration on the Rights of Indigenous Peoples, G.A. Res. 61/295, U.N. Doc. A/Res/61/295 (September 13, 2007).

Article 3. Indigenous peoples have the right of self-determination. By virtue of that right they freely determine their political status and freely pursue their economic, social and cultural development.[44]

Dr. Irene-Erica Daes, who was appointed to draft the declaration, reports that the announcement of the decision to include Article 3 was greeted with a standing ovation from the indigenous participants (Daes 2001, 261).

Although the Sub-Commission on Prevention of Discrimination and Protection of Minorities approved the draft by 1994,[45] fear of the self-determination principle contributed to a thirteen-year delay before the declaration was approved by the UN General Assembly (Daes 2001, 262). Finally, the Human Rights Council approved the declaration in June 2006, and 144 members of the General Assembly voted overwhelmingly to adopt it on September 13, 2007.[46] There were only four votes against the declaration; since then, all four of the opponents (Australia, New Zealand, Canada, and the United States) have agreed to support the declaration. Although the declaration is nonbinding, it adds significant support to arguments that its rights are a matter of enforceable international customary law.

These rights include those of meaningful citizenship and go beyond them. They emphasize freedom from discrimination, entitlement to culture and religion, as well as health and economic well-being.[47] But they also include rights not attached to individual citizens – the right to equality "as peoples," rights to self-determination (including in questions of political status and development), as well as rights of property held in common and under customary law.[48] The declaration has generated protests, like those lodged with regard to federal Indian law, that it creates a special set of privileges inconsistent with citizenship (Errico 2007, 745). It is true that the declaration creates a third status, neither state nor individual. But this status and the rights emerging from it are neither new nor inconsistent with equality. They instead reflect the mutual respect and dignity that equality requires (Daes 1995, 498).

Although the United States agreed to support the declaration on December 16, 2010, most of these international law developments have

[44] *Id.*
[45] Res. 1994/45, UN Sub-Commission on Prevention of Discrimination and Protection of Minorities, UN Doc. E/CN.4/1995/2 (1995).
[46] G.A. Res. 61/295.
[47] See, e.g., Declaration Arts. 2, 11–12 & 24.
[48] See, e.g., Declaration Arts. 2, 3, 5, 20 & 26.

had little impact on American Indians under previous administrations. As in other areas, the United States has reacted with indifference and even disdain for the constraints of international law. A telling example comes from the saga of the Dann sisters, two Shoshone women deprived of their family land by a federal claim brought by another Shoshone band. After losing before the U.S. Supreme Court,[49] the sisters brought their claim to the Inter-American Commission of Human Rights, an organ of the Organization of American States (OAS). The commission concluded that the United States had deprived the sisters of rights to equality, a fair trial, and property in violation of the American Declaration of the Rights and Duties of Man.[50] Although the United States is a member of the OAS and a signatory to the declaration, it responded by seizing and selling 252 of the sisters' cattle from the land, declaring, "The [OAS] has no jurisdiction here" (Andrersen 2002). In 2006, the United Nations condemned the United States for failing even to respond to the UN Committee for the Elimination of Racial Discrimination regarding its concerns about treatment of Western Shoshone lands.[51]

However, the actions of the Obama administration suggest the impact of international human rights norms. In 2007, Amnesty International published a report condemning the failure of the United States to address a crisis of sexual violence against American Indian women (Amnesty International 2007). Federal law limiting tribal criminal jurisdiction and creating a maze of federal, state, and tribal law helped generate the crisis by creating relative impunity for sexual offenders (Amnesty International 2007, 6–8). The year after the report, the UN Committee on the Elimination of Racial Discrimination recommended that the United States address the high rates of rape and sexual violence against Native women.[52] The Amnesty International report created the impetus for the Tribal Law and Order Act, which President Barack Obama signed into law on July 29, 2010.[53] The law strengthens tribal jurisdiction and improves federal health and law enforcement services, thus increasing tribal self-determination and increasing federal compliance with centuries-old treaty obligations. Although the United States did not cite international law as a

---

[49] *See United States v. Dann*, 470 U.S. 39 (1985).

[50] *Dann v. United States*, Case 11.140, Inter-Am. C.H.R., Report No. 113/01, para. 147 (2001).

[51] Decision 1 (68): United States of America, UN Doc. CERD/C/USA/DEC/1, April 11, 2006.

[52] Consideration of Reports Submitted by State Parties under Article 9 of the Convention: United States, UN Doc. CERD/C/USA/CO/6 (May 8, 2008).

[53] Pub. L. 111–211 § 201 (July 29, 2010).

motivation for the act, it acknowledged the role of Amnesty International in catalyzing the measure.[54] In agreeing to support the UN Declaration on Indigenous Peoples Rights, the Obama administration listed this and numerous other steps it had taken that are consistent with the goals of the declaration. Thus, despite its insistence that the norms of the declaration are non-binding and do not state current international law, the United States is finally acknowledging and responding to its political and moral force.

CONCLUSION

Historically citizenship has been used to deny human rights to indigenous peoples as often as it has been used to further them. When indigenous groups claimed self-governance rights that were distinct from those of other citizens within the states that had colonized them, colonizing states extended citizenship to further assimilate and undermine indigenous resistance to colonization. State citizenship was the triumph of assimilation and the opposite of indigeneity. Although Native people in the United States increasingly depended on citizenship for protection from abuse and discrimination, citizenship itself had an ambiguous status and often resulted in the denial of tribal rights that American Indians held equally dear.

This anomaly derives from a deeper legal and conceptual failing, one that takes individual citizen and national state as fundamental legal categories and fails to recognize nonstate collective self-governance rights. But over the last decades, both U.S. and international human rights law have begun to acknowledge and protect a fundamental right beyond citizenship. These are the rights of peoples – groups with separate culture, history, and political rights – who are within yet distinct from the states that surround them. These rights are finding halting recognition in U.S. policies of self-determination for Indian tribes, in the newly adopted UN Declaration of Indigenous Peoples Rights, and in the emerging jurisprudence of international law tribunals across the globe.

For centuries indigenous peoples' rights to self-determination have been attacked as inconsistent with both state rights and citizenship rights. But for just as long, indigenous peoples have fought for these rights and even won a measure of recognition of self-determination in domestic and

[54] Sen. Rep. No. 111–93 at 19 (Oct. 29, 2009).

international law. Historically, this acknowledgment has been inconsistent, incomplete, and rarely implemented in practice. However, it is finally beginning to secure more solid ground.

REFERENCES

Amnesty International. 2007. *Maze of Injustice: The Failure to Protect Indigenous Women from Sexual Violence in the U.S.A.* New York: Amnesty International Publications.

Anaya, S. James. 2004. *Indigenous Peoples in International Law.* New York: Oxford University Press.

Anderson, Robert T., Bethany Berger, Philip Frickey, and Sarah Krakoff. 2010. *American Indian Law: Cases and Materials.* 2nd Edition. St. Paul, MN: Thomson/West.

Andrersen, Martin Edwin. 2002. "Spat Over Federal Takeover Has Latin America Watching." *UPI Insight Magazine,* November 26.

Berger, Bethany R. 2009. "Red: Racism and the American Indian." *UCLA Law Review* 56: 591–656.

Calloway, Colin G. 1995. *The Revolution Comes to Indian Country: Crisis and Diversity in Native American Communities.* Cambridge, UK: Cambridge University Press.

Cohen, Felix S. 1942. *Handbook of Federal Indian Law.* Washington, D.C.: Government Printing Office.

Daes, Erica-Irene A. 1995. "Equality of Indigenous Peoples under the Auspices of the United Nations Draft Declaration on the Rights of Indigenous Peoples." *St. Thomas Law Review* 7: 493–99.

——— 2001. "The Concepts of Self-Determination and Autonomy of Indigenous Peoples in the Draft United Nations Declaration on the Rights of Indigenous Peoples." *St. Thomas Law Review* 14: 259–61.

Errico, Stefania. 2007. "The Draft UN Declaration on the Rights of Indigenous Peoples: An Overview." *Human Rights Law Review* 7: 741–55.

Gates, Merrill E. [1900] 1973. "Addresses at the Lake Mohonk Conferences." In *Americanizing the American Indians,* edited by F. Prucha. Cambridge, MA: Harvard University Press.

Kades, Eric. 2000. "The Dark Side of Efficiency: *Johnson v. M'Intosh* and the Expropriation of American Indian Lands." *University of Pennsylvania Law Review* 148: 1065–1190.

New York Times. 1985. "Around the Nation: 143 Renegade Kickapoos Accept Citizenship." November 22. http://www.nytimes.com/1985/11/22/us/around-the-nation-143-renegade-kickapoos-accept-us-citizenship.html.

Plane, Anne Marie, and Gregory Button. 1993. "The Massachusetts Indian Enfranchisement Act: Ethnic Contest in Historical Context, 1849–1869." *Ethnohistory* 40: 587–618.

Porter, Robert B. 1999. "The Demise of Ohnegeweh and the Rise of the Native Americans: Redressing the Genocidal Act of Forcing Citizenship on Native American Peoples." *Harvard Blackletter Journal* 15: 107–83.

Valencia-Weber, Gloria. 2004. "Racial Equality: Old and New Strains and American Indians." *Notre Dame Law Review* 80: 333–75.

Victoria, Franciscus de. [1557] 1917. *De Indis et de Ivre Belli Relectiones*. Edited by Ernest Nys, translated by J. Bate. Washington, D.C.: Carnegie Institution.

Wilkinson, Charles. 2005. *Blood Struggle: The Rise of Modern American Indian Nations*. New York: W.W. Norton & Co.

12

Human Rights Violations as Obstacles to Escaping Poverty: The Case of Lone-Mother-Headed Families

Ken Neubeck

INTRODUCTION

The United States is best characterized as an "outlier" in comparison with other affluent nations when it comes to examining and addressing domestic social and economic conditions through the lens of a human rights framework (Schulz 2009). Over the last decade, however, an energetic albeit somewhat eclectic domestic political movement has emerged within the United States whose goal is to bring this nation's domestic policies and practices into conformity with international human rights principles and standards. This movement, in effect, seeks to "bring human rights home" (Thomas 2008).

The U.S. human rights movement is spearheaded by an informal and growing coalition of more than 200 national, regional, and local social justice organizations that identify as members of the U.S. Human Rights Network (http://www.ushrnetwork.org). The network coalition is diverse, both geographically and in its composition. Member organizations address a wide range of human rights issues, including the protection of civil liberties, abolition of capital punishment, immigration reform, homelessness and affordable housing needs, health care, environmental deterioration, as well as the rights of indigenous peoples, the LGBTQ population, workers, prisoners, people with disabilities, impoverished families, women, children, and people of color (Soohoo, Albisa, and Davis 2008).

Within the U.S. human rights movement, poverty in the United States and the U.S. government's response to it are central human rights issues. Domestic poverty has not typically been framed as a human rights matter by U.S. political elites, the mass media, or most scholars. The task of bringing a human rights framework to bear on poverty has largely fallen to the poor themselves. It is a rallying cry that started with the Reverend Dr. Martin Luther King Jr.'s Poor People's Campaign of 1968 (Jackson 2006) and continues today in the grassroots Poor People's Economic Human Rights Campaign or PPEHRC (http://old.economichumanrights. org/index.shtml), an effort for which King's work provides strong inspiration. Indeed, it was King himself who, in 1967, proclaimed it time to begin the "second phase" of the civil rights movement, stating: " . . . we have moved from the era of civil rights to the era of human rights" (King 1967). More than sixty years later, this second phase is still unfolding.

PPEHRC and allied groups such as the Philadelphia-based Kensington Welfare Rights Union (http://www.kwru.org) and the Oakland (California)-based Women's Economic Agenda Project (http://www .weap.org) have insisted that poverty must be understood as a violation of human rights. PPEHRC points to the principles and standards embodied in the Universal Declaration of Human Rights (UDHR) in calling for the abolition of poverty in the United States, not simply poverty reduction or the amelioration of its most harmful effects. PPEHRC condemns domestic poverty as an international human rights violation and dismisses what it sees as the tepid response of the U.S. government to addressing it. The U.S. response to poverty is seen as hypocritical in light of political elites' frequent characterization of the United States as a world leader when it comes to respecting, protecting, and fulfilling international human rights.

Poverty-level family living conditions have long been disproportionately present among lone mothers and their children in the United States. One might expect that in such a highly affluent nation impoverished women and children would receive public assistance at a level commensurate with basic human needs. Indeed, Article 25 of the UDHR, in setting forth the principle that all people have the right to an adequate standard of living ("including food, clothing, housing, medical care and necessary social services"), clearly states: "Motherhood and childhood are entitled to special care and assistance. All children, whether born in or out of wedlock, shall enjoy the same social protection" (United Nations 1948, Article 25). Instead, the operating principle of the U.S. federal government when it comes to poverty has been characterized as "women and children last" (Sidel 1998).

Public assistance for lone-mother-headed families – of which Temporary Assistance for Needy Families (TANF), popularly known as "welfare," is the main source – does little to eliminate poverty, as we will see.

The U.S. human rights movement has, not surprisingly, come to view the U.S. system of welfare provision as in direct contradiction to fundamental human rights principles such as those set forth in Article 25 of the UDHR (Neubeck 2006, 151–76; Pollack 2008). The U.S. welfare system is equally at odds with the International Covenant on Economic, Social and Cultural Rights, a key human rights treaty that likewise recognizes "the right of everyone to an adequate standard of living" (United Nations 1966, Article 11). The United States signed this treaty but has never ratified it.

Grassroots groups such as PPEHRC have been joined in their denunciation of welfare policies by such human rights advocacy organizations as the National Economic and Social Rights Initiative (http://www.nesri.org) and the Urban Justice Center's Human Rights Project (http://hrpujc.org). Studies conducted by the latter on TANF eligibility policies and benefits have underscored the harm being done to poor families by contemporary "welfare reform" legislation (Pitcher 2002).

This chapter will critique U.S. welfare policy by examining how lone-mother-headed families have been faring during the United States' worst economic crisis since the 1930s Depression. As we will see, the nation's welfare system has proven remarkably inadequate in responding to their impoverishment and the hardships and suffering that go along with it. Even in economically healthy times, the United States lags far behind most other affluent nations when it comes to effectively addressing and reducing domestic poverty, particularly for lone mothers and their children (Neubeck 2006, 113–50).

Although the welfare system itself poses an obstacle to the ability of lone mothers and their children to escape poverty, other obstacles appear to be equally salient. Little attention has been paid to the diversity of the poverty population and variety of life circumstances characterizing its members. Thus, few scholars have addressed the multiple and intersecting sources of oppression affecting impoverished lone-mother-headed families and the ways that the welfare system contributes to such oppression (Neubeck 2006, 67–111). Impoverished lone-mother-headed families are subjected to numerous human rights violations that reinforce their inability to attain an adequate standard of living. Here we will limit our discussion to two groups of impoverished lone-mother-headed families: those containing family members with disabilities and those families with members who are immigrants to the United States. Members of such families are extremely vulnerable to impoverishment, and yet they are among those least well served by the U.S. welfare system.

We will begin by addressing the current increase in the U.S. poverty rate and the failure of the nation's welfare system to respond to the impoverishment of lone-mother-headed families in a meaningful way.

WELFARE "REFORM" AND THE GROWING POVERTY/WELFARE ASSISTANCE GAP

The plight of impoverished lone-mother-headed families and the failure of the U.S. welfare system to adequately address this plight need to be considered within the larger context of economic inequality in the United States. The gross and worsening inequality in the distribution of household wealth has been well documented (Wolff 2002). In addition, income inequality has been growing and in the last several years has reached an all-time high. In 2007, income concentration among the richest 1 percent of families was the highest it had been since 1928 (Feller and Stone 2009). Census data for 2008 showed that the top 5 percent of households received 21.5 percent of all household income that year, compared to the 3.4 percent that went to the 20 percent of households with the lowest incomes (U.S. Bureau of the Census 2009, table 3, 10). Poverty in the United States must be viewed as both an outcome and an expression of the prevailing systemic economic inequalities.

Although the nation's rich have gotten progressively richer in recent years (leaving aside their setbacks from presumably temporary downward plunges of the stock market and housing values), the plight of members of the U.S. poverty population has not significantly improved. Indeed, by all indications the situation of the impoverished has been worsened by the near-calamitous economic recession that began in December 2007. U.S. Census statistics indicate that the nation's poverty rate increased from 12.5 to 13.2 percent between 2007 and 2008, the highest rate since 1997. In 2007, prior to the recession, 37.3 million people were living in poverty in the United States. By 2008, this number had increased to 39.8 million (U.S. Bureau of the Census 2009, table 4, 14). The 2009 Census statistics show a continued upward trend in the numbers of those living below the official federal poverty line, with 43.6 million people in poverty that year (U.S. Bureau of the Census 2010, table 4, 15).

Within those officially categorized as poor in the United States, lone-mother-headed families tend to be among the poorest. Women are 40 percent more likely to be poor than men, less likely to be employed, and on average earn less than men do when they are employed (Casey et al. 2009, 2). A family consisting of one adult and two children younger than eighteen years of age was considered poor in 2008 if its income was below $17,346 (U.S. Bureau of the Census 2009, 43). According to U.S. Census data, in 2008 the poverty rate was 28.7 percent for female-headed families, more than twice the U.S. poverty rate for all individuals and families combined. These impoverished lone-mother-headed families contained 4.2 million members in 2008, most of whom were children (U.S. Bureau of the Census 2009, table 3, 10).

It would seem logical to expect that Temporary Assistance for Needy Families, the only government program providing cash assistance to impoverished families, would expand to help more families in times of increasing rates of poverty and widespread economic hardship. Indeed, for much of the time that federal and state government "welfare" benefits for poor families have been available, starting with the Depression of the 1930s, caseloads have typically expanded during economic recessions (Zedlewski 2008, 1). It is important, of course, to emphasize that such caseload expansion has never been a panacea for poverty. For a variety of reasons, cash assistance has never reached many lone-mother-headed families who are financially eligible, and the cash benefits available to such families have always been kept at a level well below the federally established poverty threshold (Neubeck 2006, 19–27; Neubeck and Cazenave 2001, 39–67).

Still, under the Social Security Act of 1935, which established "welfare" as a national federal–state program, all financially eligible families were legally *entitled* to cash benefits when and for as long as they were needed. Providing public assistance as a legal entitlement to those deemed eligible is, however, not the same as fulfilling an inalienable economic "human right." Needs-based assistance can be taken away, and this is exactly what occurred in 1990s "welfare reform" (Neubeck 2006).

In 1996, Congress passed the Personal Responsibility and Work Opportunity Reconciliation Act, which abolished Aid to Families with Dependent Children (AFDC) and replaced it with Temporary Assistance for Needy Families (TANF). Under this act, the federal government turned responsibility for administration of cash assistance over to individual states, thus eliminating any set national standard for the administration of welfare (Neubeck 2006, 30–31). This "devolution" of authority over welfare eligibility policies from the federal to the state level in effect created fifty different welfare systems. Welfare policies differ from state to state, and the amounts of cash assistance available to eligible families vary widely (Rowe and Murphy 2009).

The legal entitlement to cash assistance for eligible families that had been in existence since 1935 was abolished under TANF. Conditions for eligibility were made far more stringent than was the case for AFDC: most adult welfare recipients now had to meet mandatory work requirements to be eligible for cash assistance, and strict time limits for receiving aid were implemented for the first time. States were allowed to implement sanctions for welfare policy rule violations by recipients, including reduction or suspension of cash aid to families. They were also allowed to adopt eligibility and enrollment policies designed to divert new applicants from successfully joining the welfare rolls. From the mid-1990s on, welfare caseloads dropped significantly across the nation. This drop just barely and only temporarily slowed during the national economic recession of 2001 and continued apace when that recession was over.

The magnitude of the drop in the number of impoverished families assisted by the TANF program has been remarkable given that there has not been a similar drop in poverty rates among lone-mother-headed families in the same period. The welfare rolls have fallen "from 4.8 million families with 9 million children in 1995 to 1.7 million families with 3 million children in 2008" (Legal Momentum 2009d, 1). Moreover, fewer families who economically qualify to receive TANF cash assistance have been receiving aid: "the percent of poor children receiving welfare has declined continuously under TANF, falling from 62% in 1995 to 24% in 2007" (Legal Momentum 2009d, 1). The drop in the welfare rolls has been due to a reduction in the number of eligible families participating in TANF, not a reduction in rates of lone-mother-headed family poverty.

It should also be noted that the TANF benefits lone-mother-headed families receive have plunged in real dollar value during this same post-1996 period, falling in comparison to rising costs in living. In July 2008, for example, in all but one state a family of three (mother and two children) received a daily benefit per person of less than $8, and in thirty states the per-person benefit was below $5 per day (Legal Momentum 2009c, 1). As a consequence, the percentage of welfare-recipient families living in extreme poverty (defined as below 50 percent of the federally established poverty line) has been rising even as the TANF caseloads have been falling (Legal Momentum 2009d, 2).

The average family welfare benefit is only 29 percent of the official federal poverty threshold (Legal Momentum 2009a), an arbitrary income line most experts today believe is drawn unrealistically low. In the words of Legal Momentum, a women's advocacy group,

> Indeed, even when benefits were somewhat higher than they are now, substantial shares of recipients were reporting hardships such as being forced to move, overcrowding, utility disconnects, not having enough food to eat, inadequate winter clothing, and inability to pay for needed medical care.
>
> (2009c, 1)

The deep national recession that began in December 2007 has posed incredible challenges for lone mothers striving to support their families, given that it has been accompanied by an extremely rapid increase in unemployment (Hwang 2009). Between December 2007 and September 2009 the national unemployment rate literally doubled, going from 4.9 percent to 9.8 percent (U.S. Department of Labor 2009). Although by late 2009 many economists believed that the recession was showing signs of bottoming out, unemployment rates were expected to remain high for some time to come, and economists have predicted an extended period of "jobless recovery."

To receive cash assistance, TANF recipients must meet mandatory work requirements, a key component of federal welfare reform legislation passed in 1996. As one welfare policy expert put it, "pushing single mothers into jobs 'makes sense when unemployment is 5 percent. But if you are out of work, the welfare system in a time of recession doesn't have anything to offer'" (Eckholm 2009). Another commented, "We have a work-based safety net without work. We're really in a pickle" (DeParle 2009b).

Early in the recession, welfare rolls not only were not rising but actually *fell* in some states even as unemployment and poverty rates rose (U.S. Government Accountability Office 2010). *The New York Times* reported eighteen states cut their welfare rolls in 2008 even as the recession began to take its toll. "Of the 12 states where joblessness grew most rapidly, eight reduced or kept constant the number of families receiving [TANF]" (DeParle 2009c). In Michigan, which has led the nation with the highest unemployment rate of any state during this recession (a rate above 14 percent by mid-2009), more families were impoverished in 2009, but a smaller number of Michigan families were receiving TANF cash assistance than was the case in the previous year (Delaney 2009).

Only late in the recession did the national welfare rolls begin to show signs of rising. According to a survey conducted in mid-2009, "Twenty-three of the 30 largest states, which account for more than 88 percent of the nation's total population, see welfare caseloads above year-ago levels" (Murray 2009). Lest this be seen as evidence of a strong safety net finally engaging and extending to include more impoverished families eligible for public assistance, the main reason given for these rising welfare rolls was an increase in newly unemployed women who exhausted their eligibility for state unemployment compensation (Murray 2009).

Nor are other government programs able to do much for impoverished lone-mother-headed families. In reality, the United States' mature "welfare state" is a patchwork system at best:

> As millions of Americans seek government aid, many for the first time, they are finding it dispensed American style: through a jumble of disconnected programs that reach some and reject others, often for reasons of geography or chance rather than differences in need . . . State differences make the patchwork more pronounced . . . The result is a hit-or-miss system of relief, never designed to grapple with the pain of a recession so sudden and deep.
>
> (DeParle 2009a)

One can only react with astonishment regarding the meager cash resources the government allocates to families fortunate enough to get on the TANF rolls relative to other expenditures. In 2007 (the latest year for which such figures are available), spending for TANF cash assistance to families totaled $4.5 billion. In contrast, during a six-month period ending in April 2009, the federal government committed $700 billion to the Troubled Asset Relief Program (TARP) set up to bail out the nation's failing banks (Grabell 2009). The federal government did allocate $5 billion in economic "stimulus" funds in 2009 for emergency support of needy families; however, only twenty-three states applied because they were required to put up 20 percent in matching funds (Grabell 2009). In commenting on this disjuncture in government "welfare" spending priorities, University of Massachusetts economist Nancy Folbre noted "[t]op executives of banks bailed out this year – about 600 guys – received an estimated $1.6 billion in bonuses in 2007. That's a little over a third of what 1.6 million families got in cash from TANF that year" (Folbre 2009).

In short, by all evidence the U.S. government is seriously failing to address widespread poverty in the United States, including the impoverishment being experienced by some of U.S. society's most vulnerable members: women and children. The United States falls far short of meeting the human rights standards set forth in Article 25 of the Universal Declaration of Human Rights calling for "an adequate standard of living" for the entire nation's members. The failure of the U.S. welfare system to effectively address poverty was critically commented upon by a United Nations independent expert on human rights and extreme poverty just prior to the start of the recession. The expert observed, after visiting the United States in 2005,

> Government programmes have not effectively remedied the vulnerable situation of those groups at most risk of extreme poverty, notably African Americans, Hispanics, immigrants and women single-headed households... There is no national anti-poverty legislation in the United States... If the United States adopted a comprehensive national strategy and programmes based on human rights principles it would be possible to reduce poverty and eradicate extreme poverty.
> (United Nations Commission on Human Rights 2006)

Besides its lack of recognition of fundamental economic human rights, the United States is failing to proactively address other human rights violations that add further weight to the burdens lone mothers face. Let us examine how this plays out in the case of impoverished lone-mother-headed families with disabilities as well as immigrant families.

THE ADDED BURDENS OF DISABILITY
FOR LONE-MOTHER-HEADED FAMILIES

On July 30, 2009, the United States joined 141 other nations in signing a key human rights treaty, the Convention on the Rights of Persons with Disabilities (CRPD) (United Nations 2006). This is the first international human rights agreement the Obama Administration agreed to sign and the first human rights treaty signed by the United States in almost a decade. It remains to be seen whether the U.S. Senate will ultimately ratify the disability convention and, if it does ratify it, what reservations, understandings, and/or declarations it will attach that may weaken or undercut its domestic implementation. It is unclear whether and how this treaty will affect the treatment of people with disabilities in the United States. Nonetheless, the signing of the CRPD is a milestone: by signing it, the U.S. government acknowledges that the treatment of persons with disabilities can and should be framed as a human rights issue.

Viewing disability as a human rights issue has important implications for impoverished lone-mother-headed families because these families are far more likely than nonpoor families (mother-headed or not) to have members with a disability (Loprest and Maag 2009). Whereas disabilities vary greatly in the degree of impairment they impose and the permanence of impairment, many mental and physical disabilities can make it difficult for lone mothers to be employed. Depending upon the nature of the disability and degree of impairment, those who are able to work and who can find employment may find that they must limit the number of hours they are on the job or the types of tasks they perform (Neubeck 2006, 75–79).

According to a report prepared for the U.S. Department of Health and Human Services, "more than a quarter of TANF recipients report that they have a physical, mental, or emotional problem that keeps them from working or limits the kind or amount of work they can do" (Loprest and Maag 2009, 10). The percentage of TANF recipients reporting such work limitations is substantially higher than is the case for low-income lone mothers in general and for all adults (Loprest and Maag 2009, 10). TANF recipients also often face the challenge of caring for other adults with disabilities. Twelve percent of TANF recipient families have another adult in the household with a disability, again a higher percentage than is the case for other groups (Loprest and Maag 2009, 17).

TANF, as we have noted, contains a mandatory work requirement for recipients of cash assistance as well as time limits on receiving this assistance. The program operates under the premise that lone mothers – in return for cash assistance – will enter the labor force, begin to work, and transition off welfare by becoming workers capable of supporting themselves and their children. Women *without* disabilities often have much difficulty accomplishing the welfare-to-work feat. This is true in the best of economic times, but the feat has been made even more difficult by the virtual disappearance in the current recession of millions of jobs paying wages sufficient to adequately maintain a family.

Women *with* disabilities find moving from welfare to work even more challenging than able-bodied women. This is not solely attributable to their physical or mental limitations. Too many employers who could readily and affordably make accommodations to disability-related limitations are not interested in doing so, particularly in times of high unemployment when there are many able-bodied people available and eager to work. Moreover, the simple fact of having a disability (or even being thought to have one) can expose women to subtle employment or workplace discrimination. Consequently, women with disabilities have significantly higher rates of unemployment and underemployment than able-bodied women. At the same time, the overall financial needs of women with disabilities can be greater insofar as they face personal expenses associated with health care treatment that other women do not.

The Americans with Disabilities Act (ADA), an important U.S. civil rights law, prohibits discrimination against people with disabilities in the administration of TANF (http://www.hhs.gov/ocr/civilrights/understanding/disability/index.html). States are required under the ADA to adjust work requirements for adult TANF recipients with disabilities. At the same time, TANF policy discourages making such adjustments by threatening fiscal penalties for states that do not meet federally established employment participation standards for their total pool of recipients (disabled or not). To avoid such penalties, states must show that the adult heads of 50 percent of their TANF families are participating in work (Pavetti 2009, 2). TANF does not permit states to deem non-work activities for recipients with disabilities as counting toward the federal standard (Parrott 2007). In 2010, U.S. Congresswoman Gwen Moore introduced legislation to give states this flexibility without fiscal penalty (Moore 2010). But until such legislation becomes law, states will continue to face federal TANF policy that effectively results in unjust treatment of TANF recipients with disabilities.

It is also important to note that many children in TANF-recipient families have disabilities (Parrish, Andrews, and Rose 2010). Almost 3 percent of TANF recipients "have a child with a self-care or activity limitation" (Loprest and Maag 2009, 16). Depending on the severity of those limitations, child care responsibilities and difficulties finding outside care for special needs children may seriously hinder lone mothers' employment options, even as their families are faced with significant child health care expenses. The situation is exacerbated when, as occasionally occurs, both a mother and one or more of her children have disabilities. And, as noted in the previous section, 12 percent of TANF recipients have other adults with disabilities in their households. Many of these adults also require lone mothers' care.

In its 1996 welfare reform legislation, the federal government established a maximum lifetime limit of five years for receipt of TANF assistance but allowed individual states to set shorter eligibility time limits. Most states have done so (Rowe and Murphy 2009). Those lone mothers able to work typically leave the TANF rolls as soon as earnings from employment allow this to happen. But women with disabilities or who have children with disabilities tend to remain on the TANF rolls longer than other women and often have no choice but to rely on TANF assistance until their time-limited eligibility for cash assistance ends. Not surprisingly, over time there has been an increase in the proportion of families on the TANF rolls whose members have disabilities (Parish, Andrews, and Rose 2010).

Some mothers have been able to leave the TANF rolls and receive permanent financial assistance under Social Security Income (SSI) and Disability Insurance (DI), two federal disability-targeted programs administered by the U.S. Social Security Administration. But the eligibility requirements for these programs are onerous, not only in substance but also in form. For example, women seeking SSI or disability benefits must produce exhaustive medical records – yet many are uninsured. As more people have joined those programs and their costs to government have increased, efforts to impose *further* eligibility restrictions have emerged.

Were the United States to ratify the Convention on the Rights of Persons with Disabilities, it would be obligated to work toward the elimination of economic rights violations experienced by lone-mother-headed families burdened by disabilities. The U.S. government would need to radically change current policies if it were to conform to Article 28 of the Convention:

> States Parties recognize the right of persons with disabilities to an adequate standard of living for themselves and their families, including adequate food, clothing and housing, and to the continuous improvement of living conditions, and shall take appropriate steps to safeguard and promote the realization of this right without discrimination on the basis of disability.
>
> (United Nations 2006)

Finally, it is noteworthy that the U.S. government is one of only two United Nations members that has not ratified the Convention on the Rights of the Child (United Nations 1989). It was the first international treaty containing an article specifically addressing the human rights of children with disabilities: "a mentally or physically disabled child should enjoy a full and decent life, in conditions that ensure dignity, promote self-reliance, and facilitate the child's active participation in the community" (United Nations 2007, 4). The United States is a long way from meeting this human rights standard when it comes to providing support to impoverished mothers caring for children with disabilities.

THE ADDED BURDENS OF IMMIGRATION STATUS
FOR LONE-MOTHER-HEADED FAMILIES

Immigrant families face a dual burden: the challenge of fulfilling their basic subsistence and the challenge of transcending the negative stigma that many members of the public bestow on their immigration status (a stigma that may be informed by a combination of racism and xenophobia in the case of immigrants of color). In the current political climate, comprehensive immigration reform – whose advocates propose granting some 12 million undocumented immigrants a path to U.S. citizenship and thus to equal rights under the law – is a controversial and volatile issue.

Negative public attitudes toward immigrants are reflected in government circles by the fact that the United States has shown no interest in signing the key international treaty addressing a number of their economic human rights, the International Convention on the Protection of the Rights of Migrants and Members of their Families (ICRMW) (United Nations 1990). This indifference no doubt has much to do with the fact that current treatment of immigrants to the United States (both legal and especially undocumented) violates various human rights principles and standards, particularly when it comes to economic human rights (Satzewich 2006). As one human rights scholar recently put it:

> [T]he seeming reluctance of immigrant-receiving countries to sign the [Migrant Workers Convention] serves as a telling reminder that it is easier for well-off capitalist countries to point to where other countries are "going wrong" in the area of rights violations than it is for them to deal with economic rights violations within their own borders.
>
> (Satzewich 2006, 185)

It remains to be seen whether the federal government will adopt comprehensive immigration reforms that bring the United States into closer conformity with its human rights obligations regarding the treatment of immigrants.

Immigrants who come into and remain in the United States and who are undocumented have never been eligible for welfare benefits; those who cannot prove they reside in the country legally are specifically excluded from participating in TANF. Welfare policy in the United States is not intended to address the human right to an adequate standard of living of all people living in the country. If it were, then all U.S. residents would be eligible for welfare based on economic need, regardless of their immigration status.

But the gap between welfare and human rights extends to restrictions on public assistance that *legal* immigrants experience as well. Prior to 1996 welfare reform legislation, noncitizens who were in the United States legally and who met eligibility requirements were entitled to cash welfare assistance on par with U.S. citizens. Under TANF, this policy changed. States could opt *not* to provide TANF benefits to legal immigrants who arrived in the United States before August 22, 1996. But for those states that did opt to provide such benefits, the federal government would share their costs. Most states in fact chose to provide "pre-enactment" immigrants TANF benefits.

By contrast, legal immigrants who arrived in the United States on or after August 22, 1996, have been treated differently under TANF. Under federal welfare reform legislation, most "post-enactment" immigrants are ineligible for cash welfare assistance until they have legally resided in the United States for five years. Although individual states may provide such legal immigrants with TANF benefits during this five-year period, they have to do so using only state funds, without the benefit of federal cost sharing. Consequently, more than half the states have chosen not to offer these benefits. Clearly, many immigrants – in the United States legally or not – are being treated very differently from U.S. citizens.

One of the reasons for this differential treatment of immigrants under the 1996 welfare reform passed by Congress is the power of the erroneous stereotype that public assistance and other government benefits serve as a "magnet" for immigration, particularly immigration by poor people. Many members of Congress have taken note of the public's receptivity to this stereotype, exploited it to their political benefit, and in doing so have reinforced it.

Anti-immigrant sentiment regarding government benefits remains politically salient today. It was injected into recent debates over federal passage of health care reform, which opponents have claimed will result in more immigrants flocking into the United States. Proposals that would include all legal immigrants in plans to expand affordable health care access to the uninsured have been portrayed by reform opponents as routes to federal government bankruptcy and national economic collapse. Although President Barack Obama has proclaimed health care a "right" and not a privilege, he has not used his leadership to champion extending this right to all legal immigrants.

One of the burdens of immigration status experienced by impoverished immigrant families is directly related to the fact that many immigrants residing in the United States are undocumented. Many of the undocumented are from Latin America, primarily Mexico. Undocumented immigrants are subject to arrest and deportation by federal Immigration and Customs Enforcement (ICE) authorities, a part of the U.S. Department of Homeland Security. Government raids on homes and workplaces have created a great deal of fear in Latino communities across the nation. One consequence is that undocumented immigrants are forced to remain "within the shadows," which means they try to avoid contact with government agencies. From the perspective of persons who cannot prove they are legally in the United States, interacting with officials in a welfare office can be almost as terrifying as the prospect of interaction with local police or federal ICE agents.

The vast majority of adult immigrants come to the United States to find work and to support their families. Noncitizens, particularly undocumented workers, experience a great deal of employment and workplace discrimination even as they lack many legal protections provided under U.S. and international labor law (Atleson 2006; Lyon 2008). Impoverished lone mothers who are undocumented not only are ineligible to receive TANF benefits but also are often defenseless against workplace-based discrimination, exploitation, and harassment. Mothers who complain about such treatment are not only at risk of dismissal from employment; they also fear possible arrest and deportation if, as undocumented immigrants, they go to government agencies asking for adjudication of their complaints.

Undocumented families are legally ineligible for TANF benefits; however, many immigrant families are "mixed" in terms of the status of their household members. For example, data compiled by the Pew Research Center show that in 2008, Mexican "mixed-status family groups" (in which either the head or spouse was born in Mexico and is an undocumented immigrant, and one or more of their children is a U.S. citizen) numbered 8.8 million people: "Of these, 3.8 million are unauthorized immigrant adults and half a million are unauthorized immigrant children. The rest are US citizens (mainly children) and legal immigrants" (Passel and Cohn 2009, 8). The number of children in these families has been growing (from 3.3 million in 2003 to 4.5 million in 2008), and most of this growth represents an increase in the number of U.S. citizen children. As the Pew Research Center put it, "3.8 million unauthorized immigrants are parents of children who are US citizens" (Passel and Cohn 2009, 8).

There is no precise data showing how many mixed-status family groups are headed by undocumented immigrant women. We do know, however, that in 2006 out of almost 10 million family households in the United States headed by Latino women, 2.8 million were headed by foreign-born Latinas (Passel and Cohn 2009, table 17). Moreover, in 2007, 4 million children, or 27 percent of all Latino children, lived in lone-mother-headed households, households more than twice as likely to live in poverty than those headed by married couples (Fry and Passel 2009, table 2). We can safely assume many of the Latino women residing in the United States who are foreign-born and lone mothers are also undocumented.

In the case of impoverished lone-mother-headed families, a mother may be undocumented but one or more of her children, or others for whom she is caring, may be U.S. citizens by virtue of being born in the United States. Such native-born children are legally eligible for "child-only" TANF benefits. However, mothers without documents are often reluctant to apply for benefits for their children out of fear this could somehow lead to their own arrest and deportation, and thus family breakup.

In many instances, poverty-stricken lone-mother-headed families are forced by circumstances to share a household with others who may be family or nonfamily, some of whom are undocumented. The fear of putting other members of the household at risk may prevent mothers from applying for the TANF aid for which they or their children are legally eligible. Consequently, the percentage of eligible immigrant Latino lone-mother-headed families receiving cash assistance is lower than for similar nonimmigrant families, and they are that much poorer as a consequence.

In short, the current welfare system is not at all "immigrant-friendly," ignores many lone-mother-headed families' human rights, and essentially contributes to their impoverishment. The large immigrant Latino population is a case in point. Among ethnic groups in the United States, the poverty rate for Latinos was the fastest-growing from 2007 to 2008 (U.S. Bureau of the Census 2009, table 4, 14). Latina mothers' underrepresentation on the TANF rolls exacerbates their and their children's economic disadvantage.

CONCLUSION: MEETING NEEDS VERSUS FULFILLING RIGHTS

To many fair-minded people, including advocacy groups conscious of the shortcomings in the U.S. welfare system described here, the solution lies with reforming the current welfare system. Congress is required to pass legislation reauthorizing TANF by September 30, 2011, and national organizations such as Legal Momentum (and its EndPovertyNow Coalition) have issued proposals for reform measures they feel would address many of the program's flaws (Casey et al. 2009; Legal Momentum 2009b). The propensity of mainstream advocacy groups like Legal Momentum is to be politically "realistic" in proposing policy changes, which means the root problems of the U.S. welfare system are left unaddressed. The biggest problem, obviously, is that the welfare system simply is not structured to address poverty as a human rights issue; the system is not structured to eliminate poverty or even to make meaningful inroads into its reduction (Lower-Basch 2010).

TANF reform proposals largely entail tinkering with and adjusting existing policies to better meet the needs of impoverished lone-mother-headed families. Legal Momentum's reforms, to use an example, are framed as "an advocacy agenda aimed at rendering the program more responsive to the income and employment needs of the women and families TANF is intended to serve." This is not the same as proposing measures that would proactively and aggressively eradicate these needs so they no longer require a response. Grassroots human rights groups, by contrast, take the position that policy changes should be directed at the elimination of poverty, as opposed to its mitigation. When asked how to "reduce" poverty, members of the Poor People's Economic Human Rights Campaign ask rhetorically: "OK, if the goal is to reduce poverty instead of eliminating it, then which among your children are you going to select to remain poor?"

Reformist tinkering with the current system also does not address the fact that under 1996 federal welfare reform legislation, public assistance ceased to be an "entitlement" for eligible families. Since this entitlement was abolished and responsibility for the administration of TANF was handed off to the states to carry out as they saw fit, it has become almost impossible for welfare recipients to look to the courts for relief when individual states' TANF policies and procedures have proven harmful. As we have seen, even in the worst of national economic times, lone-mother-headed families are fortunate if they are deemed eligible for aid at all under state-run TANF programs, and those who are on the welfare rolls receive only the most minimal cash benefits, far below the federal poverty line. These benefits are for a limited period of time and continue only if mothers adhere to a variety of requirements and mandates, including the mandate to work. Yet disability or immigration status can be a huge impediment to mothers' employment and to their use of welfare as a short-term, supplemental stepping-stone toward gaining "economic independence" and "self-sufficiency," manifest goals of TANF.

A "needs-based approach" to improving TANF, which seems to be the mode of current thinking by mainstream advocacy groups, is likely to allow the needs of impoverished lone mothers and their children to be only partially met or met only under certain conditions or for certain periods of time. A human rights-based approach, by contrast, means the state is obligated by international human rights law to take measures freeing people from impoverishment. The TANF reforms proposed by advocacy organizations like Legal Momentum fall far short of addressing fundamental human rights, whether we speak of the right to an adequate standard of living, the right to protection and assistance for people with disabilities, or the right to fair employment and workplace treatment for immigrant workers.

A UN independent expert on human rights and extreme poverty has suggested "the international community recognize the existence of the conditions of extreme poverty in the United States as indications of the worst form of indignity inflicted upon human beings, which should be regarded as a denial of human rights" (United Nations Commission on Human Rights 2006). Until the United States develops a sustainable human rights culture valuing and demanding nondiscriminatory conformance with international human rights principles and standards, this nation is going to fall short of the goal of poverty elimination. Lone-mother-headed families will continue to suffer under glaringly inadequate "welfare" aid. The emergent and growing U.S. human rights movement discussed at the opening of this chapter offers hope that this culture can someday be built. This building effort deserves our collective support.

REFERENCES

Atleson, James B. 2006. "International Labor Rights and North American Labor Law." In *Economic Rights in Canada and the United States*, edited by Rhoda Howard- Hassmann and Claude E. Welch, 137–48. Philadelphia: University of Pennsylvania Press.

Casey, Timothy, Soraya Fata, Lesley Orloff, and Maya Raghu. 2009. *TANF Reauthorization Round II: An Opportunity to Improve the Safety Net for Women and Children.* New York: Legal Momentum.

Delany, Arthur. 2009. "Michigan: Surging Unemployment, Shrinking Safety Net." *Huffington Post.* June 26.

DeParle, Jason. 2009a. "For Victims of Recession, Patchwork State Aid." *New York Times.* May 10.

———. 2009b. "Slumping Economy Tests Aid System Tied to Jobs." *New York Times*. June 1.

———. 2009c. "Welfare Aid Isn't Growing as Economy Drops Off." *New York Times*. February 2.

Eckholm, Erik. 2009. "Safety Net Is Fraying for the Very Poor." *New York Times*. July 5.

Feller, Avi, and Chad Stone. 2009. *Top 1 Percent of Americans Reaped Two-Thirds of Income Gains in Last Economic Expansion*. Washington, D.C.: Center for Budget and Policy Priorities.

Folbre, Nancy. 2009. "Welfare for Bankers." *New York Times*. April 20.

Fry, Richard, and Jeffrey S. Passel. 2009. *Latino Children: A Majority Are U.S.-Born Offspring of Immigrants*. Washington, D.C.: Pew Research Center.

Grabell, Michael. 2009. "States Ignoring Stimulus Welfare Fund." *USA Today*. September 8.

Hwang, Inyoung. 2009. "Welfare Reform in a Recession." *Medill Reports*. June 4.

Jackson, Thomas F. 2006. *From Civil Rights to Human Rights: Martin Luther King Jr. and the Struggle for Economic Justice*. Philadelphia: University of Pennsylvania Press.

King, Martin Luther, Jr. 1967. "Beyond Vietnam – A Time to Break Silence." A speech presented April 4 at a meeting of Clergy and Laity Concerned, Riverside Church, New York City. http://www.americanrhetoric.com/speeches/mlkatimetobreaksilence.htm.

Legal Momentum. 2009a. *Advocate for an Improved Safety Net for Women and Children*. New York: Women's Legal Defense and Education Fund.

———. 2009b. *Improving the Federal Safety Net for Women and Children: An Agenda for TANF Reform*. New York: Women's Legal Defense and Education Fund.

———. 2009c. *Meager and Diminishing Welfare Benefits Perpetuate Widespread Material Hardship for Poor Women and Children*. New York: Women's Legal Defense and Education Fund.

———. 2009d. *The Bitter Fruit of Welfare Reform: A Sharp Drop in the Percentage of Eligible Women and Children Receiving Welfare*. New York: Women's Legal Defense and Education Fund.

Loprest, Pamela, and Elaine Maag. 2009. *Disabilities among TANF Recipients: Evidence from the NHIS*. Washington, D.C.: The Urban Institute.

Lower-Basch, Elizabeth. 2010. "Goals for TANF Reauthorization." *CLASP TANF Policy Brief*. January 6. Washington, D.C.: Center for Law and Social Policy.

Lyon, Beth. 2008. "From Sanctuary to Shaping International Law: How Unauthorized Immigrant Workers in America Are Advocating Beyond U.S. Borders." In *Bringing Human Rights Home: A History of Human Rights in the United States*, edited by Cynthia Soohoo, Catherine Albisa, and Martha F. Davis, Vol. 3, 26–34. Westport, CT: Praeger Publishers.

Moore, Gwen. 2010. "Moore Bill Would Help States Meet TANF Work Requirements for People with Disabilities." Congressional Press Release. April 20.

Murray, Sara. 2009. "Numbers on Welfare See Sharp Increase." *Wall Street Journal.* June 22.

Neubeck, Kenneth J. 2006. *When Welfare Disappears: The Case for Economic Human Rights.* New York: Routledge.

Neubeck, Kenneth J., and Noel A. Cazenave. 2001. *Welfare Racism: Playing the Race Card against America's Poor.* New York: Routledge.

Parrish, Susan L., Megan E. Andrews, and Roderick A. Rose. 2010. "TANF's Impact on Low-Income Mothers Raising Children with Disabilities." *Exceptional Children,* January 1.

Parrott, Sharon. 2007. *The New TANF Requirements and Individuals with Disabilities: State Comments to the TANF Regulations Illustrate Problems Posed by Inflexible Federal Requirements.* Washington, D.C.: Center on Budget and Policy Priorities.

Passel, Jeffrey S., and D'Vera Cohn. 2009. *A Portrait of Unauthorized Immigrants in the United States.* Washington, D.C.: Pew Research Center.

Pavetti, LaDonna. 2009. *TANF Recipients Living with a Disability: Policy Framework, Prevalence and Service Strategies.* Princeton, NJ: Mathematica Policy Research, Inc.

Pitcher, Abby. 2002. *Human Rights Violations in Welfare Legislation: Pushing Recipients Deeper into Poverty.* New York: Human Rights Project, Urban Justice Center.

Pollack, Wendy. 2008. "The Right to Social Security in the United States: Ending Welfare as We Know It." In *Bringing Human Rights Home: A History of Human Rights in The United States,* edited by Cynthia Soohoo, Catherine Albisa, and Martha F. Davis, Vol. 3, 229–63. Westport, CT: Praeger Publishers.

Rowe, Gretchen, and Mary Murphy. 2009. *Welfare Rules Databook: State TANF Policies as of July 2008.* Washington, D.C.: The Urban Institute.

Satzewich, Vic. 2006. "The Economic Rights of Migrant and Immigrant Workers in Canada and the United States." In *Economic Rights in Canada and the United States,* edited by Rhoda Howard-Hassmann and Claude E. Welch, 169–85. Philadelphia: University of Pennsylvania Press.

Schulz, William F. 2009. *Power of Justice: Applying International Human Rights Standards to American Domestic Practices.* Washington, D.C.: Center for American Progress.

Sidel, Ruth. 1998. *Keeping Women and Children Last: America's War on the Poor.* New York: Penguin.

Soohoo, Cynthia, Catherine Albisa, and Martha F. Davis, eds. 2008. *Bringing Human Rights Home: Portraits of the Movement,* Vol. 3. Westport, CT: Praeger.

Thomas, Dorothy Q. 2008. "Against American Supremacy: Rebuilding Human Rights Culture in the United States." In *Bringing Human Rights Home: A History of Human Rights in the United States,* edited by Cynthia Soohoo, Catherine Albisa, and Martha F. Davis, Vol. 1, 1–23. Westport, CT: Praeger Publishers.

United Nations. 1948. *Universal Declaration of Human Rights.* New York: United Nations General Assembly.

United Nations. 1966. *International Covenant on Economic, Social and Cultural Rights*. New York: United Nations General Assembly.

United Nations. 1989. *International Convention on the Rights of the Child*. New York: United Nations General Assembly.

United Nations. 1990. *International Convention on the Protection of the Rights of All Migrants and Members of Their Families*. New York: United Nations General Assembly.

United Nations. 2006. *International Convention on the Rights of Persons with Disabilities*. New York: United Nations General Assembly.

United Nations. 2007. *International Convention on the Rights of the Child: General Comment No. 9, The Rights of Children with Disabilities*. New York: UN Committee on the Rights of the Child. February 27.

United Nations Commission on Human Rights. 2006. *Human Rights and Extreme Poverty: Report Submitted by the Independent Expert on the Question of Human Rights and Extreme Poverty; Mission to the United States of America (October 24 to November 4, 2005); Addendum*. New York: United Nations Economic and Social Council.

U.S. Bureau of the Census. 2009. *Income, Poverty, and Health Insurance Coverage in the United States: 2008*. Washington, D.C.: U.S. Government Printing Office.

U.S. Bureau of the Census. 2010. *Income, Poverty, and Health Insurance Coverage in the United States: 2009*. Washington, D.C.: U.S. Government Printing Office.

U.S. Department of Labor. 2009. *Monthly Labor Force Statistics from the Current Population Survey*. Retrieved from http://www.bls.gov.

U.S. Government Accountability Office. 2010. *Temporary Assistance for Needy Families; Fewer Eligible Families Have Received Cash Assistance since the 1990s, and the Recession's Impact on Caseloads Varies by State*. Washington, D.C.: U.S. GAO.

Wolff, Edward N. 2002. *Top Heavy: The Increasing Inequality of Wealth in America and What Can Be Done About It*. New York: New Press.

Zedlewski, Sheila. 2008. *The Role of Welfare During a Recession*. Washington, D.C.: The Urban Institute.

13

The Human Rights of Children in Conflict with the Law: Lessons for the U.S. Human Rights Movement

Mie Lewis

INTRODUCTION

To capture many of the most widespread and egregious children's rights violations in the United States, one need only follow the early life of an African-American child born into urban poverty. The child picks up the thread of intergenerational disadvantage when she finds herself in a racially segregated neighborhood drained of resources by historical redlining and more recent racially discriminatory lending practices (Squires 1992). One or both of the child's parents may have been arrested, possibly because of racially targeted policing practices, and incarcerated for an excessive period, thereby leaving the child vulnerable to physical and sexual abuse in violation of the child's right to be protected from violence (Braman and Wood 2003; Convention on the Rights of the Child [CRC] 1989, Articles 19, 20). The parents' legal rights over the child may be terminated by the state with a minimum of due process protections and the child made a ward of the state, in violation of the child's right against arbitrary separation from her parents (Adoption and Safe Families Act of 1997 [ASFA]; CRC, Articles 7, 9, 21). Meanwhile, the child's chaotic and underfunded school may not be the life raft it otherwise could be, depriving the child of the meaningful exercise of her right to an education (*Williams v. California* 2000; CRC, Articles 28, 29). Reacting to abuse, the child may run away from a foster placement, self-medicate with street drugs, or otherwise misbehave in school or on the streets, and may as a consequence be remanded to a juvenile prison, where she is exposed to physical, sexual, and emotional abuse, this time at the hands of the state, in violation of a range of fundamental rights (Human Rights Watch

The author wishes to acknowledge the invaluable research and assistance of Deirdre McGuigan.

1995, 1996, 1997; Human Rights Watch and American Civil Liberties Union [HRW-ACLU] 2006; CRC, Articles 3, 13–16, 19, 20, 28, 37).

To illustrate the state of children's human rights in the United States and the roles that international standards can play in their protection, this chapter highlights the abuse of child prisoners and the unique guidance found in human rights norms in addressing this abuse. Part I illustrates the nature of children's rights violations in child prisons, with special attention to questions of gender and race. Child prisons are used as an illustration because within the spectrum of rights violations to which marginalized children are subjected, the moment a child enters a child prison is key. Then the child no longer merely inherits the effects of rights violations experienced by her parents but is herself exposed to direct violations, perpetrated by the state, of rights specific to children. Moreover, the pervasively coercive environment in most child prisons in the United States provides a microcosm of many common child rights violations found within and outside of state-run institutions, in areas as diverse as health, education, expression, and protection from violence. Part II analyzes the legal and nonlegal deficiencies in the domestic approach to protecting the rights of children in conflict with the law. Part III describes strengths and limitations of international law when used to enhance children's rights protection in the United States, emphasizing the analytical power of the human rights framework and its potential to correct problematic approaches currently pursued by prison administrators and reformers. The conclusion synthesizes the prior discussion and draws from it lessons relevant to the future of the U.S. human rights movement, both with respect to child prisoners and more generally.

I. THE ROOTS OF ABUSE: SEEING AND TREATING CHILDREN AS ADULTS

From the "houses of refuge" in the early nineteenth century to the varied juvenile correctional institutions of the present, child prisons in the United States have been and remain sites of human rights violations against children (Ryder and Elrod 2005, 106; Dale 1998, n.1–n.3). Although abuse of institutionalized children is widespread, it receives only sporadic public or political attention – usually when news of especially extreme abuses breaks or a child dies in custody – and even less attention from scholars, including those concerned with human rights, children's rights, and criminal justice. What academic work there is on the human rights of children in conflict with the law focuses on court processing of children accused of delinquency, particularly the referral of children to adult criminal courts for certain serious crimes and the designation by some U.S. states of sixteen or seventeen as the age of majority for criminal prosecution purposes (Rose 2003; Pagnanelli 2007). An irony of the controversy surrounding children's formal status before courts is that even those children who escape adult adjudication and are incarcerated in institutions for juvenile delinquents often find themselves in conditions similar to those found in adult prisons. Prisonlike conditions are ubiquitous among juvenile institutions, notwithstanding the rehabilitative rather than punitive mission codified in state juvenile justice statutes, as well as case authority establishing that children's conditions of confinement are subject to a different and higher standard than that applied to adult prisons (*Milonas v. Williams* 1982).

Although the character of these human rights violations and the institutional cultures from which they arise vary by state, region, prison – and in some cases even within subparts of a single institution – they typically involve physical, sexual, and emotional abuse, as well as neglect, social isolation, and educational deprivation (Human Rights Watch 1995, 1996, 1997; HRW-ACLU 2006). Underlying these abuses is the pervasive denial of children's special status as children, a denial that is both a violation of children's human rights and the basis of other subsidiary deprivations. The following examples demonstrate this problem and elucidate how the failure to distinguish between adults and children for treatment purposes while in confinement pervades the policies, practices, and language of child prisons.

One widespread feature of juvenile prisons is the excessive use of force (Human Rights Watch 1995, 1997, 1999; HRW-ACLU 2006). The governing regulations of child prisons in the United States allow physical force against children, and many define the circumstances under which such force may be used. Reflecting a punitive mentality, rules are frequently worded broadly, thereby inviting the arbitrary perpetration of violence by prison workers against their wards. For example, they permit the pepper spraying of children to "disrupt" a child's "thought process" when those thoughts are suspected of being violent (Arizona Department of Juvenile Corrections 2007, 3.a.i.7.). Other provisions permit physical force to move a child from one place to another because "the youth's behavior is escalating" to a point where facility staff believe relocation is necessary (New York Office of Children and Family Services 2007, 3247.13). Others even authorize the use of deadly force against children in some circumstances (Georgia Department of Juvenile Justice

2008, 19.3). Similarly permissive rules govern the use of "mechanical restraints," namely handcuffs, ankle cuffs, leather restraint devices, and the like.

When applied to children, who are both developmentally less able to regulate their actions – thereby triggering applications of force under broadly worded policies – and physically less able to withstand such violence, the result is frequent injury and, in some cases, death. For example, in New York a fifteen-year-old child died of a heart attack after he was pinned facedown for "verbal ranting" by two guards whose combined weight was 400 pounds (Feldman 2007; *New York Times* 2009). In Texas, a psychiatric expert recently described the effect of such punitive practices on incarcerated girls and facility workers in that state: "[S]taff recurrently act from one paradigm, and one paradigm alone – the paradigm that if you punish unwanted behavior harshly, over and over again, the behavior will eventually improve. This is a brutal and entirely counterproductive response, one that can only worsen the emotional state of the girls so treated and lead to an increasingly sadistic and overly controlling attitude by staff" (Grassian 2009). For African-American children these practices give rise to a troubling historical continuity whereby present-day child prison practices echo the shackling and state-sanctioned violence that accompanied slavery.

Another common although often unrecognized form of abuse is excessive strip- and pat-down searching of incarcerated children. Such searches are routinely performed without individual suspicion or even a generalized justification relating to institutional security. Rather, regulations governing such searches reflect practices in adult prisons, where the concealment of smuggled and improvised weapons may actually pose a threat (Texas Youth Commission [TYC] 2009, sec. 97.9). The bizarreness of imposing adultlike protocols on children as young as ten is demonstrated by what the searches yield: the vast majority turn up nothing, and what little "contraband" is discovered is almost always decidedly childlike in nature. For example, hundreds of body searches conducted over a three-month period in the largest girls' prison in Texas yielded five "contraband" discoveries: a magic marker, a pair of glasses, a note written to one child by another, lip balm, and two pieces of candy (TYC, Correctional Care Form 2008–2009). Strip and pat searches are especially harmful to incarcerated girls, the vast majority of whom have suffered sexual abuse, often severe and prolonged, prior to their incarceration (Wisdom and Maxfield 2001, 1–7; Chesney-Lind 1997, 23–29). Repeatedly being subjected to unwanted, bodywide touching – in the case of pat searches – or being compelled to remove all of their clothing and subject their bodies to inspection – in the case of strip searches – retraumatizes girls and reinforces their belief that their physical boundaries are subject to invasion. Thus, girls experience a continuity of sexual violence over their lifetimes, first in the private sphere as domestic violence then in public institutions as state violence.

This pervasive contamination of juvenile institutions by adult prison practices and culture explains much of the persistent abuse of confined children. Such contamination can be traced to several sources. As a formal matter, harsh statutory and administrative law proliferates during periods of intense public fear of violent crime committed by teenagers (Klein 1998; Butterfield 1996). During such periods, for example, the rehabilitative purpose enshrined in states' juvenile justice statutes is diluted by references to "punishment" or "public safety" (Texas Family Code 2009, sec. 51.01). These punitive provisions remain in place even in eras of relative political calm because of lawmakers' fear of being perceived as "soft on crime" (Krisberg 1994, 21).

In addition, because conditions in children's institutions have been challenged in court far less often than those in adult institutions, there is a lack of juvenile correctional case law that could clarify the distinction between adult and child prisoners and help guide child prison policies (Dale 1998, 679 and n16). Instead, juvenile justice administrators borrow policies and procedures from adult prisons. This bleeding of adult procedure into child prisons is exacerbated by staff mobility between adult and juvenile corrections fields at all levels: heads and management staff of juvenile justice agencies and individual facilities; line staff and medical and social service workers; and even government lawyers who defend facility conditions in court. Such mobility, in turn, inaptly suggests the experience of working in adult corrections is important and analogous to working with children, notwithstanding the fact that the overarching purpose of child prisons – rehabilitation – is different from the punishment aim carried out by adult prisons. Once a culture of punishment becomes entrenched, it becomes nearly impossible to eradicate (Testimony of Vincent Schiraldi 2006).

II. THE FAILURE OF DOMESTIC CHILDREN'S RIGHTS ENFORCEMENT

The persistence of these abuses suggests the domestic legal framework and the domestic mechanisms for enforcing the rights of incarcerated children are ineffective. Yet, in the abstract, domestic legal protections for children appear strong. The conditions of children's confinement are held to a higher standard under the due process clause of the Fourteenth Amendment than adult prison standards, which are subject to the largely unprotective cruel and unusual punishment test under the Eighth Amendment. More specifically, the Fourteenth Amendment has been interpreted to prohibit the confinement of children in conditions amounting to punishment, and in conditions representing a "substantial departure from generally accepted professional standards" (*Gary H. v. Hegstrom* 1987; *Jones v. Blanas* 2004; *Youngberg v. Romeo* 1982; *Bell v. Wolfish* 1979). Case authority fleshes out specific minimum standards for child prisons, including freedom from excessive force, isolation, and unnecessary searches. Existing standards in the United States also require incarcerated children to be provided adequate medical treatment, which the U.S. Department of Justice interprets to include mental health treatment and suicide prevention measures (*Youngberg v. Romeo* 1982; *Martarella v. Kelley* 1972; King 2009).

Although the existence of an entirely different and more protective rubric evinces a distinction between adult and child prisoners, there is a vast gap between these rights as articulated and conditions of confinement as experienced by confined children. The explanation for this gap is doctrinal and quasi-doctrinal. First, just as the Supreme Court's decision in *Turner v. Safley* (1987) has thwarted challenges to adult prison conditions by subjecting such conditions to an undemanding standard of review, juvenile conditions claims are vulnerable to excessive deference by courts to prison officials. Specifically, the Turner decision articulated a four-part test, a major prong of which asks whether a restriction on prisoners' rights is "reasonably related to legitimate penological interests." Similarly, where due process standards applicable to pretrial detainees and child prisoners are concerned, the Supreme Court's test in *Bell v. Wolfish* approves conditions and procedures as long as they are "reasonably related to a legitimate governmental objective," defined to include the maintenance of institutional security and order (*Bell v. Wolfish* 1979, 468–69). The question of whether and how the Wolfish reasonable relationship standard can be differentiated from the Turner standard has not been settled, but the facial similarity between the two formulations suggests that for child prisoners, as for their adult counterparts, judicial deference to institutional ends means many constitutional protections they enjoyed in free society end when they enter the prison gates. Moreover, many specific aspects of domestic legal doctrine relating to children's conditions of confinement remain unsettled or are subject to conflicting opinions among federal appeals courts. Claims asserted in the absence of settled authority establishing a particular right for children are likely to fail because federal judges accord extreme deference to child prison administrators, just as they do in the adult prison context. State court judges are often even less willing to take an antagonistic stance toward state government officials.

For its part, the requirement of adherence to generally accepted professional standards has the same weakness as the Eighth Amendment's "cruel and unusual" punishment standard: if a practice is problematic but nevertheless widespread – that is, generally accepted in the juvenile context or not unusual among adult prisons – it would presumably pass the test. In addition, the necessity of establishing in each individual case the exact content of "accepted professional standards" can require reliance on expert testimony from a class of professionals – juvenile prison administrators – who are, on the whole, adherents to the philosophy and culture of juvenile facilities as correctional rather than rehabilitative, and therefore inclined to define relevant standards leniently.

The most severe barriers to asserting child prisoners' rights are not deficiencies in applicable substantive law but practical barriers and procedural hurdles. For one, abuses of children in custody are rarely remedied because they almost never come to public attention. This is the result of three main factors: the remote location of many child prisons within the vast American countryside; prison rules isolating children from contact with adults outside the institution; and the lack of a regular mechanism of independent or even internal oversight in most child prisons (Huling 2002; HRW-ACLU 2006). This seclusion is perilous because most incarcerated children are ill-equipped to defend their own rights. Children often lack knowledge of their legal rights and the availability of legal assistance. Moreover, they tend to defer to adults and fear retribution for reporting abuse.

When abuses do become public, it is often through the investigative work of nongovernmental organizations (NGOs). However, NGOs dedicated to monitoring juvenile conditions are few and are vastly outnumbered by the hundreds of juvenile prisons, preadjudication detention facilities, and other juvenile lockups in the United States. Except in jurisdictions where a prior lawsuit has resulted in a standing court order mandating ongoing monitoring, NGOs are, with few exceptions, excluded from access to incarcerated children.[1] Moreover, although adult prisoners' identities are publicly available, making identifying and contacting them easy, child prisoners' identities are, appropriately, kept secret, making it difficult for NGO investigators to establish contact with confined children. The Special Litigation section of the U.S. Justice Department's Civil Rights Division is virtually the only body with authority to enter child prisons in the United States without prison authorities' permission.[2] The Justice Department has, however, completed only twenty investigations and filed seven complaints over the last ten years, tiny numbers in comparison with the hundreds of institutions in which children are confined (U.S. Department of Justice Civil Rights Division 2009).

The lack of transparency and enforcement resulting from the paucity of investigators and advocates has been exacerbated by the Prison Litigation Reform Act, passed in 1996. The PLRA requires prisoners, including children, to exhaust often byzantine prison grievance procedures as a precondition for filing a federal lawsuit (Prison Litigation Reform Act [PLRA] 42 USCS § 1997e[a]). It has been stringently enforced by courts (Human Rights Watch 2009, chapter VII, "The PLRA's Application to Children"). In addition, the PLRA's restrictions on attorneys' fees effectively render lawyers unable to recoup compensation for time spent challenging prison conditions, thereby discouraging private attorneys from enforcing the civil rights of both adult and child prisoners (PLRA 42 U.S.C. sec. 1997e[d]; 18 U.S.C. sec. 3626[g][3] and [5]; 42 U.S.C. sec. 1997e[h]). Incarcerated children are left without meaningful access to outside assistance. They merely accept and internalize an abusive institutional culture and either acquiesce to maltreatment or rebel, thereby triggering additional abuse.

III. THE ROLE OF HUMAN RIGHTS IN
REIMAGINING U.S. INSTITUTIONS

In light of the deeply entrenched culture of abuse existing in many child prisons in the United States and the obstacles to protecting children's

---

[1] For example, although the Correctional Association of New York is empowered by law to inspect adult prisons across the state, it has no such authority over child prisons. See New York Assembly Bill 10155A/Senate Bill 6474C (2010) (proposal, pending as of this writing, to permit correctional association to access juvenile facilities).

[2] Two minor exceptions are child advocate offices (which exist in only a few states and have varying degrees of autonomy and access to investigative resources) and federally funded "protection and advocacy" organizations charged with protecting the rights of individuals with mental illness.

rights, what role can international human rights play in achieving reform? To answer this question, many point to the formal mechanisms of human rights enforcement, such as U.S. ratification of the Convention on the Rights of the Child (CRC) and participation in the proceedings of the United Nations Committee of the Rights of the Child, or other international procedures such as the monitoring activities of the UN Special Rapporteur on Torture pursuant to the Second Optional Protocol to the Convention Against Torture. Where incarcerated girls are concerned, some point to the Convention on the Elimination of All Forms of Discrimination Against Women (CEDAW) as having ameliorative potential.

In reality, there is little likelihood the United States will participate in the international legal system to such a great extent in the foreseeable future. For example, the current presidential administration has not indicated a serious intention to pursue ratification of the CRC or the Second Optional Protocol to the Convention Against Torture. Although the administration has identified CEDAW as a priority, the prospect of the treaty moving through the executive and legislative review processes toward a U.S. Senate vote remains in doubt. Moreover, even if movement toward any of these instruments occurred, their ratification by the Senate would likely face overwhelming opposition, as it has in the past, from conservative Christian leaders who consider the CRC and CEDAW an assault on family structure, traditional gender roles, parental rights, and U.S. sovereignty (Gunn 2006, 119–27). Even if ratification were achieved, it would almost certainly be subject to sweeping reservations, understandings, and declarations curtailing the concrete implications of ratification. In sum, the outlook for ratifying treaties in a form that would subject the United States to meaningful responsibilities toward incarcerated children under international law is slim indeed.

Even if formal adoption of international legal instruments and participation in public international procedures occurs, its impact on the lives of incarcerated children in the United States would likely be slight. This is in part because international standards are not necessarily higher in substance than formal standards already articulated in domestic jurisprudence. U.S. courts have held, for example, that conditions constituting punishment are unlawful; that children can only be physically restrained under the narrowest of circumstances, with the approval of mental health staff; that the prolonged isolated confinement of children in a barren cell is barred; and that incarcerated children can maintain a claim to a minimally adequate education (*Bell v. Wolfish* 1979, 466; *Hollingsworth v. Orange County* 1990; *Lollis v. New York Department of Social Services*

1970, 482–83; *Donnell C. v. Illinois State Board of Education* 1993, 1018). As described in Part II, the failure to realize these articulated norms arises primarily from a combination of procedural impediments and non-legal barriers rather than deficiencies in the substantive law. Conversely, international tribunals interpreting human rights law have not imposed particularly high standards upon child prisons under their jurisdiction. They have held, for example, that incarcerated children may legitimately be punished and may even be subjected to that quantum of "suffering and humiliation" intrinsic to an approved punishment (*Sukhovoy v. Russia* 2008, 4). Subjecting a child to prisonlike conditions and discipline has been found permissible when characterized as "protective" rather than punitive (*D.G. v. Ireland* 2002, 23). Even the right against torture and cruel, inhuman, or degrading punishment, although phrased in absolute terms, has been applied in a relative manner. Violations are assessed based on the level of severity of the challenged ill-treatment, depending on "all the circumstances of the case" (*Sukhovoy v. Russia* 2008, 4; *D.G. v. Ireland* 2002, 23). Thus, as applied by courts, the interpretation of international children's rights norms may not boost by much, if at all, standards already in place in the United States.

Recourse to international mechanisms also poses practical problems similar to, and in some ways more severe than, those hampering domestic enforcement of U.S. civil rights law. In the international realm, it is only the most egregious cases of child prisoner abuse, usually involving death or severe injury while in custody, that reach adjudication, and only then with years-long advocacy and resource investment by NGOs or other interested parties (*Juvenile Reeducation Institute v. Paraguay*, 2004; *Matter of Children Deprived of Liberty in the "Complexo do Tatuapé" of FEBEM* 2008). Moreover, even a favorable judgment raises the question of how enforcement could be carried out or overseen when most child prisoner abuses lie in the minutiae of the day-to-day operation of a closed institution. Not surprisingly, the European Commission on Human Rights has repeatedly emphasized the primary role played by national governments in the enforcement of international norms (Schinas 2008; Hennis-Plasschaert 2008).

In light of these realities, reform possibilities attending greater formal U.S. participation in international law and institutions are easily overstated, and it is incumbent upon those within the domestic human rights movement to develop other ways of bringing human rights into child prisons. Perhaps paradoxically, one fruitful means of bringing concrete benefits to incarcerated children lies in the informal influence human rights norms – and the insights underlying such norms – can assert over domestic children's rights discourse. Human rights norms represent a considered and detailed compendium of key principles and best practices in juvenile justice administration effectuating the basic principle that children are fundamentally different from adults and entitled to protections over and above those accorded to adults. The adoption by states of these treaties, or by the United Nations in the case of subsidiary rules and guidelines, demonstrates an international consensus regarding such norms, even by states that do not achieve compliance with the norms in practice. Indeed, much useful content appears in lower order instruments having no binding effect on any state, except to the extent they are understood as providing interpretive guidance on the implementation of the rights addressed in treaty law. The oldest of these instruments is the Standard Minimum Rules for the Treatment of Prisoners, passed in 1955 and approved by the UN Economic and Social Council in 1957 and 1977, concerning conditions of confinement for adults and children. The UN Minimum Standard Rules for the Administration of Juvenile Justice, known as the Beijing Rules, were adopted in 1985 and share many principles in common with the Convention on the Rights of the Child. The UN Rules for the Protection of Juveniles Deprived of Their Liberty and the UN Guidelines for the Prevention of Juvenile Delinquency, known as the Riyadh Guidelines, were adopted in 1990.

The approach taught in these documents represents a better method of administering juvenile justice than those currently in use, as well as some of the alternatives being pursued by reformers in the United States. One important example of the beneficial shift in perspective human rights norms offer over existing domestic paradigms is that while U.S. law derives any heightened protections applied to incarcerated children from the formal procedural distinction between criminal conviction and juvenile adjudication, human rights norms enshrine the special status of children as an independent and fundamental right (CRC Preamble, Article 3). The subsidiary norms governing various aspects of juvenile justice administration and conditions of confinement are, in turn, all grounded in the recognition of the special status of children. This principle implies a high degree of suspicion any time a procedure employed in a child prison is borrowed from, or even merely resembles, that in an adult prison.

This fundamental principle gives rise to another tenet that provides useful guidance for the operation of child prisons in the United States, namely, the dual standard of basic rights protection and individualized care provision as primary benchmarks of juvenile justice performance

(United Nations Standard Minimum Rules for the Administration of Juvenile Justice ["Beijing Rules"] 1985, 2.3a). This deceptively simple formulation, that child prisons must "meet the varying needs of juvenile offenders, while protecting their basic rights," can, if taken seriously, provide a key to maintaining genuinely humane and rehabilitative conditions of confinement. It takes into account an essential but often overlooked truth: it is impossible to achieve rehabilitative goals without respecting basic rights. For example, education and counseling cannot succeed when the right against chemical restraints is violated. This author personally observed group counseling sessions where some of the children were so sedated that their heads and bodies lolled in their seats. For the children whose basic right to protection from abusive medical practices was infringed, the counseling session was obviously useless. Likewise, trauma services and other mental health care support cannot succeed when children's physical safety and privacy are not assured, because under such circumstances it is difficult to impossible to form trusting therapeutic relationships. Nevertheless, child prisoners report the disclosure of personal information such as abuse histories and diagnoses of sexually transmitted infections by prison staff (HRW-ACLU 2006, 73–75). This violation of a basic right undermines the potential effectiveness of such rehabilitative services as are provided.

The second requirement, that of individualized care, demands that child prisons conduct a competent needs assessment of each child in custody and that such needs as are discovered be met with highly individualized services provided by competent professionals and sustained over the course of the child's imprisonment. Implementing this criterion requires intensive fact-gathering on the part of juvenile justice agencies regarding each child's history and needs. It also requires agencies to study broader trends such as characteristics of the population of children entering the system, and what evidence-based interventions actually provide children with the tools they need to thrive outside the institution.

Although the notion of shaping institutions around the principles of basic rights protection coupled with individualized care appears straightforward, it is actually overlooked by domestic child prison agencies and, more worryingly, by many reformers (Office of Juvenile Justice and Delinquency Prevention [OJJDP] 1998). In particular, two reform models currently being advocated, and to varying degrees implemented, in child prisons in the United States show failings that could be avoided by referring to the basic rights/individualized care model. The first of these is the medicalized model, under which incarcerated children are viewed principally as sufferers of mental illness. With respect to girls, there is increasing emphasis on high rates of trauma and attendant problems, particularly posttraumatic stress disorder (PTSD). A grave consequence associated with the medical model is the overmedication of children or the ratification of overmedication already taking place, whether for sedation or merely as the result of low-quality psychiatric care and poor coordination between caregivers (King 2009). The inappropriate administration of powerful psychoactive medications is especially a problem for girls, who are much more medicated within institutions than boys, even though they are less often prescribed psychiatric medication outside the prison context. Other dangers of this view of child prisoners include overpathologizing, that is, describing as medical conditions states and behavior that in many children are likely to be largely social and situational in nature. The medical model insinuates that the problems leading to incarceration and those occurring within prison walls are personal and physical in nature, despite evidence they are social and legal creations, and in some cases even the product of medication itself (Holsinger and Holsinger 2005, 213–17; Von Zielbauer 2005).

Another abusive practice related to the medicalized mindset is the administrative extension of a child's placement in custody because she is deemed not to be completely "rehabilitated," as if being rehabilitated were an objectively determinable state achieved with the eradication of the disease of delinquency. The medicalization of juvenile delinquency amounts to a continuation of the double-edged role of the psychiatric profession's relationship with prisons, a conundrum that has been observed since the earliest days of mass imprisonment (Foucault [1975] 1995). In contrast, by remaining agnostic about whether the causes of delinquent behavior in any particular case are medical or something else, and by demanding prison officials determine in each child's case what is in fact the root of delinquency, the basic rights/individualized care model avoids these pitfalls, proving a safer and more responsive alternative to prison culture.

The second reform model in vogue is that of providing "gender-specific" services. Given the large number of girls incarcerated in every U.S. state, it is clear the traditional emphasis on boys to the exclusion of girls is no longer an appropriate approach to conceptualizing juvenile justice. Yet the recent emphasis on "girl-specific programming" or "girl-centered services" threatens to distract from abuses and other fundamental concerns and perpetuate stereotypes about the backgrounds and needs of both girls and boys. For example, guiding tenets of gender-specific models of carceral care are that girls, as opposed to boys, are focused on interpersonal relationships, and that girls are more likely to be sufferers of abuse and its psychological consequences than boys (Zaplin 1998, 119; OJJDP 1998). Such beliefs are not only dubious, as some girls in the system may not focus as intently as others on relationships and may not have abuse histories, they also imply the opposite, namely, that boys are not relationship focused and are not likely to have a background of abuse and trauma. In other words, the gender-specific approach, as practiced, neglects both girls' individuality and the shared aspects of girls' and boys' experiences (Goodkind 2005).

In contrast, the individualized care aspect of the international model avoids such problems by demanding an inquiry into the needs of each individual child. It bypasses the problems of gender-specific models, such as needlessly sex-segregated environments, the perpetuation of stereotypes, and the implementation of programming based on such stereotypes. More importantly, gender-specific rhetoric threatens to distract from basic rights violations. For example, the New York juvenile justice agency has for years boasted of its "girls task force," a group of senior staff members who discuss gender-specific issues, such as whether girls should be made to wear similar uniforms to boys.[3] At the same time, various independent investigations have found agency failing toward girls and boys alike, including the excessive use of physical force and isolation practices and the lack of adequate internal and external oversight. Both are more fundamental and more complex than the question of what girls wear.

In short, the gender-neutral yet individually responsive human rights framework is useful because it demands rights protection and individualized care, thereby avoiding the conundrum of whether to demand equality between boys and girls or respect for gender differences. Such a framework is important when confronting institutions that have an admittedly powerful male bias and where equal treatment would mean only parity with the poor, and often abusive, conditions to which boys are subjected. Recalibrating reform efforts along these lines also avoids the unintended consequence of transforming one form of abuse into another – such as physical restraint into pharmaceutical restraint – as well as escaping the futility of gaining hard-won improvements in services only to have such

[3] In a meeting with HRW/ACLU, OCFS administrators cited the purchase of uniforms for girls different from those issued to boys as an example of interdepartmental cooperation in the interest of girls. HRW/ACLU meeting with OCFS senior administrators, Albany, NY, April 18, 2006.

advances rendered ineffective by the continuing violation of children's fundamental rights.

IV. DIRECTIONS FOR THE FUTURE OF HUMAN RIGHTS-BASED SCHOLARSHIP AND ACTIVISM

The foregoing discussion suggests a number of conclusions regarding directions for the human rights movement in the United States as it relates to children, persons deprived of their liberty, and other constituencies affected by human rights deprivations. First, it highlights the availability of human rights principles and logic, as embodied in human rights instruments, for incorporation into theory, practice, and rhetoric, even absent any formal legislative adoption or judicial ratification. The task of absorbing human rights into American political consciousness is a critical one, because, as with domestically recognized legal rights, widespread awareness of the rights and the expectation that the rights be observed are arguably preconditions to their formal recognition and, in reality, the ultimate goal of the movement.

The prior discussion also suggests that to make the best use of scarce resources, human rights analysis and activism undertaken in the United States must be carried out with a high level of legal and political sophistication. In some respects, the exuberance of the domestic human rights movement, understandable in light of the failures of rights protections within the domestic framework, has not been matched by an equivalent zeal for strategic analysis of what human rights law actually is, and what it can do. For example, considerable resources have been and continue to be expended on campaigns for treaty ratification, including the Second Optional Protocol to the Convention Against Torture, the CRC, and CEDAW. Yet, as described previously in connection with the European Court of Human Rights' interpretation of the rights of incarcerated children, human rights instruments are similar to domestic statutory law in that their text is subject to interpretation and sometimes considerable weakening by courts. The promise that any particular provision of international law holds for any marginalized group within the United States must therefore be measured not only by a facial analysis of the instrument but also by means of a thorough examination of judicial interpretation, the history of the instrument's formulation and adoption, and other relevant information necessary to realistically assess whether and how human rights can help in any given situation. In short, the U.S. human rights community should take frequent stock of ways in which it expends scarce institutional resources to ensure that the "human" – the lived experiences of oppressed people – remains central to the work of human rights.

Finally, discussion in this chapter is intended to be both cautionary and encouraging. It demonstrates that in some ways the real work of human rights is independent of the degree of interest or acceptance those rights can have among judges, legislators, prison administrators, and others who wield authority. The human rights movement is a mass movement, and a great deal of work can be done from the grassroots upward. Although the informal work of elucidating, spreading, and demanding compliance with human rights principles can appear less concrete than legislative or judicial efforts, it is in some ways this arm of the movement whose effect will most likely be felt by incarcerated children and other groups whose experiences are defined, illuminated, and ideally regulated by human rights standards.

CONCLUSION

Children in conflict with the law suffer a range of rights abuses that purely domestic approaches have failed to remedy. The ineffectiveness of the domestic regime has both legal and practical causes that, when realistically compared with a hypothetical United States in which greater formal adherence to human rights standards has been achieved, suggest such formal participation may not greatly improve the lives of incarcerated children. When competing legal regimes are bypassed and the roots of the abuse themselves examined, they appear cultural as well as legal and include a failure to squarely recognize the special status of children. As a result, children are subjected to practices designed for adult prisons and wholly inappropriate to them. At the same time, reform efforts embodying medicalized or gender-specific models of understanding juvenile delinquency offer inadequate alternatives to the prevailing penal model. Despite the low likelihood that participation in the formal mechanisms of international human rights law will elevate the standards of treatment seen in U.S. child prisons, the framework embodied in human rights norms offers clear guidance for child prison administrators, politicians, and reformers alike. It recognizes the distinct status of children and, as a matter of implementation, requires the protection of children's fundamental rights and the provision of tailored rehabilitative care to each and every child.

The availability of such an alternative framework and the potential for its effective implementation in the United States (even absent approval by state organs) gives credence to a less formalistic and more strategic, creative, and tailored approach taken within the domestic human rights movement. This approach has value for child constituencies in the United States not just in the prison context, but in other areas where children's rights are infringed – for example, in educational and foster care settings. Indeed, its potential application is not limited to children in conflict with the law but extends to human rights advocacy more generally.

REFERENCES

Adoption and Safe Families Act. 1997. 42 USCS § 675(5)(E).

Arizona Department of Juvenile Corrections. 2007. Procedure 4058.01 ("Use of Force Continuum").

Bell v. Wolfish. 441 U.S. 520 (1979).

Braman, Donald, and Jennifer Wood. 2003. "From One Generation to the Next: How Criminal Sanctions Are Reshaping Family Life in Urban America." In *Prisoners Once Removed: The Impact of Incarceration and Reentry on Children, Families, and Communities,* edited by Jeremy Travis and Michelle Waul, 157–88. Washington, D.C.: Urban Institute Press.

Butterfield, Fox. 1996. *All God's Children.* New York: Harper Perennial.

Chesney-Lind, Meda. 1997. *The Female Offender: Girls, Women and Crime.* Thousand Oaks, CA: SAGE Publications.

Convention on the Rights of the Child. 1989. Adopted November 20, 1989, G.A. Res. 44/25, U.N. Doc. A/RES/44/25, entered into force September 2, 1990, signed by the United States of America on February 16, 1995.

D.G. v. Ireland. App. no. 39474/98, European Court of Human Rights (2002).

Dale, Michael J. 1998. "Lawsuits and Public Policy: The Role of Litigation in Correcting Conditions in Juvenile Detention Centers." *University of San Francisco Law Review,* 32: 675.

Donnell C. v. Illinois State Board of Education. 829 F. Supp. 1016 (N.D. Ill. 1993).

Feldman, Cassi. 2007. "State Facilities' Use of Force Is Scrutinized After a Death." *New York Times,* March 4.

Foucault, Michel. [1975] 1995. *Discipline & Punish: The Birth of the Prison.* New York: Vintage Books.

Gary H. v. Hegstrom. 831 F.2d 1430, 1432 (9th Cir. 1987).

Georgia Department of Juvenile Justice. 2008. Policy 19.3 ("Use of Force").

Goodkind, Sarah. 2005. "Gender-Specific Services in the Juvenile Justice System: A Critical Examination." *Affilia* 20(1): 52–70.

Grassian, Stuart. 2009. Declaration filed in *K.C. v. Townsend,* 6:09-CV-012-C, U.S. District Court, Northern District of Texas on August 21, 2009.

Gunn, T. Jeremy. 2006. "The Religious Right and the Opposition to U.S. Ratification of the Convention on the Rights of the Child." *Emory International Law Review* 20(1): 111–28.

Hennis-Plasschaert, Jeanine. 2008. Written Question to the European Commission on Human Rights (E-2231/08).

Hollingsworth v. Orange County. No. 51-08-65 (Superior Court Orange County, California 1990).

Holsinger, Kristi, and Alexander M. Holsinger. 2005. "Differential Pathways to Violence and Self-Injurious Behavior: African American and White Girls in the Juvenile Justice System." *Journal of Research in Crime and Deliquency* 42: 211–42.

Huling, Tracy. 2002. "Building a Prison Economy in Rural America." In *Invisible Punishment: The Collateral Consequences of Mass Imprisonment*, edited by Marc Mauer and Meda Chesney-Lind, 197–213. New York: The New Press.

Human Rights Watch. 1995. *Children in Confinement in Louisiana.* New York: Human Rights Watch.

———. 1996. *Modern Capital of Human Rights? Abuses in the State of Georgia.* New York: Human Rights Watch.

———. 1997. *High Country Lockup: Children in Confinement in Colorado.* New York: Human Rights Watch.

———. 1999. *No Minor Matter: Children in Maryland's Jails.* New York: Human Rights Watch.

———. 2009. *No Equal Justice: The Prison Litigation Reform Act in the United States.* New York: Human Rights Watch.

Human Rights Watch and the American Civil Liberties Union. 2006. *Custody and Control: Conditions of Confinement in New York's Juvenile Prisons for Girls.* New York: Human Rights Watch.

Jones v. Blanas. 393 F.3d 918, 931 (9th Circuit 2004).

Juvenile Reeducation Institute v. Paraguay. Inter-American Court of Human Rights, Judgment of September 2, 2004.

King, Loretta. 2009. Letter from Acting Assistant Attorney General Loretta King to New York Governor David Patterson. "Investigation of the Lansing Residential Center, Louis Gossett, Jr. Residential Center, Tryon Residential Center, and Tryon Girls Center," August 14, 2009.

Klein, Eric K. 1998. "Dennis the Menace or Billy the Kid: An Analysis of the Role of Transfer to Criminal Court in Juvenile Justice." *American Criminal Law Review* 35: 371–410.

Krisberg, Barry. 1994. "Distorted by Fear: The Make Believe War on Crime." *Social Justice* 21(3): 38–49.

Lollis v. New York Department of Social Services. 322 F. Supp. 473 (S.D. N.Y. 1970), modified, 328 F. Supp. 1115 (S.D.N.Y. 1971).

Martarella v. Kelley. 349 F. Supp. 575, 598 (S.D.N.Y. 1972).

Matter of Children Deprived of Liberty in the "Complexo do Tatuapé" of FEBEM. Order of the Inter-American Court of Human Rights (November 25, 2008).

Milonas v. Williams. 691 F.2d 931 (10th Circuit 1982).

New York Office of Children and Family Services. 2007. Policy and Procedures Manual 3247.13 ("Use of Physical Restraint").

New York Times. 2009. "Editorial: New York's Disgrace," August 25.

Office of Juvenile Justice and Delinquency Prevention. 1998. Guiding Principles for Promising Female Programming. http://ojjdp.ncjrs.gov/pubs/principles/contents.html.

Pagnanelli, Enrico. 2007. "Children as Adults: The Transfer of Juveniles to Adult Courts and the Potential Impact of *Roper v. Simmons*." *American Criminal Law Review* 44: 175–94.

Prison Litigation Reform Act. 42 U.S.C. §1997e(a)(requirement of exhaustion of administrative grievance procedures); 18 U.S.C. sec. 3626(g)(3) and (5)(applicability to children); 42 U.S.C. sec. 1997e(h)(same); 42 U.S.C. sec. 1997e(d)(limiting attorneys fees award).

Rose, Joshua T. 2003. "Innocence Lost: The Detrimental Effect of Automatic Waiver Statutes on Juvenile Justice." *Brandeis Law Journal* 41: 977–95.

Ryder, R. Scott, and Preston Elrod. 2005. *Juvenile Justice: A Social, Historical, and Legal Perspective.* 2nd Edition. Sudbury: Jones and Bartlett Publishers.

Schinas, Margaritis. 2008. Written Question to the European Commission on Human Rights (E-3686/08).

Squires, Gregory D. ed. 1992. *From Redlining to Reinvestment: Community Responses to Urban Disinvestment.* Philadelphia: Temple University Press.

Sukhovoy v. Russia. App. no. 63955/00, European Court of Human Rights (2008).

Testimony of Vincent Schiraldi. Department of Youth Rehabilitation Services, before the District of Columbia, Committee on Human Services, February 16, 2006 (on file with the author).

Texas Family Code §51.01. 2009. ("Purpose and Interpretation").

Texas Youth Commission. 2009. General Administrative Policy Manual.

Texas Youth Commission, Correctional Care Form. Search Log, Dec. 23, 2008 – March 19, 2009 (on file with the author).

Turner v. Safley. 482 U.S. 78 (1987).

United Nations Standard Minimum Rules for the Administration of Juvenile Justice ("Beijing Rules"). Adopted November 29, 1985, by General Assembly Resolution 40/33.

U.S. Department of Justice, Civil Rights Division, Special Litigation Section. 2009. Documents and Publications. http://www.usdoj.gov/crt/split/findsettle .php#CRIPAletters.

Von Zielbauer, Paul. 2005. "A Spotty Record of Health Care for Children in City Detention." *New York Times*, March 1.

Williams v. California. Sup. Ct. California, Docket No. 312236 (filed 2000).

Wisdom, Cathy S., and Michael G. Maxfield. 2001. "An Update on the 'Cycle of Violence.'" *Research in Brief.* U.S. Department of Justice, Office of Justice Programs, National Institute of Justice.

Youngberg v. Romeo. 457 U.S. 307 (1982).

Zaplin, Ruth T. 1998. *Female Offenders: Critical Perspectives and Effective Interventions.* Gaithersburg, MD: Aspen Publishers.

14

LGBT Rights as Human Rights in the United States: Opportunities Lost

Julie Mertus

*One night, my family was eating dinner and talking about the new princi-
pal at my children's school. My then-nine-year-old daughter had her own
concerns. "Do you think he knows we're lesbians?" Lynne wondered.
"Oh honey, YOU and Daniel are not lesbians, WE are," I said, pointing to my partner and myself. The conversation took a strange turn as I
fumbled, "Well, you could be a lesbian, there is nothing . . . errr . . . wrong
with that." "And so what about me?" five-year-old Daniel chimed in. I
couldn't control a chuckle as Lynne admonished him, "Boys can't be lesbians!" "Oh, I remembered that," Dan responded, with a disappointed
tone in his voice, "I just forgot why."*

Lesbian, gay, bisexual, and transgendered (LGBT) people have quietly
realized some success in arguing their claims in human rights terms in
U.S. courts. Shunning the media, LGBT lawyers fear the public backlash that might occur should the extent of their victories become a
matter for broad public comment. Yet even with the voluntary, self-
imposed restrictions and the unevenness of advocacy victories, it is hard
to deny that LGBT rights have come a long way in the U.S. legal system. But this is only a recent phenomenon; for three decades the movement for LGBT concerns was grounded less in human rights terms
(i.e., the belief that all human beings have equal moral worth) and
more in terms of participation through liberation rhetoric, displays of
self-discovery, self-help strategies against two main threats (i.e., disease
and public violence), and political campaigns. In the United States, the
LGBT movement has continually wavered between legal and institutional approaches that attempt to achieve liberal equality within existing identity categories and social–political structures, and more radical
approaches that demand a rethinking of existing structures and a search
for alternative approaches more reflective of actually lived identities

and relationships. This chapter seeks to unravel this complex story by analyzing the ways in which LGBT advocacy in the United States has evolved across four time periods: the 1970s (a time for liberation and self-discovery); 1980s (a relapse into "survival mode, and the creation of new avenues for participation"); the 1990s (entry into popular culture); and, the first decade of the 2000s (finally, advocacy campaigns and litigation invoking human rights norms). Human rights exposes the injustice of stigma based on arbitrary characteristics and, in so doing, provides the grounds for people classified as lesbian, gay, bisexual, or transgendered (LGBT) to claim their entitlement to being treated as having equal moral worth.

Herein lies the catch: we are not all the same, and we are rarely discriminated against or abused based on one "essential" characteristic. Our claims for being treated with dignity are complex. There is no single LGBT way of being or thinking, and therefore, there is no single way to define being treated with dignity. Members of the Log Cabin Republicans, an influential conservative gay group, are as gay as the men dancing in brightly colored, feathered costumes in the street in the rainbow parade. Nor can one identify a single set of LGBT "experiences." To be LGBT, one need not reject the heterosexual program for marriage or the patriarchal militarization of society. On the contrary, one may seek to participate in traditional family structures and support military organizations and not sacrifice their "LGBT-ness." The attempt to force LGBT concerns to fit within the human rights framework has floundered because many people do not view their identity in terms of the hetero/homo dichotomy. LGBT activists in the United States, running slightly behind their European counterparts (Council of Europe 2010), have only recently begun to frame their struggles in terms of fundamental human rights principles such as "human dignity" and "equality" (Zeidan 2006, 74).

The LGBT advocacy strategy that has emerged in the United States over the last forty years has continually emphasized the importance of safeguarding the capacity of individuals and groups to define themselves as they participate in society, safely and openly, according to their own terms (i.e., as publicly or privately as they desire). This is not at odds with a human rights framework's requirement that individuals be treated with dignity and as having equal moral worth. But it does challenge human rights advocates to adjust their tactics. As time has progressed, decade by decade, one can see the rights-based claims of LGBT advocates coming into sharper focus.

THE 1970s: SEEKING SELF-RESPECT AND LIBERATION

The gay liberation movement that emerged in the United States in the 1970s rarely used a rights-based approach – and certainly never used international human rights as its lodestar. Instead, it was focused inward, fostering collective identity while at the same time providing space for the formation of new interest groups within that identity (Engel 2001). As this process of self-discovery and action evolved, so did the politics and discourse informing it. The movements embodying the New Left (in the 1970s) – the student movement, the antiwar movement, the black power movement, and the feminist movement – began to utilize a new vocabulary. Engel observes: "Instead of viewing their goals in terms of anti-discrimination, minority groups spoke in terms of the structural oppression inherent in the capitalist system... aiming for equality and integration, the goal shifted to liberation and self-determination" (2001, 47).

Adherents to the gay liberation movement endeavored to build new organizations with a more leftist orientation. The manifesto of one of the most influential groups of the times, the Gay Liberation Front (GLF), declared itself to be:

> a revolutionary homosexual group of men and women formed with a realization that a complete sexual liberation for all people cannot come about unless existing social institutions are abolished. We reject society's attempt to impose sexual roles and definitions on our nature... Babylon has forced us to commit ourselves to one thing... revolution.
>
> (GLF Statement of Purpose 1969, as quoted in
> D'Emilio and Freedman 1998)

However, the movement's actions did not match the GLF's revolutionary rhetoric. The main tactic of GLF was internalized consciousness raising (Jay and Young 1992), a nonconfrontational and "inward" experience that brought gay men and women together to discuss their experiences with the aim of "cognitive liberation" (Engel 2001; Marotta 1981). Interestingly, more public and strident actions were undertaken by GLF's main competitor, the Gay Activist Alliance (GAA), which was considerably less radical in tone. In fact, GAA was formed as a counterweight to GLF; it sought to work within the system to promote legal and social change. Through the efforts of GAA and other organizations, protests, "kiss-ins" in restaurants refusing to serve gay customers, publicized applications by gay and lesbian couples for marriage licenses, intense "zaps" against media establishments refusing to acknowledge the homosexual community all increased in frequency (Marotta 1981).

During this period, academic activism met with remarkable success. A gay group within the American Library Association publicly argued for changes in the library practice of classifying homosexuality as an abnormality. But the real triumph came in 1973 when the Board of Trustees of the American Psychiatric Association voted to delete homosexuality as a mental disorder from the seventh printing of the second edition of the *Diagnostic and Statistical Manual of Mental Disorders*, or DSM-II (Bayer 1988; D'Emilio and Freedman 1998). This move facilitated the creation of a more open association of lesbian and gay psychiatrists, the Caucus of Gay, Lesbian, and Bisexual Members of the American Psychiatric Association (Association of Gay and Lesbian Psychiatrists).

By the mid-1970s, more than 1,000 gay and lesbian organizations existed in the United States (D'Emilio 1983, 2). Although the GLF collapsed in 1973 and the GAA disbanded in 1974, other single- and multi-issue organizations were ready to take their place. One organization established during this time, the National Gay Task Force, would, under its new name, National Gay and Lesbian Task Force (changed in 1986), become one of the leading U.S.-based LGBT advocacy groups (National Gay and Lesbian Task Force 1984). The 1970s closed with the largest manifestation of gay pride ever in the nation's capital: more than 100,000 gay and lesbian activists marched on Washington, D.C., in 1979. The placards they waved and chants they sang were focused less on radical liberation and more on traditional rights-based goals. They might have continued this trend toward human rights if not for a major obstacle blocking their path: a public health crisis surrounding a disease known as HIV-AIDS.

THE 1980s: STRUGGLING FOR SURVIVAL, CREATING NEW AVENUES FOR PARTICIPATION

For many LGBT activists, and especially for gay men, the 1980s were a time of literally struggling to survive. The social climate of the 1980s was conservative and hostile, but even more significantly, a devastating new public health crisis disproportionately affecting gay men challenged LGBT activists to provide new leadership and strategies. The first five cases of a new, untreatable form of cancer were reported by *The New York Times* in 1981. By the end of the decade more than 300,000 would die from what would be identified as acquired immune deficiency syndrome (AIDS); 220,000 of them would be gay men (Vaid 1996, 81). The fact that gay men were dying in large numbers from a disease believed to be transmitted primarily through homosexual sexual acts provided fodder for hateful conservatives who blamed them for their own deaths (Herek 1991, 13).

Seemingly impervious to human rights frameworks, LGBT activists in the 1980s once again turned inward for self-help and mutual support to confront the health crisis. Numerous community-based health organizations formed to offer direct services and to promote better information on "safe sex" practices (Adam 1995, 157). One group begun at the time to fill the gap in the health care establishment, the Gay Men's Health Crisis (GMHC), would eventually become the largest AIDS service organization in the world and a significant proponent of the right to access to health care (Letellier 2004).

New avenues for political participation opened as, increasingly, gay men and lesbians were viewed by American politicians as an interest group and a voter block (Bailey 1998). One of the most influential lobbyist-oriented LGBT groups to arise in this period was the Human Rights Campaign Fund (HRC). Although it prominently uses the words "human rights" in its title, HRC was not at its onset a "human rights" organization in the traditional sense of promoting specific international human rights standards and using international human rights institutions. Even to this day, its webpage (www.hrc.org) does not mention international human rights, except for issues related to immigration. Rather, it has always been an issue-focused lobby advocating for gay and gay-friendly political candidates on local, state, and national levels, as well as lobbying for gay-related national legislation. And, by not being overtly gay (its moniker is a mathematical equal sign), it has provided a new path to participation for more conservative and moderate gay men and lesbians.

Despite continual efforts of the LGBT community to present a positive and acceptable picture of their lives, being open continued to involve risk. The academic research on gay and lesbian lives that flourished in the 1980s presented a stark picture. For example, a 1984 study of gay men and lesbians in eight U.S. cities found 24 percent of gay men and 9 percent of lesbians reported being punched, hit, kicked, or beaten at least once in their lives because of their sexual orientation; 42 percent of gay men were threatened with physical violence and 93 percent had experienced some type of victimization for the same reason (National Gay and Lesbian Task Force 1984). Students who described themselves as lesbian, gay, bisexual, or transgender were five times more likely to miss school because of feeling unsafe, and 28 percent felt that they were forced to drop out of school (National Gay and Lesbian Task Force 1984).

Noting the power of the media to shape opinions about gays and lesbians, a group of writers formed the Gay and Lesbian Alliance Against Defamation (GLAAD) in 1985. The group worked to promote "fair, accurate, and inclusive representation as a means of challenging discrimination based on sexual orientation or identity" (GLAAD 1996). Their activism involved monitoring media depictions of gays and lesbians and responding to those images, positive or negative, wherever they are used.

Many gay and lesbian activists viewed these new professional organizations with suspicion. GLAAD, to take one illustration, was perceived as not radical or sincere enough in its struggle for the advancement of gays and lesbians. GLAAD was known for its "orchestrated demonstrations," according to Maxine Wolf, an original member of the more militant organization ACT UP (AIDS Coalition to Unleash Power). Wolf complained the demonstrations were:

> negotiated with the cops, [where the GLAAD officers] basically told you when to show up, when to go home, and there was absolutely no input from anybody into what was going to be done. The board of directors made the decisions. Women coming to their meetings eventually just stopped because they were huge meetings and no one would even get a chance to get up and speak.
>
> (Ingram and Retter 1997)

Widespread disillusionment with the results of traditional nonviolent protests, as well as the relative lack of visibility in the mainstream press, created pressure for the resurgence of confrontational strategies. Most notably, ACT UP, founded in 1987, derided the work of reform-oriented organizations like GLAAD, GMHC, and the Human Rights Campaign Fund (Vaid 1996, 94). The methods of ACT UP were "disruptive" and garnered a great deal of attention in the media.

Galvanized by the Washington, D.C. march and angered by the lack of response by government officials to their concerns, activists concluded the 1980s with a flash of militancy. Four activists from ACT UP, who had personally experienced antigay violence, chose to form Queer Nation. Queer Nation declared itself to be a nonviolent direct action network believing in an ideology of fluid sexuality (neither gay, nor straight, but queer). One controversial "in your face" campaign involved "outing" public officials who were gay and lesbian in hopes of convincing the American public that gays and lesbians were already in influential positions and acting as effective leaders (Marech 2004).

For a period of time, Queer Nation (QN) and its NYC spin-off The Lesbian Avengers were incredibly successful in rekindling pride and excitement among LGBT communities. Although Queer Nation "struggled to find an organizational premise" (Engel 2001, 56), it was certainly a phenomenon challenging traditional LGBT politics. As Urvashi Vaid explains:

> QN had a dress code (leather, shaved heads, Doc Martens, and T-shirts with big lettering), an antiestablishment stand...and an attitude that spoke to the nineties (postmodern, in their faces, militant). The flourishing underground 'zines published by defiant queers ranted against the assimilation stance of those who used the words gay and lesbian to identify themselves. Queer became the vanguard; everything else was retro (1996, 237).

The popularity of Queer Nation among LGBT youth made it clear that despite the professionalization of many LGBT organizations there was still a need for highly participatory organizations and activities that steered clear of a focus on rights and instead permitted inward-looking self-identification (Fraser 1996, 32–35).

THE 1990S: ENTERING MAINSTREAM CULTURE

Self-identification mixed potently with pop culture's imagination in the 1990s. By the middle of that decade, gay and lesbian visibility became a

> pop-culture phenomenon with the public with the "coming out" of such celebrities as k.d. Lang, Lea Delaria, Melissa Etheridge, and WBZ news anchor Randy Price. In film and theater, *The Crying Game*, *The Wedding Banquet*, and the award-winning play *Angels in America* all addressed homosexual issues in mainstream venues, while popular television shows such as *Roseanne*, *Melrose Place*, and MTV's *Real World* regularly featured openly gay, lesbian, and bisexual characters.
>
> (Joyce 1993)

Over the past few years, American pop culture has embraced the openly lesbian comedienne Ellen DeGeneres, the popular television show *Queer Eye for the Straight Guy*, and the Oscar-nominated film *Brokeback Mountain*. This cultural shift met a strong conservative backlash. In 1992, conservative Pat Buchanan proposed that the United States was entering a "culture war," in which issues surrounding LGBT persons played a pivotal role. At the Republican National Convention in Houston that year, he asserted that "there is a religious war going on in this country . . . it is a cultural war as critical to the kind of nation we shall be as the Cold War itself, for this war is for the soul of America" (Buchanan 1992).

In the 1990s, LGBT advocates (well-fortified by years of George H. W. Bush) decided the best method for taking on the religious right was to engage from within instead of protest from outside. Although a few gay and lesbian activists continued the confrontational strategies of the 1980s, many others explored possibilities for working with and within the political establishment (Witt, Thomas, and Marcus 1995). Instead of seeking to prevent the state from interfering in negative ways in gay and lesbian lives, this strategy encouraged the state to become engaged in gay-related issues in a positive way (Adam 1995; Sherrill 1996; Wilcox and Wolpert 1996).

Another 1990s strategy involved lobbying and support for openly gay or LGBT-friendly political candidates who would be expected to vote on legislation in line with LGBT concerns. For example, in 1993 HRC's heavy lobbying and constituency pressure led Congress to pass the Hate Crimes Sentencing Enhancement Act. This law strengthened sentences for federal hate crimes – including those targeting gays and lesbians. The Hate Crimes Act was the first federal statute to use the term "sexual orientation" to define a protected group. And in 1994, HRC supported U.S. Representatives and Senators who introduced a bill for the Employment Non-Discrimination Act, which prohibited "employment agencies, labor organizations, and training programs from engaging in specified unlawful employment practices (discrimination) based upon sexual orientation" (U.S. Library of Congress 2001). The HRC, concentrating heavily on political pressure and lobbying, soon became the largest civil rights organization in the United States working for gay, lesbian, bisexual, and transgender equality (Human Rights Campaign 2004).

The third-largest gay and lesbian organization in the United States, the Lesbian and Gay Victory Fund (LGVF), was also founded in 1991 and also focused entirely on encouraging gay men and lesbians to run for political office. As the decade closed, LGVF was one of a handful of LGBT organizations providing an easy (and effective) means for participation in mainstream LGBT politics at the national level. Other groups were more focused on the burgeoning field of same-sex marriage, including the National Center for Lesbians, Equality California, and the Lambda Legal Defense and Education Fund Marriage Project. Bolstered by their increased visibility in political and social culture, LGBT activists ended the 1990s closer to the human rights framework than ever before. LGBT activists demanded nothing short of nondiscrimination and equality in all aspects of their lives.

THE 2000s: LITIGATION, NONDISCRIMINATION EVERYWHERE

By the time the new century unfolded, the notion that human rights included LGBT rights had already been embraced by human rights activists in the United States, South Africa, and many European states. But a tremendous difference on this issue existed between activists in the United States and those in other countries. Activists in other countries applied human rights principles to their own country's laws and practices, often with great success. For example, activists in South Africa successfully lobbied for the inclusion of sexual orientation within their post-apartheid constitution (SouthAfrica Info.com 2010). By contrast, American activists began by investigating and reporting on LGBT rights violations in *other* countries (Rosenblum 1994). As this chapter has explained, application of human rights tenets *at home* was more slow in coming.

There are three main trends marking the domestic application of human rights law by American LGBT activists: (1) the widening of nondiscrimination principles to encompass more people and issues, including immigration and asylum; (2) political and legal efforts to lift restrictions on gay men and lesbians freely serving in the military; and (3) a concerted focus on everyday family life and same-sex marriage.

THE WIDENING OF NONDISCRIMINATION

Antidiscrimination laws have forced Americans to face the fundamental unfairness of judging people according to a particular personal characteristic that has nothing to do with the issue at hand. In a competitive American society, certainly people were judged based on their ability to perform – for instance, only kids who can play basketball really well can make the "A Team." However, judgments based on irrelevant characteristics are not permitted – no Jews or no Hispanics on this basketball team (regardless of how well they play). From an early age, American children are taught that they live in a meritocracy. It simply makes no sense, then, to prejudge gay people. Opponents of this line of thinking had long responded with a variation of "the criminal" exception: nondiscrimination is fine for most people, but the principle does not apply to groups of people who threaten morality through their conduct and, indeed, their existence. This class of people – derelicts, criminals, and the like – are outside the law and cannot claim its protection.

The appeal of the "criminal exception" had worn off by the 1990s, when people came out of the closet in record numbers and, as noted earlier, queer media icons like Ellen Degeneres made being gay or lesbian acceptable, if not stylish. Suddenly everyone knew someone who was gay – Aunt Betty, who has been living with that nice sorority sister for years; the two impeccably dressed men who always sit in the third row in church; a daughter who has a passion for motorcycles. Colorful or plain, these people could not be considered criminals. The early 2000s provided opportunities to test this line of thinking.

In some instances, advocates pushed for the creation of new antidiscrimination laws specific to gay men and lesbians, or for an even more inclusive grouping including not only gay men and lesbians but also transgendered, bisexual, or gender-ambiguous people. Where antidiscrimination laws already existed, advocates adopted the strategy of using existing legislation, either by adding a new category to an already broad list of groups protected from discrimination or by suggesting a category in existing law that should be interpreted to include at least some in the LGBT community. (For example, sex or gender discrimination could be seen as encompassing discrimination based on gender identity.)

The regime of protection under antidiscrimination law did give the LGBT movement "a presence in both the law and culture of equality in the United States." A seasoned activist professor Nan Hunter has observed, warning that only some LGBT Americans are covered by antidiscrimination law, and those who are covered often receive inadequate protection (Hunter 2000, 565).

The nature of discrimination against LGBT people differs greatly from other forms of discrimination more often covered by U.S. antidiscrimination legislation. To trigger a workplace protection, African Americans rarely need to declare their race, but sexual minorities most often must declare their orientation. "The entire 'don't ask, don't tell' nature of dominant American sexual culture hinges on keeping the silence," observes Hunter. "The structure of civil rights laws do not accommodate the dynamic of silence very well" (Hunter 2000, 576–77). One must "come out" in order to claim the rights to nondiscrimination and equality, but once a person does "come out" in the workplace, they risk being fired for "flaunting their sexuality," provoking a response, and disturbing the work flow. Then, when they are fired, the alleged reason is not for their sexual orientation but for their speech/conduct. Thus, although the presence of antidiscrimination laws has pushed American employers and American judges to align themselves with human rights principles, progress has been limited.

THE MILITARY BAN

It took 17 years to lift the Clinton formulation for gay men and lesbians in the military. This policy, conceived as a compromise, prohibited anyone who demonstrated a propensity or intent to engage in homosexual acts from serving in the armed forces of the United States. The regulation prohibited military recruiters from asking armed forces applicants if they were homosexual. At the same time, the regulation also prohibited gay and lesbian soldiers from disclosing their sexual orientation or from speaking about any homosexual conduct, including their relationships, marriages, or other familial attributes, while serving in the U.S. armed forces. "Many people on both the left and right would agree that the 'Don't Ask, Don't Tell' (DADT) policy was perhaps the greatest blunder of the Clinton administration" (Belkin and Bateman 2003, 4–5). Proponents of including gay men and lesbians in the military contended that the new policy, by forcing people into the closet and keeping them paranoid of being discovered at any time, was worse than an explicit ban. Opponents of DADT argued that it made military service too open for homosexuals and in so doing undermined group cohesion.

In his first State of the Union address on January 27, 2010, President Barack Obama explicitly stated his plans to end the military's "Don't Ask, Don't Tell" (DADT) policy on homosexuals serving in the armed forces: "This year, I will work with Congress and our military to finally repeal the law that denies gay Americans the right to serve the country they love because of who they are." Well into his presidency, DADT discharges continued. In fiscal year 2009 alone, 428 service members were discharged (Wilson 2010). Finally, in December 2010, after repeated Republican attempts to block any legislation authorizing a change, the U.S. Senate voted 65–31 to repeal DADT.

EQUALITY IN THE FAMILY

Surprisingly, LGBT advocates had greater success in tackling another American nondiscrimination stronghold: equal rights to marriage. The "marriage campaign" deeply worried the more radical LGBT advocates who viewed marriage as a deeply flawed institution that LGBT persons might want to avoid, not join. But LGBT people wanted their relationships and families to be recognized as equally worthy as other families. They accepted and even desired the responsibility, stability, and fidelity demanded by marriage. The argument circulating through center/left advocates was that equal access to marriage must be an option for those who desire it (Edgington 2010). After all, "we're just like you," gay families contended.

The campaign for same-sex marriages in the United States has been fought in the legislatures and the courts. The 1990s and 2000s were important both for the creation of laws banning marriage between two people of the same sex and for litigation as to the constitutionality of such laws. The case kicking off this spate of litigation was *Goodridge v. Massachusetts Dept. of Public Health* (2003). In November 2003, in a hard fought three to four decision, the Massachusetts Supreme Judicial Court found that the state may not "deny the protections, benefits and obligations conferred by civil marriage to two individuals of the same sex who wish to marry." The explanation of the majority decision came close to a human rights approach when it reasoned that the state's constitution "affirms the dignity and equality of all individuals. It forbids the creation of second-class citizens," and that "the right to marry is not a privilege conferred by the State, but a fundamental right that is protected against unwarranted State interference."

In this case, the Massachusetts Supreme Court gave the legislature six months to change the law so that it no longer improperly discriminated. When the legislature suggested civil unions as an alternative, the Massachusetts Supreme Court flatly rejected the plan as inadequate. Same-sex couples in Massachusetts were permitted to enter into the same civil marriage arrangement as heterosexual couples. Additional states following suit included Connecticut, Iowa, and Vermont. In Iowa, for example, the Supreme Court ruled unanimously that the state's law limiting marriage to opposite-sex couples was unconstitutional and same-sex couples must have access to marriage. Vermont, in contrast, became the first state to enact marriage equality through legislative action and, in March 2010, the District of Columbia's City Council vote in favor of same-sex marriage became effective after it survived the Congressional approval period mandated for such cases.

Cases where same-sex marriage was put to a popular vote, however, have been largely unsuccessful. In one prominent example, the Maine legislature passed a same-sex marriage bill in May 2000. Governor John

Baldacci, long opposed to same-sex marriage, came to view it as a matter of fairness and thus had no problem signing it. Scheduled to take effect in September 2009, the bill was put on hold pending a November 2009 popular vote. In an extremely tight race, Maine residents opposed to same-sex marriage edged out those who supported the measure and Maine "returned to being a 'marriage lite' state, where same-sex couples have some of the rights of marriage but don't share equal rights with opposite-sex couples" (Doskow 2010).

Attorney Emily Moscow explains that marriage-lite states offer either civil unions or domestic partnerships (i.e., New Jersey) said to provide the same rights and responsibilities as marriage, including rights under family laws, such as annulment, divorce, child custody, child support, alimony, domestic violence, adoption, and property division; rights to sue for wrongful death, loss of consortium, and under any other tort or law concerning spousal relationships; family leave benefits; joint state tax filing; and property inheritance when one partner dies without a will.

In the United States, these rights apply only to couples living in those states accepting same-sex civil unions, and not all of the rights apply in all states in the same manner. Rhode Island and Wisconsin, for example, provide limited rights and benefits for same-sex partners. However, rights and benefits under federal law are not included. Therefore, same-sex couples are not eligible for such benefits as Social Security, immigration privileges, or the marriage exemption to some federal taxes. Perhaps most significantly, same-sex civil unions do not provide the same respect for families made by same-sex partners as that afforded traditional families.

The demand for fully equitable same-sex marriage continues to be strong. During the short window of time in which same-sex marriage was legal in California (five-and-a-half months, from June until November 2008), an estimated 18,000 same-sex couples were wed in California. The California Supreme Court ruled that limiting marriage to persons of the opposite sex violates the California Constitution, but the electorate expressed its disagreement with the legislature by voting for Proposition 8, a measure limiting marriage in California to opposite-sex couples.

Whether the same-sex relationships formalized in either "marriage-lite" states or full marriage equivalent states will be recognized in other states is in debate. The U.S. Constitution requires each state to give "full faith and credit" to the laws of other states. However, in 1996 Congress passed a law to undermine the "full faith and credit" requirement, the federal Defense of Marriage Act (DOMA). The intent was clearly stated in DOMA's legislative history:

> H.R. 3396, the Defense of Marriage Act, has two primary purposes. The first is to defend the institution of traditional heterosexual marriage. The second is to protect the right of States to formulate their own public policy regarding the legal definition of same-sex unions, free from any federal constitutional implications that might attend the recognition by one State of the right for homosexual couples to acquire marriage licenses.
>
> (U.S. Library of Congress 1995, 2)

Many states have also passed their own DOMA laws barring same-sex marriages in those states. Any state with a DOMA law – even those providing some form of same-sex relationship recognition – will not recognize a same-sex marriage from any of the states that allow it, and states with so-called Super-DOMA laws will not recognize a same-sex relationship of any kind. With so many states enacting DOMA laws and so few adopting fully equitable marriage laws, the campaign for gay marriage cannot be considered a human rights success. It remains one area in which the United States lags behind progressive countries that are more comfortable viewing their own behavior through a human rights lens (Slovenia 2009).

CONCLUSION

Understanding where the movement for LGBT human rights can go means understanding where the movement has been. This historical analysis supports three points: first, the tension between human rights and gay identity politics runs deep; second, this tension has an impact on what is valued as meaningful political participation; and third, the methodology of human rights advocates has changed over time, but the conditions under which human rights advocacy is most successful at advancing LGBT concerns remain constant. Where the actions of advocacy groups are open to diverse participation and are transparent, accountable, and highly participatory, LGBT rights advocacy has greater success.

Two forms of advocacy inform LGBT activism at the domestic level in the United States: (1) assimilation approaches that accept categories and emphasize the "normal" nature of LGBT lives; and (2) confrontational approaches that reject binary categories and stress "difference" over "sameness." Given that domestic politics are overwhelmingly more informed by the approach most compatible with human rights claims – the assimilation approach – one would expect that human rights framings would play a key role in domestic LGBT politics today. Yet LGBT advocates are only beginning to tap human rights, relying instead on civil rights law reform and litigation as the primary vehicles for social change (Rosenblum 1994, 19). To become more relevant and successful, the human rights framework will have to bend enough to accommodate the diversity of lived realities captured under the LGBT umbrella.

REFERENCES

Adam, Barry D. 1995. *The Rise of a Gay and Lesbian Movement*. New York: Twayne.

Bailey, Robert. 1998. "Out and Voting, The Gay, Lesbian and Bisexual Vote in Congressional House Elections, 1990–1996." *The National Gay and Lesbian Task Force*. http://www.thetaskforce.org/downloads/outnvoting.pdf.

Bayer, Ronald. 1988. *Homosexuality and American Psychiatry: The Politics of Diagnosis*. Princeton, NJ: Princeton University Press.

Belkin, Aaron, and Geoffrey Bateman. 2003. *Don't Ask, Don't Tell: Debating the Gay Ban in the Military*. Boulder, CO: Lynne Rienner.

Buchanan, Patrick J. 1992. "Republican National Convention Speech." August 17. http://www.buchanan.org/pa-92-0817-rnc.html.

Council of Europe. 2010. *The Toolkit to Promote and Protect the Enjoyment of Human Rights by Lesbian, Gay, Bisexual and Transgender (LGBT) People*. Council of the European Union Working Party on Human Rights. June 8, Brussels.

D'Emilio, John. 1983. *Sexual Politics, Sexual Communities*. Chicago: Chicago University Press.

D'Emilio, John, and Estelle Freedman. 1998. *Intimate Matters: A History of Sexuality in America*. New York: Harper and Row.

Doskow, Emily. 2010. "Same-Sex Marriage: Developments in the Law." *Nolo*. http://www.nolo.com/legal-encyclopedia/article-29828.html.

Edgington, Byron. 2010. "Is Gay Marriage a Conservative Issue?" *The Lantern*. January 24. http://www.thelantern.com/opinion/is-gay-marriage-a-conservative-issue-1.1084438.

Engel, Stephen M. 2001. *The Unfinished Revolution: Social Movement Theory and the Gay and Lesbian Movement*. Cambridge, UK/New York: Cambridge University Press.

Fraser, Michael R. 1996. "Identity and Representation as Challenges to Social Movement Theory: A Case Study of Queer Nation." In *Mainstreams and Margins: Cultural Politics in the 1990s*, edited by Michael Morgan and Susan Leggett, 32–44. Westport, CT: Greenwood Press.

GLAAD. 1996. Media Release. New York City. August 7. http://www.uky.edu/StudentOrgs/QueerInfo/glaad.htm.

Goodridge v. Massachusetts. Dept. of Public Health. 2003. 79 N.E.2d 941.

Herek, G.M. 1991. "Stigma, Prejudice, and Violence Against Lesbians and Gay Men." In *Homosexuality: Research Implications for Public Policy*, edited by John C. Gonsiorek and James W. Weinrich, 60–80. Newbury Park, CA: SAGE Publications.

Human Rights Campaign. 2004. "The Human Rights Campaign Turns 20." *The Human Rights Campaign.* http://www.hrc.org/Content/NavigationMenu/ About_HRC/HRC_History_Timeline_1980–1989.htm.

Hunter, Nan D. 2000. "Sexuality and Civil Rights: Re-Imagining Anti-Discrimination Laws." *New York Journal of Human Rights* 1(17): 565–87.

Ingram, Anne-Marie Bouthillette, and Yolanda Retter, eds. 1997. *Queers in Space: Communities, Public Places, Sites of Resistance.* Seattle, WA: Bay Press.

Joyce, Jacqueline. 1993. "Introduction Latent Image." *Latent Image.* Emerson College. http://pages.emerson.edu/organizations/fas/latent_image/issues/1993–12/intro.htm.

Letellier, Patrick. 2004. "Groups United in Gay Men's Health Institute." *Gay.com.* June 29. http://www.gay.com/news/article.html?2004/06/29/1.

Marech, Rona. 2004. "Activists Consider Ethics, Efficacy of Outing, after Voters Frown on Same-Sex Marriages, Gay Rights Proponents Take Stock of Options." *San Francisco Gate*, SFGate.com. November 14. http://www.sfgate .com/cgi-bin/article.cgi?file=/c/a/2004/11/14/MNGF69RDS R1.DTL.

Marotta, Toby. 1981. *The Politics of Homosexuality.* Boston: Houghton Mifflin.

National Gay and Lesbian Task Force. 1984. *National Anti-Gay/Lesbian Victimization Report.* New York: National Gay and Lesbian Task Force.

Rosenblum, Darren. 1994. "Queer Intersectionality and the Failure of Recent Lesbian and Gay 'Victories.'" *Law and Sexuality Review, Lesbian and Gay Legal Issues* 4(83): 84–120.

Sherrill, Kenneth. 1996. "The Political Power of Lesbians, Gays and Bisexuals." *PS: Political Science and Politics* 29(3): 469–73.

"Slovenia to Legalize Soon Same-Sex Marriage: Minister." 2009. AFP – July 2. http://www.google.com/hostednews/afp/article/ALeqM5hjrgMMgg 5JR4WuLYjqWx5dRrRGOQ.

SouthAfrica Info.com. 2010. http://www.southafrica.info/about/democracy/ constitution.htm.

U.S. Library of Congress. 1995. *Committee Reports, 104th Congress (1995–1996) House Report 104–664.* http://www.congress.gov/cgi-bin/cpquery/R? cp104:FLD010:@1(hr664).

U.S. Library of Congress. 2001. "A Bill to Prohibit Employment Discrimination on the Basis of Sexual Orientation. – July 31. http://thomas.loc.gov/ cgi-bin/bdquery/z?d107:SN01284:@@@L&summ2=m&.

Vaid, Urvashi. 1996. *Virtual Equality: The Mainstreaming of Gay and Lesbian Politics.* New York: Doubleday.

Wilcox, Clyde, and Robin M. Wolpert. 1996. "President Clinton, Public Opinion and Gays in the Military." In *Gay Rights, Military Wrongs: Political Perspectives on Lesbians and Gays in the Military*, edited by Craig A. Rimmerman, 127–46. New York: Garland.

Wilson, Evan. 2010. *International Legal Updates: Repealing Don't Ask/Don't Tell*, 40. http://www.wcl.american.edu/hrbrief/17/3legal.pdf?rd=1.

Witt, Lynn, Sherry Thomas, and Eric Marcus, eds. 1995. *Out in All Directions: The Almanac of Gay and Lesbian America.* New York: Time Warner Books.

Zeidan, Sami. 2006. "The Limits of Queer Theory in LGBT Litigation and International Human Rights Discourse." *Willamette Journal of International Law and Dispute Resolution* 14(73): 1–96.

15

No Shelter: Disaster Politics in Louisiana and the Struggle for Human Rights

Davida Finger and Rachel E. Luft

Following U.S. government failures before, during, and after Hurricane Katrina, social justice organizers and advocates increasingly turned to human rights frameworks to challenge the state. The 2005 hurricane revealed the human cost of domestic disaster policy, with regard to both disaster evacuation and shelter. Almost exactly three years later, Hurricane Gustav hit the Gulf Coast, triggering the largest evacuation in Louisiana history. As the first significant post-Katrina disaster event in the greater New Orleans area, Gustav provides an important opportunity to examine the ways in which community organizers have contested domestic disaster policy. Using sheltering policy as an example, we explore social movement efforts to resist and transform U.S. disaster politics. In particular, we examine the emergence of a human rights discourse for reframing disaster-related social problems. In light of the expansion of domestic human rights activity sparked by the Gulf Coast hurricanes (Luft 2009; Soohoo, Albisa, and Davis 2008), we believe this local case study has broader significance for both the practice and the scholarship of U.S. human rights.

For at least ten years before Hurricane Katrina, there was a growing resurgence of domestic human rights movement activity (Soohoo et al. 2008). Katrina laid bare not only the limitations of U.S. disaster policy but also the social contract to provide well-being more generally. These contradictions further inspired national and local movement actors to

Author names in alphabetical order. We would like to thank the following activists, advocates, and scholars for their input: Kali Akuno, Rhoda Howard-Hassmann, Ken Neubeck, Eric Tars, and Tracie Washington, along with gracious editors Shareen Hertel and Kathryn Libal. Rachel also acknowledges the Office of Research and Sponsored Programs at the University of New Orleans and Oxfam America for research awards that helped to support her work on this project.

turn to human rights frameworks to contest the state's handling of both the disaster and the recovery.

Domestic disaster policy generally focuses on providing hazard mitigation assistance to states to help reduce risks of future disasters, to aid harmed individuals, and to assist with infrastructure repair (Robert T. Stafford Disaster Relief and Emergency Assistance Act, 42 U.S.C. § 5170 *et seq.* 1988). Sociology's four-part disaster response model tracks domestic policy emphasizing mitigation, preparedness, response, and recovery. Sheltering – the slice of this trajectory we focus on – straddles preparedness and response. The significance of sheltering, however, extends beyond these stages, for "[a]ctions taken during the mitigation, preparedness, and response phases always influence recovery efforts" (Phillips 2009, 21). The government's early decisions regarding sheltering produce a broad array of longer-term outcomes, from housing to mental and physical health.

In conformity with domestic policy, disaster scholars identify four postdisaster housing stages: emergency shelter, temporary shelter, temporary housing, and permanent housing (Quarantelli in Phillips 2009, 200). For our discussion, sheltering refers to the first two of these – emergency and temporary shelter – because after both Katrina and Gustav, they blurred into each other. Despite the fact that they are underexamined in disaster literature (Phillips 2009; Nigg and Torres 2006), emergency and temporary sheltering are of significant human consequence. In the postdisaster Gulf Coast, sheltering is a notable site where those with the least access to resources have disproportionately faced humanitarian violations.

Disaster policy alone does not account for the government's failures in the Gulf Coast. The subject of "social vulnerability to disaster" – caused by race, class, gender, age, disability, and citizenship status – has been widely discussed with regard to the Gulf Coast hurricanes (Luft 2009; Laska and Morrow 2006). Flaws in domestic policy are exacerbated by social, economic, and political inequalities. In this way, the social experience of disaster is a function of already existing injustices. In focusing on postdisaster sheltering, we highlight a stage in the disaster cycle that, although briefer than others, dramatically reveals disaster inequality, or the way disaster is differentially experienced. The ability to avoid use of a public shelter during evacuation, for example, depends heavily on factors such as private car ownership, the ability to self-evacuate, caretaking responsibilities, and the financial or social capital to acquire private accommodation. In pre-Katrina New Orleans, one in four residents did not own a vehicle, a number stratified by race as well as by class; 27 percent of blacks did not own a car versus 5 percent of whites (Berube and Raphael 2005, 1). If 20 percent of the average disaster-affected community is expected to end up in an emergency shelter, it follows that poorer regions such as New Orleans, where a greater proportion of the population faces obstacles to self-evacuation, are likely to send far more (Philips 2009, 200). This examination of shelter policy, therefore, is not only a snapshot of the differential impact of disaster and disaster policy, but also of social inequality more broadly.

We pursue this project with an interdisciplinary approach linking macro-policy analysis to qualitative exploration of local social movement activity. In the first section, we provide a framework for domestic disaster policy, highlighting Louisiana and emergency sheltering. We then introduce the international human rights document that pertains to internal displacement and that provides a strong comparison to domestic disaster policy: the United Nations Guiding Principles on Internal Displacement (Guiding Principles 1998). In the final third of the chapter we discuss post-Katrina New Orleans-based human rights activity, focusing on the period during and after Hurricane Gustav, because it provides the opportunity to track changes – both in policy and in movement organization – since Katrina. We find a budding local culture of human rights whose discursive features exceed its strategic and tactical embrace of human rights practice.

Before the discussion of U.S. disaster policy we briefly situate this study and review our methods. Davida Finger is an attorney and Rachel E. Luft is a sociologist. Data for our interdisciplinary analysis come from dozens of public records requests spanning a period of six months in 2009; video recordings of two city council hearings; hundreds of hours of participant observation in social movement groups; eleven formal interviews with New Orleans residents who evacuated from Gustav through the City Assisted Evacuation Program, as well as informal conversations with dozens of others; and six formal interviews with movement leaders, advocates, and attorneys.

U.S. DISASTER POLICY

This overview of domestic disaster policy establishes the framework for U.S. disaster response. It highlights the delegation of duties from the federal government to state and local governments and the discretionary nature of the federal role. The broad array of policies discussed here establishes, in part, the structural conditions that produced inequitable hurricane outcomes in the case of Katrina and Gustav.

The U.S. domestic emergency response is governed by the 1988 Robert T. Stafford Disaster Relief and Emergency Assistance Act (Stafford Act), which authorizes the president to provide disaster-related assistance, including housing (Stafford Act, 42 U.S.C. §§ 5170(b), 5174(b)(c)). By executive order, the president has delegated disaster response duties to the Federal Emergency Management Authority (FEMA) as the primary federal coordinating agency for disaster response (Stafford Act, 42 U.S.C. § 5170a). Informed by "new federalism," significant disaster authority is also granted to state and local governments (Ryan 2009).

With regard to sheltering, the Stafford Act authorizes federal "essential assistance" including for "emergency shelter" (Stafford Act, 42 U.S.C. § 5170b(a)(3)(b)). This sheltering assistance is discretionary: "Federal agencies may on the direction of the President, provide assistance essential to meeting threats to life and property resulting from a major disaster" (Stafford Act, 42 U.S.C. § 5170b(a)). Actual emergency sheltering of individuals is accomplished by state and local governments in a cost-share arrangement with FEMA and supported by nonprofit organizations.

In Louisiana, the state's duties for emergency preparedness and disaster-response functions are obligatory. Approximately six months after Katrina, the state agency responsible for preparedness and response reorganized as an independent office of the governor called the Governor's Office of Homeland Security and Emergency Preparedness (GOHSEP) (LA. REV. STAT. § 29:721 *et seq.*). GOHSEP, in turn, tasks the Louisiana Department of Social Services (DSS) with sheltering prior to and immediately following a disaster. Under the purview of DSS, Emergency Support Function No. 6 (ESF 6), Mass Care, Housing, and Human Services provides the structure for coordination and support of local government and nongovernmental efforts to address sheltering. Ultimately, much disaster response in the United States remains a state and local responsibility. As we saw during Katrina, this is a potentially unmanageable task for regions experiencing catastrophe (Ryan 2009).

GUSTAV SHELTERING FAILURES

The grave problems with evacuation and sheltering following Hurricane Katrina were demonstrated graphically in the haunting images of people in flood waters, on interstate overpasses, and amassed at the Superdome and Convention Center. Because there were no mechanisms in place to evacuate people who did not have transportation, residents who wound up in shelters were either self-evacuating but had nowhere else to go or were stranded in New Orleans during the hurricane and subsequent flooding and were brought to shelters by FEMA.

Almost three years later, on September 1, 2008, Hurricane Gustav made landfall near Cocodrie, Louisiana, and triggered the largest evacuation in Louisiana history (GOHSEP 2008). By the time Gustav struck, there had been post-Katrina disaster policy revisions at the federal, state, and local levels along with extensive government and nongovernmental assessments and critiques of the federal government's failed Katrina response. Despite analyses and policy changes, there were significant remaining flaws with the state's sheltering plan, which led to new humanitarian violations.

After the egregious humanitarian violations and public relations debacle of the Superdome and Convention Center during Katrina, New Orleans would no longer provide local shelters. New mechanisms for evacuation procedures were implemented, such as the City Assisted Evacuation Program (CAEP) and the Critical Transportation Needs Shelters (CTNS), which are "large capacity sheltering facilities that will house all non-medical evacuees who do not have the ability to self-evacuate" (DSS 2009a, 1). During Gustav, approximately 37,000 residents utilized the new CTNS (DSS 2009b, 5; GOHSEP 2009).

To analyze the humanitarian failures in the Gustav shelters, we turn to the report of a grassroots social movement group. STAND with Dignity, a project of the New Orleans Workers' Center for Racial Justice, is "a grassroots group of elders, farmers, skilled workers, and fathers who have formerly experienced or are experiencing homelessness in New Orleans" (STAND 2008, 25). As low-income residents, STAND members boarded the CAEP buses and were taken to CTNS around the Gulf Coast. They stayed in close contact by cell phone, calling in to a lead organizer who drove from shelter to shelter monitoring conditions. They conducted "hundreds of interviews" at twelve shelters in three states, and ten days later presented a petition to the city with 1,500 signatures, decrying humanitarian violations (STAND 2008, 2). Within a few weeks of the storm they also produced a report called "Never Again: Lessons from Louisiana's Gustav Evacuation." The document captures the experience of evacuees in the CTNS and urges reform.

"Never Again" makes three sets of demands. The first is for equity, specifically a call to terminate the CTNS differential sheltering policy. Arguing that the CTNS policy produced "differential treatment" and "startling inequity," STAND insisted it be revoked: "The present differential treatment shelters policy plays out to proactively disadvantage poor and working class African Americans – whether by intention or by impact" (STAND 2008, 7, 8).

The second demand is for improved humanitarian conditions and the fulfillment of basic needs. The long list of grievances includes the absence of: indoor running water and toilets; showers until the fifth day of evacuation in some shelters; separate quarters for the elderly, sick, disabled, and children's play; distinct spaces for eating and sleeping; and information on both the disaster and the evacuees' family members. "We're not asking for silver and gold," said a young woman in the Sam's Club warehouse shelter in Shreveport, Louisiana, "just to be treated like human beings" (STAND 2008, 4). The third demand sought democratic participation in decision making, toward including _"the directly affected communities –_ those who have the hardest time evacuating – in creating the plans for shelters during disaster" (STAND 2008, 7–8; emphasis in the original).

In acknowledgment of the gross mismanagement of the shelters, the DSS secretary and deputy secretary were forced to resign within weeks of Gustav (Reckdahl 2008; Barrow 2008). By September 22, 2008, the DSS' own review recognized significant failures, deeming its post-Katrina emergency sheltering plan "inadequate," "poorly executed," and one that caused "unnecessary and inexcusable hardships on individuals that [sic] chose to seek emergency shelter provided by the state" (DSS 2008, 1). The review found an insufficient number of in-state shelters and diminished trust among evacuees based on the substandard resources at shelters, inadequate care for the elderly, and problems with reentry (DSS 2008, 4). The objective of the review was to make "immediate changes to the state's emergency sheltering process." However, it remains unclear what has been accomplished in terms of concrete policy changes and functional improvements.

We summarize here only the highlights of our efforts to acquire and assess Louisiana post-Gustav evacuation and shelter policy. On August 4, 2009, after months of public promises and delays, DSS finally announced the "release" of the policy. This was midway through the 2009 hurricane season and just weeks before the one-year Gustav anniversary. In response to our request for the revised policy, which was not available on the DSS website, we eventually received various versions of the ESF 6 document for both 2008 and 2009, including two versions of Appendix N, the Shelter Plan Summary for 2009. One was dated June 29, 2009, and came with track changes, and the other June 31, 2009 (a date which, we note for good measure, does not actually exist). These Shelter Plan Summary documents, issued two (fictional) days apart, contain vastly different information regarding the number and location of shelters and the number of available shelter beds, including CTNS beds. Our requests for additional documents and attempts to make sense of the ones we received produced hundreds of additional documents but little added clarity.

It is difficult, in sum, to know with any certainty how many CTNS beds were either guaranteed or actually secured for the 2009 hurricane season, or whether Louisiana fulfilled its commitment to standardize shelter conditions and bring them in line with basic humanitarian guidelines. During this period, however, DSS was still bound by substantive obligations regarding sheltering. Its mandate to maintain an inventory of pre-identified shelters and to pre-position resources did not vary. Although there are nuanced differences between the 2008 and the multiple revised 2009 plans, there is no data indicating significant policy changes to shelter conditions. Indeed, in documents produced by the state there are blank forms related to shelter facility assessment; it is not indicated whether and how these evaluation tools were utilized.

A HUMAN RIGHTS FRAMEWORK FOR DISASTER

We turn now to a discussion of disaster and sheltering from a human rights perspective. We begin by highlighting the key features of the core international standard for internal displacement: the United Nations Guiding Principles on Internal Displacement[1] (United Nations 1998). We then examine some of the ways local advocates and grassroots groups have engaged a human rights framework in response to Katrina and Gustav, focusing on post-Gustav sheltering contestation.

Guiding Principles on Internal Displacement

A disaster response governed by human rights norms prioritizes and guarantees postdisaster shelter and humane, dignified treatment of displaced persons. The primary international document detailing these rights is the

---

[1] Note: We use the term "Guiding Principles" to refer alternately to the instrument and to the principles themselves. The former takes a singular verb and the latter a plural verb.

UN Guiding Principles on Internal Displacement, which explains that internally displaced persons (IDPs) are:

> Persons or groups of persons who have been forced or obliged to flee or leave their homes or places of habitual residence, in particular as a result of or in order to avoid the effects of armed conflict, situations of generalized violence, violations of human rights or natural or human-made disasters, and who have not crossed an internationally recognized State border.
>
> (United Nations 1998, 2)

Prepared by a team of experts and submitted to the Human Rights Commission in 1998, the thirty Guiding Principles are grounded in international law and have been affirmed as an international norm by the UN member states. According to Walter Kalin, now Representative of the UN Secretary-General on Internally Displaced Persons, "the Guiding Principles are not a UN declaration on the rights of internally displaced persons, nor do they constitute, as such, a binding instrument. However, they reflect and are consistent with international human rights law and international humanitarian law" (Kalin 2008, 22). The Guiding Principles restate existing international law while generating more broadly applicable norms for displacement situations. Thus, they provide important minimum standards in situations of internal displacement along with an overall framework for identifying protection needs and, critically, implementation of protection mechanisms.

After Katrina, the UN Human Rights Committee urged member states to accept the Guiding Principles and explicitly advised the U.S. government to apply them to maximize protection of the rights of hurricane victims (HRC 2006). The United States, however, has still not recognized those displaced by the Gulf Coast hurricanes as internally displaced persons. Although it has embraced the Guiding Principles in its policies toward other nations (USAID 2004), it has chosen not to utilize this framework in its disaster response in the Gulf Coast.

The Guiding Principles offer an alternative to U.S. disaster policy in four significant ways. First, a key aspect of disaster sheltering from the perspective of international human rights law is that the primary duties remain with the national government agency (United Nations 1998, Principles 3, 9). The Stafford Act, with its delegation of both authority and financial responsibility for disaster response to various federal and state agencies, structurally avoids this responsibility. The second way in which the Guiding Principles differ from domestic policy is in their rights-based framework. Where U.S. displacement protections and provisions under federal policy are general and discretionary, the Guiding Principles detail thirty separate categories of rights of displaced persons. This entitlement to a wide swath of rights simply by virtue of being human is the heart of what distinguishes a human rights framework from other political paradigms.[2] Another core contribution of the rights framework is its recognition of the indivisibility and intersectionality of different dimensions of human experience, or different kinds of rights – economic, social, and cultural, as well as civil and political.

The third key difference is the Guiding Principles' adherence to explicit humanitarian standards (United Nations 1998, Section IV). In a rights-based framework, humanitarianism is neither discretionary nor subjective, but rather obligatory and standardized, based on the right to life. Since publication of the Guiding Principles in 1998, efforts have been made to clarify the relationship between a humanitarian and a rights paradigm in a disaster context. The Inter-Agency Standing Committee (IASC) Operating Guidelines explain that:

> Human rights are the legal underpinning of all humanitarian work pertaining to natural disasters. There is no other legal framework to guide such activities, especially in areas where there is no armed conflict. If humanitarian assistance is not based on a human rights framework, it risks having too narrow a focus, and cannot integrate all the basic needs of the victims into a holistic planning process.
>
> (IASC 2006, 9)

According to Kali Akuno of the U.S. Human Rights Network, the human right to shelter and to related humanitarian protections politicizes humanitarianism by anchoring it in the right to a dignified life. As a right, it becomes the government's responsibility and a legitimate object of legal struggle.

The fourth key difference is the Guiding Principles' broad definition of displacement – and therefore of the duration of government obligation – for the complete period that extends until full "resettlement and reintegration" (United Nations 1998, Section V). Further, they specify that "Competent authorities have the primary duty and responsibility to establish conditions, as well as provide the means, which allow internally displaced persons to return voluntarily, in safety and with dignity, to their homes or places of habitual residence" (United Nations 1998, Principle 28).

[2] For example, see Robert J. Rhee for a discussion of public and private disaster compensation outside of the context of human rights (Rhee 2009).

Two regional human rights organizations leading the human rights movement response to Katrina have highlighted these and other contributions of the Guiding Principles. The first is Advocates for Environmental Human Rights (AEHR), which seeks to build a community-based campaign for (the right to) a healthy environment. Based in New Orleans, AEHR was founded by two lawyers in 2003. The second is the national U.S. Human Rights Network (USHRN), which functions as a steering body for domestic human rights movement-building. Both groups have called for U.S. adherence to the Guiding Principles on the grounds that the principles are superior to domestic disaster policy. And both groups use formal human rights instruments and grassroots political education to build a human rights culture.

Following Katrina, AEHR produced a critique of the Stafford Act based on the Guiding Principles (AEHR n.d.). Soon after, the USHRN launched a "Hold the US Accountable Campaign" that pursued many of the same points. Both groups continue to petition the U.S. government through shadow reporting and position papers and also engage in human rights movement-building through popular education and training.

HUMAN RIGHTS MOVEMENT RESPONSES IN NEW ORLEANS, POST-KATRINA

Within days of Hurricane Katrina's landfall, AEHR, USHRN, and other U.S. social justice advocates and organizers were framing the disaster in human rights terms. They emphasized different rights frameworks in accord with their respective organizational orientations. For example, the National Economic and Social Rights Initiative concentrated on the absence of economic rights that even prior to the hurricane had produced poverty and greatly enhanced disaster vulnerability. A notable number of black liberation organizations condemned the events in the language of human rights and national oppression. Saladin Muhammad of Black Workers for Justice, for instance, issued a searing critique of national policy called "The Black Nation's 9/11" (Muhammad 2005). He placed Katrina in a long history of racism and imperialism, concluding with the link between human rights and black self-determination that has been central to black liberation human rights articulations. The political diversity of this early Katrina framing reflects the vibrancy and heterogeneity of the U.S. human rights movement.

In this section, we describe the development of these frameworks within the grassroots movement struggling for a just reconstruction in

New Orleans. In the five years since Hurricane Katrina, some local movement groups have begun to adopt the discourse of human rights in their
resistance efforts. We find a hybrid approach: local groups use some
human rights *language* but have not for the most part adopted human
rights *strategy* or *tactics*, staying focused instead on conventional civil
rights-based goals and methods. We begin with some general trends post-
Katrina and then narrow the rest of the discussion to the role of human
rights in response to hurricane sheltering after Gustav.

When Katrina struck land in August 2005, New Orleans was already
home to legal advocates working on a domestic human rights agenda.
Few though they were, these advocates had strong ties to local grassroots organizers. Although New Orleans movement culture itself was
overwhelmingly oriented to local issues of racial and economic justice
and cultural survival,[3] the human rights advocates were part of broader
national networks. These ties would be important conduits of human
rights activity after the storm.

Days after Hurricane Katrina, dozens of local and regional far left
groups came together to form a movement coalition called the People's
Hurricane Relief Fund (PHRF). It was founded by leaders of the black
liberation movement, some of whom had political roots in the black liberation human rights tradition (Luft 2009). Within weeks PHRF organizers
had carefully chosen the language of "Right to Return" as their motto.
Coined to assert the contested, political, and interconnected web of obstacles to returning home, the phrase placed displacement at the center of
the recovery and rights at the center of displacement. The saying became
the slogan of local and national Katrina resistance activity. By December
2005, at the height of PHRF's role as the New Orleans post-Katrina justice movement coalition, the human rights orientation was central to its
articulation of grievances and its reconstruction agenda. One significant
action was to convene human rights tribunals – part of a two-pronged
effort to sustain international attention on Katrina-related U.S. rights violations and to advance a local, popular, human rights political education
campaign.

Between Hurricane Katrina in 2005 and Hurricane Gustav in September 2008, human rights activism in New Orleans proliferated. It included
the use of traditional human rights tactics such as testimony before UN

---

[3] A noteworthy exception to this local focus was the work of the New Orleans INCITE!
Women of Color Against Violence chapter, which had a transnational analysis of reproductive justice and gender violence. Just six months before Katrina, local INCITE!
organized a national INCITE! conference in New Orleans.

committees and the submission of shadow reports, visits by several UN Special Rapporteurs, a proposed resolution to the People's Assembly of the United States Social Forum, the PHRF Tribunals, and grassroots public forums designed to educate New Orleanians about international human rights standards and to demand U.S. accountability to them. In addition to these more formal human rights mechanisms, this period also witnessed a growing use of human rights language in meetings, rallies, and marches supporting the movement for a just reconstruction. This discursive development suggests a cultural shift that human rights advocates and scholars have argued is a central component of human rights movement-building (Soohoo et al. 2008). Post-Katrina New Orleans, we found, is the site of an emergent human rights culture.

By human rights culture we mean an engagement – philosophical, moral, and political, if not legal or systematic – with the notion that human beings are entitled to a broader category of rights than those promised by the U.S. Constitution. This orientation reveals itself in the growing use of human rights framing devices by grassroots movement activists. We believe this development has the potential to become part of what Cass Sunstein terms "constitutive commitments" (Sunstein 2004) toward what USHRN calls the necessary "transform[ation of] U.S. political culture" (USHRN n.d.).

The human rights agenda was still foreign to most New Orleanians and the community's grassroots leadership before Katrina, steeped like most U.S. citizens in a civil rights framework. But at the time of this writing, at the fifth anniversary of Katrina, the effects of the popular education campaign are discernable. In the rest of this chapter, we examine this development and describe two characteristics. The first is that human rights frames are entering communities through professional human rights advocates via local movement leadership; it is not a bottom-up phenomenon. Human rights do not constitute the political *habitus* of most Americans for specific historical reasons documented by Carol Anderson and others (Anderson 2003). However, the advocates who have played the greatest role in New Orleans are those with strong movement ties; their priority is domestic human rights movement-building in and among poor black communities. The second characteristic is the coexistence of proto-human rights consciousness with more conventional strategies and tactics. Discursive inclusion of human rights in the political vocabulary of movement participants does not necessarily signal a human rights strategic orientation or use of formal human rights instruments. Instead, we find a hybrid approach. We take each of these characteristics in turn.

Human rights consciousness is spreading in top-down fashion as movement leaders become educated to human rights frameworks through the explicit efforts of local and nonlocal advocates. Monique Harden of AEHR and Kali Akuno of PHRF and USHRN have each played an instrumental role in introducing human rights concepts and reframing local issues in human rights terms. Each has pursued formal human rights mechanisms – shadow reports, Special Rapporteur visits, tribunals – as political education and base-building opportunities for local activists and residents. Local movement leadership, in turn, has taken to the framework more quickly than the base.

An example of the vertical nature of the flow of human rights acculturation is apparent in Voice of the Ex-Offender (V.O.T.E.), a local criminal justice reform organization. Founder Norris Henderson does not draw directly on human rights frameworks in his own work, which is focused on civil and political rights, but he understands their value:

> The first word is human. Everyone is on the same level. That gives us more protection. We've been fascinated by civil rights. And it did that, it got us civically engaged. But we're still shut out. So we need something else. I see the benefits of being called an IDP. If I'm an IDP, then all these things should happen. We have a lack of human rights education. We need more training. People just get accustomed to what they've been doing.

Although Henderson appreciates the political possibilities offered by human rights frames, they are still foreign to his membership. Two days after Henderson voiced the distinction between civil and human rights, when one member of his organization was asked the same question about whether human rights had a role in V.O.T.E.'s work, the member replied, "Absolutely. We fight for human rights more than anything. We're not supposed to see a color. We see this happening with Mexicans now. They're not getting what they deserve." His answer suggested a conflation of human rights with a civil rights politic and a post-civil rights color-blindness; he responded from the domestic framework with which he was familiar. There is still a gap in familiarity with human rights between the leadership and its constituency. We describe this feature of local human rights culture because of the political delicacy of movement-building with non-indigenous frames. Because of the history of political culture in the United States, spontaneous human rights discourse is unlikely. We have sought to document patterns in its reception once the framework is introduced.

The second characteristic of the emergent human rights culture is a burgeoning human rights consciousness that exists together with traditional

U.S.-based movement strategies and tactics rooted in local or domestic agendas. Adoption of human rights terms does not necessarily signal adoption of the legal, formal, or transnational agenda and methods that have usually accompanied them. Instead, at this stage, they communicate a more general sense that people betrayed by the U.S. government have rights that transcend its jurisdiction and to which it must be accountable. Henderson, for example, the grassroots organizer who founded V.O.T.E., has a national vision for enfranchising formerly incarcerated persons. The work is consummate political rights activity based on voter education and registration, although he understands it to be a part of the broader struggle for human rights. Although most New Orleans movement groups maintain their strategic and programmatic focus locally and domestically, we see signs that the language of human rights is becoming a more generalized movement vocabulary for politicizing hurricane-related events and other forms of injustice.

The second characteristic is consistent with the literature on grassroots domestic human rights movements in the United States (Soohoo et al. 2008; Neubeck 2006). Use of formal human rights instruments such as international rights documents and presentations to international human rights bodies still represents quintessential human rights activity. However, as the U.S. human rights movement grows, formal mechanisms are becoming de-centered, taking their place in a larger repertoire of social movement tactics. Human rights scholarship suggests that it is ultimately human rights framing more than strategy, and strategy more than tactics, that marks a shift in political culture, at least at the emergent stage. In New Orleans, human rights strategy and tactics are still the purview of professional human rights advocates.

Gustav and the Contestation over State Sheltering: An Example of Human Rights Hybridity

By the time of Hurricane Katrina's third anniversary, the effort to advance human rights standards and build a popular human rights movement was in evidence – if highly decentralized – and moving slowly among weary Katrina survivors. When Gustav struck three days later, it infused life into the battered movement, providing new opportunities for movement mobilization. This time, advocates and organizers were better prepared for monitoring government emergency operations and directing movement actions (Luft 2009). The pre-Gustav effort that would prove most influential was mobilized by STAND, the grassroots group that exposed the problems in Critical Transportation Needs Shelters. These early actions placed STAND in a leadership role in the contestation over state evacuation and sheltering policy.

After Gustav, resistance activity converged on evacuation, sheltering, and return. Although the city's evacuation procedure contrasted sharply with the lack of transportation provisions during Katrina, the post-Katrina plan produced a fresh round of humanitarian violations as documented earlier in this chapter. Early post-Gustav grassroots movement response ranged from providing relief to residents who had endured financial hardship due to the evacuation to challenging the state over the evacuation and sheltering policy itself. The former approach included a landlord/tenant agreement drawn up by Tracie Washington (a local civil rights lawyer and director of the Louisiana Justice Institute) and Bill Quigley (local social justice lawyer), together with grassroots groups, with which tenants could ask landlords to accept payment deferral for the month that began during the mandatory evacuation. Washington and others also pressed FEMA to provide funding to DSS for emergency food stamps after the evacuation, which it eventually did in a reversal that activists credited to their protestations (Greater New Orleans Organizers' Roundtable 2008). Seeking to turn this one-time award into a disaster entitlement in advance of future crises, Washington proposed to city and state officials that FEMA create a debit card for heads of households. Drawing on the threat heard often among CTNS evacuees that they would be less likely to evacuate in the future due to the economic strain and humanitarian violations they experienced with Gustav, she called her proposal "Suggestions to Incentivize Evacuations in the Future" (Washington 2008).

A year after Gustav, however, Washington noted that the city council resolution to study these and other reforms had foundered. Some of the other measures, like the rental agreement, were limited at best, because, as she put it, "you don't have any real rights." For local activists, Gustav confirmed the realization laid bare by Katrina that the government's disaster policy was fundamentally flawed. The failures of Louisiana's revised sheltering plan three years after Katrina made this clear, calling into question the possibility of viable reform under existing legal frameworks (Soohoo 2008, xviii). As Akuno of USHRN explained:

> I think there is a consensus, an underlying consensus that the civil rights narrative has run its course and is very limited.... The right wing control of the courts ... which would adjudicate things around civil rights and civil rights protections, definitely is not in our favor.... There is a consensus around that which has kind of compelled folks ... to seek a broader phase.

By the time of humanitarian violations after Gustav, more local leadership was realizing it had to look beyond traditional channels. Because of groundwork done by local and regional human rights advocates in the years since Katrina, the human rights framework was an available discursive repository.

Movement response to Hurricane Gustav thus produced another step forward in the development of local human rights culture. The African American Leadership Project of New Orleans used human rights language in its call for a town hall meeting after Gustav: "Obviously it is time to think outside the box. Perhaps we should view evacuation as a human rights and public safety issue, rather than simply as an individual and personal choice" (African American Leadership Project 2008). STAND also began to use the language of rights. Its first report on shelter conditions issued in September 2008 made no explicit mention of rights but instead anchored its claims in humanitarian terms and the notion of dignity. Eleven months later, however, when it issued its second report after monitoring shelter reforms, its thirteen-page document used the word *rights* nineteen times and *human rights* explicitly an additional two times (STAND 2009). As these examples demonstrate, social movement responses to the state's violations during Gustav were increasingly informed by new human rights terms for articulating their grievances. But the relationship between discourse and grassroots action was less clear. This slippage begs the question of what ultimately constitutes U.S. human rights movement activity. Review of U.S. human rights movements suggests there may be three levels (Soohoo et al. 2008; Neubeck 2006; Merry 2006):

1) *Framing*: Invocation of human rights language in a local context and exploratory adoption of human rights language for local grievances;
2) *Framing, Strategy*: Translation of local movement objectives to a substantive human rights agenda; reorientation of local strategy;
3) *Framing, Strategy, Tactics*: Use of conventional tactics for human rights goals; synthesis of local tactics and formal human rights instruments.

We apply this template to the post-Gustav moment to explore what a more expansive repertoire of human rights responses might have included.

Framing. The turn to human rights language by people resisting state policy is an important part of human rights movement-building, according to national advocates and scholars. "Adding a rights perspective," explains Cynthia Soohoo, "to discourses currently dominated by market-based commodity or charity models" contributes to changing the political culture (Soohoo 2008, xix). Human rights advocate Eric Tars of National Law Center on Homelessness and Poverty (NLCHP), which has supported human rights efforts in New Orleans, understands framework transformation as a critical step in organizing for far-reaching policy change: "It's that slow kind of building of new frameworks that in the end allows you to push for the larger pieces." For him, building human rights consciousness is more important than any particular movement victory: "We're not working just to revise the Stafford Act, but also to build that consciousness.... The consciousness is very important, so people can demand [rights].... [and] that will help you with overall goals down the road." Although we have seen professional human rights advocates use formal human rights instruments in the movement for a just reconstruction, most human rights activity in New Orleans reflects the framing level.

Framing, Strategy. In her study of human rights and gender violence, Sally Engle Merry defines "translation" as "the process of adjusting the rhetoric and structure of [human rights] programs or interventions to local circumstances" (Merry 2006, 135). We have already suggested that key human rights advocates have functioned as translators in New Orleans. Here we move beyond individual advocates to the political process of translating human rights strategies to local struggles.

In the post-Gustav context, for example, translation could have occurred more broadly if human rights strategy had informed the production of political demands. Advocates and activists could have used the rights assured by the Guiding Principles to streamline grievances. For purposes of this hypothetical exploration, we focus on the economic grievances that emerged after Gustav as framed by the economic rights articulated in the principles and reinforced by the International Covenant on Economic, Social, and Cultural Rights. The Guiding Principles recognize economic threats posed by displacement and guarantee a set of rights to mitigate them (United Nations 1998, Principles 7, 22, 29).

A post-Gustav strategy informed by these rights might have articulated and channeled grievances accordingly, focusing on economic compensation for personal finances spent to subsidize inadequate shelter, food and other provisions, housing and employment protection, rent adjustment, and so forth. At the broader level, a post-Gustav human rights strategy might have linked the economic rights promised to IDPs in the Guiding Principles (which the United States has affirmed), to the economic grievances so many New Orleanians face outside of the context of disaster. That is, the principles, which have nominal U.S. support, could be linked to economic rights more generally.

The irony that the Guiding Principles include more rights and protections than U.S. citizens have outside of the context of disaster should not be lost on anyone agitating for IDP rights; instead, it could be an important bridge for economic rights beyond disaster. One significant contribution a human rights approach makes is linking issues traditionally segregated by our political system. As the report by the NLCHP put it after a human rights training session in New Orleans in 2006, "For people to be able to live in their houses, they need services – health clinics, schools, water and grocery stores. This is where the human rights framework is especially useful, as it makes the connections between all these rights in a context of interdependence and universality" (NLCHP 2006, 3). In this way human rights disaster organizing becomes a tool in a broader, holistic movement for rights-based justice.

Framing, Strategy, Tactics. The third level utilizes human rights tactics to operationalize human rights strategy. At the most narrow level, human rights tactics refer to formal instruments that draw on international documents and engage international bodies. But, according to advocates, they also refer to the use of conventional domestic movement methods reframed in human rights terms (Asbed 2008, 21; Foscarinis and Tars 2008, 157–58; Neubeck 2006, 165–70).

A post-Gustav human rights strategy using human rights frameworks to inform tactics might have differently weighed short-term and long-term gains. For example, the egregious conditions of the Gustav shelters and the well-organized exposé by social justice activists created a window of opportunity while the state was scrambling to demonstrate accountability and reform. Traditional tactics – public outcry, petitions, town hall meetings, and public statements – earned several movement groups and advocates a seat at city and state tables to discuss reforms. At that point, the activists' goals – enhanced shelter conditions, greater subsidies from the state, equal protection and due process in sheltering – were for the most part familiar to the U.S. struggles of social service reform and civil rights accountability. Human rights advocates, however, had a different strategic and tactical vision based on a broader human rights agenda. Their vision entailed moving beyond the limits of humanitarian and civil rights paradigms. One advocate suggested pressuring the state to agree to human rights training for disasters and partnering with civil society and UN agencies to do so. The goal of the trainings would be to overhaul Louisiana's evacuation and sheltering policy based on human rights protocols. Several human rights advocates noted the importance from a litigation perspective of getting human rights language into the policy as the basis for future claims. Another suggestion was to create autonomous councils of CTNS residents who would be charged with independent monitoring in keeping with the idea of human rights participation.

Human rights advocates recognize that this paradigm shift in movement strategy and tactics sometimes requires sacrificing short-term gains for longer-term goals. Both Akuno and Tars, for example, observed that although a focus on humanitarian provisions during disaster is important to human dignity and more winnable than other demands, it does not fundamentally change the balance of power. Activists may be "making short term gains," explained Tars, "at the expense of long term progress." In a broader human rights campaign, he noted, sometimes "the short term gains are to be sacrificed for the long term. It's a tough decision to make." Similarly, Akuno noted, those making humanitarian claims can get distracted and think that the number of Porta-Potties per shelter is the point, when it is actually just the "baseline": "I just painted the prison walls from blue to black, and I have more toilet paper." The real goal, he added, is to change "the fundamental questions of power." It is no small feat, for "a tragic sense of history teaches that . . . the rescue of individuals is often more feasible than the transformation of whole societies" (Schulz 2008, 17). Tars, Akuno, and others emphasize that movement-building is a long-term process. They cite the decades of struggle between Reconstruction and the civil rights movement. Said Tars, "In the human rights movement, we're where the Civil Rights movement was in the 1930s. *Brown v. Board of Education* is still twenty years away."

To identify three levels of human rights movement-building is not to assert they are necessarily linear or inevitable, nor that every community beginning to frame its struggles in human rights terms will invariably use international instruments. Indeed, some of the hybridity we describe reflects ambivalence or even skepticism regarding human rights (Goodale and Merry 2007; Goodale 2006). Several movement groups that use the language of rights are not interested in building a connection to a human rights movement. Others describe confusion about what human rights offers to social justice struggles above and beyond familiar tools. As one local black leader confessed, "The move from civil rights to human rights seems like the change from Negro to Black to African American. The person hasn't changed, the label has changed." What we do know is that the early signs of a political cultural shift are apparent in post-Katrina New Orleans movement circles. Whether it develops into a full blown human rights movement depends on a variety of factors, including capacity, funding streams, relations between movement groups, national civil and human rights politics, and future hurricanes.

CONCLUSION

Sheltering functions as a microcosm of both disaster and inequality. It is the literal site through which the most vulnerable pass as they travel between pre- and postdisaster lives. This bridge between disaster and nondisaster is most illuminated – and potentially transformed – by a human rights approach. Whereas domestic policy refers to sheltering as a discrete time, place, and limited set of possible actions, the IDP framework links the displacement experience to conditions before (e.g., social vulnerability) and after it (e.g., facilitated return and economic restitution). Indeed, the human rights perspective reveals the absurdity of caring for displaced persons during a disaster when the lack of rights before the disaster is a prime contributor to disaster vulnerability, and the lack of rights after makes "recovery" nonsensical – recovery to what?

From this perspective it is not difficult to understand that New Orleanians are exploring human rights frameworks. As people who live in a world where the line between pre-hurricane and post-hurricane is all too blurry, the holistic nature of human rights makes a kind of cultural sense.

REFERENCES

Advocates for Environmental Human Rights. n.d. "US Disaster Response Law vs. Human Rights Standards on Internal Displacement." Accessed August 1, 2010. http://www.ehumanrights.org/ourwork_residents_USDRLvHRS.html.

African American Leadership Project. 2008. Gustav Town Hall Meeting on Wednesday October 8th in City Council Chambers. The New Orleans Agenda, online newsletter. Sylvain Solutions.

Anderson, Carol. 2003. *Eyes Off the Prize: The United Nations and the African American Struggle for Human Rights, 1944–1955.* Cambridge, UK: Cambridge University Press.

Asbed, Greg. 2008. "Coalition of Immokalee Workers: 'Golpear a Uno Es Golpear a Todos' To Beat One of Us Is to Beat Us All!" In *Bringing Human Rights Home: Portraits of the Movement,* edited by Cynthia Soohoo, Catherine Albisa, and Martha F. Davis, Vol. 3, 1–24. Westport, CT: Praeger Publishers.

Barrow, Bill. 2008. "State Social Services Secretary Ann Williamson Resigns." *Times Picayune,* Sept. 15, 1.

Berube, Alan, and Steven Raphael. 2005. *Access to Cars in New Orleans*. Washington, D.C.: Brookings Institution.

Department of Social Services, State of Louisiana. 2008. Assessment of Louisiana's Sheltering Plan and Operations Post Hurricanes Gustav and Ike. September 22.

_____. 2009a. ESF-6 Shelter Operations Timeline and Narrative. June 25.

_____. 2009b. Louisiana Shelter Summit Report: Shelter Planning Recommendations and Feedback.

Foscarinis, Maria, and Eric Tars. 2008. "Housing Rights and Wrongs: The United States and the Right to Housing." In *Bringing Human Rights Home: Portraits of the Movement*, edited by Cynthia Soohoo, Catherine Albisa, and Martha F. Davis, Vol. 3, 149–72. Westport, CT: Praeger Publishers.

Goodale, Mark. 2006. "Toward a Critical Anthropology of Human Rights." *Current Anthropology* 47: 485–98.

Goodale, Mark, and Sally Engle Merry, eds. 2007. *The Practice of Human Rights: Tracking Law between the Global and the Local*. New York: Cambridge University Press.

Governor's Office of Homeland Security and Emergency Preparedness. 2008. Governor Jindal's 5:30 Update on Hurricane Gustav's Preparedness Efforts. August 31.

_____. 2009. *Emergency Operations Plan, ESF 6–1*. Baton Rouge, LA: Governor's Office of Homeland Security and Emergency Preparedness.

Greater New Orleans Organizers' Roundtable. 2008. Gustav Flyer. September.

Inter-Agency Standing Committee. 2006. Protecting Persons Affected by Natural Disasters: IASC Operational Guidelines on Human Rights and Natural Disasters. Washington, D.C.: Brookings-Bern Project on Internal Displacement, 1–36.

Kalin, Walter. 2008. "Guiding Principles on Internal Displacement: Annotations." *Studies in Transnational Legal Policy* 38: 1–173.

Laska, Shirley, and Betty Morrow. 2006. "Social Vulnerabilities and Hurricane Katrina: An Unnatural Disaster in New Orleans." *Marine Technology Society Journal* 40: 16–26.

LA. REV. STAT. ANN. § 29;769 (2007).

Luft, Rachel E. 2009. "Beyond Disaster Exceptionalism: Social Movement Developments in New Orleans after Hurricane Katrina." *American Quarterly. Special Volume: In the Wake of Hurricane Katrina: New Paradigms and Social Visions* 61: 499–528.

Merry, Sally Engle. 2006. *Human Rights & Gender Violence: Translating International Law into Local Justice*. Chicago: The University of Chicago Press.

Muhammad, Saladin. 2005. "Hurricane Katrina: The Black Nation's 9/11." http://www.greens.org/s-r/39/39–05.html.

National Law Center on Homelessness & Poverty. 2006. *Human Rights Training Report*. Washington, D.C.: National Law Center on Homelessness & Poverty.

Neubeck, Kenneth J. 2006. *When Welfare Disappears: The Case for Economic Human Rights*. New York: Routledge.

Nigg, Joanne M., and Manuel R. Torres. 2006. "Hurricane Katrina and the Flooding of New Orleans: Emergent Issues in Sheltering and Temporary Housing."

The ANNALS of the American Academy of Political and Social Science 604: 113–28.

Office of the United Nations Disaster Relief Coordinator. 2006. *Exploring Key Changes and Developments in Post-Disaster Settlement, Shelter and Housing, 1982–2006.* United Nations: Office of the United Nations Disaster Relief Coordinator.

Phillips, Brenda D. 2009. *Disaster Recovery.* Boca Raton, FL: Auerbach Publications.

Reckdahl, Katy. 2008. "Thousands Get Double Food Stamps; Even More Still Await Disaster Assistance." *Times Picayune.* September 16, 1.

Rhee, Robert J. 2009. "Participation and Disintermediation in a Risk Society." In *Law and Recovery from Disaster: Hurricane Katrina,* edited by Robin Paul Malloy, 103–26. Burlington, VT: Ashgate.

Robert T. Stafford Disaster Relief and Emergency Assistance Act. 1988. (Pub. L. 93–288) 42 U.S.C. § 5170 *et seq.,* amended by Pub. L. 109–295.

Ryan, Erin. 2009. "How the New Federalism Failed Katrina Victims." In *Law and Recovery from Disaster: Hurricane Katrina,* edited by Robin Paul Malloy, 174–211. Burlington, VT: Ashgate.

Schulz, William F., ed. 2008. *The Future of Human Rights: U.S. Policy for a New Era.* Philadelphia, PA: University of Pennsylvania Press.

Soohoo, Cynthia. 2008. "Introduction to Volume 3." In *Bringing Human Rights Home: Portraits of the Movement,* edited by Cynthia Soohoo, Catherine Albisa, and Martha F. Davis, Vol. 3, xv–xxii. Westport, CT: Praeger Publishers.

Soohoo, Cynthia, Catherine Albisa, and Martha F. Davis, eds. 2008. *Bringing Human Rights Home: Portraits of the Movement,* Vols. 1, 2, 3. Westport, CT: Praeger Publishers.

STAND. 2008. *Never Again: Lessons from Louisiana's Gustav Evacuation.* New Orleans, LA: New Orleans Workers' Center for Racial Justice.

———. 2009. *Through My Eyes: Louisiana's First Independent Evacuation Shelter Monitoring Report.* New Orleans, LA: New Orleans Workers' Center for Racial Justice.

Sunstein, Cass. 2004. *The Second Bill of Rights: FDR's Unfinished Revolution and Why We Need It More Than Ever.* New York: Basic Books.

United Nations Guiding Principles on Internal Displacement. 1998. U.N. Doc. E/CN.4/1998/53/Add.2. Geneva, Switzerland: Office of the United Nations High Commissioner for Human Rights.

United Nations Human Rights Committee. Concluding Observations of the Human Rights Committee: United States of America, P 18, U.N. Doc. CCPR/C/USA/CO/3/Rev.1 (Dec. 18, 2006).

U.S. Agency for International Development. 2004. *USAID Assistance to Internally Displaced Persons Policy.* USAID, 16.

United States Human Rights Network. n.d. About Us. Accessed December 16, 2010. http://www.ushrnetwork.org/about_us.

Washington, Tracie. 2008. Letter on Suggestions to Incentivize Evacuations in the Future. New Orleans.

Universal Declaration of Human Rights

Preamble

Whereas recognition of the inherent dignity and of the equal and inalienable rights of all members of the human family is the foundation of freedom, justice and peace in the world,

Whereas disregard and contempt for human rights have resulted in barbarous acts which have outraged the conscience of mankind, and the advent of a world in which human beings shall enjoy freedom of speech and belief and freedom from fear and want has been proclaimed as the highest aspiration of the common people,

Whereas it is essential, if man is not to be compelled to have recourse, as a last resort, to rebellion against tyranny and oppression, that human rights should be protected by the rule of law,

Whereas it is essential to promote the development of friendly relations between nations,

Whereas the peoples of the United Nations have in the Charter reaffirmed their faith in fundamental human rights, in the dignity and worth of the human person and in the equal rights of men and women and have determined to promote social progress and better standards of life in larger freedom,

Whereas Member States have pledged themselves to achieve, in cooperation with the United Nations, the promotion of universal respect for and observance of human rights and fundamental freedoms,

Whereas a common understanding of these rights and freedoms is of the greatest importance for the full realization of this pledge,

Now, therefore,

The General Assembly,

Proclaims this Universal Declaration of Human Rights as a common standard of achievement for all peoples and all nations, to the end that every individual and every organ of society, keeping this Declaration constantly in mind, shall strive by teaching and education to promote respect for these rights and freedoms and by progressive measures, national and international, to secure their universal and effective recognition and observance, both among the peoples of Member States themselves and among the peoples of territories under their jurisdiction.

Article 1
All human beings are born free and equal in dignity and rights. They are endowed with reason and conscience and should act towards one another in a spirit of brotherhood.

Article 2
Everyone is entitled to all the rights and freedoms set forth in this Declaration, without distinction of any kind, such as race, colour, sex, language, religion, political or other opinion, national or social origin, property, birth or other status.

Furthermore, no distinction shall be made on the basis of the political, jurisdictional or international status of the country or territory to which a person belongs, whether it be independent, trust, non-self-governing or under any other limitation of sovereignty.

Article 3
Everyone has the right to life, liberty and security of person.

Article 4
No one shall be held in slavery or servitude; slavery and the slave trade shall be prohibited in all their forms.

Article 5
No one shall be subjected to torture or to cruel, inhuman or degrading treatment or punishment.

Article 6
Everyone has the right to recognition everywhere as a person before the law.

Article 7
All are equal before the law and are entitled without any discrimination to equal protection of the law. All are entitled to equal protection against any discrimination in violation of this Declaration and against any incitement to such discrimination.

Article 8
Everyone has the right to an effective remedy by the competent national tribunals for acts violating the fundamental rights granted him by the constitution or by law.

Article 9
No one shall be subjected to arbitrary arrest, detention or exile.

Article 10
Everyone is entitled in full equality to a fair and public hearing by an independent and impartial tribunal, in the determination of his rights and obligations and of any criminal charge against him.

Article 11
Everyone charged with a penal offence has the right to be presumed innocent until proved guilty according to law in a public trial at which he has had all the guarantees necessary for his defence.

No one shall be held guilty of any penal offence on account of any act or omission which did not constitute a penal offence, under national or international law, at the time when it was committed. Nor shall a heavier penalty be imposed than the one that was applicable at the time the penal offence was committed.

Article 12
No one shall be subjected to arbitrary interference with his privacy, family, home or correspondence, nor to attacks upon his honour and reputation. Everyone has the right to the protection of the law against such interference or attacks.

Article 13
Everyone has the right to freedom of movement and residence within the borders of each State.

Everyone has the right to leave any country, including his own, and to return to his country.

Article 14

Everyone has the right to seek and to enjoy in other countries asylum from persecution.

This right may not be invoked in the case of prosecutions genuinely arising from non-political crimes or from acts contrary to the purposes and principles of the United Nations.

Article 15

Everyone has the right to a nationality.

No one shall be arbitrarily deprived of his nationality nor denied the right to change his nationality.

Article 16

Men and women of full age, without any limitation due to race, nationality or religion, have the right to marry and to found a family. They are entitled to equal rights as to marriage, during marriage and at its dissolution.

Marriage shall be entered into only with the free and full consent of the intending spouses.

The family is the natural and fundamental group unit of society and is entitled to protection by society and the State.

Article 17

Everyone has the right to own property alone as well as in association with others.

No one shall be arbitrarily deprived of his property.

Article 18

Everyone has the right to freedom of thought, conscience and religion; this right includes freedom to change his religion or belief, and freedom, either alone or in community with others and in public or private, to manifest his religion or belief in teaching, practice, worship and observance.

Article 19

Everyone has the right to freedom of opinion and expression; this right includes freedom to hold opinions without interference and to seek, receive and impart information and ideas through any media and regardless of frontiers.

Article 20

Everyone has the right to freedom of peaceful assembly and association.

No one may be compelled to belong to an association.

Article 21

Everyone has the right to take part in the government of his country, directly or through freely chosen representatives.

Everyone has the right to equal access to public service in his country.

The will of the people shall be the basis of the authority of government; this will shall be expressed in periodic and genuine elections which shall be by universal and equal suffrage and shall be held by secret vote or by equivalent free voting procedures.

Article 22

Everyone, as a member of society, has the right to social security and is entitled to realization, through national effort and international co-operation and in accordance with the organization and resources of each State, of the economic, social and cultural rights indispensable for his dignity and the free development of his personality.

Article 23

Everyone has the right to work, to free choice of employment, to just and favourable conditions of work and to protection against unemployment.

Everyone, without any discrimination, has the right to equal pay for equal work.

Everyone who works has the right to just and favourable remuneration ensuring for himself and his family an existence worthy of human dignity, and supplemented, if necessary, by other means of social protection.

Everyone has the right to form and to join trade unions for the protection of his interests.

Article 24

Everyone has the right to rest and leisure, including reasonable limitation of working hours and periodic holidays with pay.

Article 25

Everyone has the right to a standard of living adequate for the health and well-being of himself and of his family, including food, clothing, housing and medical care and necessary social services, and the right to security in the event of unemployment, sickness, disability, widowhood, old age or other lack of livelihood in circumstances beyond his control.

Motherhood and childhood are entitled to special care and assistance. All children, whether born in or out of wedlock, shall enjoy the same social protection.

Article 26
Everyone has the right to education. Education shall be free, at least in the elementary and fundamental stages. Elementary education shall be compulsory. Technical and professional education shall be made generally available and higher education shall be equally accessible to all on the basis of merit.

Education shall be directed to the full development of the human personality and to the strengthening of respect for human rights and fundamental freedoms. It shall promote understanding, tolerance and friendship among all nations, racial or religious groups, and shall further the activities of the United Nations for the maintenance of peace.

Parents have a prior right to choose the kind of education that shall be given to their children.

Article 27
Everyone has the right freely to participate in the cultural life of the community, to enjoy the arts and to share in scientific advancement and its benefits.

Everyone has the right to the protection of the moral and material interests resulting from any scientific, literary or artistic production of which he is the author.

Article 28
Everyone is entitled to a social and international order in which the rights and freedoms set forth in this Declaration can be fully realized.

Article 29
Everyone has duties to the community in which alone the free and full development of his personality is possible.

In the exercise of his rights and freedoms, everyone shall be subject only to such limitations as are determined by law solely for the purpose of securing due recognition and respect for the rights and freedoms of others and of meeting the just requirements of morality, public order and the general welfare in a democratic society.

These rights and freedoms may in no case be exercised contrary to the purposes and principles of the United Nations.

Article 30
Nothing in this Declaration may be interpreted as implying for any State, group or person any right to engage in any activity or to perform any act aimed at the destruction of any of the rights and freedoms set forth herein.

International Covenant on Economic, Social and Cultural Rights

Adopted and opened for signature, ratification and accession by General Assembly resolution 2200A (XXI) of 16 December 1966

entry into force 3 January 1976, in accordance with article 27

Preamble

The States Parties to the present Covenant,

Considering that, in accordance with the principles proclaimed in the Charter of the United Nations, recognition of the inherent dignity and of the equal and inalienable rights of all members of the human family is the foundation of freedom, justice and peace in the world,

Recognizing that these rights derive from the inherent dignity of the human person,

Recognizing that, in accordance with the Universal Declaration of Human Rights, the ideal of free human beings enjoying freedom from fear and want can only be achieved if conditions are created whereby everyone may enjoy his economic, social and cultural rights, as well as his civil and political rights,

Considering the obligation of States under the Charter of the United Nations to promote universal respect for, and observance of, human rights and freedoms,

Realizing that the individual, having duties to other individuals and to the community to which he belongs, is under a responsibility to strive for the promotion and observance of the rights recognized in the present Covenant,

Agree upon the following articles:

PART I

Article 1

1. All peoples have the right of self-determination. By virtue of that right they freely determine their political status and freely pursue their economic, social and cultural development.

2. All peoples may, for their own ends, freely dispose of their natural wealth and resources without prejudice to any obligations arising out of international economic co-operation, based upon the principle of mutual benefit, and international law. In no case may a people be deprived of its own means of subsistence.

3. The States Parties to the present Covenant, including those having responsibility for the administration of Non-Self-Governing and Trust Territories, shall promote the realization of the right of self-determination, and shall respect that right, in conformity with the provisions of the Charter of the United Nations.

PART II

Article 2

1. Each State Party to the present Covenant undertakes to take steps, individually and through international assistance and co-operation, especially economic and technical, to the maximum of its available resources, with a view to achieving progressively the full realization of the rights recognized in the present Covenant by all appropriate means, including particularly the adoption of legislative measures.

2. The States Parties to the present Covenant undertake to guarantee that the rights enunciated in the present Covenant will be exercised without discrimination of any kind as to race, colour, sex, language, religion, political or other opinion, national or social origin, property, birth or other status.

3. Developing countries, with due regard to human rights and their national economy, may determine to what extent they would guarantee the economic rights recognized in the present Covenant to non-nationals.

Article 3
The States Parties to the present Covenant undertake to ensure the equal right of men and women to the enjoyment of all economic, social and cultural rights set forth in the present Covenant.

Article 4
The States Parties to the present Covenant recognize that, in the enjoyment of those rights provided by the State in conformity with the present Covenant, the State may subject such rights only to such limitations as are determined by law only in so far as this may be compatible with the nature of these rights and solely for the purpose of promoting the general welfare in a democratic society.

Article 5
1. Nothing in the present Covenant may be interpreted as implying for any State, group or person any right to engage in any activity or to perform any act aimed at the destruction of any of the rights or freedoms recognized herein, or at their limitation to a greater extent than is provided for in the present Covenant.

2. No restriction upon or derogation from any of the fundamental human rights recognized or existing in any country in virtue of law, conventions, regulations or custom shall be admitted on the pretext that the present Covenant does not recognize such rights or that it recognizes them to a lesser extent.

PART III

Article 6
1. The States Parties to the present Covenant recognize the right to work, which includes the right of everyone to the opportunity to gain his living by work which he freely chooses or accepts, and will take appropriate steps to safeguard this right.

2. The steps to be taken by a State Party to the present Covenant to achieve the full realization of this right shall include technical and vocational guidance and training programmes, policies and techniques to achieve steady economic, social and cultural development and full and productive employment under conditions safeguarding fundamental political and economic freedoms to the individual.

Article 7
The States Parties to the present Covenant recognize the right of everyone to the enjoyment of just and favourable conditions of work which ensure, in particular:

(a) Remuneration which provides all workers, as a minimum, with:

(i) Fair wages and equal remuneration for work of equal value without distinction of any kind, in particular women being guaranteed conditions of work not inferior to those enjoyed by men, with equal pay for equal work;

(ii) A decent living for themselves and their families in accordance with the provisions of the present Covenant;

(b) Safe and healthy working conditions;

(c) Equal opportunity for everyone to be promoted in his employment to an appropriate higher level, subject to no considerations other than those of seniority and competence;

(d) Rest, leisure and reasonable limitation of working hours and periodic holidays with pay, as well as remuneration for public holidays

Article 8
1. The States Parties to the present Covenant undertake to ensure:

(a) The right of everyone to form trade unions and join the trade union of his choice, subject only to the rules of the organization concerned, for the promotion and protection of his economic and social interests. No restrictions may be placed on the exercise of this right other than those prescribed by law and which are necessary in a democratic society in the interests of national security or public order or for the protection of the rights and freedoms of others;

(b) The right of trade unions to establish national federations or confederations and the right of the latter to form or join international trade-union organizations;

(c) The right of trade unions to function freely subject to no limitations other than those prescribed by law and which are necessary in a democratic society in the interests of national security or public order or for the protection of the rights and freedoms of others;

(d) The right to strike, provided that it is exercised in conformity with the laws of the particular country.

2. This article shall not prevent the imposition of lawful restrictions on the exercise of these rights by members of the armed forces or of the police or of the administration of the State.

3. Nothing in this article shall authorize States Parties to the International Labour Organisation Convention of 1948 concerning Freedom of Association and Protection of the Right to Organize to take legislative measures which would prejudice, or apply the law in such a manner as would prejudice, the guarantees provided for in that Convention.

Article 9
The States Parties to the present Covenant recognize the right of everyone to social security, including social insurance.

Article 10
The States Parties to the present Covenant recognize that:

1. The widest possible protection and assistance should be accorded to the family, which is the natural and fundamental group unit of society, particularly for its establishment and while it is responsible for the care and education of dependent children. Marriage must be entered into with the free consent of the intending spouses.

2. Special protection should be accorded to mothers during a reasonable period before and after childbirth. During such period working mothers should be accorded paid leave or leave with adequate social security benefits.

3. Special measures of protection and assistance should be taken on behalf of all children and young persons without any discrimination for reasons of parentage or other conditions. Children and young persons should be protected from economic and social exploitation. Their employment in work harmful to their morals or health or dangerous to life or likely to hamper their normal development should be punishable by law. States should also set age limits below which the paid employment of child labour should be prohibited and punishable by law.

Article 11
1. The States Parties to the present Covenant recognize the right of everyone to an adequate standard of living for himself and his family, including adequate food, clothing and housing, and to the continuous improvement

of living conditions. The States Parties will take appropriate steps to ensure the realization of this right, recognizing to this effect the essential importance of international co-operation based on free consent.

2. The States Parties to the present Covenant, recognizing the fundamental right of everyone to be free from hunger, shall take, individually and through international co-operation, the measures, including specific programmes, which are needed:

(a) To improve methods of production, conservation and distribution of food by making full use of technical and scientific knowledge, by disseminating knowledge of the principles of nutrition and by developing or reforming agrarian systems in such a way as to achieve the most efficient development and utilization of natural resources;

(b) Taking into account the problems of both food-importing and food-exporting countries, to ensure an equitable distribution of world food supplies in relation to need.

Article 12
1. The States Parties to the present Covenant recognize the right of everyone to the enjoyment of the highest attainable standard of physical and mental health.

2. The steps to be taken by the States Parties to the present Covenant to achieve the full realization of this right shall include those necessary for:

(a) The provision for the reduction of the stillbirth-rate and of infant mortality and for the healthy development of the child;

(b) The improvement of all aspects of environmental and industrial hygiene;

(c) The prevention, treatment and control of epidemic, endemic, occupational and other diseases;

(d) The creation of conditions which would assure to all medical service and medical attention in the event of sickness.

Article 13
1. The States Parties to the present Covenant recognize the right of everyone to education. They agree that education shall be directed to the full development of the human personality and the sense of its dignity, and shall strengthen the respect for human rights and fundamental freedoms. They further agree that education shall enable all persons to participate

effectively in a free society, promote understanding, tolerance and friendship among all nations and all racial, ethnic or religious groups, and further the activities of the United Nations for the maintenance of peace.

2. The States Parties to the present Covenant recognize that, with a view to achieving the full realization of this right:

(a) Primary education shall be compulsory and available free to all;

(b) Secondary education in its different forms, including technical and vocational secondary education, shall be made generally available and accessible to all by every appropriate means, and in particular by the progressive introduction of free education;

(c) Higher education shall be made equally accessible to all, on the basis of capacity, by every appropriate means, and in particular by the progressive introduction of free education;

(d) Fundamental education shall be encouraged or intensified as far as possible for those persons who have not received or completed the whole period of their primary education;

(e) The development of a system of schools at all levels shall be actively pursued, an adequate fellowship system shall be established, and the material conditions of teaching staff shall be continuously improved.

3. The States Parties to the present Covenant undertake to have respect for the liberty of parents and, when applicable, legal guardians to choose for their children schools, other than those established by the public authorities, which conform to such minimum educational standards as may be laid down or approved by the State and to ensure the religious and moral education of their children in conformity with their own convictions.

4. No part of this article shall be construed so as to interfere with the liberty of individuals and bodies to establish and direct educational institutions, subject always to the observance of the principles set forth in paragraph I of this article and to the requirement that the education given in such institutions shall conform to such minimum standards as may be laid down by the State.

Article 14
Each State Party to the present Covenant which, at the time of becoming a Party, has not been able to secure in its metropolitan territory or other territories under its jurisdiction compulsory primary education, free of

charge, undertakes, within two years, to work out and adopt a detailed plan of action for the progressive implementation, within a reasonable number of years, to be fixed in the plan, of the principle of compulsory education free of charge for all.

Article 15

1. The States Parties to the present Covenant recognize the right of everyone:

(a) To take part in cultural life;

(b) To enjoy the benefits of scientific progress and its applications;

(c) To benefit from the protection of the moral and material interests resulting from any scientific, literary or artistic production of which he is the author.

2. The steps to be taken by the States Parties to the present Covenant to achieve the full realization of this right shall include those necessary for the conservation, the development and the diffusion of science and culture.

3. The States Parties to the present Covenant undertake to respect the freedom indispensable for scientific research and creative activity.

4. The States Parties to the present Covenant recognize the benefits to be derived from the encouragement and development of international contacts and co-operation in the scientific and cultural fields.

PART IV

Article 16

1. The States Parties to the present Covenant undertake to submit in conformity with this part of the Covenant reports on the measures which they have adopted and the progress made in achieving the observance of the rights recognized herein.

2.

(a) All reports shall be submitted to the Secretary-General of the United Nations, who shall transmit copies to the Economic and Social Council for consideration in accordance with the provisions of the present Covenant;

(b) The Secretary-General of the United Nations shall also transmit to the specialized agencies copies of the reports, or any relevant parts therefrom,

from States Parties to the present Covenant which are also members of these specialized agencies in so far as these reports, or parts therefrom, relate to any matters which fall within the responsibilities of the said agencies in accordance with their constitutional instruments.

Article 17

1. The States Parties to the present Covenant shall furnish their reports in stages, in accordance with a programme to be established by the Economic and Social Council within one year of the entry into force of the present Covenant after consultation with the States Parties and the specialized agencies concerned.

2. Reports may indicate factors and difficulties affecting the degree of fulfilment of obligations under the present Covenant.

3. Where relevant information has previously been furnished to the United Nations or to any specialized agency by any State Party to the present Covenant, it will not be necessary to reproduce that information, but a precise reference to the information so furnished will suffice.

Article 18

Pursuant to its responsibilities under the Charter of the United Nations in the field of human rights and fundamental freedoms, the Economic and Social Council may make arrangements with the specialized agencies in respect of their reporting to it on the progress made in achieving the observance of the provisions of the present Covenant falling within the scope of their activities. These reports may include particulars of decisions and recommendations on such implementation adopted by their competent organs.

Article 19

The Economic and Social Council may transmit to the Commission on Human Rights for study and general recommendation or, as appropriate, for information the reports concerning human rights submitted by States in accordance with articles 16 and 17, and those concerning human rights submitted by the specialized agencies in accordance with article 18.

Article 20

The States Parties to the present Covenant and the specialized agencies concerned may submit comments to the Economic and Social Council on any general recommendation under article 19 or reference to such general recommendation in any report of the Commission on Human Rights or any documentation referred to therein.

Article 21
The Economic and Social Council may submit from time to time to the General Assembly reports with recommendations of a general nature and a summary of the information received from the States Parties to the present Covenant and the specialized agencies on the measures taken and the progress made in achieving general observance of the rights recognized in the present Covenant.

Article 22
The Economic and Social Council may bring to the attention of other organs of the United Nations, their subsidiary organs and specialized agencies concerned with furnishing technical assistance any matters arising out of the reports referred to in this part of the present Covenant which may assist such bodies in deciding, each within its field of competence, on the advisability of international measures likely to contribute to the effective progressive implementation of the present Covenant.

Article 23
The States Parties to the present Covenant agree that international action for the achievement of the rights recognized in the present Covenant includes such methods as the conclusion of conventions, the adoption of recommendations, the furnishing of technical assistance and the holding of regional meetings and technical meetings for the purpose of consultation and study organized in conjunction with the Governments concerned.

Article 24
Nothing in the present Covenant shall be interpreted as impairing the provisions of the Charter of the United Nations and of the constitutions of the specialized agencies which define the respective responsibilities of the various organs of the United Nations and of the specialized agencies in regard to the matters dealt with in the present Covenant.

Article 25
Nothing in the present Covenant shall be interpreted as impairing the inherent right of all peoples to enjoy and utilize fully and freely their natural wealth and resources.

PART V

Article 26

1. The present Covenant is open for signature by any State Member of the United Nations or member of any of its specialized agencies, by any State Party to the Statute of the International Court of Justice, and by any other State which has been invited by the General Assembly of the United Nations to become a party to the present Covenant.

2. The present Covenant is subject to ratification. Instruments of ratification shall be deposited with the Secretary-General of the United Nations.

3. The present Covenant shall be open to accession by any State referred to in paragraph 1 of this article.

4. Accession shall be effected by the deposit of an instrument of accession with the Secretary-General of the United Nations.

5. The Secretary-General of the United Nations shall inform all States which have signed the present Covenant or acceded to it of the deposit of each instrument of ratification or accession.

Article 27

1. The present Covenant shall enter into force three months after the date of the deposit with the Secretary-General of the United Nations of the thirty-fifth instrument of ratification or instrument of accession.

2. For each State ratifying the present Covenant or acceding to it after the deposit of the thirty-fifth instrument of ratification or instrument of accession, the present Covenant shall enter into force three months after the date of the deposit of its own instrument of ratification or instrument of accession.

Article 28

The provisions of the present Covenant shall extend to all parts of federal States without any limitations or exceptions.

Article 29

1. Any State Party to the present Covenant may propose an amendment and file it with the Secretary-General of the United Nations. The Secretary-General shall thereupon communicate any proposed amendments to the States Parties to the present Covenant with a request that they notify him whether they favour a conference of States Parties for the purpose of considering and voting upon the proposals. In the event that at least one

third of the States Parties favours such a conference, the Secretary-General shall convene the conference under the auspices of the United Nations. Any amendment adopted by a majority of the States Parties present and voting at the conference shall be submitted to the General Assembly of the United Nations for approval.

2. Amendments shall come into force when they have been approved by the General Assembly of the United Nations and accepted by a two-thirds majority of the States Parties to the present Covenant in accordance with their respective constitutional processes.

3. When amendments come into force they shall be binding on those States Parties which have accepted them, other States Parties still being bound by the provisions of the present Covenant and any earlier amendment which they have accepted.

Article 30
Irrespective of the notifications made under article 26, paragraph 5, the Secretary-General of the United Nations shall inform all States referred to in paragraph I of the same article of the following particulars:

(a) Signatures, ratifications and accessions under article 26;

(b) The date of the entry into force of the present Covenant under article 27 and the date of the entry into force of any amendments under article 29.

Article 31
1. The present Covenant, of which the Chinese, English, French, Russian and Spanish texts are equally authentic, shall be deposited in the archives of the United Nations.

2. The Secretary-General of the United Nations shall transmit certified copies of the present Covenant to all States referred to in article 26.

International Covenant on Civil and Political Rights

Adopted and opened for signature, ratification and accession by General Assembly resolution 2200A (XXI) of 16 December 1966

entry into force 23 March 1976, in accordance with Article 49

Preamble

The States Parties to the present Covenant,

Considering that, in accordance with the principles proclaimed in the Charter of the United Nations, recognition of the inherent dignity and of the equal and inalienable rights of all members of the human family is the foundation of freedom, justice and peace in the world,

Recognizing that these rights derive from the inherent dignity of the human person,

Recognizing that, in accordance with the Universal Declaration of Human Rights, the ideal of free human beings enjoying civil and political freedom and freedom from fear and want can only be achieved if conditions are created whereby everyone may enjoy his civil and political rights, as well as his economic, social and cultural rights,

Considering the obligation of States under the Charter of the United Nations to promote universal respect for, and observance of, human rights and freedoms,

Realizing that the individual, having duties to other individuals and to the community to which he belongs, is under a responsibility to strive for the promotion and observance of the rights recognized in the present Covenant,

Agree upon the following articles:

PART I

Article 1

1. All peoples have the right of self-determination. By virtue of that right they freely determine their political status and freely pursue their economic, social and cultural development.

2. All peoples may, for their own ends, freely dispose of their natural wealth and resources without prejudice to any obligations arising out of international economic co-operation, based upon the principle of mutual benefit, and international law. In no case may a people be deprived of its own means of subsistence.

3. The States Parties to the present Covenant, including those having responsibility for the administration of Non-Self-Governing and Trust Territories, shall promote the realization of the right of self-determination, and shall respect that right, in conformity with the provisions of the Charter of the United Nations.

PART II

Article 2

1. Each State Party to the present Covenant undertakes to respect and to ensure to all individuals within its territory and subject to its jurisdiction the rights recognized in the present Covenant, without distinction of any kind, such as race, colour, sex, language, religion, political or other opinion, national or social origin, property, birth or other status.

2. Where not already provided for by existing legislative or other measures, each State Party to the present Covenant undertakes to take the necessary steps, in accordance with its constitutional processes and with the provisions of the present Covenant, to adopt such laws or other measures as may be necessary to give effect to the rights recognized in the present Covenant.

3. Each State Party to the present Covenant undertakes:

(a) To ensure that any person whose rights or freedoms as herein recognized are violated shall have an effective remedy, notwithstanding that the violation has been committed by persons acting in an official capacity;

(b) To ensure that any person claiming such a remedy shall have his right thereto determined by competent judicial, administrative or legislative authorities, or by any other competent authority provided for by the legal system of the State, and to develop the possibilities of judicial remedy;

(c) To ensure that the competent authorities shall enforce such remedies when granted.

Article 3
The States Parties to the present Covenant undertake to ensure the equal right of men and women to the enjoyment of all civil and political rights set forth in the present Covenant.

Article 4
1. In time of public emergency which threatens the life of the nation and the existence of which is officially proclaimed, the States Parties to the present Covenant may take measures derogating from their obligations under the present Covenant to the extent strictly required by the exigencies of the situation, provided that such measures are not inconsistent with their other obligations under international law and do not involve discrimination solely on the ground of race, colour, sex, language, religion or social origin.

2. No derogation from articles 6, 7, 8 (paragraphs I and 2), 11, 15, 16 and 18 may be made under this provision.

3. Any State Party to the present Covenant availing itself of the right of derogation shall immediately inform the other States Parties to the present Covenant, through the intermediary of the Secretary-General of the United Nations, of the provisions from which it has derogated and of the reasons by which it was actuated. A further communication shall be made, through the same intermediary, on the date on which it terminates such derogation.

Article 5
1. Nothing in the present Covenant may be interpreted as implying for any State, group or person any right to engage in any activity or perform any act aimed at the destruction of any of the rights and freedoms recognized herein or at their limitation to a greater extent than is provided for in the present Covenant.

2. There shall be no restriction upon or derogation from any of the fundamental human rights recognized or existing in any State Party to the present Covenant pursuant to law, conventions, regulations or custom on the pretext that the present Covenant does not recognize such rights or that it recognizes them to a lesser extent.

PART III

Article 6

1. Every human being has the inherent right to life. This right shall be protected by law. No one shall be arbitrarily deprived of his life.

2. In countries which have not abolished the death penalty, sentence of death may be imposed only for the most serious crimes in accordance with the law in force at the time of the commission of the crime and not contrary to the provisions of the present Covenant and to the Convention on the Prevention and Punishment of the Crime of Genocide. This penalty can only be carried out pursuant to a final judgement rendered by a competent court.

3. When deprivation of life constitutes the crime of genocide, it is understood that nothing in this article shall authorize any State Party to the present Covenant to derogate in any way from any obligation assumed under the provisions of the Convention on the Prevention and Punishment of the Crime of Genocide.

4. Anyone sentenced to death shall have the right to seek pardon or commutation of the sentence. Amnesty, pardon or commutation of the sentence of death may be granted in all cases.

5. Sentence of death shall not be imposed for crimes committed by persons below eighteen years of age and shall not be carried out on pregnant women.

6. Nothing in this article shall be invoked to delay or to prevent the abolition of capital punishment by any State Party to the present Covenant.

Article 7
No one shall be subjected to torture or to cruel, inhuman or degrading treatment or punishment. In particular, no one shall be subjected without his free consent to medical or scientific experimentation.

Article 8

1. No one shall be held in slavery; slavery and the slave-trade in all their forms shall be prohibited.

2. No one shall be held in servitude.

3.

(a) No one shall be required to perform forced or compulsory labour;

(b) Paragraph 3 (a) shall not be held to preclude, in countries where imprisonment with hard labour may be imposed as a punishment for a crime, the performance of hard labour in pursuance of a sentence to such punishment by a competent court;

(c) For the purpose of this paragraph the term "forced or compulsory labour" shall not include:

(i) Any work or service, not referred to in subparagraph (b), normally required of a person who is under detention in consequence of a lawful order of a court, or of a person during conditional release from such detention;

(ii) Any service of a military character and, in countries where conscientious objection is recognized, any national service required by law of conscientious objectors;

(iii) Any service exacted in cases of emergency or calamity threatening the life or well-being of the community;

(iv) Any work or service which forms part of normal civil obligations.

Article 9

1. Everyone has the right to liberty and security of person. No one shall be subjected to arbitrary arrest or detention. No one shall be deprived of his liberty except on such grounds and in accordance with such procedure as are established by law.

2. Anyone who is arrested shall be informed, at the time of arrest, of the reasons for his arrest and shall be promptly informed of any charges against him.

3. Anyone arrested or detained on a criminal charge shall be brought promptly before a judge or other officer authorized by law to exercise judicial power and shall be entitled to trial within a reasonable time or to release. It shall not be the general rule that persons awaiting trial shall be

detained in custody, but release may be subject to guarantees to appear for trial, at any other stage of the judicial proceedings, and, should occasion arise, for execution of the judgement.

4. Anyone who is deprived of his liberty by arrest or detention shall be entitled to take proceedings before a court, in order that that court may decide without delay on the lawfulness of his detention and order his release if the detention is not lawful.

5. Anyone who has been the victim of unlawful arrest or detention shall have an enforceable right to compensation.

Article 10
1. All persons deprived of their liberty shall be treated with humanity and with respect for the inherent dignity of the human person.

2.

(a) Accused persons shall, save in exceptional circumstances, be segregated from convicted persons and shall be subject to separate treatment appropriate to their status as unconvicted persons;

(b) Accused juvenile persons shall be separated from adults and brought as speedily as possible for adjudication.

3. The penitentiary system shall comprise treatment of prisoners the essential aim of which shall be their reformation and social rehabilitation. Juvenile offenders shall be segregated from adults and be accorded treatment appropriate to their age and legal status.

Article 11
No one shall be imprisoned merely on the ground of inability to fulfil a contractual obligation.

Article 12
1. Everyone lawfully within the territory of a State shall, within that territory, have the right to liberty of movement and freedom to choose his residence.

2. Everyone shall be free to leave any country, including his own.

3. The above-mentioned rights shall not be subject to any restrictions except those which are provided by law, are necessary to protect national security, public order (ordre public), public health or morals or the rights

and freedoms of others, and are consistent with the other rights recognized in the present Covenant.

4. No one shall be arbitrarily deprived of the right to enter his own country.

Article 13
An alien lawfully in the territory of a State Party to the present Covenant may be expelled therefrom only in pursuance of a decision reached in accordance with law and shall, except where compelling reasons of national security otherwise require, be allowed to submit the reasons against his expulsion and to have his case reviewed by, and be represented for the purpose before, the competent authority or a person or persons especially designated by the competent authority.

Article 14
1. All persons shall be equal before the courts and tribunals. In the determination of any criminal charge against him, or of his rights and obligations in a suit at law, everyone shall be entitled to a fair and public hearing by a competent, independent and impartial tribunal established by law. The press and the public may be excluded from all or part of a trial for reasons of morals, public order (ordre public) or national security in a democratic society, or when the interest of the private lives of the parties so requires, or to the extent strictly necessary in the opinion of the court in special circumstances where publicity would prejudice the interests of justice; but any judgement rendered in a criminal case or in a suit at law shall be made public except where the interest of juvenile persons otherwise requires or the proceedings concern matrimonial disputes or the guardianship of children.

2. Everyone charged with a criminal offence shall have the right to be presumed innocent until proved guilty according to law.

3. In the determination of any criminal charge against him, everyone shall be entitled to the following minimum guarantees, in full equality:

(a) To be informed promptly and in detail in a language which he understands of the nature and cause of the charge against him;

(b) To have adequate time and facilities for the preparation of his defence and to communicate with counsel of his own choosing;

(c) To be tried without undue delay;

(d) To be tried in his presence, and to defend himself in person or through legal assistance of his own choosing; to be informed, if he does not have legal assistance, of this right; and to have legal assistance assigned to him, in any case where the interests of justice so require, and without payment by him in any such case if he does not have sufficient means to pay for it;

(e) To examine, or have examined, the witnesses against him and to obtain the attendance and examination of witnesses on his behalf under the same conditions as witnesses against him;

(f) To have the free assistance of an interpreter if he cannot understand or speak the language used in court;

(g) Not to be compelled to testify against himself or to confess guilt.

4. In the case of juvenile persons, the procedure shall be such as will take account of their age and the desirability of promoting their rehabilitation.

5. Everyone convicted of a crime shall have the right to his conviction and sentence being reviewed by a higher tribunal according to law.

6. When a person has by a final decision been convicted of a criminal offence and when subsequently his conviction has been reversed or he has been pardoned on the ground that a new or newly discovered fact shows conclusively that there has been a miscarriage of justice, the person who has suffered punishment as a result of such conviction shall be compensated according to law, unless it is proved that the non-disclosure of the unknown fact in time is wholly or partly attributable to him.

7. No one shall be liable to be tried or punished again for an offence for which he has already been finally convicted or acquitted in accordance with the law and penal procedure of each country.

Article 15
1. No one shall be held guilty of any criminal offence on account of any act or omission which did not constitute a criminal offence, under national or international law, at the time when it was committed. Nor shall a heavier penalty be imposed than the one that was applicable at the time when the criminal offence was committed. If, subsequent to the commission of the offence, provision is made by law for the imposition of the lighter penalty, the offender shall benefit thereby.

2. Nothing in this article shall prejudice the trial and punishment of any person for any act or omission which, at the time when it was committed,

was criminal according to the general principles of law recognized by the community of nations.

Article 16
Everyone shall have the right to recognition everywhere as a person before the law.

Article 17
1. No one shall be subjected to arbitrary or unlawful interference with his privacy, family, home or correspondence, nor to unlawful attacks on his honour and reputation.

2. Everyone has the right to the protection of the law against such interference or attacks.

Article 18
1. Everyone shall have the right to freedom of thought, conscience and religion. This right shall include freedom to have or to adopt a religion or belief of his choice, and freedom, either individually or in community with others and in public or private, to manifest his religion or belief in worship, observance, practice and teaching.

2. No one shall be subject to coercion which would impair his freedom to have or to adopt a religion or belief of his choice.

3. Freedom to manifest one's religion or beliefs may be subject only to such limitations as are prescribed by law and are necessary to protect public safety, order, health, or morals or the fundamental rights and freedoms of others.

4. The States Parties to the present Covenant undertake to have respect for the liberty of parents and, when applicable, legal guardians to ensure the religious and moral education of their children in conformity with their own convictions.

Article 19
1. Everyone shall have the right to hold opinions without interference.

2. Everyone shall have the right to freedom of expression; this right shall include freedom to seek, receive and impart information and ideas of all kinds, regardless of frontiers, either orally, in writing or in print, in the form of art, or through any other media of his choice.

3. The exercise of the rights provided for in paragraph 2 of this article carries with it special duties and responsibilities. It may therefore be

subject to certain restrictions, but these shall only be such as are provided by law and are necessary:

(a) For respect of the rights or reputations of others;

(b) For the protection of national security or of public order (ordre public), or of public health or morals.

Article 20

1. Any propaganda for war shall be prohibited by law.

2. Any advocacy of national, racial or religious hatred that constitutes incitement to discrimination, hostility or violence shall be prohibited by law.

Article 21

The right of peaceful assembly shall be recognized. No restrictions may be placed on the exercise of this right other than those imposed in conformity with the law and which are necessary in a democratic society in the interests of national security or public safety, public order (ordre public), the protection of public health or morals or the protection of the rights and freedoms of others.

Article 22

1. Everyone shall have the right to freedom of association with others, including the right to form and join trade unions for the protection of his interests.

2. No restrictions may be placed on the exercise of this right other than those which are prescribed by law and which are necessary in a democratic society in the interests of national security or public safety, public order (ordre public), the protection of public health or morals or the protection of the rights and freedoms of others. This article shall not prevent the imposition of lawful restrictions on members of the armed forces and of the police in their exercise of this right.

3. Nothing in this article shall authorize States Parties to the International Labour Organisation Convention of 1948 concerning Freedom of Association and Protection of the Right to Organize to take legislative measures which would prejudice, or to apply the law in such a manner as to prejudice, the guarantees provided for in that Convention.

Article 23

1. The family is the natural and fundamental group unit of society and is entitled to protection by society and the State.

2. The right of men and women of marriageable age to marry and to found a family shall be recognized.

3. No marriage shall be entered into without the free and full consent of the intending spouses.

4. States Parties to the present Covenant shall take appropriate steps to ensure equality of rights and responsibilities of spouses as to marriage, during marriage and at its dissolution. In the case of dissolution, provision shall be made for the necessary protection of any children.

Article 24

1. Every child shall have, without any discrimination as to race, colour, sex, language, religion, national or social origin, property or birth, the right to such measures of protection as are required by his status as a minor, on the part of his family, society and the State.

2. Every child shall be registered immediately after birth and shall have a name.

3. Every child has the right to acquire a nationality.

Article 25

Every citizen shall have the right and the opportunity, without any of the distinctions mentioned in article 2 and without unreasonable restrictions:

(a) To take part in the conduct of public affairs, directly or through freely chosen representatives;

(b) To vote and to be elected at genuine periodic elections which shall be by universal and equal suffrage and shall be held by secret ballot, guaranteeing the free expression of the will of the electors;

(c) To have access, on general terms of equality, to public service in his country.

Article 26

All persons are equal before the law and are entitled without any discrimination to the equal protection of the law. In this respect, the law shall prohibit any discrimination and guarantee to all persons equal and effective protection against discrimination on any ground such as race, colour, sex, language, religion, political or other opinion, national or social origin, property, birth or other status.

Article 27

In those States in which ethnic, religious or linguistic minorities exist, persons belonging to such minorities shall not be denied the right, in community with the other members of their group, to enjoy their own culture, to profess and practise their own religion, or to use their own language.

PART IV

Article 28

1. There shall be established a Human Rights Committee (hereafter referred to in the present Covenant as the Committee). It shall consist of eighteen members and shall carry out the functions hereinafter provided.

2. The Committee shall be composed of nationals of the States Parties to the present Covenant who shall be persons of high moral character and recognized competence in the field of human rights, consideration being given to the usefulness of the participation of some persons having legal experience.

3. The members of the Committee shall be elected and shall serve in their personal capacity.

Article 29

1. The members of the Committee shall be elected by secret ballot from a list of persons possessing the qualifications prescribed in article 28 and nominated for the purpose by the States Parties to the present Covenant.

2. Each State Party to the present Covenant may nominate not more than two persons. These persons shall be nationals of the nominating State.

3. A person shall be eligible for renomination.

Article 30

1. The initial election shall be held no later than six months after the date of the entry into force of the present Covenant.

2. At least four months before the date of each election to the Committee, other than an election to fill a vacancy declared in accordance with article 34, the Secretary-General of the United Nations shall address a written invitation to the States Parties to the present Covenant to submit their nominations for membership of the Committee within three months.

3. The Secretary-General of the United Nations shall prepare a list in alphabetical order of all the persons thus nominated, with an indication of the States Parties which have nominated them, and shall submit it to the States Parties to the present Covenant no later than one month before the date of each election.

4. Elections of the members of the Committee shall be held at a meeting of the States Parties to the present Covenant convened by the Secretary General of the United Nations at the Headquarters of the United Nations. At that meeting, for which two thirds of the States Parties to the present Covenant shall constitute a quorum, the persons elected to the Committee shall be those nominees who obtain the largest number of votes and an absolute majority of the votes of the representatives of States Parties present and voting.

Article 31
1. The Committee may not include more than one national of the same State.

2. In the election of the Committee, consideration shall be given to equitable geographical distribution of membership and to the representation of the different forms of civilization and of the principal legal systems.

Article 32
1. The members of the Committee shall be elected for a term of four years. They shall be eligible for re-election if re-nominated. However, the terms of nine of the members elected at the first election shall expire at the end of two years; immediately after the first election, the names of these nine members shall be chosen by lot by the Chairman of the meeting referred to in article 30, paragraph 4.

2. Elections at the expiry of office shall be held in accordance with the preceding articles of this part of the present Covenant.

Article 33
1. If, in the unanimous opinion of the other members, a member of the Committee has ceased to carry out his functions for any cause other than

absence of a temporary character, the Chairman of the Committee shall notify the Secretary-General of the United Nations, who shall then declare the seat of that member to be vacant.

2. In the event of the death or the resignation of a member of the Committee, the Chairman shall immediately notify the Secretary-General of the United Nations, who shall declare the seat vacant from the date of death or the date on which the resignation takes effect.

Article 34
1. When a vacancy is declared in accordance with article 33 and if the term of office of the member to be replaced does not expire within six months of the declaration of the vacancy, the Secretary-General of the United Nations shall notify each of the States Parties to the present Covenant, which may within two months submit nominations in accordance with article 29 for the purpose of filling the vacancy.

2. The Secretary-General of the United Nations shall prepare a list in alphabetical order of the persons thus nominated and shall submit it to the States Parties to the present Covenant. The election to fill the vacancy shall then take place in accordance with the relevant provisions of this part of the present Covenant.

3. A member of the Committee elected to fill a vacancy declared in accordance with article 33 shall hold office for the remainder of the term of the member who vacated the seat on the Committee under the provisions of that article.

Article 35
The members of the Committee shall, with the approval of the General Assembly of the United Nations, receive emoluments from United Nations resources on such terms and conditions as the General Assembly may decide, having regard to the importance of the Committee's responsibilities.

Article 36
The Secretary-General of the United Nations shall provide the necessary staff and facilities for the effective performance of the functions of the Committee under the present Covenant.

Article 37
1. The Secretary-General of the United Nations shall convene the initial meeting of the Committee at the Headquarters of the United Nations.

2. After its initial meeting, the Committee shall meet at such times as shall be provided in its rules of procedure.

3. The Committee shall normally meet at the Headquarters of the United Nations or at the United Nations Office at Geneva.

Article 38
Every member of the Committee shall, before taking up his duties, make a solemn declaration in open committee that he will perform his functions impartially and conscientiously.

Article 39
1. The Committee shall elect its officers for a term of two years. They may be re-elected.

2. The Committee shall establish its own rules of procedure, but these rules shall provide, inter alia, that:

(a) Twelve members shall constitute a quorum;

(b) Decisions of the Committee shall be made by a majority vote of the members present.

Article 40
1. The States Parties to the present Covenant undertake to submit reports on the measures they have adopted which give effect to the rights recognized herein and on the progress made in the enjoyment of those rights:

(a) Within one year of the entry into force of the present Covenant for the States Parties concerned;

(b) Thereafter whenever the Committee so requests.

2. All reports shall be submitted to the Secretary-General of the United Nations, who shall transmit them to the Committee for consideration. Reports shall indicate the factors and difficulties, if any, affecting the implementation of the present Covenant.

3. The Secretary-General of the United Nations may, after consultation with the Committee, transmit to the specialized agencies concerned copies of such parts of the reports as may fall within their field of competence.

4. The Committee shall study the reports submitted by the States Parties to the present Covenant. It shall transmit its reports, and such general comments as it may consider appropriate, to the States Parties. The Committee may also transmit to the Economic and Social Council these

comments along with the copies of the reports it has received from States Parties to the present Covenant.

5. The States Parties to the present Covenant may submit to the Committee observations on any comments that may be made in accordance with paragraph 4 of this article.

Article 41

1. A State Party to the present Covenant may at any time declare under this article that it recognizes the competence of the Committee to receive and consider communications to the effect that a State Party claims that another State Party is not fulfilling its obligations under the present Covenant. Communications under this article may be received and considered only if submitted by a State Party which has made a declaration recognizing in regard to itself the competence of the Committee. No communication shall be received by the Committee if it concerns a State Party which has not made such a declaration. Communications received under this article shall be dealt with in accordance with the following procedure:

(a) If a State Party to the present Covenant considers that another State Party is not giving effect to the provisions of the present Covenant, it may, by written communication, bring the matter to the attention of that State Party. Within three months after the receipt of the communication the receiving State shall afford the State which sent the communication an explanation, or any other statement in writing clarifying the matter which should include, to the extent possible and pertinent, reference to domestic procedures and remedies taken, pending, or available in the matter;

(b) If the matter is not adjusted to the satisfaction of both States Parties concerned within six months after the receipt by the receiving State of the initial communication, either State shall have the right to refer the matter to the Committee, by notice given to the Committee and to the other State;

(c) The Committee shall deal with a matter referred to it only after it has ascertained that all available domestic remedies have been invoked and exhausted in the matter, in conformity with the generally recognized principles of international law. This shall not be the rule where the application of the remedies is unreasonably prolonged;

(d) The Committee shall hold closed meetings when examining communications under this article;

(e) Subject to the provisions of subparagraph (c), the Committee shall make available its good offices to the States Parties concerned with a view to a friendly solution of the matter on the basis of respect for human rights and fundamental freedoms as recognized in the present Covenant;

(f) In any matter referred to it, the Committee may call upon the States Parties concerned, referred to in subparagraph (b), to supply any relevant information;

(g) The States Parties concerned, referred to in subparagraph (b), shall have the right to be represented when the matter is being considered in the Committee and to make submissions orally and/or in writing;

(h) The Committee shall, within twelve months after the date of receipt of notice under subparagraph (b), submit a report:

(i) If a solution within the terms of subparagraph (e) is reached, the Committee shall confine its report to a brief statement of the facts and of the solution reached;

(ii) If a solution within the terms of subparagraph (e) is not reached, the Committee shall confine its report to a brief statement of the facts; the written submissions and record of the oral submissions made by the States Parties concerned shall be attached to the report. In every matter, the report shall be communicated to the States Parties concerned.

2. The provisions of this article shall come into force when ten States Parties to the present Covenant have made declarations under paragraph I of this article. Such declarations shall be deposited by the States Parties with the Secretary-General of the United Nations, who shall transmit copies thereof to the other States Parties. A declaration may be withdrawn at any time by notification to the Secretary-General. Such a withdrawal shall not prejudice the consideration of any matter which is the subject of a communication already transmitted under this article; no further communication by any State Party shall be received after the notification of withdrawal of the declaration has been received by the Secretary-General, unless the State Party concerned has made a new declaration.

Article 42
I.

(a) If a matter referred to the Committee in accordance with article 41 is not resolved to the satisfaction of the States Parties concerned, the Committee may, with the prior consent of the States Parties concerned, appoint an ad hoc Conciliation Commission (hereinafter referred to as the Commission). The good offices of the Commission shall be made available to the States Parties concerned with a view to an amicable solution of the matter on the basis of respect for the present Covenant;

(b) The Commission shall consist of five persons acceptable to the States Parties concerned. If the States Parties concerned fail to reach agreement within three months on all or part of the composition of the Commission, the members of the Commission concerning whom no agreement has been reached shall be elected by secret ballot by a two-thirds majority vote of the Committee from among its members.

2. The members of the Commission shall serve in their personal capacity. They shall not be nationals of the States Parties concerned, or of a State not Party to the present Covenant, or of a State Party which has not made a declaration under article 41.

3. The Commission shall elect its own Chairman and adopt its own rules of procedure.

4. The meetings of the Commission shall normally be held at the Headquarters of the United Nations or at the United Nations Office at Geneva. However, they may be held at such other convenient places as the Commission may determine in consultation with the Secretary-General of the United Nations and the States Parties concerned.

5. The secretariat provided in accordance with article 36 shall also service the commissions appointed under this article.

6. The information received and collated by the Committee shall be made available to the Commission and the Commission may call upon the States Parties concerned to supply any other relevant information.

7. When the Commission has fully considered the matter, but in any event not later than twelve months after having been seized of the matter, it shall submit to the Chairman of the Committee a report for communication to the States Parties concerned:

(a) If the Commission is unable to complete its consideration of the matter within twelve months, it shall confine its report to a brief statement of the status of its consideration of the matter;

(b) If an amicable solution to the matter on the basis of respect for human rights as recognized in the present Covenant is reached, the Commission shall confine its report to a brief statement of the facts and of the solution reached;

(c) If a solution within the terms of subparagraph (b) is not reached, the Commission's report shall embody its findings on all questions of fact relevant to the issues between the States Parties concerned, and its views on the possibilities of an amicable solution of the matter. This report shall also contain the written submissions and a record of the oral submissions made by the States Parties concerned;

(d) If the Commission's report is submitted under subparagraph (c), the States Parties concerned shall, within three months of the receipt of the report, notify the Chairman of the Committee whether or not they accept the contents of the report of the Commission.

8. The provisions of this article are without prejudice to the responsibilities of the Committee under article 41.

9. The States Parties concerned shall share equally all the expenses of the members of the Commission in accordance with estimates to be provided by the Secretary-General of the United Nations.

10. The Secretary-General of the United Nations shall be empowered to pay the expenses of the members of the Commission, if necessary, before reimbursement by the States Parties concerned, in accordance with paragraph 9 of this article.

Article 43
The members of the Committee, and of the ad hoc conciliation commissions which may be appointed under article 42, shall be entitled to the facilities, privileges and immunities of experts on mission for the United Nations as laid down in the relevant sections of the Convention on the Privileges and Immunities of the United Nations.

Article 44
The provisions for the implementation of the present Covenant shall apply without prejudice to the procedures prescribed in the field of human rights by or under the constituent instruments and the conventions of the United Nations and of the specialized agencies and shall not prevent the States Parties to the present Covenant from having recourse to other procedures for settling a dispute in accordance with general or special international agreements in force between them.

Article 45
The Committee shall submit to the General Assembly of the United Nations, through the Economic and Social Council, an annual report on its activities.

PART V

Article 46
Nothing in the present Covenant shall be interpreted as impairing the provisions of the Charter of the United Nations and of the constitutions of the specialized agencies which define the respective responsibilities of the various organs of the United Nations and of the specialized agencies in regard to the matters dealt with in the present Covenant.

Article 47
Nothing in the present Covenant shall be interpreted as impairing the inherent right of all peoples to enjoy and utilize fully and freely their natural wealth and resources.

PART VI

Article 48
1. The present Covenant is open for signature by any State Member of the United Nations or member of any of its specialized agencies, by any State Party to the Statute of the International Court of Justice, and by any other State which has been invited by the General Assembly of the United Nations to become a Party to the present Covenant.

2. The present Covenant is subject to ratification. Instruments of ratification shall be deposited with the Secretary-General of the United Nations.

3. The present Covenant shall be open to accession by any State referred to in paragraph 1 of this article.

4. Accession shall be effected by the deposit of an instrument of accession with the Secretary-General of the United Nations.

5. The Secretary-General of the United Nations shall inform all States which have signed this Covenant or acceded to it of the deposit of each instrument of ratification or accession.

Article 49

1. The present Covenant shall enter into force three months after the date of the deposit with the Secretary-General of the United Nations of the thirty-fifth instrument of ratification or instrument of accession.

2. For each State ratifying the present Covenant or acceding to it after the deposit of the thirty-fifth instrument of ratification or instrument of accession, the present Covenant shall enter into force three months after the date of the deposit of its own instrument of ratification or instrument of accession.

Article 50

The provisions of the present Covenant shall extend to all parts of federal States without any limitations or exceptions.

Article 51

1. Any State Party to the present Covenant may propose an amendment and file it with the Secretary-General of the United Nations. The Secretary-General of the United Nations shall thereupon communicate any proposed amendments to the States Parties to the present Covenant with a request that they notify him whether they favour a conference of States Parties for the purpose of considering and voting upon the proposals. In the event that at least one third of the States Parties favours such a conference, the Secretary-General shall convene the conference under the auspices of the United Nations. Any amendment adopted by a majority of the States Parties present and voting at the conference shall be submitted to the General Assembly of the United Nations for approval.

2. Amendments shall come into force when they have been approved by the General Assembly of the United Nations and accepted by a two-thirds majority of the States Parties to the present Covenant in accordance with their respective constitutional processes.

3. When amendments come into force, they shall be binding on those States Parties which have accepted them, other States Parties still being bound by the provisions of the present Covenant and any earlier amendment which they have accepted.

Article 52

1. Irrespective of the notifications made under article 48, paragraph 5, the Secretary-General of the United Nations shall inform all States referred to in paragraph I of the same article of the following particulars:

(a) Signatures, ratifications and accessions under article 48;

(b) The date of the entry into force of the present Covenant under article 49 and the date of the entry into force of any amendments under article 51.

Article 53

1. The present Covenant, of which the Chinese, English, French, Russian and Spanish texts are equally authentic, shall be deposited in the archives of the United Nations.

2. The Secretary-General of the United Nations shall transmit certified copies of the present Covenant to all States referred to in article 48.

Index